T. S. ELIOT: THE CRITICAL HERITAGE

VOLUME 2

THE CRITICAL HERITAGE SERIES

GENERAL EDITOR: B. C. SOUTHAM, M.A., B.LITT. (OXON.)
Formerly Department of English, Westfield College, University of London

For a list of books in the series see the back end paper

T. S. ELIOT

THE CRITICAL HERITAGE

VOLUME 2

Edited by

MICHAEL GRANT

Lecturer in English and American Literature
The University of Kent at Canterbury

ROUTLEDGE & KEGAN PAUL
LONDON, BOSTON, MELBOURNE AND HENLEY

First published in 1982
by Routledge & Kegan Paul Ltd
39 Store Street, London WC1E 7DD,
9 Park Street, Boston, Mass. 02108, USA,
296 Beaconsfield Parade, Middle Park,
Melbourne, 3206, Australia, and
Broadway House, Newtown Road,
Henley-on-Thames, Oxon RG9 1EN.
Printed in Great Britain by
The Thetford Press Ltd, Thetford, Norfolk
Compilation, introduction, notes, bibliography and index
© Michael Grant 1982

Library of Congress Cataloging in Publication Data

T. S. Eliot, the critical heritage.

(Critical heritage series)
Bibliography: p.
Includes index.
1. Eliot, T. S. (Thomas Stearns), 1888-1965—
Criticism and interpretation—Addresses, essays,
lectures. I. Grant, Michael 1940-
II. Series.
PS3509.L43Z8732   821'.912   82-3842

ISBN 0-7100-9224-5 (v. 1)   AACR2
ISBN 0-7100-9225-3 (v. 2)

General Editor's Preface

The reception given to a writer by his contemporaries and near-contemporaries is evidence of considerable value to the student of literature. On one side we learn a great deal about the state of criticism at large and in particular about the development of critical attitudes towards a single writer; at the same time, through private comments in letters, journals or marginalia, we gain an insight upon the tastes and literary thought of individual readers of the period. Evidence of this kind helps us to understand the writer's historical situation, the nature of his immediate reading-public, and his response to these pressures.

The separate volumes in the *Critical Heritage Series* present a record of this early criticism. Clearly, for many of the highly productive and lengthily reviewed nineteenth- and twentieth-century writers, there exists an enormous body of material; and in these cases the volume editors have made a selection of the most important views, significant for their intrinsic critical worth or for their representative quality—perhaps even registering incomprehension!

For earlier writers, notably pre-eighteenth century, the materials are much scarcer and the historical period has been extended, sometimes far beyond the writer's lifetime, in order to show the inception and growth of critical views which were initially slow to appear.

In each volume the documents are headed by an Introduction, discussing the material assembled and relating the early stages of the author's reception to what we have come to identify as the critical tradition. The volumes will make available much material which would otherwise be difficult of access and it is hoped that the modern reader will be thereby helped towards an informed understanding of the ways in which literature has been read and judged.

B.C.S.

For Theresa

Contents

ACKNOWLEDGMENTS   xvii

ABBREVIATIONS   xx

INTRODUCTION   1

NOTE ON THE TEXT   66

'Prufrock and Other Observations' (June 1917)

1 ARTHUR WAUGH, The New Poetry, 'Quarterly Review', October 1916   67

2 EZRA POUND, Drunken Helots and Mr. Eliot, 'Egoist', June 1917   70

3 Unsigned review, 'Times Literary Supplement', June 1917   73

4 Unsigned review, 'Literary World', July 1917   74

5 Unsigned review, 'New Statesman', August 1917   75

6 EZRA POUND, T. S. Eliot, 'Poetry', August 1917   75

7 CONRAD AIKEN, Divers Realists, 'Dial', November 1917   80

8 EZRA POUND, A Letter from Remy de Gourmont, 'Little Review', December 1917   81

9 MAY SINCLAIR, 'Prufrock and Other Observations': A Criticism, 'Little Review', December 1917   83

10 BABETTE DEUTSCH, Another Impressionist, 'New Republic', February 1918   88

11 MARIANNE MOORE, A Note on T. S. Eliot's Book, 'Poetry', April 1918   89

12 EDGAR JEPSON, Recent United States Poetry, 'English Review', May 1918   91

13 WILLIAM CARLOS WILLIAMS, Prologue, 'Little Review', May 1919   92

'Poems' (May 1919)

14 Unsigned review, Not Here, O Apollo, 'Times Literary Supplement', June 1919   96

15 Unsigned review, Is This Poetry?, 'Athenaeum', June 1919   99

113 PHILIP HORTON, Speculations on Sin, 'Kenyon Review', Summer 1939 — 393

114 JOHN CROWE RANSOM, T. S. Eliot as Dramatist, 'Poetry', August 1939 — 396

115 HORACE GREGORY, The Unities and Eliot, 'Life and Letters', October 1939 — 400

'Old Possum's Book of Practical Cats' (October 1939)

116 STEPHEN SPENDER, Cats and Dog, 'Listener', October 1939 — 406

'East Coker' (first Faber edition September 1940)

117 G. W. STONIER, Mr. Eliot's New Poem, 'New Statesman', September 1940 — 409

118 JAMES KIRKUP, Eliot, 'Poetry London', January 1941 — 412

119 STEPHEN SPENDER, The Year's Poetry, 1940, 'Horizon', February 1941 — 415

120 JAMES JOHNSON SWEENEY, 'East Coker': A Reading, 'Southern Review', Spring 1941 — 418

121 ETHEL M. STEPHENSON, T. S. Eliot and the Lay Reader (II), 'Poetry Review', March–April 1942 — 438

'Burnt Norton' (first separate edition February 1941)

122 ANDREWS WANNING, from Criticism and Principles: Poetry of the Quarter, 'Southern Review', Spring 1941 — 443

123 ETHEL M. STEPHENSON, T. S. Eliot and the Lay Reader (I), 'Poetry Review', October 1941 — 446

'The Dry Salvages' (September 1941)

124 J. P. HOGAN, Eliot's Later Verse, 'Adelphi', January–March 1942 — 451

125 MURIEL BRADBROOK, The Lyric and Dramatic in the Latest Verse of T. S. Eliot, 'Theology', February 1942 — 458

126 ROLFE HUMPHRIES, Salvation from Sand in Salt, 'Poetry', March 1942 — 468

127 HELEN GARDNER, a study of Eliot's more recent poetry, 'New Writing and Daylight', 1942 — 469

128 GEORGE ORWELL, Points of View: T. S. Eliot, 'Poetry London', October–November 1942 — 483

129 KATHLEEN RAINE, Points of View: Another Reading, 'Poetry London', October–November 1942 — 488

34 CONRAD AIKEN, An Anatomy of Melancholy, 'New
   Republic', February 1923   156
35 HAROLD MONRO, Notes for a Study of 'The Waste Land':
   An Imaginary Dialogue with T. S. Eliot, 'Chapbook',
   February 1923   162
36 HARRIET MONROE, A Contrast, 'Poetry', March 1923   166
37 J.M., review, 'Double Dealer', May 1923   170
38 JOHN CROWE RANSOM, Waste Lands, 'New York Evening
   Post Literary Review', July 1923   172
39 ALLEN TATE, a reply to Ransom, 'New York Evening
   Post Literary Review', August 1923   180
40 HELEN MCAFEE, The Literature of Disillusion, 'Atlantic',
   August 1923   182
41 EDGELL RICKWORD, unsigned review, A Fragmentary
   Poem, 'Times Literary Supplement', September 1923   184
42 CLIVE BELL, T. S. Eliot, 'Nation and Athenaeum',
   September 1923   186
43 J. C. SQUIRE on Eliot's failure to communicate, 'London
   Mercury', October 1923   191
44 WILLIAM ROSE BENÉT, Among the New Books. Poetry Ad
   Lib, 'Yale Review', October 1923   192
45 CHARLES POWELL, review, 'Manchester Guardian',
   October 1923   194
46 F. L. LUCAS, review, 'New Statesman', November 1923   195
47 HUMBERT WOLFE, Waste Land and Waste Paper, 'Weekly
   Westminster', November 1923   200
48 GORHAM B. MUNSON, The Esotericism of T. S. Eliot,
   '1924', July 1924   203

          'Poems 1909–1925' (November 1925)
49 LEONARD WOOLF, 'Jug Jug' to Dirty Ears, 'Nation and
   Athenaeum', December 1925   213
50 EDGELL RICKWORD, The Modern Poet, 'Calendar of
   Modern Letters', December 1925   215
51 LOUISE MORGAN, The Poetry of Mr. Eliot, 'Outlook'
   (London), February 1926   219
52 JOHN MIDDLETON MURRY on Eliot and the 'Classical'
   revival, 'Adelphi', February–March 1926   222
53 I. A. RICHARDS, Mr. Eliot's Poems, 'New Statesman',
   February 1926   234

54 EDMUND WILSON, Stravinsky and Others, 'New
   Republic', March 1926   239
55 J. C. SQUIRE on Eliot's meaninglessness, 'London
   Mercury', March 1926   240
56 ALLEN TATE, A Poetry of Ideas, 'New Republic', June
   1926   242
57 CONRAD AIKEN, from The Poetic Dilemma, 'Dial', May
   1927   246

'Ash-Wednesday' (April 1930)
58 GERALD HEARD, T. S. Eliot, 'Week-end Review', May
   1930   249
59 FRANCIS BIRRELL, Mr. T. S. Eliot, 'Nation and
   Athenaeum', May 1930   251
60 EDA LOU WALTON, T. S. Eliot Turns to Religious Verse,
   'New York Times Book Review', July 1930   253
61 ORGILL MCKENZIE, review, 'New Adelphi', June–August
   1930   255
62 EDMUND WILSON, review, 'New Republic', August 1930   259
63 MORTON D. ZABEL, T. S. Eliot in Mid-Career, 'Poetry',
   September 1930   261
64 THOMAS MOULT, from Contrasts in Current Poetry,
   'Bookman' (London), September 1930   265
65 WILLIAM ROSE BENÉT, from Round about Parnassus,
   'Saturday Review', October 1930   267
66 E. G. TWITCHETT, review, 'London Mercury', October
   1930   268
67 BRIAN HOWARD, Mr. Eliot's Poetry, 'New Statesman',
   November 1930   269
68 ALLEN TATE, Irony and Humility, 'Hound and Horn',
   January–March 1931   272

'Marina' (September 1930)
69 MARIANNE MOORE, A Machinery of Satisfaction, 'Poetry',
   September 1931   280

'Triumphal March' (October 1931)
70 MORTON D. ZABEL, The Still Point, 'Poetry', December
   1932   282

'Sweeney Agonistes' (December 1932)

71 D. G. BRIDSON, review, 'New English Weekly', January
1933   286

72 GEORGE BARKER, from a review, 'Adelphi', January 1933   288

73 MORTON D. ZABEL, A Modern Purgatorio,
'Commonweal', April 1933   290

74 MARIANNE MOORE, review, 'Poetry', May 1933   291

'The Rock' (May 1934)

75 Unsigned review, 'Listener', June 1934   294

76 Unsigned review, Mr. Eliot's Pageant Play, 'Times
Literary Supplement', June 1934   295

77 MICHAEL SAYERS, Mr. T. S. Eliot's 'The Rock', 'New
English Weekly', June 1934   298

78 Unsigned editorial on 'The Rock', 'Theology', July
1934   302

79 Unsigned review, 'Tablet', August 1934   303

80 Unsigned review, 'Everyman', August 1934   303

81 A.M., review, 'Blackfriars', September 1934   304

82 Unsigned review, 'Sunday Times', September 1934   305

83 D. W. HARDING, 'The Rock', 'Scrutiny', September 1934   306

84 CONRAD AIKEN, After 'Ash-Wednesday', 'Poetry',
December 1934   310

'Murder in the Cathedral' (June 1935)

85 Unsigned review, Mr. Eliot's New Play, 'Times Literary
Supplement', June 1935   313

86 I. M. PARSONS, from Poetry, Drama and Satire,
'Spectator', June 1935   315

87 JAMES LAUGHLIN, Mr. Eliot on Holy Ground, 'New
English Weekly', July 1935   317

88 EDWIN MUIR, New Literature, 'London Mercury', July
1935   320

89 MARK VAN DOREN, The Holy Blisful Martir, 'Nation'
(New York), October 1935   323

90 F. O. MATTHIESSEN, T. S. Eliot's Drama of Becket,
'Saturday Review', October 1935   324

91 EDWARD SHILLITO, review, 'Christian Century', October
1935   328

92 FREDERICK A. POTTLE, from Drama of Action, 'Yale
Review', December 1935   332

'Collected Poems 1909–1935' (April 1936)

93 JOHN HAYWARD, London Letter, 'New York Sun', March 1936 — 335

94 EDWIN MUIR, Mr. Eliot's Poetry, 'Spectator', April 1936 — 336

95 PETER QUENNELL, Mr. T. S. Eliot, 'New Statesman', April 1936 — 339

96 CYRIL CONNOLLY, A Major Poet, 'Sunday Times', May 1936 — 344

97 MALCOLM COWLEY, Afterthoughts on T. S. Eliot, 'New Republic', May 1936 — 347

98 MARIANNE MOORE, It Is Not Forbidden to Think, 'Nation' (New York), May 1936 — 350

99 MORTON D. ZABEL, from Poets of Five Decades, 'Southern Review', Summer 1936 — 353

100 ROLFE HUMPHRIES, Eliot's Poetry, 'New Masses', August 1936 — 356

101 D. W. HARDING, T. S. Eliot, 1925–1935, 'Scrutiny', September 1936 — 359

102 LOUIS UNTERMEYER, from New Poetry, 'Yale Review', September 1936 — 364

103 R. P. BLACKMUR, The Whole Poet, 'Poetry', April 1937 — 366

'The Family Reunion' (first produced and published March 1939)

104 Unsigned review, Mr. Eliot in Search of the Present, 'Times Literary Supplement', March 1939 — 369

105 DESMOND MacCARTHY, Some Notes on Mr. Eliot's New Play, 'New Statesman', March 1939 — 371

106 IVOR BROWN, review, 'Observer', March 1939 — 375

107 Unsigned review, 'Listener', April 1939 — 377

108 MICHAEL ROBERTS, Mr. Eliot's New Play, 'London Mercury', April 1939 — 379

109 LOUIS MacNEICE, Original Sin, 'New Republic', May 1939 — 381

110 MAUD BODKIN, The Eumenides and Present-Day Consciousness, 'Adelphi', May 1939 — 384

111 FREDERICK A. POTTLE, A Modern Verse Play, 'Yale Review', June 1939 — 387

112 CLEANTH BROOKS, Sin and Expiation, 'Partisan Review', Summer 1939 — 390

113 PHILIP HORTON, Speculations on Sin, 'Kenyon Review', Summer 1939 — 393

114 JOHN CROWE RANSOM, T. S. Eliot as Dramatist, 'Poetry', August 1939 — 396

115 HORACE GREGORY, The Unities and Eliot, 'Life and Letters', October 1939 — 400

'Old Possum's Book of Practical Cats' (October 1939)

116 STEPHEN SPENDER, Cats and Dog, 'Listener', October 1939 — 406

'East Coker' (first Faber edition September 1940)

117 G. W. STONIER, Mr. Eliot's New Poem, 'New Statesman', September 1940 — 409

118 JAMES KIRKUP, Eliot, 'Poetry London', January 1941 — 412

119 STEPHEN SPENDER, The Year's Poetry, 1940, 'Horizon', February 1941 — 415

120 JAMES JOHNSON SWEENEY, 'East Coker': A Reading, 'Southern Review', Spring 1941 — 418

121 ETHEL M. STEPHENSON, T. S. Eliot and the Lay Reader (II), 'Poetry Review', March–April 1942 — 438

'Burnt Norton' (first separate edition February 1941)

122 ANDREWS WANNING, from Criticism and Principles: Poetry of the Quarter, 'Southern Review', Spring 1941 — 443

123 ETHEL M. STEPHENSON, T. S. Eliot and the Lay Reader (I), 'Poetry Review', October 1941 — 446

'The Dry Salvages' (September 1941)

124 J. P. HOGAN, Eliot's Later Verse, 'Adelphi', January–March 1942 — 451

125 MURIEL BRADBROOK, The Lyric and Dramatic in the Latest Verse of T. S. Eliot, 'Theology', February 1942 — 458

126 ROLFE HUMPHRIES, Salvation from Sand in Salt, 'Poetry', March 1942 — 468

127 HELEN GARDNER, a study of Eliot's more recent poetry, 'New Writing and Daylight', 1942 — 469

128 GEORGE ORWELL, Points of View: T. S. Eliot, 'Poetry London', October–November 1942 — 483

129 KATHLEEN RAINE, Points of View: Another Reading, 'Poetry London', October–November 1942 — 488

130 A correspondent intervenes, 'Poetry London',
     February–March 1943   493

          'Little Gidding' (December 1942)
131 Unsigned review, Midwinter Spring, 'Times Literary
     Supplement', December 1942   496
132 ROBERT SPEAIGHT, a review, 'Tablet', December 1942   497
133 LUKE TURNER, O.P., a review, 'Blackfriars', February
     1943   500
134 EDWIN MUIR, 'Little Gidding', 'New Statesman',
     February 1943   502
135 JAMES KIRKUP, Eliot, 'Poetry London', February–March
     1943   505
136 MURIEL BRADBROOK, review, 'Theology', March 1943   510
137 D. W. HARDING, We Have Not Reached Conclusion,
     'Scrutiny', Spring 1943   515
138 R. N. HIGINBOTHAM's objections to Harding's review,
     'Scrutiny', Summer 1943   519
139 F. R. LEAVIS replies to Higinbotham, 'Scrutiny', Summer
     1943   521
140 JAMES JOHNSON SWEENEY, 'Little Gidding': Introductory
     to a Reading, 'Poetry', July 1943   529
141 JOHN SHAND, Around 'Little Gidding', 'Nineteenth
     Century', September 1944   536

          'Four Quartets' (May 1943)
142 CHARLES WILLIAMS, A Dialogue on Mr. Eliot's Poem,
     'Dublin Review', April 1943   552
143 HORACE GREGORY, Fare Forward, Voyagers, 'New York
     Times Book Review', May 1943   560
144 MALCOLM COWLEY, Beyond Poetry, 'New Republic',
     June 1943   563
145 DELMORE SCHWARTZ, Anywhere Out of the World,
     'Nation' (New York), July 1943   567
146 PAUL GOODMAN, T. S. Eliot: The Poet of Purgatory,
     'New Leader', August 1943   570
147 JOHN GOULD FLETCHER, Poems in Counterpoint, 'Poetry',
     October 1943   573
148 LOUIS UNTERMEYER, a review, 'Yale Review', December
     1943   576

149 REGINALD SNELL, T. S. Eliot and the English Poetic
Tradition, 'New English Weekly', December 1944   577
150 E. J. STORMAN, S.J., Time and Mr. T. S. Eliot, 'Meanjin',
Winter 1944   581

*'The Cocktail Party' (first produced 22–7 August 1949
and published March 1950)*

151 I.H., Mr. T. S. Eliot's New Play, 'Manchester Guardian',
August 1949   591
152 PETER RUSSELL, A Note on T. S. Eliot's New Play,
'Nine', Autumn 1949   592
153 DESMOND SHAWE-TAYLOR, from a review of the Edinburgh
Festival production, 'New Statesman', September 1949   594
154 ROBERT SPEAIGHT, a review, 'Tablet', September 1949   597
155 WILLIAM CARLOS WILLIAMS, It's About 'Your Life and
Mine, Darling', 'New York Post', March 1950   601
156 E. M. FORSTER, Mr. Eliot's 'Comedy', 'Listener', March
1950   602
157 Unsigned review, 'Times Literary Supplement', March
1950   604
158 WILLIAM BARRETT, Dry Land, Dry Martini, 'Partisan
Review', April 1950   606
159 BONAMY DOBRÉE, Books and Writers, 'Spectator', April
1950   612
160 JOHN PETER, Sin and Soda, 'Scrutiny', Spring 1950   615
161 Unsigned review, Writing for the Theatre, 'Times
Literary Supplement', August 1950   622
162 WILLIAM ARROWSMITH, Notes on English Verse Drama,
'Hudson Review', Autumn 1950   624
163 JOHN MIDDLETON MURRY, Mr. Eliot's Cocktail Party,
'Fortnightly', December 1950   643

'The Complete Poems and Plays 1909–1950' (November 1952)

164 V. S. PRITCHETT, An American Puritan in England, 'New
York Times Book Review', November 1952   653
165 MARY COLUM, St Louis over Bloomsbury, 'Saturday
Review', December 1952   656

*'The Confidential Clerk' (first produced 25 August–5 September 1953
and published March 1954)*

166 HENRY DONALD, Edinburgh Festival, 'Spectator',
September 1953   660

167 T. C. WORSLEY, a review, 'New Statesman', September
    1953   662

168 J. G. WEIGHTMAN, from a report on the Edinburgh
    Festival, 'Twentieth Century', October 1953   665

169 RICHARD FINDLATER, The Camouflaged Drama,
    'Twentieth Century', October 1953   667

170 BONAMY DOBRÉE, a review, 'Sewanee Review', January
    1954   675

171 NICHOLAS BROOKE, 'The Confidential Clerk': A
    Theatrical Review, 'Durham University Journal', March
    1954   689

172 HELEN GARDNER, a review, 'New Statesman', March 1954   697

*'The Elder Statesman' (first produced 25–30 August 1958
and published April 1959)*

173 HENRY HEWES, T. S. Eliot at Seventy, and an interview
    with Eliot, 'Saturday Review', September 1958   702

174 J. G. WEIGHTMAN, After Edinburgh, 'Twentieth
    Century', October 1958   707

175 FRANK KERMODE, What Became of Sweeney?, 'Spectator',
    April 1959   709

176 DENIS DONOGHUE, Eliot in Fair Colonus: 'The Elder
    Statesman', 'Studies', Spring 1959   712

177 NONA BALAKIAN, Affirmation and Love in Eliot, 'New
    Leader', May 1959   722

178 HUGH KENNER, For Other Voices, 'Poetry', October 1959   725

'Collected Poems 1909–1962' (September 1963)

179 DONALD DAVIE, Mr Eliot, 'New Statesman', October
    1963   731

180 JOHN FREDERICK NIMS, Greatness in Moderation, 'Saturday
    Review', October 1963   736

181 FRANK KERMODE, Reading Eliot Today, 'Nation' (New
    York), October 1963   743

SELECT BIBLIOGRAPHY   746
INDEX   750

Acknowledgments

I should like to express my gratitude to my colleague Professor R.A. Foakes, whose advice and encouragement have proved invaluable. I should also like to acknowledge my debt to the Library at the University of Kent and especially to Miss Enid Dixon. My thanks are due also to my secretary, Mrs Freda Vincent.

It has not always proved possible to locate the owners of copyright material. However, all possible care has been taken to trace ownership of the selections printed and to make full acknowledgment for their use. For permission to reprint, and for answering queries, thanks are due to the following: The Trustees of Amherst College for No. 100; Edward Arnold (Publishers) Ltd for No. 156, from E.M. Forster, 'Two Cheers for Democracy'; 'Atlantic Monthly' for No. 40 (Copyright © 1923, by The Atlantic Monthly Company, Boston, Mass. Reprinted with permission); Brandt & Brandt for Nos 7 and 57, reprinted from 'Collected Criticism of Conrad Aiken' published by Oxford University Press; Cambridge University Press for Nos 138, 139 and 160; Carcanet Press Ltd for No. 50, from Edgell Rickword, 'Essays and Opinions 1921-31', ed. Alan Young; Chatto & Windus Ltd for Nos 83, 101 and 137, from D.W. Harding, 'Experience into Words'; The Christian Century Foundation for No. 91 (Copyright 1935 Christian Century Foundation. Reprinted by permission from the 2 October 1935 issue of 'The Christian Century'); 'Commonweal' for No. 73; Contemporary Review Company Ltd for No. 163; J.M. Dent & Sons Ltd for No. 80; Dodd, Mead & Company for No. 25; The University of Durham for No. 171 by Nicholas Brooke, from 'Durham University Journal', March 1954, xlvi, 66-70; Farrar, Straus & Giroux, Inc., for No. 30 (reprinted with the permission of Farrar, Straus & Giroux, Inc. Copyright 1922 by Edmund Wilson); George Firmage and Nancy T. Andrews for No. 22, from E.E. Cummings, 'A

Miscellany' (Copyright © 1958 by E.E. Cummings); Helen
Ransom Forman for No. 38; Dame Helen Gardner for No. 127;
Horace Gregory for No. 115; the 'Guardian' for Nos 45 and
151; A.M. Heath & Company Ltd and Mrs Sonia Brownell Orwell
for No. 128; David Higham Associates Ltd for No. 142;
Hodder & Stoughton Ltd for No. 64; 'The Hudson Review' for
No. 162, English Verse Drama (II): 'The Cocktail Party', by
William Arrowsmith, reprinted by permission from 'The
Hudson Review', vol. III, no. 3, Autumn, 1950 (Copyright ©
1950 by The Hudson Review, Inc.); Hutchinson Publishing
Group Ltd for Nos 9 and 51; John Johnson for No. 72; James
Kirkup for Nos 118 and 135; James Laughlin for No. 87; 'The
Nation' (New York) for Nos 23, 31, 89, 98, 145 and 181;
'New Blackfriars' for Nos 81 and 133; New Directions Pub-
lishing Corporation for Nos 13 and 155, William Carlos
Williams, Prologue, 'Little Review', vol. 6, May 1919, and
It's About 'Your Life and Mine, Darling', 'New York Post',
12 March 1950 (All rights reserved. Reprinted by permis-
sion of New Directions, New York, Agents); New Directions
Publishing Corporation and Faber & Faber Ltd for Nos 2
and 8, Ezra Pound, Drunken Helots and Mr. Eliot, 'Egoist',
vol. 4, June 1917, and A Letter from Remy de Gourmont,
'Little Review', vol. 4, December 1917 (All rights
reserved. Reprinted by permission of New Directions
Publishing Corporation, New York, Agents for the Ezra
Pound Literary Property Trust, and Faber & Faber Ltd);
'The New Leader' for Nos 146 and 177, reprinted with permission from 'The New Leader', 14 August 1943 and 11 May
1959 (Copyright © The American Labor Conference on Inter-
national Affairs, Inc.); 'The New Republic' for Nos 10,
20, 26, 34, 54, 56, 62, 97, 109 and 144; 'New Statesman'
for Nos 5, 15, 16, 19, 42, 46, 49, 53, 59, 67, 95, 105,
117, 134, 153, 167 and 172, from the 'Athenaeum', the
'Nation and Athenaeum' and the 'New Statesman'; 'New
Statesman' and Carcanet Press Ltd for No. 179, from Donald
Davie, 'The Poet in the Imaginary Museum'; 'New York Post'
for Nos 33 and 39, reprinted from the 'New York Post';
'The New York Times' for Nos 28, 60, 143 and 164 (© 1922,
1930, 1943, 1952 by The New York Times Company. Reprinted
by permission); Mrs Diana M. Oakeley for No. 93; 'The
Observer' for Nos 18 and 106; Ohio University Press and
Allen Tate for No. 68, Allen Tate, Irony and Humility, from
'Collected Essays' (© 1959); 'Partisan Review' and William
Barrett for No. 158 (Copyright © April, 1950, by Partisan
Review); 'Partisan Review' and Cleanth Brooks for No. 112
(Copyright © July, 1939, by Partisan Review); A.D. Peters
& Co. Ltd for Nos 116 and 119 (reprinted by permission of
A.D. Peters & Co. Ltd); 'Poetry' for Nos 11, 21, 36, 69,
74 and 103 (Copyright 1918, 1920, 1923, 1931, 1933, 1937 by

The Modern Poetry Association); 'Poetry' and the Trustees
of Amherst College for No. 126 (Copyright 1942 by The
Modern Poetry Association); 'Poetry' and Brandt & Brandt
for No. 84, first published in 'Poetry' (Copyright 1934
by The Modern Poetry Association), reprinted from 'Collected Criticism of Conrad Aiken' published by Oxford University Press; 'Poetry' and Mrs John Gould Fletcher for No.
147 (Copyright 1943 by The Modern Poetry Association);
'Poetry' and Helen Ransom Forman for No. 114 (Copyright
1939 by The Modern Poetry Association); 'Poetry' and Hugh
Kenner for No. 178 (Copyright 1959 by The Modern Poetry
Association); 'Poetry', New Directions Publishing Corpora-
tion, and Faber & Faber Ltd for No. 6, Ezra Pound, T.S.
Eliot, from 'Poetry', vol. 10, August 1917 (Copyright 1917
by The Modern Poetry Association. All rights reserved.
Reprinted by permission of the Editor of 'Poetry', New
Directions Publishing Corporation, New York, Agents for the
Ezra Pound Literary Property Trust, and Faber & Faber Ltd);
'Poetry' and Mrs Alta Fisch Sutton for Nos 63 and 70
(Copyright 1930, 1932 by The Modern Poetry Association);
'Poetry' and James Johnson Sweeney for No. 140 (Copyright
1943 by The Modern Poetry Association); The Poetry Society
for Nos 121 and 123; Kathleen Raine for No. 129; 'Saturday
Review' for Nos 65, 90, 165, 173 and 180; the 'Sewanee
Review' for No. 170, Bonamy Dobrée, 'The Confidential
Clerk', from the 'Sewanee Review', 62 (Winter 1954) (Copy-
right 1954 by the University of the South, reprinted by
permission of the Editor); Janet Adam Smith for No. 108;
The Society for Promoting Christian Knowledge for No. 78;
The Society for Promoting Christian Knowledge and M.C.
Bradbrook for Nos 125 and 136; The Society of Authors as
the literary representative of the Estate of John Middle-
ton Murry for No. 52; 'Southern Review' for Nos 99, 120
and 122; 'Spectator' for Nos 86, 94, 159, 166 and 175;
Father E.J. Stormon, S.J., for No. 150, from 'Meanjin';
'Studies' for No. 176; 'The Tablet' for Nos 79, 132 and
154; Times Newspapers Ltd for Nos 82 and 96, reproduced
from 'The Sunday Times', and for Nos 3, 14, 17, 27, 41,
76, 85, 104, 131, 157 and 161, reproduced from 'The Times
Literary Supplement' by permission; Louis Untermeyer for
Nos 24 and 32; Weidenfeld & Nicolson Ltd and A.P. Watt and
Son for No. 169; John Weightman for Nos 168 and 174; 'The
Yale Review' for Nos 92 and 111, from 'The Yale Review'
(Copyright Yale University Press); 'The Yale Review' and
Louis Untermeyer for Nos 102 and 148, from 'The Yale
Review' (Copyright Yale University Press).

Abbreviations

'Bibliography'   Donald Gallup, 'T.S. Eliot: A Biblio-
                   graphy' (London, 1969).
Browne   E. Martin Browne, 'The Making of T.S.
                   Eliot's Plays', second impression
                   (Cambridge, 1970).
CPP   'The Complete Poems and Plays of T.S.
                   Eliot' (London, 1969).
Unger   'T.S. Eliot: A Selected Critique', edited
                   with an introduction by Leonard Unger
                   (New York, 1966).

'The Family Reunion'

First produced at the Westminster Theatre, London, 21 March 1939;
first published, London, 21 March 1939, and New York, 30 March 1939

104. UNSIGNED REVIEW, MR. ELIOT IN SEARCH OF THE PRESENT, 'TIMES LITERARY SUPPLEMENT'

25 March 1939, no. 1938, 176

Mr. Eliot must be admired for his persistence in making experiments for a modern verse drama. The box-office success of 'Murder in the Cathedral' may have given him an unexpected and fortunate filip. It is possible, indeed, that he, more than other poets on the scene at the moment, may establish an altered theatre. His work is ritualistic, a thing which will be increasingly appropriate, without doubt, in the coming years. Yet, strangely enough, in his new play, 'The Family Reunion' (produced at the Westminster Theatre this week), he clings in the text to naturalism of surface and the naturalistic time. For all the versification, he may be said to have hardly broken with the main tenets of Shaftesbury Avenue.

Here we have the fixed drawing-room and library of an English country house. The slight ceremonies of such a place may make a preliminary appeal to Mr. Eliot. The verse is so apologetic it might often hardly be noticed.

She's a nice girl; but it's a difficult age for her.
I suppose she must be getting on for thirty?

This is perhaps an experiment in infiltration, of 'getting by' with verse before the Philistines suspect it. It has the flat simplicity of Frost, the studied casualness of certain Frenchmen, but it does not seem especially dramatic; nor is it compact. At times it is both clumsy and

diffuse, reminding us rather of the novel of analysis, now
passing, than of a possible poetic drama. It has less
natural music than that of certain dramatists who take
conversation and subtilize it and make it dance to its inherent tunes. Too often he imposes rather than educes the
music. What the theatre requires is the dance of the text;
whether verse or prose does not matter. Crommelynck's
prose, for instance, has more lively poetry than this
Eliotian verse.

'The Family Reunion', to some extent, reflects the
state of the modern theatre, both in its treatment and
story. Old appearances are kept up, but always there is a
sense of another thing, in this case horrible, ready to
explode beneath. At intervals a choric frankness breaks
forth, and the Eumenides are sighted for a second in a
window embrasure. We realise it is inevitable that the
surface will break completely, in the end, and that is
all: a negative approach. The general effect is static
and descriptive. We had imagined a dynamic and cursive
drama, learning from the Greek, but moving away from it
too. This is the contrary. Characters are erected like
statues (made at Madame Tussaud's) here and there about
the desiccated stage. They are the statues of an intellectual commentary, not bold complete figures in Greek
sunshine, but tenebrous with nineteenth-century Gothic
guilt.

A group of cohering relatives in an English mansion,
paying tribute to an old property that has become more
important than their life, is disturbed by a son who has
twitched his wife over a ship's rail at sea, cleverly,
without being found out (except by the Eumenides). What,
then, is the play? A few bad thoughts in a good family.
The son goes off again, as if led now by the Eumenides to
redemption.

> Somewhere on the other side of despair.
> To the worship in the desert, the thirst and depriva-
>   tion,
> A stony sanctuary and a primitive altar,
> The heat of the sun and the icy vigil,
> A care over lives of humble people,
> The lesson of ignorance, of incurable diseases ...
> I must follow the bright angels.

Mr. Eliot is a poet with a sense of the past in search of
an equivalent present. His poems contrasted slick modernism with ancient greatness, to the former's disadvantage.
Here he has tried to insert guilt in the ancient style,
into a drawing-room. He spoke in an essay once of Hamlet
being

dominated by an emotion which is inexpressible, because
it is in *excess* of the facts as they appear. And the
supposed identity of Hamlet with his author is genuine
to this point; that Hamlet's bafflement at the absence
of objective equivalent to his feelings is a prolongation of the bafflement of his creator in the face of
his artistic problem.

His own words describe the impression that 'The Family
Reunion' makes.
     Again, this is the past looking for a present, not the
present reabsorbing the past (compare, on this point,
Cocteau's 'Les Parents Terribles'). Mr. Eliot is perhaps
an illustration of the Orpheus legend. He has visited the
world of the dead and is bringing back what he needs to
enrich the modern time. But it is ordained that the poet
must keep his eyes well on his own brief day lest, ironically, the world of the dead should cease to help him.

105. DESMOND MacCARTHY, SOME NOTES ON MR. ELIOT'S NEW
PLAY, 'NEW STATESMAN'

25 March 1939, vol. xvii, 455-6

On Tuesday the 21st the first performance of Mr. T.S.
Eliot's new verse play, 'The Family Reunion,' was given at
The Westminster Theatre. It is a drama of the inner life.
The character contrast which runs through it - the test
applied to all the characters in the play - is whether he
or she attempts to live on the surface and *pretends* (that
is all that is possible) to ignore the spiritual destiny
of man, or accepts a predicament which is essentially
tragic. If I had grasped this while in the theatre instead of only when on my return home, I should not have
been so perplexed by the play. The characters who wilfully shut their eyes and seek to enjoy sham happiness by
living superficially are the mother (Lady Monchensey,
excellently acted by Miss Helen Haye), two of her sisters,
her two brothers-in-law and Dr. Warburton; those who face
the obligations and pain of living in reality in various
degrees are Lady Monchensey's third sister, Agatha
(amazingly well interpreted by Miss Catharine Lacey), her
young cousin, Mary, and, of course, her eldest son, Harry
(Michael Redgrave: surprisingly good in a most difficult

part) whose conscience is, so to speak, the seat of the
drama.

The theme of this drama is retribution and expiation.
It postulates a supernatural conception of sin. The dramatic method employed is (a) a blending of symbolism and
realism (Ibsen's later method and the most poetic way of
dealing with dramas of the inner life) and (b) a device
which Eugene O'Neill used in that extraordinarily interesting experiment, 'Strange Interlude,' namely, that of making
the characters on the stage speak their thoughts and feelings aloud, not as in traditional drama in the form of
brief conventional asides or set soliloquies, but in order
to convey to the audience a running contrast between what
they are saying to each other, and those thoughts and
feelings they are withholding or even stifling unconsciously in themselves.

This is obviously an extremely difficult device to
handle. I cannot say that Mr. Eliot has employed it
throughout with that psychological tact towards his audience which is absolutely essential if the effect is not to
be more grotesque than impressive. In a sense, too, it is
a 'get-out.' It is a way of circumventing what is the
great difficulty in handling on the stage a drama of the
inner life; namely, of writing dialogue which shall be
realistically plausible and yet every line of which, however commonplace and natural, shall *suggest* to us what is
going on privately at the back of the speakers' minds.
Ibsen was the great master of this art. Chehov hit upon a
device which was a sort of half-way compromise, realistically justified by the Russian temperament – that of the
soliloquy à *deux*. Recall how often in his plays conversation between two or more characters takes the form of each
pursuing aloud their own thoughts instead of answering
directly what is said to them. They don't listen to each
other, but continue to speak out of themselves as though
they were alone or as if the other person (who is also
talking in the same way) were passively listening. In fiction Virginia Woolf uses this monologistic form of dialogue at points where traditional novelists (claiming the
privileges of an omniscient observer) would have simply
stated what was going on inside the heads of people,
while they were *talking* about something else. The O'Neill
experiment, which Mr. Eliot has followed, is deliberately
to make the thoughts or feelings of his characters audible
to the audience, without attempting to make soliloquy, as
Chehov did, consonant with the realistic surface of the
dialogue. Indeed, Mr. Eliot goes a step further. At certain points in the dialogue where a group of people are
presented as embodying the same reactions, they are made

to speak the same words in chorus. Thus, suddenly, in the
middle of humorously realistic chit-chat, to which in turn
each of them has contributed some characteristic trifle,
Harry's uncles and aunts (always with the exception of
Agatha, who does not cling to the make-belief surface of
life) will start speaking the same words in chorus. This
device is a failure, and for two reasons. It weakens
still further the actuality of the scene before our eyes,
and thus the intensity of what we feel about it; and
secondly, words muttered in unison have the inevitable
effect of ritual responses - as it might be, 'Lord, have
mercy upon us and incline our hearts to obey this Law.'
Realism, whether on the stage or on the written page, is
primarily a means to increasing our fellow-feeling with
imaginary characters and strengthening our faith in the
situation presented. It is a very powerful means indeed,
never to be lightly sacrificed, except in order to gain
another intensity, poetic or symbolic, more valuable still.
Here the destruction of plausibility is complete. The
audience may have adapted their imaginations to the new
convention of characters speaking their private thoughts
aloud; but when a London clubman, a Bayswater boarding-
house lady, a retired colonel and a well-to-do widow, who
the moment before have been making typical remarks, suddenly start murmuring in chorus, then the last refuge of
willing make-believe in us is destroyed. It is hard enough
for actors to mark by their delivery from the stage the
difference between the spoken *thoughts* and the spoken *words*
which the author puts in their mouths. It can only be done
by uttering the former with a peculiarly personal self-
withdrawn intonation, and this is impossible when they are
made to speak in unison, when to be audible they have to
keep in strict time with each other. It is the difference
between walking and marching. A man may express his individuality by his gait, but not in the ranks. Thus in
this play at times when the words should seem to be pro-
ceeding out of the depths of an individual mind, they
reach our ears like a singing-lesson or a liturgy. Mr.
Eliot's 'chorus' of uncles and aunts implies a violation
of auditory psychology.

How did he come to make it? That is an interesting
question connected with my fundamental criticism of his
play. Evidently his theme - retribution and expiation -
occurred to him first in the form of Greek drama. Eugene
O'Neill had adapted in 'Mourning Becomes Electra' with
extraordinary, tragic effect the Greek conception of
Destiny and the whole of the Clytemnestra-Agamemnon story.
It was a masterpiece, thanks fundamentally to the

inspiration which made him perceive in the modern theory
of the Unconscious - a power which pushes us into
behaving against our will - a close parallel to the Greek
conception of Destiny. Mr. Eliot has perceived a relation
between the Greek Furies and remorse or a maddened conscience. But note this. O'Neill got his effect without
using *Greek* mythology. Had he introduced the Eumenides in
the last Act as symbols of Orry's remorse, they would not
only have left us cold but made nonsense of an intensely
tragic situation. The Eumenides are not for us recognised
symbols of remorse and retribution. They are not part of
the furniture of our minds as, in a shadowy way, guardian
angels and devils still are. They carry no guns, so to
speak; the mention of their name, let alone a glimpse of
them through a modern drawing-room window, awakes no sensation of dim disgust and terror in our hearts. They are
hopeless symbols for Mr. Eliot's purpose. If he had put
his story of remorse and expiation into a Greek setting,
Furies would have been in place, but he could not expect
us to shiver at the idea of a young lord being pursued on
his travels by those monsters (visible also to his chauf-
feur and a young lady cousin) and of his finding them
waiting in his old home.

It is the greatest pity that Mr. Eliot in writing this
play about the place of the conscience in life ever took off
on a Greek foot. The temper of his mind, too, is entirely
Christian, not Greek. I know the Greeks to propitiate
evil powers called them by flattering names, and the
Eumenides were superstitiously referred to as 'the good
ones' for fear of being dogged by them. But the whole
point of Mr. Eliot's play is that they (these embodiments
of remorse and thwarted spiritual aspirations) are really
guiding angels which must be welcomed and followed, if man
is to find peace. Why in that case introduce Greek mythology at all? It is maddening. This play shows that Mr.
Eliot has it in him to write a masterpiece on a theme
nearer his thoughts than any other: on the problem of
wickedness and the salvation of the soul. But the Greeks
are the last people in the world to help him in that. He
might have presented this young man, who perhaps - it is
even left in doubt whether he ever did more than contemplate doing it - pushed his silly wife overboard, as
haunted on his return to take up his life as a country
squire. We can still suspend disbelief in regard to
revengeful ghosts, and be interested in them too, if they
stand at the same time for spiritual torture. But (*vide*
Macbeth) certainly no one else ought to see the spectre of
his conscience.

There was another less fundamental flaw in 'The Family

Reunion' which threw me for a long time off the track. In
the opening scenes the family are presented as living in
dread. The mother says, 'We must not mention to Harry
anything that has happened during the last eight years,'
and one of the others says, 'That will be difficult.' Of
course, the audience thinks that there is a ghastly family
secret. But the only skeleton in the cupboard let loose
is Harry's own confession on his arrival that, while away,
he had drowned his detested wife. Why, then, should the
family be under a curse? The mother turns out to be more
sinned against than sinning - except in so far as she is
one of those who deny the importance of the spiritual life.
It was Harry's dead father who, before Harry was born, had
thought of murdering *her*, and had been restrained by
Agatha who loved him. Surely this is confusing. But -
and that 'but' is an enormous one - there are passages of
intense significance concerned with the difference between
ignoring spiritual realities and facing them. The play is
also an example of how to write a modern play in verse.
Mr. Eliot has used a kind of subtle verse, based on iambic
blank verse, which can be delivered as prose, or at
moments of high emotion, stressed rhythmically so as to
carry us into the region of poetry: a great achievement
and one of pioneer importance. The diction, too, is
fine, clear and impeccable.

106. IVOR BROWN, REVIEW, 'OBSERVER'

26 March 1939, 15

Brown (1891-1974), an English novelist and critic, was
drama critic for the 'Observer' from 1929 to 1954, and
editor from 1942 to 1948.

Amy, Lady Monchensey.........................Helen Haye
Agatha.................................Catharine Lacey
Ivy.......................................Henzie Raeburn
Violet.............................Marjorie Gabain
Charles Piper...........................Stephen Murray
Gerald Piper......................Colin Keith-Johnston
Mary...Ruth Lodge
Harry, Lord Monchensey................Michael Redgrave

```
Denman.....................................Pamela Kelly
Downing....................................Robert Harris
Dr. Warburton.........................E. Martin Browne
Sergeant Winchell.......................Charles Victor
```
                Directed by E. Martin Browne.

Life, chez Lady Monchensey, is not gay: her tribe have the
gloomiest of family seats, and the starkest of family
curses. They are people of property - and doom. They are
Forsytes who will suddenly speak in chorus, like the
elders of Argos. It is as though a play of John Galsworthy's had collided with something of Sophocles. That
confusion is accompanied by the blending of a pagan idea
(the family curse) with Christian ideas of expiation,
'by intercession, by pilgrimage,' and by accepting as
'bright angels' the seeming Furies who haunt young Harry
Monchensey. The curse concerns a family proclivity to
willing or achieving the murder of a wife - a serious matter for a decent lot of landed gentry and their estimable
women-folk. Into the Monchensey country Mr. Eliot makes a
curious Anglo-Hellenic tour and comes back with as strange
a piece of poetical drama as ever set a Forsyte quartette
confessing themselves in choric form.
     Here then is abundance of fine, confused feeling. The
best of it, to my mind, comes on the fringes. Mr. Eliot
has written some really exquisite passages, one about old
age, spoken by Miss Helen Haye as the Dowager with all
Miss Haye's firm mastery of pathos, and others about the
childhood of the family ('The rule of conduct was simply
pleasing mother') and their games and pleasures. These
things and more can be easily revealed because Mr. Eliot
employs a convention whereby the characters are living on
two levels, one of normal, self-suppressing, polite, For-
sytish behaviour, the other of self-revelation to the
audience. That convention makes things easy for a dramatist. Many technical problems are abolished at a stroke.
But that convention also has its price, at least with a
British public accustomed to realism. The urgency and
intimacy of naturalistic stagecraft bring the characters
straight to us. Destroy that intimacy and the characters
are apt to seem remote, fragments of an experimental technique, something to argue over later, not something to feel
and feel poignantly now.
     Mr. Eliot's play, when it comes to doctrines of expia-
tion and methods of curse-lifting, fades into a misty,
muddled enigmatic exaltation; inevitably, for Christian
and pagan do not mix. How can a Christian accept the idea
of a family curse at all? But it does go wandering off
with musical honours and leaves the memory of some most
moving passages. The dramatist has raised an enormous
number of issues, doctrinal, and technical. He uses, with

very good effect, a series of metres in which the trochaic
and anapaestic feet do more of the marching than the familiar iambic. (By the way, it is amusing to find that the
scholarly Mr. Eliot does not know that the word 'fruition'
means enjoyment and has nothing to do with ripeness.)
Whether or no you are bored by the story of the curse and
its expiation, there is so much innovation of style and
such skilled use of words and rhythms that the play is
arresting and important. Furthermore, it suggests that Mr.
Eliot might write an excellent light comedy. (I preferred
his fun to his Furies.) Naturally, it sets the actors some
problems, and these are extremely well surmounted by a
strong company, of whom Mr. Michael Redgrave, Miss Helen
Haye, and Miss Catharine Lacey are the chief ornaments,
all blending strength with sensibility, and firmly, quietly
assisting Mr. Eliot's play on its strange, uneven passage
to the mind and heart.

107. UNSIGNED REVIEW, 'LISTENER'

6 April 1939, vol. xxi, 750

No one should miss reading this play, if it happens, as
may well be, to prove a failure on the stage. As an
imaginative work of art, a book to read, it compares with
the most sensitive of the short novels by Henry James.
It is fashionable to say boldly that there is no place in
the library for the dramatic poem; poetic drama is written
for the stage, we are told, and if it fails there, it is
useless. But just conceivably the poetic drama is developing in two directions; one, in the plays of Auden and
Isherwood, certainly towards the theatre; the other, of
which this play is a striking example, towards narrative
poetry.
   The plot of 'A Family Reunion' is extremely simple. The
scene is a family party to celebrate the birthday of its
senior member, Lady Monchensey, the mother of the hero,
Harry. A shadow is cast over the proceedings by the fact
that Harry's wife, whom the family always disliked, has
been drowned by falling overboard during a voyage at sea.
Everyone assumes that this is either suicide or an accident. However, when Harry returns, he disconcertingly
reveals that he either has, or believes he has, pushed
her overboard. The family assures him that this is the

working of his fevered imagination. However, he is a
modern Orestes, pursued by the Eumenides. Moreover, the
crime is not just his, for it has been repeated in the
family; his father has also wished to murder his mother.
This leads us to think that in all probability neither of
these murders exists outside the hearts of the protagonists. But Harry has to suffer:

                                        It is possible
  You are the consciousness of your unhappy family,
  Its bird sent flying through the purgatorial flame.
  Indeed it is possible. You may learn hereafter,
  Moving alone through flames of ice, chosen
  To resolve the enchantment under which we suffer.

The upshot is that Harry leaves his family to follow the
'bright angels' of the Eumenides and to atone for his crime
in isolation.
     Various features of this plot must surely mar it on the
stage. In the first place, the main piece of action, the
murder, is an unexplained mystery, which may even not have
happened. It has only a symbolic significance. The actual
action on the stage is of a quiet, domestic drama, in which
one of the characters has a load of guilt on his mind: and
yet one feels that there is more than that to it, that
something violent ought to *happen*. The Eumenides idea, and
the idea of the repeated crime, are surely purely academic:
it would be much simpler if one member of the family was
faced with the problem of his own sin, and the rest of the
family were spectators, entering into his consciousness at
various levels. These things do not bother one so much
when one reads the play; although the obscurity of the
action sometimes makes it a little tiresome to follow.
But what is wonderful is the marvellous opening out of
consciousness, the flowering of meaning, which makes this
play an account of a spiritual experience. There are
passages of great poetic beauty, and statements which are
the fruits of a lifetime devoted to poetry. To find any
parallel to Mr. Eliot's moral sensitivity, to his capacity
for feeling life and opening out layer after layer of
consciousness, we are brought back again to his great com-
patriot the New Englander, Henry James.

108. MICHAEL ROBERTS, MR. ELIOT'S NEW PLAY, 'LONDON MERCURY'

April 1939, vol. xxxix, 641-2

Roberts (1902-48) was a poet, critic and anthologist. His 'Collected Poems' was published by Faber & Faber in 1958. In his introduction to 'The Faber Book of Modern Verse' (1936), which he edited, he gave sympathetic attention to Eliot's work up to that date.

It is a relief to be able to read a new verse drama with interest, to be fairly confident that no revolutionary flood is going to get the dramatist out of a tight corner and that nobody is going to die in the last ditch. In Mr. Eliot's new play the characters are *there*, in Lord Monchensey's country house, and their problems have to be solved on the given data. The main problem is Lord Monchensey himself, returning to an unhappy family after seven years' absence; but when he returns we see that the problem is not any of those his mother or his uncles and aunts have foreseen - what he will do with the house, will he marry again, and so on - but a problem he carries inside himself.

The versification is an advance on anything Mr. Eliot has so far written. The epic poet or the novelist can afford to be longwinded once in a while - the reader can always skip a dozen pages - but the dramatist has to hold his audience all the time, or the whole reality of the play vanishes. If he chooses to write in verse, the verse must be flexible enough to carry trivialities as well as meditations and flashes of insight, and the passages of poetry must carry the action forward quite as much as the passages of backchat: if the audience becomes conscious of being jolted up to the poetic level, or jerked down, the play becomes an anthology. Mr. Eliot has worked out a kind of verse that allows him to be trivial without becoming silly:

I hear that Harry has arrived already
And he was the only one that was uncertain.
Arthur or John may be late, of course.
We may have to keep the dinner back ...

The same verse, without any strain, is capable of carrying

statements that are pitched higher than prose would stand:

> We do not pass twice through the same door
> Or return to the door through which we did not pass.
> I have seen the first stage: relief from what happened
> Is also relief from the unfulfilled craving
> Flattered in sleep, and deceived in waking.

It is not only that the verse will carry off short, sententious thoughts like a thought from Pascal:

> Everything is true, only in a different sense

without ever raising in the reader's mind the awkward thought that people do not talk like that, but also that it allows Mr. Eliot to move into poetry as serious as anything he has written:

> A curse is like a child, formed
> In a moment of unconsciousness
> In an accidental bed
> Or under an elder tree
> . . . .
> O my child, my curse,
> You shall be fulfilled:
> The knot shall be unknotted
> And the crooked made straight.

Readers familiar with Mr. Eliot's will have a smile of recognition for the imagery: the sun shining on the rose garden, 'I would go south in the winter, if I could afford it,' death by water, '*You* don't see them, but I see them,' the noises in the cellar, 'a door opens at the end of a corridor.' But this repetition is not a sign of poverty. Mr. Eliot is a poet rather than a novelist or dramatist: the material of his thought is imagery rather than characters and situations, and in this play the imagery is not merely repeated but developed. Each of the themes mentioned above occurs in a context that throws new light on the similar phrases in Mr. Eliot's poems.

The characters are none the less real and distinct, and when they are used as a chorus they are convincing because we already know them as individuals. As chorus, they are free to speak the thoughts of which they are barely conscious as individuals. The propriety of this may not be *understood* in a stage production, but it is likely to be *felt*: and it gives the chorus real work to do in the development of the play.

At a first reading, one wonders whether the denouement
is strong enough, whether it throws enough new light on
the past, alters Lord Monchensey's relations to all the
other characters, and paves the way for a dissolution of
all the 'situations' as we have seen them. Perhaps it
does: it has not the brutal directness of a revelation
in Greek tragedy, but there is no doubt that it solves
the problems by breaking them up, so that each character
is left with the responsibility of fending for himself.
This may not be easy to put across the footlights, but it
comes out clearly on re-reading the play, and it reveals
the comparative triviality of the motor accidents that
pointed the climax of Part One.

There is much more that might be said about what happens at Wishwood - 'Seek only there... The hermit's
chapel, the pilgrim's prayer' - and it is a pity that this
important book has to be reviewed briefly and in haste.

109. LOUIS MacNEICE, ORIGINAL SIN, 'NEW REPUBLIC'

3 May 1939, vol. xcviii, 384-5

MacNeice (1907-63) was a poet associated with Auden and
Spender during the 1930s. From 1941 to 1949 he was a
producer for the BBC. His 'Collected Poems, 1925-1948'
was published by Faber & Faber in 1949. Poems and
reviews by him appeared in the 'Criterion'.

'The Family Reunion' seems to be a better play than
'Murder in the Cathedral,' better integrated, less of a
charade. This time the subordinate characters are real
persons, fuller, more differentiated, more sympathetic;
and the ideas behind the play are fused into the action
and the characters; it is difficult (and this is as it
should be) to divorce the theme or the moral from the play
itself. It would be an easy play to ridicule - a hag-
ridden hero who appears in a vague mess and disappears
toward a vague solution - but such ridicule would be mis-
placed. Aristotle thought that the soul of a play is
action. If we interpret action in the narrow or external
sense, then according to Aristotle this play is not dramatic. But Mr. Eliot has always been more interested in

action, and in the correlative suffering, on the spiritual
plane. His religious beliefs, as can be seen from such
books as his notorious 'After Strange Gods,' have opposed
him to 'liberalism,' to any basically utilitarian doctrine
of progress. From one point of view, then, Mr. Eliot is a
reactionary, but he is at the same time a corrective to the
facile optimism of many Leftist writers. We may regret
that he seems to put all his money on the religious conscience as distinct from practical morality, but at the
same time we must recognize that he asserts certain truths
(even if these are the truths of the Unknown God) which
are now commonly neglected and whose neglect may in the
long run sap the life from our utilitarian ethics:

> ...the circle of our understanding
> Is a very restricted area
> Except for a limited number
> Of strictly practical purposes
> We do not know what we are doing.

Though the subject of his play is Original Sin, Mr.
Eliot has embodied it in characters who on the surface
plane also are involved in dramatically interesting
relationships to each other (this set of characters in
the same situation could in fact have been treated by
Chekhov). There is a compromise here between naturalism
and mysticism. The definite surface facts - the mother's
birthday, the family house, the brothers' accidents, the
hero's home-coming, the previous death of his wife, the
death in the last scene of his mother - may be from Mr.
Eliot's point of view merely incidental, but they act as
girders to the play. Thus the hero, like Orestes, has
apparently committed (or thinks he has committed) a murder; this murder is merely incidental to, or at most
symptomatic of, a far more basic and less particularized
sin which he has to expiate. The Eumenides who haunt him
appear at first sight to be subjective phantoms but are
discovered, to the hero's own belief, to be forces outside
him. His expiation on the face of it seems to consist in
leaving his home forever; this is in fact the outward and
visible sign of a profound spiritual change. This change
being still obscure, Mr. Eliot was of course right to
stress the outward and visible signs. For this reason the
play seems to me more suited to the stage than 'Murder in
the Cathedral.'
The trouble with 'Murder in the Cathedral' was that the
essential conflict was between Becket and himself as
represented by the Tempters; the murderers merely arrived
out of a machine. In 'The Family Reunion,' the hero is

again struggling with himself, but the conflict is made
more palpable by the antipathies between various members
of his own family - between the hero and his family in
general or his mother in particular, between his mother
and the aunts and uncles, between the dead father and the
mother, between the inhibited young cousin Mary and the
mother and aunts. These characters are not treated satirically; even the stupidest uncle is allowed a certain
human feeling and an inkling of truth outside himself.
The old mother, who in a sense has been a vampire to her
son, yet compares favorably with the mother in Messrs.
Auden and Isherwood's 'Ascent of F-6,' who is almost a
Freudian dummy.

Technically the verse of this play is most successful,
though some people have accused it of not being verse at
all. Mr. Eliot has quite rightly avoided inserting any
hunks of obvious prose; no prose-plus-verse play in
recent times has as yet managed to be homogeneous. He has
therefore had to contrive a versification elastic enough
to be incantatory at one moment and to represent the
banalities of conversation at another. This is a very
considerable achievement. He uses his favorite devices -
hypnotic repetition, antithesis, paradox, the overrunning
of sentences from line to line, the simple and sharp but
yet mysterious use of imagery:

>...the sobbing in the chimney
>The evil in the dark closet?

And there are echoes from his previous poetry - 'south in
the winter,' 'You don't see them, but I see them' (the
key line from the 'Choephoroe' of Aeschylus). It is
foolish to cavil at these echoes when they are so well
integrated into the present piece. Thus the scene between
Harry and his Aunt Agatha is a reminiscence of 'Burnt
Norton,' but is a magnificent presentation of the world of
unfulfilled choices:

>I was not there, you were not there, only our phantasms
>And what did not happen is as true as what did happen,
>O my dear and you walked through the little door
>And I ran to meet you in the rose garden.

Most of the characters speak at one time or another as
if they were a chorus; this is one of the advantages of a
poetic play. Further, Mr. Eliot here has not introduced
any external chorus (a disrupting influence on the modern
stage) but on occasions (with a certain irony?) he makes
the four stupidest characters step out of their proper

parts and speak a commentary in unison. I am not sure if
this will succeed on the stage, but it is at least a hopeful experiment. It is probable, however, that this could
have been dispensed with and that characters like Agatha
could have been left to speak the commentary singly and
still more or less in character.

Lastly, this is a very moving play both as a whole and
in its passing pictures, its ironic comments, its pregnant
understatements, its bursts into liturgy. Witness Mary's
criticism of Henry:

> ...you attach yourself to loathing
> As others do to loving; an infatuation
> That's wrong, a good that's misdirected.

Or Henry's comment on himself as a person that his family
has conspired to invent. Or one of his first remarks on
re-meeting them after eight years: 'You all look so
withered and young.' Or his mother's dying words: 'The
clock has stopped in the dark.' Or the brilliant reminiscences of a neurotic childhood. Or Henry's indication of
his apparently eccentric conduct:

> In a world of fugitives
> The person taking the opposite direction
> Will appear to run away.

Mr. Eliot's own poetry may appear to be taking the opposite direction, but the reader of this play cannot, I
think, object to it, as he could to 'The Waste Land,' that
it is essentially defeatist; it embodies a sincere belief
and a genuine courage.

110. MAUD BODKIN, THE EUMENIDES AND PRESENT-DAY CONSCIOUS-
NESS, 'ADELPHI'

May 1939, vol. xv, 411-13

Bodkin (1875-1967) was an English critic best known for
her Jungian analyses of poetry, as exemplified by 'Arche-
typal Patterns in Poetry' (1934) and by her study of 'The
Family Reunion' in relation to the 'Eumenides' of Aeschylus, 'The Quest for Salvation in an Ancient and a Modern
Play' (1941).

Of T.S. Eliot's play, 'The Family Reunion,' at the Westminster Theatre, one critic - in the 'Observer' - wrote
'Christian and Pagan do not mix. How can a Christian
accept the idea of a family curse at all?' Another - Desmond MacCarthy in the 'New Statesman' - similarly questions: Why introduce the Furies - 'hopeless symbols for
Mr. Eliot's purpose' - in a play of Christian temper
'about the place of the conscience in life'? A vengeful
ghost, visible, as in 'Macbeth,' to the haunted sinner
alone, would, Mr. MacCarthy suggests, win from us a readier
response.
     A play by Mr. Eliot is more than an event of the
theatre. A critic reviewing the play - in the 'Listener'
- as 'an imaginative work of art,' that 'no one should miss
reading,' praising Eliot's 'moral sensitivity,' his 'capacity for feeling life and opening out layer after layer
of consciousness,' yet repeats the complaint concerning the
use of the myth of the Eumenides. He pronounces it 'purely
academic; it would be much simpler if one member of the
family was faced with the problem of his own sin and the
rest of the family were spectators.'
     Does it not seem a little odd that critics, recognising
the poet's moral sensitivity and power to bring new
issues to consciousness, should yet so lightly propose
change in the play's central imagery, as if they knew
better than the author what experience this imagery
should illumine?
     Is this a play about an individual conscience haunted
by an individual sin? Eliot - I think - tries to guard
against just such an apprehension of his theme. The play's
chief character, Harry, the returning heir, speaking to his
assembled family, dismayed to find him, as it seems,
conscience-haunted, believing himself guilty of the murder
of his wife - insists that they do not understand:

                              It goes a good deal deeper
     Than what people call their conscience; it is just the
          cancer
     That eats away the self. I knew how you would take it.
     First of all, you isolate the single event.

                              It is not my conscience,
     Not my mind, that is diseased, but the world I have to
          live in.

And again:

     You go on trying to think of each thing separately,
     Making small things important, so that everything
     May be unimportant....

    I was like that in a way, so long as I could think
    Even of my own life as an isolated ruin,
    A casual bit of waste in an orderly universe.
    But it begins to seem just part of some huge disaster.

Of the haunting to which these words refer we can best
gain understanding, it seems to me, if we search our own
spirits, and putting aside demands of theatrical convention, use the poet's fable and imaginative speech to
objectify our own deeper experience at this moment of our
individual and collective destiny. For us, too, horror
grows of overshadowing disaster. Our world is diseased,
constrained to self-destroying violence; and when we question: 'Can devastation of our own homes be averted? Can
we, if war comes, refuse part in it?' do we not feel that
our questions falsely 'isolate the single event,' 'making
small things important'?
    It is indeed one necessity of life to isolate, concen-
trating upon our small individual range; yet there is
another need: to be aware of a reality more comprehensive.
There is a vision of the real pressing on our spirits that
only myth and imagery can convey. At a time like the present, in a world where - as I think some journalist put it
- the air around us is dark with the wings of curses coming home to roost, surely the myth of the Eumenides -
dread pursuers that avenge not private but communal crime
- far from being academic, has dreadful relevance.
    Of the pursuing forces in Eliot's play the fugitive
says:

                              Were they simply outside,
    I might escape somewhere, perhaps. Were they simply
        inside
    I could cheat them perhaps with the aid of Dr.
        Warburton -

But this is too real for your words to alter.
    So with us; when the horror of reported events becomes
unendurable, we escape to private interests; when the pain
of our own spirits overwhelms us, we practise devices of
mental hygiene. But our trouble is both within us and
without. For such modes of escape it is too real. Is any
escape possible?
    The play suggests an answer. For such a problem any
solution a poet may suggest can be no more than a hint,
partial and tentative, to which an individual spirit may
respond.
    Harry learns that his sin against the wife he hated was
foreshadowed in his father's sin of intention against his

mother; that his suffering has its counterpart in that of
the woman, his aunt, who loved his father, and had known
and loved himself as though he had been her son. She
tells him:

[Quotes 'The Family Reunion', II, ii, CPP, p. 333, 'It is
possible that you have not known' to 'which we suffer'.]

The revelation of the nature of the haunting sin, with
fellowship in suffering, is found to liberate. The spectres seen again by their victim, released from the 'awful
privacy of the insane mind,' are seen without fear or wonder.

> This time, you are real, this time, you are outside me,
>   and just endurable....

> Now I see at last that I am following you,
> And I know that there can be only one itinerary and one
>   destination.

So of this horror laid on us; though we do not know,
individually or collectively, the path we must tread, we
perhaps know this at least: that what horrifies us is real.
We cannot escape it; we must not, like the unseeing aunts
and uncles of Eliot's chorus refuse to know what lies beyond our narrow circle, blindly insisting 'that the world
is what we have always taken it to be.' We have to seek
knowledge of the sin - in ourselves and in our world -
that now is fulfilling itself in such monstrous shape.
In conscious fellowship with others, enduring sin's consequences that cannot be averted, we also may sustain hope
hereafter to achieve expiation of the curse, resolution of
the enchantment under which we suffer.

111. FREDERICK A. POTTLE, A MODERN VERSE PLAY, 'YALE
REVIEW'

June 1939, vol. xxviii, 836-9

Mr. Eliot's experiment in domestic drama is an even more
decisive technical triumph than 'Murder in the Cathedral,'
not because it contains actually better verse but because
the problem to be solved was more difficult and he does

well with it. The martyrdom of Thomas, the subject of his
first play, seems naturally 'poetic,' but it is another
thing to make credible an apparition of the Eumenides at
Wishwood. We have known the specifications of this kind
of play for a long time: it must give us a prevailing surface of dialogue so close to prose in its rhythms and sen-
timents as to create the illusion of common reality, but
it must also manage to invest its matter with the urgency
which we associate with verse. To be prosaic: to be
literary: - these are the poet's Scylla and Charybdis. It
seems pretty certain that Mr. Eliot has come through more
prosperously than any of his predecessors. His conversational lines have a surface which we recognize as the
familiar level of prose, but when we venture on it, we
feel it to be precarious; maintained, as it were, not by
gravitation but by an unnatural tension. Beneath, and
momentarily breaking through, is the real world, a world
of poetry in which people see strange sights and say
things never heard in any drawing-room.

The device for the chorus is masterly. It was perhaps
suggested by 'Strange Interlude,' but in its effect is
quite original. The four characters who compose it express, in their normal rôles, no sentiment not strictly
in prose character. The 'choruses' consist not of what
they would ever actually say, but of what they are thinking - or would be thinking if they had the poet's power of
expression. I find no verse here so memorable as parts
of 'The Rock' and 'Murder in the Cathedral,' but that was,
no doubt, Mr. Eliot's intention. He had to be extremely
careful in this piece not to pitch any passages so high as
to make them seem verse interludes in a prose context.

A brilliant feat; but if my own feelings can be trusted,
the least satisfactory of Mr. Eliot's long poems. I do
not feel in it that strong current of excitement which has
previously swept me on through dense and rare. One should
have seen the piece presented before attempting to diag-
nose its faults, and I have not had that opportunity. But
I venture the following criticisms.

The exposition should be clearer. This is emphatically
not closet drama. It deals, as Mr. Eliot's chief character
is at pains to point out, with states of mind, not with
events; but without knowledge of certain crucial events, a
good deal of the language is radically ambiguous. The
explanation of the mystery comes very late: the play is
more than two-thirds over before Agatha reveals the crucial
bit of information that makes sense of what has gone before. Anyone reading and pondering the text will probably
convince himself that the central character, Lord Monchensey (Harry), really did push his wife over the steamer-rail,

though we are to think of the crime as not his but the sin
of his father, mother, and aunt coming to completion
through him. No person merely seeing the play presented
will be sure that Harry did not imagine the whole thing.
It makes a difference. And we do not know what Harry is
going to do at the end of the play. His mother, not un-
naturally, infers that he plans to be a missionary; he
says that is not it. He has 'not yet had the precise
directions.' It is very hard, if not impossible, to feel
that any act is expiatory until we know what it is. In
neither case does the ambiguity result from clumsiness;
ambiguity is Mr. Eliot's deliberate intention. To object
to this is not to raise the old cry against his 'obscurity,' it is merely to insist that a play to be acted is a
different thing from a poem to be read. There seems no
escape from the conclusion that the people who are to witness a play must be quite clear as to the gross actions
which constitute the plot. If these are not part of history or notorious legend, they must be unequivocally set
forth by the author. And 'unequivocal' is not the word
for Mr. Eliot.

In the second place, I do not think Mr. Eliot so
successful as usual in his religious framework. Current
criticism charges him with having dwindled into a Christian poet, and some will feel that he is showing his versa-
tility by writing a play from which Christian dogma is
entirely excluded and in which Christian phraseology is
allowed to appear only in the last scene. It is more
probable that he has yielded to a dramatic exigency: having chosen to write a play of modern life, he had to reconcile himself to the religious paucity of the skeptical
mind. At Wishwood the stark Greek conception of the
ripening curse may barely seem in character, but to add
the rest - the massive pagan faith of Aeschylus or Sophocles - would be too much. This makes for dramatic difficulties.

'What we have written,' says Agatha in lines that are
clearly to be taken as an epigraph,

What we have written is not a story of detection,
Of crime and punishment, but of sin and expiation.

Crime and detection have meaning without expressed religious values, but sin and expiation have none. It is too
late to bring in the Christian reference at the very end
by ritual (a parody of the service of *tenebrae*) and by
such words as 'intercession,' 'pilgrimage,' and 'redemption.' The result is to make 'The Family Reunion' more
than superficially like the works of a dramatist whom

I cannot think Mr. Eliot wished to resemble: Ibsen.
There is the same plot of inexorable destiny, the same
visiting of the sins of the fathers on the children, the
same bad manners (I do not remember reading any play in
which the chief characters were so consistently rude), the
same flaying of bourgeois virtues, the same obsessions -
almost, one would say, the same ghosts. The intent, no
doubt, was to effect a resolution: to show the solemn
forms of Christian faith emerging through disbelief,
petulance, and horror to invest the curse with meaning;
but the end seems rather a surprise than a resolution.

112. CLEANTH BROOKS, SIN AND EXPIATION, 'PARTISAN REVIEW'

Summer 1939, vol. vi, 114-16

Brooks (b. 1906), a well-known American critic, was Professor of English at Louisiana State University from 1932
to 1947. His publications include 'Modern Poetry and the
Tradition' (1939) and 'The Well Wrought Urn' (1947). He
has written extensively on Eliot and his aesthetic presuppositions have been profoundly influenced by his understanding of both Eliot's poetry and criticism.

The work of few poets shows the intense continuity which
we have learned to expect in the work of T.S. Eliot. It
was to be predicted that 'The Family Reunion' would contain a recapitulation of the symbols which dominate
Eliot's earlier poetry. They are here: the purposeless
people moving in a ring ('in an overcrowded desert,
jostled by ghosts') of 'The Waste Land'; the 'hellish,
sweet smell' that accompanies the apprehension of the
supernatural from 'Murder in the Cathedral'; the purgatorial flame of 'Ash-Wednesday.' But most of all, perhaps, the play is illuminated by that rather dry and not
sufficiently appreciated poem, 'Burnt Norton'; and in one
sense, at least, the play may be said to be a restatement
of 'Burnt Norton' in terms of drama.
   The world of the play is the world of 'The Waste Land':
a world inhabited by thoroughly respectable upper-class
English ladies and gentlmen, 'people to whom nothing has
ever happened,' and who consequently 'cannot understand

the unimportance of events,' people whose 'life' is 'the
keeping up of appearances. The making the best of a bad
job.'

But to Harry, the young head of the family, something
has happened, something which breaks through the death-in-
life in which he has lived, and his return to the family
home completes his birth into the real world. At the end
of the play, like Arnaut, he is, with joy, committing
himself to the purgatorial flame, but he despairs of making
the family understand what has happened to him, and why he
cannot take up his place as head of the family and master
of Wishwood. As he says late in the play

> ...when one has just recovered sanity,
> And not yet assured in possession, that is when
> One begins to seem the maddest to other people.

His is essentially the position of the protagonist at the
end of 'The Waste Land' - 'Hieronymo's mad againe.'

But Harry's difficulty is Eliot's difficulty. The audience for whom he writes are quite as secularized as are the
characters of the play, and they are far more hard-boiled
in their rationalism. They are not more likely to understand the treatment of the relation of time to eternity expressed in 'Burnt Norton'; they are even less likely to be
sympathetic with it. Eliot has set himself a very difficult task in the play. For many readers, Harry's action
will be quite incredible, and the play will consequently
be murky and dull - another instance of Eliot's retreat
into Anglo-Catholic mysticism.

But precisely because Eliot has faced this basic problem frankly, the play is a triumph. The dramatic fact,
kept steadily in focus, is Harry's awareness that, intense
and meaningful as the experience is to him, it is quite
impossible for his uncles and aunts to understand it.
There is even a grim humor in the fact that the revelation
has come through Harry's sin (One remembers Eliot's comment in the essays, 'and it is better in a paradoxical
way to do evil than to do nothing; at least we exist.')
Harry is conscious of the humor, just as he is willing to
entertain the belief that he may be mad. The play does
not turn into preaching. It remains focused on Harry's
exploration of his experience.

It is symptomatic of the play's closeness of texture
that one cannot separate out gobbets of poetry and have
them retain the intensity which they undoubtedly possess
in the context. The poetry is very closely integrated
with the other elements of the play. The verse is one
which allows Eliot to shift from the casual, fatuous,

after-dinner conversation into the passionate language of
Harry's colloquies with Agatha.   There is a sense of
dramatic acceleration, but not of strain; and this, in
part, of course, is because the contrast is not superficial and external, but a part of the central dramatic
fact.   The contrasts occur, therefore, at the proper level,
and thus allow Harry's experience to grow out of the
family history, as they allow his crisis to grow legiti-
mately out of the rather boring normality of a family
reunion.

By the same token, the choruses are natural: the
characters do not strike a pose as they begin their
choruses.   They are merely speaking aloud (by conversation) their unspoken thoughts in the awkward silences
which occur as they wait for dinner.   I have not seen the
play performed, but my feeling is that it would gain from
being acted, and this, again, is further testimony to the
fact that Eliot has conscientiously subordinated every
detail to the total effect of the play as a play.

A review so brief as this cannot hope to penetrate very
far into the more interesting problems of organization
which the play raises.   Perhaps it is more important to
try to say a further word about the reader's problem of
belief.   The play obviously has something to say to people
who cannot accept Eliot's metaphysic.   It would be folly
to argue that his metaphysic is of no importance in this
play in which it finds, perhaps, its most explicit statement.   But it is also folly to prejudge the play as
representing an intolerable narrowness of interest by
narrowing our own interests in advance.   For the reader
who is likely to be troubled by this problem, one may suggest some such approach to the play as the following.
Eliot has not lost touch with the realities.   The desiccation, the fatuousness, the deadening complacency of the
British upper classes are revealed in this play quite as
mercilessly as Auden reveals them.   Harry's vision of a
different world is certainly not Auden's vision, but he
occupies a position with relation to society basically
similar to that occupied by Auden's characters.   (Auden's
'converted' characters have their problem of communication
too, and their problem of expiation.)   There will be time
enough, and room enough outside the play, to argue the
relative truth of the two visions.   Suffice it to say here
that Eliot, with a dramatic consistency and integrity
which rarely lapses, has exploited the dramatic values inherent in the situation.   And it is ultimately by a test
which takes this dramatic integrity into account that his
play will have to be appraised.

113. PHILIP HORTON, SPECULATIONS ON SIN, 'KENYON REVIEW'

Summer 1939, vol. i, 330-3

Horton, an American critic, published a biography of Hart
Crane in 1937.

It is perhaps scarcely legitimate to compare 'Murder in
the Cathedral,' which is more properly a pageant than a
play, with Eliot's latest work, yet at one point such a
comparison will serve to illustrate what I feel to be the
radical weakness of 'The Family Reunion.' Doubtless there
are several reasons for the surprising stage success of
the earlier piece, including its character as pageant, but
not the least of them is the fact that the audience is at
once put in possession of the knowledge why the action is
necessary. Whatever else may escape them - the further
reaches of theology and irony - they know that Thomas is
to become a martyr, and understand at least enough of the
circumstances and the character of the man to make the
action seem plausible, if not, indeed, necessary.

It is precisely here - in point of adequate motivation
- that 'The Family Reunion' seems to me to fail. To be
sure, we know the general subject of the play; it 'is not
a story of detection / Of crime and punishment, but of sin
and expiation.' But this is not enough. In order that
the action be convincing, the sin must be sufficiently defined to make clear not only the nature of the relations
between the characters, but also the terms of the central
conflict. Without such elementary definition, it seems to
me, there can be no adequate motivation. What Eliot
offers in its stead - a complex of possible sins almost
Jamesian in its ambiguities - hardly constitutes, however
rich its materials, a workable substitute.

These are the essential facts of the play. Harry, the
eldest son of Lady Monchensey, returns from abroad after
an absence of eight years. During this time he has taken
a wife whom he later murdered (or thought he murdered),
and since then has been pursued, like Orestes, by the Eumenides. Presently he becomes aware of some 'origin of
wretchedness' behind his childhood, and upon questioning
Agatha, one of his mother's sisters, learns that his
father, long since dead, had really been in love with her,
Agatha, had lived with his wife for a few years only under
duress, and had wished and even planned to murder her.

After this revelation Harry comes to a decision to leave
home again in pursuit of expiation - a decision that is
directly responsible for his mother's death at the end of
the play.

Now, however it may be for theology, it is not enough,
I think, for the purpose of dramatic motivation simply to
name the sin; it is also necessary to ground it in circumstance, to supply its rationale. Admitting that it is immaterial whether Harry actually caused his wife's death,
why did he desire it? Had she been unfaithful to him; or
was their marriage, like that of his parents, corrupted by
a less patent immorality; or have we to deal here with a
Freudian situation where the desire for the death of the
wife represents the desire for the death of the mother?
(There is some support for the last suggestion in the
highly effective scene where Harry plays grimly upon the
phrase, Her Ladyship, which may refer equally to his dead
wife and to his mother.) Nowhere in the play are these
questions answered. With the family sin, however, things
are a little more clear. Harry's father is also guilty of
desiring his wife's death; but in his case the motive is
supplied: he was in love with Agatha. In the eyes of a
theologian like Eliot - if one wishes to press matters -
this might well make him guilty of three sins: murder,
adultery (since he lusted after another woman), and forni-
cation (since there was no love between him and his wife).
But though the rationale of the family sin is relatively
clear, I still do not feel that it serves as adequate
motivation, for the reason that Eliot does not indicate on
Harry's part any decisive or commensurate reaction to it.
Neither in speech nor in behavior does he betray any in-
crement of guilt or horror at Agatha's revelations, nor is
one made to feel that this knowledge radically changes or
determines his course of action. It contributes to it, to
be sure; but neither the family sin nor the 'murder' of
his wife is clearly defined in terms of the dramatic conflict (i.e., in terms of Harry's consciousness). The burden of motivation seems to fall somewhere between the two.
The resulting ambiguity may be seen in Agatha's tentative
statement of the central problem in the next to the last
scene. Its very tentativeness may serve as a measure of
my objections.

[Quotes 'The Family Reunion', II, ii, CPP, p. 333, 'It is
possible that you have not known' to 'purgatorial flame'.]

From this passage it would appear that the ambiguity
was deliberate on Eliot's part. If this is true, one may
perhaps find an explanation for it in the fact that the

sin and the expiation are spoken of variously in terms of
Christian dogma (defilement, pilgrimage, intercession,
redemption), in terms of pagan thought and ritual (the
season of sacrifice, the Eumenides, exorcism, consummation
of the curse), and possibly in terms of psychoanalysis as
well (the creeping back through the little door, the private worlds of make-believe and fear, the wife-mother, the
search for the father).

All this would seem to indicate that Eliot, instead of
supplying the play with a *definition* of the specific sin
in question, has used the play as a vehicle of *speculation*
on the nature of sin. It is important to note that the
one does not necessarily exclude the other. The speculation, if indulged through the consciousness of the hero,
as in 'Hamlet,' might well have become a legitimate and
effective agent in the dramatic conflict. But Eliot has
carried on his speculation *in his own person as playwright*
by his manipulation of the materials and structure of the
play: by the incantations assigned variously to Agatha,
Mary, and Harry; by his treatment of the Eumenides (he has
followed Aeschylus in transforming the spirits from the
Erinyes, the 'sleepless hunters,' who pursue, into the
'bright Angels,' who guide, without, however, making clear
the logic of the transformation); and by the deliberate
ambiguity with which he has cloaked the nature both of the
sin and of the expiation that is to follow. Now for the
'higher levels of significance' in drama such mysteries
and ambiguities are often highly desirable, but only provided that the action, far from depending upon them for
its motivation, is supported, as in 'Hamlet,' by a relatively simple rationale that will be immediately available
to the audience. Furthermore, it seems to me that such
ambiguities should not be left implicit in the structure
of the play, but should be made explicit through the characters. In failing to do this, Eliot has, to my mind,
handled his materials as if he were writing, not a poetic
drama, but a dramatic or philosophical poem, like 'The
Waste Land,' with the unfortunate result that the ideas,
the speculation, tend to take precedence over the characters both as the principal agents of the action and the
center of interest.

The radical weakness of the play is all the more regret-
table since in other respects - in the richness and complexity of its subject, in its flexible adaptation of
simple idiomatic speech to blank verse, in the skilful
manipulation of dramatic materials in certain scenes - it
represents a distinct achievement in the advance of contemporary poetic drama.

114. JOHN CROWE RANSOM, T.S. ELIOT AS DRAMATIST, 'POETRY'

August 1939, vol. liv, 264-71

A new creative work by T.S. Eliot is not going to be
simple, even if he has reverted to a simpler literary
form, and simple judgments by the critics will misrepresent it. His latest work is the play, 'The Family
Reunion.' He may be said by this time to have entered
upon a new literary career, as playwright. But it would
be idle to expect that the new plays will be out of relation with the old poems and critical prose. He keeps a
foot in each of two worlds: the new world of naturalistic
or realistic psychological drama, and the old world of
poetry which, for him, means metaphysics. He will soon
make ordinary drama look cheap because of its lack of metaphysical interest, just as he had part in making the
ordinary shallow poetry of twenty years ago look the same
way, and for the same reason.

As a dramatist working in the contemporary, Mr. Eliot
resembles Ibsen much more than Shaw, to call names of comparable stature with his. His satiric touch is devastat-
ing, and he turns it onto living English types to show up
their social and political silliness, among other things.
That sounds like Shaw, and in fact as a satirist he compares unfavorably with Shaw only in that he does not sustain the satire uproariously; but Shaw does that because
he has nothing else to do; for Shaw is a social gospeler,
except that we must allow something also for his miscel-
laneous and professional wit. Ibsen could confine himself
to social satire, but characteristically he was deeper
than that; he quickly got to the point where he could make
scornful play with his fighting terms, 'Ideal' and
'Liberal'; he was really a poet, and had the metaphysical
dimension in his thinking.

Shaw inherited a part of Ibsen. It might be quite mistaken to say that Eliot has inherited any of him, since he
has come to drama by his own private ways. But there is
common property between the two, if we compare 'The Family
Reunion' with many Ibsen plays, such as 'The Wild Duck'
and 'Rosmersholm.' Each is a poet working in an age which
is metaphysically innocent and childlike. Or should I
say, working in a medium which rejects the metaphysics?
But for a few schools, such as the Greek tragedy and the
Japanese noh-drama, the statement would not be, I think,
wide. So each tries to import the metaphysical into the
dramatic structure, which without it already is formally

complete, and to the satisfaction of its customary audi-
tors. When Mr. Eliot abandoned the loaded materials of
'Murder in the Cathedral,' handpicked out of Catholic
history, and came to the contemporary setting, he knew
that he was not inviting success. But when he had abandoned formal poetry and taken to drama in the first place,
he must have known that the medium was not the one calculated to favor his peculiar intentions. Milton as a
religious poet risked failure in one Greekish pageant and
one dramatic adaptation of Scripture. Mr. Eliot is bold
enough to try a stage representing a modern English
country house.

On the realistic level Mr. Eliot is superb in his mastery of characterization (both the satiric and the sympathetic), handling of plot-sequence, exposition of background through dialogue, and, I imagine, such other tech-
niques as belong to an oral form like drama. It is com-
forting to find that an intellectualist, so strict and
unconceding that he has been accused of living in a tower,
has picked up without any fuss the knack for the close
structural effects of drama; it argues that his famous and
original capacity as poet was inclusive rather than exclusive, and that our popular stage-drama, with whatever
rigor it may claim, is not a very wonderful exercise of
genius, and not a thing to which first-rate minds need
feel under obligations to become addicted. Success on
that level is a hollow triumph for Eliot.

But the success is unquestionable. Such is the cogency
of the play as a mere drama, that deals with the individual characters and collective fortunes of a family. It
does not need a great deal of documentation here, and I
will only point out that Mr. Eliot knows how to epitomize
a poor lot with very terse exhibits indeed. In the first
scene the family is waiting for the return of Harry, Lord
Monchensey, now master of the house, who has been absent
for eight years. Agatha, an aunt, knowing and sympathetic
beyond any other woman character that Eliot has drawn, expects that Harry will not find it altogether a pleasure to
review the scenes of his childhood.

[Quotes 'The Family Reunion', I, i, CPP, pp. 288-9, 'I mean
that at Wishwood' to 'at home, I say!']

There you have what must be life to the drama, in the close
exchange of the personal styles and attitudes. You also
have the conflict between the metaphysical (and rather ineffectual) character and the natural Englishman, and that
is of central importance in the mind of Eliot, and in the
play.

From there we may as well go the Eliot metaphysics; for
Agatha has said something about *spectres*. Now Harry does
not see any ordinary spectres, not even the spectre of his
wife, whom he has murdered. Nor does Agatha see any at
all, though she is psychic, and thought she almost connived
with Harry's father a murder at the expense of Harry's
mother, Amy. What Harry is constantly seeing, and what we
the audience must see, if the play is acted according to
the stage-directions, but what nobody else on the stage
including Agatha can see at all though Harry implores them
to look, is a band of Hunters, Bright Angels, Eumenides,
or Furies. They drive him over the earth. They have
driven him home to obtain the sense that the curse is on
his house and not on him alone; and they will drive him
away presently to expiate the curse by going out into the
world and performing deeds of goodness and heroism. They
never speak, and if they extend their claws that seems the
most they do. Before they put in their appearances Harry
knows it by the feel of a stirring 'underneath the air,'
and by a scent 'direct to the brain,' and other premoni-
tions.

The men of Harry's family are Oxford men, and some of
them must know their Greek. At one point in the play the
Chorus doesn't know whether there is any way to exorcise
the evil out of old houses either 'in Argos or in England.'
There is of course the fact itself that the play does have
a Chorus, like Greek plays; for the minor and insensitive
characters have a way of talking themselves into a passage
where they can talk in unison, to an effect that is often
burlesque, as in Auden's plays, but is sometimes solemn
and fearful as in Greek. And these features constitute
all the Greek that attaches to this English play, except
the Furies, who cannot quite be assimilated into it by
these means, for the literal reader like myself.

I do not know how genuinely Mr. Eliot is under conviction about ancestral curses and their expiation. He may
feel that the necessity of the doctrine, given such situations as these, is very deep in the nature of things. It
is certain that dramatically the terror of the mysterious
curse is very much more emphasized than the beauty of the
idea of expiation, which comes in almost as an after-
thought. But I think there is a rule of dramatic propriety by which these Eumenides are not sustained as
vehicles of the curse. They belong not only to an age of
faith, but to an age when faith was different from what
it is likely to be again. In other words, the audience,
I think, will see them and will not believe in them. The
hardboiled audience, I mean; and as for the sensitive and
literary people, who will infallibly constitute much of

the audience for this kind of play, even they will think
these creatures too 'literary' to express the metaphysical
realities, and too readily picked up from another context.
They belong in a more imaginative order of literature than
realistic drama if they are to be vitalized.

I like the air of mystery that thickens steadily
throughout the play. We see the 'natural' action gathering
occult significances. I think there will not be an intelligent auditor who can resist being powerfully impressed;
not by the Furies, but by the talk and actions of the
characters. As in all metaphysical speculations, a reality
deeper than the visible world is indicated.

I remark that there is nothing particularly Christian
in this play. A Christian entity to do the work of the
Eumenides probably was not forthcoming; or if it was, it
seemed unavailable for this drama, for drama now. Ibsen
many times experimented with mysterious symbols in trying
to express the occult effects by which he proposed to explode the naturalism of drama. They were not apparitions
but words; words which had power with the actors in the
main action, therefore with the other actors, and with the
audience. It is my impression that when there are no
orthodox supernatural beings in the vogue of drama at the
time, fresh symbols - which it is as wrong to push to a
high visibility as it is not to have them at all - are the
best recourse that dramatists have. Unless, at least,
they want to leave drama for forms in which imagination
need not be so constrained.

The poetic diction probably does well enough - for a
play. The metrics are execrable, except in the light of
the same qualification. They are not too tight but too
loose, which means, nevertheless, that they do not really
encroach on the prose feeling of a realistic play, and are
quite prepared to abdicate entirely if necessary. There
is just occasional poetic language independent of drama,
or in set and undramatic speeches. But it is an atmo-
spheric play. Mary, the cousin who would have married
Harry, and who is made sensitive by the slight, says:

> The cold spring now is the time
> For the ache in the moving root
> The agony in the dark
> The slow flow throbbing the trunk
> The pain of the breaking bud.
> These are the ones that suffer least:
> The aconite under the snow
> And the snowdrop crying for a moment in the wood.

Harry replies:

> Spring is an issue of blood
> A season of sacrifice
> And the wail of the new full tide
> Returning the ghosts of the dead
> Those whom the winter drowned
> Do not the ghosts of the drowned
> Return to land in the spring?
> Do the dead want to return?

And I like that on the whole, and in a play especially, because it is better than I had bargained for. But it is not the Eliot we knew as a poet. It is that Eliot warmed over, for 'theatre.'

115. HORACE GREGORY, THE UNITIES AND ELIOT, 'LIFE AND LETTERS'

October 1939, vol. xxiii, 53-60

Gregory (b. 1898), an American poet and critic, was a freelance writer during the 1930s, contributing to the major periodicals.

Whatever else Mr. T.S. Eliot has done or has not done, he has frequently given his critics an excuse to exercise their feelings or opinions, their wit or will, either good or bad, or their ingenuity. In America, book reviewers have been unusually hospitable to his new play and dramatic critics who have read it have assumed the attitude of the lady in Frederick Watts's painting who is said to represent Hope in a million bourgeois living-rooms. I strongly suspect, however, that 'The Family Reunion' will finally turn out to be one of the more conspicuous of Mr. Eliot's successful failures. Nor do I believe that its arrival has been spontaneously conceived, for it may be said that Mr. Eliot has had designs on the theatre since 1919 and that his serious intentions toward the general direction of the modern stage have been foreshadowed in his two essays, Rhetoric and Poetic Drama and A Dialogue on Dramatic Poetry. 'The Family Reunion' is his first full-length play, and is, therefore, the first sustained proof of his willingness to test his theories concerning

poetic drama before an audience. If mere failure were all
that it accomplished, or if Mr. Eliot were another kind of
poet than he is, his adverse critics could drop back into
the brief security of the moment in 1922 that followed the
spectacular publication of 'The Waste Land.' It now seems
clear that 'The Waste Land' was neither a hoax nor the
greatest poem of its time, but was the first success that
Mr. Eliot had achieved through failure. Both 'Prufrock'
and 'Ash-Wednesday' are better poems, yet 'The Waste Land'
represents the turning point in Mr. Eliot's career and its
very title has become identified with the literary decade
preceding 1930.

I can think of no poet of Mr. Eliot's generation who
has gained or learned so much from failure as he, or who
has become more formidable after his critics have
announced him dead and buried. It is for this reason,
among others, that I believe 'The Family Reunion' should
be regarded with particular wariness, and whatever should
be said against it demands some recognition of the serious
intentions which lie behind it. For the moment we have no
proof that Mr. Eliot will continue to write plays, but if
he does, 'The Family Reunion' contains a promise of being
the most important event in the English speaking theatre
since a certain evening in 1893 when non-paying guests
were invited to see a performance of Mr. Bernard Shaw's
'Mrs Warren's Profession.' The continued failure of modern plays written in good verse is almost equal to a ban
placed upon them by an officious censor; in one case we
have a bewildered audience, in the other we have a confused and overtly anxious custodian of public morals, and
if the playwright continues to improve his work beyond the
evening of either disapproval, the very play that once
earned disparise will receive applause beyond the proportion of its actual value. 'The Family Reunion' seems to
be that kind of play; so far as its failure may be predicted, its London audience has already registered a jus-
tifiable dislike of it, yet I doubt if that audience, or
a New York audience, can measure, at one sitting, the
potentialities of (and, I might almost say, threat that
lies behind) Mr. Eliot's new play.

I can well imagine that Mr. Eliot's desire to restore
the Greek unities of time and place seem genuinely foreign
on the British stage. But here again we must look for an
American precedent in viewing Mr. Eliot's intentions. If,
as D.H. Lawrence once remarked, early American novelists
were haunted by the ghost of the American Indian, it
should also be remarked that American poets have been
haunted by the perfection, the remoteness, the undying
vitality of Greek poetry. One might say that it is almost

natural to discover in Whitman an embryonic attempt to
reproduce the sound of the Greek hexameter beneath the
Biblical rhythms of his unrhymed verse. The curious passion concealed within the phrase, 'the glory that was
Greece / And the grandeur that was Rome,' owes its first
expression to Edgar Allan Poe. To the American public
that reads contemporary verse and goes to see a modern
play, the revival of a Greek theme in Mr. Eliot's new
play is no more extraordinary than Mr. Robinson Jeffers's
adaptation of the Orestes myth in 'The Tower Beyond
Tragedy,' or H.D.'s translation of the 'Ion of Euripides,'
or the Homeric undertones of Mr. Ezra Pound's first Canto
or Mr. Eugene O'Neill's 'Mourning Becomes Electra.' The
theme of Mr. Eliot's new play takes its place within that
tradition, if it may be called so; meanwhile its setting
recalls the atmosphere of the bourgeois melodrama as it was
once conceived by Sir Arthur Wing Pinero. There is neither
a Mrs. Tanqueray nor a notorious Mrs. Ebbsmith (or should I
say a Mrs. Patrick Campbell?) to enliven its performance
and make its setting plausible to a London audience. What
we have instead is a mixture of at least two insoluble
elements over which a dark blood-stained atmosphere floats,
reproducing something that has the obvious intention of
arousing discomfort and fear; what seems to be aimed at is
the quality of wit that entered 'Volpone,' leaving its
mark upon each character within the play, until at last
one hears only the reiterations of the chorus. What
actually emerges are two things in conflict: the contemporary environment of a country house in the North of England and a vision of the Eumenides.

In theory Mr. Eliot's play appears well disciplined. A
certain Harry, Lord Monchensey, returns to his family
house, his mother's home, for a reunion with his mother,
his aunts, his uncles and his brothers, who, by the way,
never arrive but are withheld by accidents. The first act
is kept alive by the anticipation of Harry's entrance and
the surprise of his early arrival: but in the unfolding of
the Orestes story, Harry's conviction of his responsibility
for his wife's death, his inheritance of that same sense of
guilt from his father, his vision of the Eumenides, the
play drags and becomes increasingly unreal and 'experimental', quite as though one were witnessing an amateur performance given in a 'little Theatre'. One waits for the
fine choruses, one of which is written for the last act,
and then and only then does one feel at ease. Part of the
discomfort is, of course, the deliberate intention of the
author. His characters are stripped of their security with
the same critical perception that is conveyed when one
reads in 'The Waste Land':

>   One of the low on whom assurance sits
>   As a silk hat on a Bradford millionaire

The same harsh light of irony plays over the people who
move behind the footlights of 'The Family Reunion.'
And realizing this, it would be an easy matter to interpret the play in terms of social irony. Its commentary on
the British upper middle class is obvious enough: the
characters that Mr. Eliot has called together for a family
reunion are terrible and terrifying people and my regret
is that they do not terrify us with the absolute conviction
we desire. The Eumenides who uncover Harry's guilt and
disclose the theme of the play to the spectators' eyes are
untranslated elements in the environment where they
appear. They are as significant and as false as Mr. Eugene
O'Neill's use of masks in 'The Great God Brown' and should
not be tolerated for a single moment.

If the Eumenides in 'The Family Reunion' seem imposed by
the will of the author from outside the play, then why do
we accept the witches in 'Macbeth,' the dead king's ghost
in 'Hamlet' or the hovering, invisible presence of the
White Horses in 'Rosmersholm'? These, too, are the supernatural signs of an internal conflict within the human
heart and mind and are the springs of dramatic action
within the play. I need not, I hope, go into the detail of
why or how they are made to seem inevitable within their
separate plays; commentators on Shakespeare and on Ibsen
have already done so to the satisfaction of their col-
leagues as well as to the understanding of the public.
The witches, the White Horses, and the king's ghost convey
their power through the very conventions of the play that
they inhabit, they are in the language of the play's
worldly environment, they are of that world and of none
other. In 'The Family Reunion' we are forced to take specific creatures of a distant time and culture on larger
faith than anything within the play implies; nor is there
anything in the cast of Harry's imagination, as we hear
him speak, that points inevitably to a selection of the
winged sisters, leaping to being from the blood of muti-
lated Uranus to follow him until he turns upon them at the
country seat of his name and household. This is not to
argue against his sense of guilt, nor against the fact that
his state of mind may be one which is commonly called
'possessed by furies'. That reality is granted at the
moment of his first confession. The unreality is attached
to the specific symbol of his guilt; unlike the White
Horses of 'Rosmersholm,' who signified within the neigh-
bourhood of Rosmer's guilt-ridden threshold the grief and
madness that possessed his mind, Harry's Eumenides are

neither of earth nor air, and though he is careful not to
name them, his author has, so that the reader is forced to
struggle with them against unbelief.

Whatever flaws Mr. Eugene O'Neill's 'Mourning Becomes
Electra' contains, and those of inflated language and
loose writing are among them, the play solves the very
problem in translation that Mr. Eliot leaves undone, and
until he does so, his intention to revive poetic drama in
full stature on the modern stage will remain a brilliant
amateur's performance in the theatre. In contrast to Mr.
Eliot's version of the Orestes myth, 'Mourning Becomes
Electra' is omnibus drama, each situation overdramatized
at such length that its great energy loses meaning in protracted violence. But the translation of the Orestes cycle
is fully realized in the terms of the New England setting
re-created by Mr. O'Neill - and for that reason, I believe,
Mr. O'Neill's critics and audiences felt or saw something
of a true vision of guilt and horror that Mr. Eliot's
audiences do not.

The unities of time and place for which Mr. Eliot pleads
so eloquently in his dialogue on dramatic poetry and which
appear as though a promise had been fulfilled in 'The
Family Reunion,' display their usefulness in the writing of
poetic drama, and it is good to rediscover their merits on
the modern stage. They cannot save a bad play, but they do
tend to conserve the energy required in hearing verse spoken on the stage, and above all they concentrate the attention of the audience upon individual lines of poetry.
There are other unities, of course, and not the least of
them (which Shakespeare's quick intelligence discovered)
are unities of human motive, speech, and imagination that
exist within the play itself and are not to be destroyed.
The dramatic reality of Mr. Eliot's 'Murder in the Cathedral' suddenly evaporated when its four Knights stepped to
the footlights and spoke their reasons for killing Becket
as though they had walked out of a script conceived and
written by Mr. Bernard Shaw. Something of the same violation of the play's integrity - and I am speaking of the
play's integrity and not its author's - occurs when Harry
sets out to pursue the Eumenides in his car.

'Go face the Furies, turn tables on them and track them
down,' says Mr. Eliot. This is surely excellent advice to
many members of Mr. Eliot's generation who fear to face any
reality within themselves. The advice contains the same
perception into the world that Mr. Eliot now inhabits as the
mere title of 'The Waste Land' once conveyed to its immediate contemporaries. The same restless sensibility is alive
within it, the same disquiet note of warning is heard above
the ruins of a notably imperfect play. It is the quality

of Mr. Eliot's failures in verse and on the stage that
endow them with unusual distinction. What this may mean
if one considers a probable future of poetic drama in
English is, as I have already suggested, something like a
threat, and the very least that we can expect from it is
the continuation of an Anglo-American influence upon
poetry that is written for the stage.

The last impression to be carried away from 'The Family
Reunion' and its revival of the Orestes story is that Mr.
Eliot never seems more American than when he is most European. The divided, sleepless sensibility that creates a
play and then destroys it, that is most un-British in its
seeking-out of an absolute, a classical serenity, still
evokes emotions of significant discomfort on both sides of
the Atlantic.

'Old Possum's Book of Practical Cats'

London, 5 October 1939; New York, 16 November 1939

116. STEPHEN SPENDER, CATS AND DOG, 'LISTENER'

26 October 1939, vol. xxii, supplement viii

Spender (b. 1909), an English poet, critic and man of
letters, was co-editor of 'Horizon' from 1939 to 1941.
His 'Collected Poems' appeared from Faber & Faber in 1955.
He published a full-length study of Eliot in the Fontana
Modern Masters series (London, 1975).

On the wrapper, the publishers give an explanation for
offering a book under this title, instead of the originally announced 'Pollicle Dogs and Jellicle Cats'. Mr.
Eliot, they say, 'has been fortified by a growing desire
for the company of *cats*, and a growing perception that it
would be improper to wrap them up with *dogs*'. As though
this lame excuse were not injury enough to the canine
world, insult is added to it by the publication of one
poem about dogs, to thirteen about cats. Yet it is difficult to think that the Pollicle dogs of the original
title slipped in by an oversight, since the poem which
records their fight with the Pekes and (it must be ad-
mitted) the intervention of the Great Rumpuscat, has a
heading of six lines of magnificent 18-pt. capitals.
However, doubtless the injustice committed by Messrs.
Faber and Faber and Mr. Eliot to the race of Pollicles
will not pass in silence, since, as the poet himself
admits:

                                        they
     Bark bark bark bark
     Bark bark BARK BARK
     Until you can hear them all over the Park.

They are probably barking in Gloucester Road and Russell
Square at this moment.
     The truth is that poets have always shown a marked pre-
ference for cats, whilst dogs have been treated either
satirically, or else sentimentally, tearfully even.
Baudelaire, Christopher Smart, Cowper, Eliot, are only a
few of the army on the side of cats, whilst Shakespeare
heaped invective on dogs. Dogs are themselves too like
little satiric poems on the behaviour of their masters to
need much interpreting. But cats are mysterious and need
interpretation, as Mr. Eliot knows:

     When you notice a cat in profound meditation,
         The reason, I tell you, is always the same:
     His mind is engaged in a rapt contemplation
         Of the thought, of the thought, of the thought of
             his name:
             His ineffable effable
             Effanineffable
     Deep and inscrutable singular name.

     The grown-up reader will notice the influence of Poe
in the last few lines, and ballad influences are evident
in such lines as:

     Woe to the weak canary, that fluttered from its
         cage;
     Woe to the pampered Pekinese, that faced Growl-
         tiger's rage.
     Woe to the bristly Bandicoot, that lurks on foreign
         ships,
     And woe to any cat with whom Growltiger came to grips!

     But doubtless the majority of readers of these poems
will not be keen inquirers into modern poetry and tradition. Sufficient to them that 'cat' rhymes with 'mat':

     All day she sits upon the stair or on the steps or on
         the mat;
     She sits and sits and sits and sits - and that's what
         makes a Gumbie cat!

They will delight in names such as Growltiger, Gus,
Bustopher Jones, Skimbleshanks, Macavity and Old

Deuteronomy. The story of Growltiger's last stand will
thrill them to the marrow, whilst they will deplore the
snobbishness of Bustopher Jones, the Cat about town.

This is a charming book, charmingly produced, and very
moderately priced. The author's illustrations on the
cover, raise hopes that when a new edition is produced,
he will illustrate 'The Battle of the Pekes and the
Pollicles', and The Theatre Cat, to say the least, even if
it takes him all his time between now and then to work at
the drawings.

'East Coker'

First Faber edition, London, 12 September 1940

117. G.W. STONIER, MR. ELIOT'S NEW POEM, 'NEW STATESMAN'

14 September 1940, vol. xx, 267-8

Stonier (b. 1903), critic and journalist, was literary
editor of the 'New Statesman' from 1928 to 1945.

It is five years since the publication of Mr. Eliot's last
poem - a period occupied by criticism, two plays and a
volume of light verse - but 'East Coker' takes us back to
'Burnt Norton', in something more than title, as though
scarcely a day had passed. Or rather, since Mr. Eliot is
not a writer who repeats himself, it would be better to
say that we resume from the earlier point. There is a
similar cluster of experience: problems of time and eternity clutched at from the sliding second; the return to
country scenes in childhood - a moment is held and then
let go with a gesture of resignation; permanence sought in
solitude and in art hung like a Chinese vase in time; the
desire to escape from a twilit consciousness into bright
daylight or darkness; the struggle to fix ever-shifting
experiences with words which also break and slip. No need
to remark, at this time of day, that the expression, the
amalgamation of such attitudes is sharp and poignant, as
final as Mr. Eliot can make it; or that the poem carries
an authority which marks the work of no other living poet
except Claudel. This authority has been compared more
than once to that of Arnold, but it seems to me even more
powerful and exclusive. We do not approach a new poem by
Mr. Eliot as single-mindedly as, for example, we used to

409

open the 'London Mercury' to discover a new poem of Yeats.
Whether Yeats or Eliot is the 'better' poet is beside the
point. We expect, and find, a criticism both of literature and life. As we read, the hint of passages in Milton
and Spenser carry the mind back to criticism he has written in the past; the nature of writing itself is put to
the test:

[Quotes 'East Coker', V, CPP, p. 182, 'So here I am' to
'seem unpropitious'.]

Here, it seems to me, is an integrity as inflexible and
moving as Baudelaire's, involving however a confession of
failure which no poet of earlier date has dared venture;
the mask of eloquence - the only questionable part of
Baudelaire's achievement - has been dropped altogether,
with masterly effect. If one says that Mr. Eliot has set
an example to modern poets, it is in this sense of self-
discipline and sacrifice and not of course with the meaning that anyone should follow or attempt to follow his
manner of writing.

There are many threads in Mr. Eliot's poetry. The
mingled nostalgia and caricature of the Prufrock period
have vanished never perhaps to reappear; the roots of his
later poetry, 'East Coker' and 'Burnt Norton' are to be
found in 'The Hollow Men'. There the lyric, the sardonic
jingle, the austere response, were set nakedly side by
side; the successes -

    Eyes I dare not meet in dreams,
    In death's dream kingdom,
    These do not appear:
    There, the eyes are
    Sunlight on a broken column, etc.

- were offset by passages in which fragments from different worlds merely clashed and grated. Since then Mr.
Eliot has marshalled his material more harmoniously, and
as a whole 'East Coker' is a more satisfactory poem than
'The Hollow Men', though it contains no passage to equal
the lines quoted above. The greater homogeneity is due
chiefly of course to religious contemplation which has
smoothed many corners. Pessimistic though Mr. Eliot is
even in his acceptances, there is a difference of tone between the following lines and the bleak intrusion of
Jehovah in 'The Hollow Men':

[Quotes 'East Coker', III, CPP, p. 180, 'I said to my
soul' to 'in the waiting'.]

In another section of the poem, a similar stoicism
leads to one of those catalogues of theological paradox -
'what you do not know is the only thing you know, And what
you own is what you do not own' - from which Mr. Eliot derives consolation but which are rather blankly depressing
to the reader. His thought seems, at such times, to run
into a verbal palindrome from which there is escape.
Having abjured ecstasy, he yet allows himself to fall into
a neutral trance; the bare words do not carry all the
weight and meaning which they are meant to carry; and here,
I think, one can put one's finger on his main weakness.
Everyone who has read Mr. Eliot with some enthusiasm and
care must have discovered for himself that in almost
everything he writes there are dumb notes; notes dumb, I
mean, to us, not to Mr. Eliot, for they appear at important junctures and are repeated. Certain passages are in-
operative: such, I believe, are many of his statements of
faith, the affectation of disjointedness, the use of words
like 'Shantih' at the end of the end of 'The Waste Land',
where obviously more intensity went to putting down the
word than comes off the page.
    Again his use of quotation, by which he so often im-
parts a nostalgic flavour to his verse, has curious lapses.
In 'East Coker' there are examples of both success and
failure. The section beginning

    O dark, dark, dark. They all go into the dark,
    The vacant interstellar spaces, the vacant into
        the vacant;
    The captains, merchant bankers, eminent men of
        letters....

makes excellent use of a well-known passage in 'Samson'
('Dark, dark, dark! The moon ... hid in her vacant inter-
lunar cave'). But how do the last lines of the following
passage, delightful in its scene, strike the reader?

[Quotes, 'East Coker', I, CPP, pp. 177-8, 'In that open
field' to 'betokeneth concorde'.]

There the Elizabethan spelling imparts no flavour save
perhaps one of pedantry; its only effect is to make us
think, 'Well, I suppose Eliot, when he wrote that, was
thinking of passages in Spenser's "Epithalamion".' Yet
obviously to Eliot the whiff of the antique has an
immediate, an emotional effect, like the reminiscences
of Haydn in Profokiev's Classical Symphony. This is a
purely literary failure and the more odd because of all
poets Eliot is in certain directions the most precise in

his effects. The drawbacks I have mentioned will not come
as any surprise to Mr. Eliot's admirers.

Taken as a whole, though, 'East Coker' is one of its
author's best and most mature poems. Who else now writing
in English could have packed into 214 lines so many disparate things? And despite blemishes and minor lapses,
the effect is homogeneous. Perhaps I am wrong in applying
the word stoical to consolations which for Mr. Eliot may
have a theological reference, but 'East Coker' seems to me
the sombre and moving utterance of a man looking round him
as he grows old.

Sois sage, O ma Douleur, et tiens-toi plus tranquille.
Tu réclamais le soir; il descend; le voici.

118. JAMES KIRKUP, ELIOT, 'POETRY LONDON'

15 January 1941, vol. i, 115-16

Kirkup (b. 1923), an English poet, translator and novelist,
has taught in Malaya and Japan.

Mr. Eliot is the only great English poet living. That is,
the only poet who in years to come will be read even when
it is fashionable to ignore him. Among the likeable set
of brilliant hoaxers and endearing cleversides who have
succeeded in charming and bewildering the distracted *entre
deux guerres* audience, he alone stands out, with Lawrence,
as a genuine poet, one of major importance.

His early satirical verse, even in its most frivolous
and disconcerting moments, hints at the qualities and the
philosophy which distinguish his latest poem. In 'East
Coker' we find again the metaphysical anguish of the early
poems, the obsession with death and the vision of existence as a state in which death is life and life death:

Earth feet, loam feet, lifted in country mirth
Mirth of those long since under earth
Nourishing the corn.

The grimness and grinning of Webster are still there,
only the lines are longer, the vision mellower and the

accent less despairing. Man and beast, rotting victims on the treadmill of birth, copulation and death, are levelled to a common dust:

> The time of the coupling of man and woman
> And that of beasts ...
> ...Dung and death.

And again:

> Old fires to ashes, and ashes to the earth
> Which is already flesh, fur and faeces,
> Bone of man and beast, cornstalk and leaf.

Matter exists whether it is dead or living, and must triumph. But the implied protest of the early poems and of the 'Waste Land' is not to be found in 'East Coker.' Instead there is, not ennui or lassitude in the face of the inevitable, but a wise humility. The prospect of dying inspires no fear, no raptures, but a calm resignation, comparable to the 'Gelassenheit' of the aged Goethe and the visionary humility of Rilke in the 'Duineser Elegien.' Mr. Eliot is not the first to have realised that life is not all life, and death not all death, and that existence does not merely consist of one state following on the other, but that both states are one.

> And what there is to conquer
> In strength and submission, has already been discovered
> Once or twice, or several times, by men whom one cannot
>   hope
> To emulate ...

This humility which the poet endeavours to attain is an attitude devoid of any conscious nobility, but which is essentially noble. It is a religious or Christian humility, the fruit of patience. We are reminded of the significant line in 'What the Thunder Said':

> He who was living is now dead
> We who were living are now dying
> With a little patience

We begin to see that the stage of humility is an organic development out of an initial despair and an acquired patience. Humility is the keynote of the poem. Only humility can make endurable a vision of unending existence in which 'here and now cease to matter.' We are reminded again of the lines in 'The Burial of the Dead':

> I was neither
> Living nor dead, and I knew nothing.

And the conclusion drawn by the poet, the germ of the poem:

> The only wisdom we can hope to acquire
> Is the wisdom of humility; humility is endless.

'East Coker' impresses us by that quality which we have come to expect of Mr. Eliot - beauty of language, of which the most dominant characteristic is a hypnotic repetitiveness:

> O dark dark dark. They all go into the dark,
> The vacant interstellar spaces, the vacant into the
>   vacant ...

These are Miltonic echoes, recalling the dark of 'Samson Agonistes.' And near the beginning of the poem:

[Quotes 'East Coker', I, CPP, p. 177, 'there is a time' to 'silent motto'.]

In parts the intricate weaving and commingling of sounds and the knitting of line into line, expressive of the merged state of life and death, is effected by a frequent use of the present participle:

[Quotes 'East Coker', I, CPP, p. 178, 'Keeping time' to 'Dung and death'.]

The above passage is also a good example of the chasteness of Mr. Eliot's vocabulary. And then we see at the conclusion of the third section of the poem how well the death-life paradox adapts itself again to poetically impressive treatment:

> In order to arrive at what you are not
> You must go through the way in which you are not.
> And what you do not know is the only thing you know
> And what you own is what you do not own
> And where you are is where you are not.

It is this essentially simple nature of thought and language which surprises and satisfies. Here and there, standing out from the serious, almost monotone background of the poem with a lucid sweetness, are controlled lyrical or elegiac passages:

> Whisper of running streams, and winter lightning,
> The wild thyme unseen and the wild strawberry,
> The laughter in the garden, echoed ecstasy ...

In 'East Coker,' Mr. Eliot has written a poem of major
importance, moving, serious, sincere, and above all,
poetical. It reveals, as 'Ash-Wednesday' and 'Burnt Norton' revealed to us, the most precious and enduring aspect
of his genius. It is the poetry of a mature mind, showing
depth of understanding and much humanity, as well as a
perfection of the most appealing quality in Mr. Eliot's
technique, a reverent and impressive use of words.

He brings us a sure proof of the true nature of poetry,
for which, at present especially, we are grateful.

119. STEPHEN SPENDER, THE YEAR'S POETRY, 1940, 'HORIZON'

February 1941, vol. iii, 138-41

This is an extract from a longer article.

Ever since Matthew Arnold wrote his critical essays, and
perhaps since Shelley, poets have suffered from uneasy
consciences. In an age when science produces theoreti-
cians who are either specialists or else who disinterest-
edly invent the means of corrupting the mind and then
destroying the fabric of civilization; when the myths of
religion seem to have been exploded; when philosophy is
an exploration of words corresponding to no known reality;
at such a time poetry might step forward, take the place
of religion, understand, absorb and criticize science, and
create a synthesis in which thought was related to the
needs of society and the psychology of individuals, instead of being departmentalized.

The poets, seeing pitfalls opening round them, have
protested. A poetic myth which is a description of life
based on a hypothetical situation cannot take the place of
religion, which is dogmatic. If it did, religion would be
without any centre of literal truth, because all poetic
myths would have an equal religious value. If you treat
the Bible simply as poetry, then all poetry equal aesthetically to the Bible is as true as the Bible. Incidentally,

all poets would be promoted to the position of major or
minor prophets: a very uncomfortable thought.

Other objections, which have for some years been can-
vassed by the younger writers, are raised and disputed by
the poet as politician. T.S. Eliot protests both against
the substitution of poetry for religion, and against
Shelley's conception of poets as the 'unacknowledged legislators of mankind'. Nevertheless, his view that poetry
is merely a highly organized form of intellectual amuse-
ment does not really dispose of the issues, any more than
it would to say that poetry was just a pattern of words.

Of course, there are various kinds of poetry, and one
must avoid saying that poetry must do this or that. Yet
the fact remains that one kind, and perhaps the most enduring kind, of poetry has been a particular use of language to describe the situation of that part of humanity
which happens to be living at a particular time, struggling
with the circumstances of its environment. The first
essential of this kind of poetry is a somewhat naive consciousness of being alive; naive, because this sense of
being alive is kept separate from the actual circumstances
of living, which are regarded partly as an expression of
being alive, partly as an impediment to a full awareness of
it. A poet is a person who is conscious of the possibility
of living at any time, because he isolates the sense of
living from the sense of environment. This means also
that he is specially aware of the conflict with his
environment, because he is always trying to alter, or perhaps even accept, his environment by interpreting it into
terms of a more general and less transitory continuity of
existence.

Poetry, then, cannot evade the responsibility of interpreting the significance of life at a particular time and
relating it to life at other times. The poetry of the past
is a very freshly preserved record of the reactions of men
who were alive in the same way as we are to sets of circumstances different from ours. How different? They can tell
us only if we can also tell them. We have to establish our
own value in relation to theirs. We rapidly lose the significance of life in the past if we lose it in the present.

The problem that confronts poets - and, indeed, everyone
who is aware and alive - is that external circumstances may
arise which destroy the continuity of life sensed by
poetry. If it is conceded that this is possible - that the
destruction of the values of living, and their supersession
by machinery, aims of power, and materialism, might make
life meaningless - is the poet justified in stepping out of
his poetry, as it were, and taking a hand in altering the
world? Is he justified in using poetry as a means of

propaganda for traditional values which may, in fact, be
revolutionary?

Most contemporary poets seem to have been faced by these
these questions. Some have replied by abandoning poetry
altogether and joining revolutionary movements. Those who
have continued to write poetry have often been forced to
use their poetry as an affirmation of values rather than
as an interpretation of values which they find generally
recognized by society.

Eliot is a case in point. As I have indicated, he has
protested in his criticism against the suggestion that the
poet is concerned with aims outside poetry. Nevertheless,
his recent poetry, especially 'Burnt Norton' and 'East
Coker', shows a tendency to move outside itself and question its own use. After a passage in a dancing measure,
he writes, in 'East Coker':

[Quotes 'East Coker', II, CPP, p. 179, 'That was a way' to
'wisdom of age?'.]

'East Coker' lacks, perhaps, some of the essentially
poetic merits of Eliot's earlier poetry. If one can say
it is a successful poem without being completely poetic,
this is not really a contradiction, for it is a poem whose
aim is not entirely poetry. What the poem does is to re-
create an experience; and this experience lies outside the
poetry, within religion and philosophy; that is to say, it
could be created by other than poetic means: in prose, in
music, or in a philosophic treatise. For 'East Coker' is
not merely an experience, it is also a statement. It
succeeds in producing the sense of man's isolation in the
midst of darkness, and his desire to achieve union with
God. These phrases are meaningless, or, rather, are outworn, in themselves; but they are not meaningless in
Eliot's poem: he has re-created the experience which they
imply.

But what is the effect of poetry which uses poetry as a
medium to re-create an experience which is outside the
poetry itself? It is, that poetry is stepping out of a
world of isolated poetic experiences and insisting on the
significance of the kind of truth that poetry can describe
in the real world, and, quite literally, in the contemporary situation.

O dark, dark, dark. They all go into the dark,
The vacant interstellar spaces, the vacant into the
    vacant,
The captains, merchant bankers, eminent men of letters,

In this passage the poetry seems to say, 'This is poetic truth, but also it is literal truth, on which religion is based, existing in the world, which you cannot get away from.' Throughout 'East Coker' Eliot makes use of religious experience to insist on external and univer- sal truths which have always existed and which exist like shining and rather terrible jewels in the sombre contem- porary setting which he can convey with greater ease than any other of the moderns.

So, to some extent, Eliot's poetry insists on its pre- sence in the world of actuality. Yet although it invokes religion, and might even invoke politics, it is not a sub- stitute for religion or a loudspeaker of a political party. No. What it insists on is the reality of the kind of truth which poetry can describe: the human situation. It is as though there might be a party of poets bearing not the slogans of politics and psycho-analysis, but the slo- gans of poetry: 'In His will is our peace'; 'Ripeness is all'; and Rilke's 'You must change your life'. These can be insisted on as statements about reality, and they are also poetic statements. A time is coming when, without being a substitute for anything or propaganda of any cause, they might play their part in giving the world a sense of values.

120. JAMES JOHNSON SWEENEY, 'EAST COKER': A READING, 'SOUTHERN REVIEW'

Spring 1941, vol. vi, 771-91

Sweeney (b. 1900) is a distinguished American art critic and museum director.

Curtis B. Bradford supplemented Sweeney's work in Foot- notes to 'East Coker', 'Sewanee Review' (Winter 1944), lii, 169-75. Both essays were reprinted in 'T.S. Eliot: "Four Quartets"', a Casebook, edited by Bernard Bergonzi (London, 1969), pp. 36-63.

Since its first appearance in the spring of 1940, (1) T.S. Eliot's 'East Coker' has been widely applauded as his most considerable poetic achievement of the last eighteen years. Since the publication of 'The Waste Land' Eliot's

use of literary allusion and adapted quotation has become
familiar and expected. In spite of this, with the publication of 'East Coker' in book form we again began to hear
criticisms and complaints reminiscent of those which
greeted 'The Waste Land' two decades ago.

In his essay Tradition and the Individual Talent re-
published in 'The Sacred Wood' (1920) we read: 'the historical sense involves a perception, not only of the past-
ness of the past, but of its presence.' Again in his
introduction to Mark Wardle's translation of Valéry's 'Le
Serpent' (1924) he wrote: 'One of the qualities of a
genuine poet ... is that in reading him we are reminded of
remote predecessors, and in reading his remote predecessors we are reminded of him.'

Between the publication of these two statements 'The
Waste Land' appeared, when the presence and necessity of
notes provoked impatience and censure on the part of many
critics. But as I.A. Richards put it in his 'Principles
of Literary Criticism': 'A more reasonable complaint would
have been that Mr. Eliot did not provide a larger apparatus of elucidation.'

But it appears that the reviewers are still reluctant
to make the effort to read him carefully before passing
judgment on him. For example, in the 'New Statesman and
Nation' of September 14, 1940, we have such a perceptive
critic as G.W. Stonier writing in the body of a generally
sympathetic review as follows:

> Again his [Eliot's] use of quotation, by which he so
> often imparts a nostalgic flavour to his verse, has
> curious lapses. In 'East Coker' there are examples of
> both success and failure. The section beginning
>
> > O dark dark dark. They all go into the dark,
> > The vacant interstellar spaces, the vacant into the
> >   vacant,
> > The captains, merchant bankers, eminent men of
> >   letters ...
>
> makes excellent use of a well-known passage in 'Samson'
> ('Dark, dark, dark! The moon ... hid in her vacant
> interlunar cave'). But how do the last lines of the
> following passage, delightful in its scene, strike the
> reader?
>
> [Quotes 'East Coker', I, CPP, pp. 177-8, 'In that open
> field' to 'betokeneth concorde'.]
>
> There the Elizabethan spelling imparts no flavour save

perhaps one of pedantry; its only effect is to make us
think, 'Well, I suppose Eliot, when he wrote that was
thinking of passages in Spenser's "Epithalamion".' Yet
obviously to Eliot the whiff of the antique has an
immediate, an emotional effect, like the reminiscences
of Haydn in Profokiev's Classical Symphony. This is a
purely literary failure...

Such a conclusion is an injustice. And it is particularly difficult to understand since Stonier concludes this
sentence with the words: '...the more odd because of all
poets Eliot is in certain directions the most precise in
his effects.'
A reader who has confidence in Eliot's precision that
Stonier claims to have and is as familiar with Eliot's
allusive technique, should not be satisfied to identify
such a pointed emphasis on the archaic as a mere willful
infusion of pedantry. He should endeavor to find what
specific allusion is embodied in the passage and why the
poet sought to underscore these lines in the text by
setting them apart from the rest in archaic spelling.
In Eliot's manner of doing it there is certainly no
attempt at disguise or mystification. We are clearly invited to associate the lines with some specific feature
of the literary past. And had Stonier seriously considered this point he would have had to look no further
for a cue than the poem's title and the author's name.
Coker is a small village near Yeovil on the borders of
Dorsetshire and Somersetshire in England, reputedly the
birthplace of Sir Thomas Elyot (?-1546), the author of
'The Boke named The Gouvernour' (1531). Chapter XXI of
The Firste Boke is entitled 'Wherefore in the good
ordre of daunsinge a man and a woman daunseth to gether.'
And the opening paragraph of this chapter reads:

It is diligently to be noted that the associatinge of
man and woman in daunsing, they bothe obseruinge one
nombre and tyme in their meuynges, was not begonne without a speciall consideration, as well for the *neces-
sarye coniunction* of those *two persones*, as for the
intimation of sondry vertues, whiche be by them represented. And for as moche as *by the association of a
man and a woman in daunsinge may be signified matri-
monie*, I coulde in declarynge *the dignitie and com-
moditie of that sacrament* make intiere volumes...

Then further along we come across a passage:

In euery daunse, of a moste auncient custome, there

daunseth to gether a man and a woman, *holding eche
other by the hande or the arme, whiche betokeneth
concorde.*

Here we have clearly the source of those lines. Their
roots turn out to be Tudor not Elizabethan. And thanks
to that 'flavour of pedantry,' or more exactly archaism,
to which Stonier objects, one aspect of Eliot's approach
to his theme in 'East Coker' begins to take shape for us.
'The Boke named The Gouvernour' was one of the first of
those works partly on politics, partly on education, which
the study of the classics and more particularly that of
Plato, multiplied at the end of the Renaissance throughout
Europe. 'The Gouvernour' has been described as the earliest treatise on moral philosophy in the English language.
Sir Thomas Elyot was an ardent monarchist, a scholar
deeply influenced by the writings of such continental
humanists as Pico della Mirandola and Erasmus, and a
thorough churchman – at one time the intimate of Sir
Thomas More, but always a loyal adherent to the Church of
his sovereign. We are at once struck by the link between
Sir Thomas Elyot's interests and T.S. Eliot's famous
declaration of faith as a 'Classicist in literature, royalist in politics, and anglo-catholic in religion' which
appeared in his 1928 preface to 'For Lancelot Andrewes.'
A common emphasis is apparent in the title of T.S. Eliot's
essay 'The Idea of a Christian Society' and Elyot's translation of Pico della Mirandola's 'Rules of a Christian
Life'; just as we find a community of viewpoint between
T.S. Eliot's later poems and Sir Thomas Elyot's work entitled 'Cyprianus, a Swete and Devoute Sermon of the Holy
Saynt Cyprian on the Mortality of Man.'
Finally, a fundamental feature of Sir Thomas Elyot's
interests was language – words in particular. He was very
conscious of the poverty of the Anglo-Saxon of his time as
compared with other languages and desired above all things
to augment its vocabulary. In 1536 he undertook the compilation of a dictionary, the 'Bibliotheca Eliotae' subsequently known as 'Eliotes Dictionarie.' And from a
purely linguistic viewpoint 'The Gouvernour' may be regarded as a connecting link between the English of the
time of Chaucer and the English of the time of Bacon. Its
style for the period is peculiar; for many of the words or
phrases it employed were even then going out of use,
while, on the other hand, many new words are recognizable,
apparently original importations.
We now see the picture beginning to arrange itself: a
twentieth century Eliot, who feels he has certain spiritual links with a Tudor Elyot, communing with himself in

the dark spring following the outbreak of the second world war within little more than two decades. Although Sir Thomas Elyot of Coker may have died without issue, there is a sufficient kinship in their interests to draw the contemporary Eliot to him in thought. Something is amiss with contemporary civilization, its mode of conduct or philosophy of life. The elder Elyot had tried through 'The Boke named The Gouvernour' to suggest for his period a pattern of harmonious living and concord based on the Platonic ideals of the Renaissance. The younger man, faced by the darkness of the present moment, feels a certain irony in the parallels which he recognizes between his own interests and those of his precursor. In spite of all the confidence in intellectual progress of Sir Thomas Elyot's time, it is evident, today, that the neo-classical, individualist approach of the Renaissance led to a mechanical view and a spiritual poverty and produced the cataclysm which has overwhelmed the present age.

In my beginning is my end.

This is the theme which dominates the whole work. Like a musical phrase it is woven back and forth through the entire texture of the composition, now stated in one key of meaning, now in another.

The actual wording of the theme is possibly an echo of the inscription

En ma fin est mon commencement

embroidered upon the chair of state of Mary, Queen of Scots. In 1931 Maurice Baring published an historical study of the Scottish queen under this title. In his preface we read:

The title of this book needs some explanation. The inscription:

'In my End is my Beginning'

was the motto embroidered upon the Chair of State of Mary, Queen of Scots. This inscription perplexed Mr. Nicholas White, a friend of Cecil's, who, on his road to Ireland in the spring of the year 1569, paid a visit of curiosity to the Queen of Scots during her captivity at Tutbury, the house of the Earl of Shrewsbury.

He wrote as follows: 'In looking upon her cloth of estate, I noticed this sentence embroidered: "en ma fin est mon commencement", which is a riddle I understand not'...

Baring continues:

> Her motto was symbolic in more ways than one. Putting
> aside the question of whether the death of the Queen of
> Scots was, as some think, the triumph of a martyred
> saint awaiting canonization in the future, or a consum-
> mate piece of playacting, there is no doubt that prac-
> tically and politically the end of the Queen of Scots
> was her beginning; for at her death her son, James
> Stuart, became heir to the crowns of England and Scot-
> land and he lived to wear both crowns.

A more remote source of the theme, yet a source which
has been rich in suggestion for so much of Eliot's mature
poetry, is the philosophical remains of Heraclitus of
Ephesus. For example here we read:

> The beginning and the end are common. (LXX)
> Fire lives in the death of earth, air lives in the
> death of fire, water lives in the death of air, and
> earth lives in the death of water. (XXV)

Throughout the poem we find this theme given two contrasting interpretations: a spiritual one, and a material
or temporal one. In the spiritual interpretation the
'beginning' is seen as that 'highest type of knowledge -
the intuition of pure being' which Christopher Dawson regards as 'the starting point of human progress' in his
study 'Progress and Religion'; and man's end - goal or
purpose - is the knowledge of the Divine Order, or God,
which can only come by intuition, through love. The
material or temporal interpretation stresses the cyclic
nature of history, the temporality of material achievement, and the mortality of man in the spirit of the
admonition: 'Remember, man, that thou art dust and unto
dust thou shalt return.'
These two interpretations of the dominant theme are
played back and forth until their final combination in
that victorious reversal of the introductory statement
that closes the poem:

> In my end is my beginning.

I

Man as a physical being has his cycle of life; its
opening predicates its close.
Like every other form of animal life man is the

creature of environment, heredity and function. 'Consequently his culture is not an abstract intellectual construction, but a material organization of life, which is
submitted to the same laws of growth and decay, of "generation and corruption," as the rest of the material world.'
(Christopher Dawson, *op cit.*, p. 74) As in Heraclitus'
view, all is one eternal flux, all is involved in ceaseless
round of life, death, growth, and decay. The Logos, the
element of law or order, is the only stable factor in the
ever shifting world:

>   ...In succession
>   Houses rise and fall, crumble, are extended,
>   Are removed, destroyed, restored ...

Houses - whether the term be taken literally to signify
buildings, the material components of a village such as
Coker, or figuratively, as dynasties - houses rise and
fall, houses live and die.

>   ...there is a time for building
>   And a time for living and for generation
>   And a time for the wind to break the loosened pane
>   And to shake the wainscot where the field-mouse trots
>   And to shake the tattered arras woven with a silent
>   motto.

In the passing of Mary Queen of Scots, we see the fugitive
character of temporal glory and we have its symbolization
in the fluttering of the tattered arras embroidered with
her motto.

To Eliot, as he looks back from the dark moment after
the outbreak of a new, disillusioning war, the village of
Coker in its association with Sir Thomas Elyot represents
a beginning - the beginning of a period which had looked
forward idealistically and hopefully to a future of intellectual achievement and conquest. You can still imagine
Sir Thomas Elyot's ideal dancers in their dance 'around
the bonfire' symbolizing human harmony and concord, yet at
the same time reminding us, through 'the rhythm of their
dancing,' of the laws of growth and decay, of generation
and corruption -

>   Eating and drinking. Dung and death.

And the poet is brought back to the reality of the present.
For that period is completely behind us,

>   Dawn points, and another day
>   Prepares for heat and silence.

All that survives, from the period just closed, on which
we can hope to build for the future, is what that period
already had at its outset - 'the intuition of pure being.'

> Out at sea the dawn wind
> Wrinkles and slides. I am here
> Or there, or elsewhere. In my beginning.

II

So what has the present day to do with these hopes of a
younger time? Eliot asks himself in the opening lines of
the second section

> What is the late November doing
> With the disturbance of the spring
> And creatures of the summer heat ...?

In these 'sproutings' of

> That corpse you planted last year in your garden,

we feel an echo of 'The Waste Land' and a renunciation of
the earlier attitude of that poem and of 'Gerontion.'

> Do not let me hear ...

The pattern and content of these poems he sums up in the
first seventeen lines of Section II of 'East Coker,' with
subtle echoes of their rhythms and imagery. Late November, like 'The Waste Land's' 'winter dawn,' now hears
'thunder rolled by the rolling stars ... whirled in a
vortex that shall bring' the world, eventually, through
fire, as preached in the 'Fire Sermon,' and through
devastation to 'the peace that passeth understanding,'
even as 'The Waste Land' saw this prefigured in

> The sound of horns and motors, which shall bring
> Sweeney to Mrs. Porter in the spring

But 'the poetry does not matter.' To start again is
the important thing. As Christopher Dawson says in 'Progress and Religion': '...intellectually, at least, man's
development is not so much from the lower to the higher
as from the confused to the distinct.' The materialist
approach did not help us to this. In spite of Sir Thomas
Elyot's enthusiasm, zeal and optimism, things did not work
out as they were expected to. The autumn of civilization

did not bring the serenity and calm that was expected.
Did those quiet-voiced elders, such as Sir Thomas Elyot and
the Renaissance leaders, deceive us more with their confidence in man and his powers of intellectual achievement, or
the despairful author of 'Gerontion'?

> There is, it seems to us,
> At best, only a limited value
> In the knowledge derived from experience.
> The knowledge imposes a pattern, and falsifies,
> For the pattern is new every moment.

For in the Heraclitean saying, no man ever bathes twice in
the same stream, just as we may speak of the ever-changing
bather the stream receives. Or according to the late F.H.
Bradley, for whom Eliot has long had a great admiration:
If views are dependent on needs and needs are culturally
and individually determined,

> the whole Universe seems too subject to the individual
> knower. What is given counts for so little and the
> arrangement counts for so much, while in fact the
> arranger, if we are to have real knowledge, seems so
> dependent on the world. But the individual who knows
> is here wrongly isolated, and then, because of that, is
> confronted with a mere alien Universe. And the indi-
> vidual, as so isolated, I agree, could do nothing, for
> indeed he is nothing. My real personal self which
> orders my world is in truth inseparably one with the
> Universe. Behind me the absolute reality works through
> and in union with myself, and the world which confronts
> me is at bottom one thing in substance and in power
> with this reality. There *is* a world of appearance and
> there *is* a sensuous curtain, and to seek to deny the
> presence of this or to identify it with reality is mis-
> taken. But for truth I come back always to that doc-
> trine of Hegel, that 'there is nothing behind the cur-
> tain other than that which is in front of it.'

Again we read in Eliot's 1939 essay 'The Idea of a Christian Society':

> ...so long as we consider 'education' as a good in
> self ..., without any ideal of the good life for society
> or for the individual, we shall move from one uneasy
> compromise to another. To the quick and simple organi-
> zation of society for ends which, being only material
> and worldly, must be as ephemeral as worldly success,
> there is only one alternative. As political philosophy

derives its sanction from ethics, and ethics from the
truth of religion, it is only by returning to the
eternal source of truth that we can hope for any social
organization which will not, to its ultimate destruction, ignore some essential aspect of reality.

In other words, the solution is clearly not through
the accumulation of encyclopaedic knowledge in accord
with the ideal of the Renaissance, or a scientific
exploration of our physical world in keeping with that of
the last two centuries, but through a return to the
beginning - through the intuition of pure being - to the
eternal source of truth. The increase of human knowledge
only brings us the satisfaction of feeling ourselves undeceived.

Of that which, deceiving, could no longer harm.

At the same time the passionate pursuit of material knowledge which has characterized the last five centuries of
European history has steadily more and more discouraged
any interest in spiritual values. As a result we find
ourselves today like Dante in the opening lines of the
'Inferno'.

In the middle of the journey of our life
I found myself in a dark wood,
having lost the straight path.

'Life has become' for us, as it had for Dr. Watson in
A. Conan Doyle's 'The Hound of the Baskervilles,' 'like
that great Grimpen Mire, with little green patches everywhere into which one may sink and with no guide to point
the track.' And Eliot has both these pictures in mind
when he sees himself in 'East Coker'

In the middle, not only in the middle of the way
But all the way, in a dark wood, in a bramble,
On the edge of a grimpen, where there is no secure
    foothold,
And menaced by monsters, fancy lights,
Risking enchantment.

And in this predicament after depending so long on the
misleading advice and the empty promises of our elders,
Eliot resolves that we should put aside all notions of
'the wisdom of old men.' 'Do not let me hear' he writes,
'Of the wisdom of old men, but rather of their folly...,'
which is their vanity. In reality they are nothing more

than infinitesimal details of the Divine pattern. And
their notion of their importance as individuals, their
dread of losing their imagined spiritual autonomy - their
fear 'of belonging to another, or to others or to God' is
only another heritage of the Renaissance individualist
approach. At best it is merely the wisdom of the children
of this world in their generation - a short term wisdom.
For if we face facts frankly we will realize that

    The only wisdom we can hope to acquire
    Is the wisdom of humility: humility is endless.

This is especially clear today when we consider the
emptiness of the material civilization we have so long
adulated. It was a dream, a delusion even as Eliot's
present-day vision of Sir Thomas Elyot's dancers. And
in the concluding lines of Section II of 'East Coker'
Eliot caustically underscores its fragile passing with a
parody of the line of Stevenson's 'Requiem': 'Home is the
sailor, home from the sea, / And the hunter home from the
hill' -

    The houses are all gone under the sea.

      The dancers are all gone under the hill.

             III

    The third section of the poem opens on this note - the
darkness in which the disappearance of these illusions has
left the world:

[Quotes 'East Coker', III, CPP, p. 180, 'O dark' to 'all
go with them'.]

    In the present world-crisis Eliot sees illustrated the
broader spiritual problem which faces us. In his editorial valedictory Last Words in the final issue of the
'Criterion,' January, 1939, he wrote: 'The period
immediately following the war of 1914 is often spoken of
as a time of disillusionment: in some ways and for some
people it was rather a period of illusions.' And in the
concluding paragraph of 'The Idea of a Christian Society'
published in the autumn of 1939, we read:

    I believe that there must be many persons who, like
    myself, were deeply shaken by the events of September
    1938; persons to whom that month brought a profounder

> realization of a general plight ... a feeling of
> humiliation which seemed to demand an act of personal
> contrition, of humility, repentance and amendment; a
> doubt of the validity of a civilization... Was our
> society, which had always been so assured of its
> superiority and rectitude, so confident of its un-
> examined premises, assembled round anything more
> permanent than a congeries of banks, insurance com-
> panies, and industries, and had it any beliefs more
> essential than a belief in compound interest and the
> maintenance of dividends?

And in this context - its association with the present
eclipse of such formerly powerful sources of information
as the 'Almanach de Gotha,' the 'Stock Exchange Gazette'
and the 'Directory of Directors' - the line

> And cold the sense and lost the motive of action

affords a subtle, ironic commentary through an echo it
brings us of the line from Swinburne's 'The Last Oracle'
('Poems and Ballads - Second Series'): 'Dark the shrine
and dumb the fount of song thence welling.'
  To Milton's Samson the darkness in his eyes was a
source of lamentation:

> O dark, dark, dark, amid the blaze of noon,
> Irrecoverably dark, total Eclipse
> Without all hope of day!

To Eliot, on the contrary, the first closing-in of
darkness brings promise of a sounder road to truth and
enlightenment. We already have a suggestion of this in
the echo of Vaughan's 'Ascension Hymn' -

> They are all gone into the world of light!

- in the first line of Section III:

> O dark dark dark. They all go into the dark.

The clearing away of material, distracting ambitions, the
blacking-out of the 'fancy lights,' open a way to the poet
to return to his beginning - to 'the starting point of
human progress, the intuition of pure being.'

> I said to my soul, be still, and let the dark come upon
>   you
> Which shall be the darkness of God.

For the poet, this darkness is the darkness of the Isa
Upanishad:

> Into blind darkness enter they
> That worship ignorance;
> Into darkness, as it were, greater
> They that delight in knowledge.
> Other, indeed, they say, than knowledge!
> Other, they say, than non-knowledge!

It is the transitional stage between periods - Jung's
'Night Journey' of the Rebirth Pattern - with a suggestion
of the present war in the possible ambiguity of interpretation afforded by the 'hollow rumble of wings':

> As, in a theatre,
> The lights are extinguished, for the scene to be
>   changed
> With a hollow rumble of wings, with a movement of
>   darkness on darkness ...

But from a spiritual viewpoint such a darkness and such a
realization of the emptiness of material achievement
awaken in Eliot above all thoughts of 'The Dark Night of
the Soul,' that passive night, that intense purification
with which God, according to St. John of the Cross, visits
the soul. To such as desire purification St. John of the
Cross says:

> Advice must be given to learn to abide attentively and
> to pay no heed either to imagination or its workings;
> for here, as we may say, the faculties are at rest,
> and are working not actively but passively by receiving
> that which God works in them.

And in this spirit Eliot tells us

> I said to my soul, be still, and wait without hope
> For hope would be hope for the wrong thing; wait
>   without love
> For love would be love of the wrong thing; there is
>   yet faith
> But the faith and the love and the hope are all in the
>   waiting.
> Wait without thought, for you are not ready for
>   thought:
> So the darkness shall be the light, and the stillness
>   the dancing.

In the first half of this line we hear once again an
echo of Milton's 'Samson':

O first created Beam, and thou great Word,
Let there be light, and light was over all;
Why am I thus bereav'd thy prime decree?

And in the concluding clause – 'And the stillness the dancing,' another echo of Sir Thomas Elyot of Coker: 'There
daunseth to gether a man and a woman, holding eche other by
the hande or the arme, which betokeneth concorde.'
    To recover purity of vision, which must not be regarded
as hopelessly lost, we must learn from nature the need of
undergoing

        the agony
Of death and birth

– that is to say 'rebirth' – a return through the agony of
death (near at hand for 'old men') to 'the beginning,' 'the
intuition of pure being.' The way to this, according to
Eliot, is St. John of the Cross' 'Dark Night of the Soul'
as we have it explained in the concluding lines of Section
III:

    In order to arrive there,
To arrive where you are, to get from where you are not,
    You must go by a way wherein there is no ecstasy.
In order to arrive at what you do not know
    You must go by a way which is the way of ignorance.

    And it is clear that Eliot wants the source of these
lines to be readily recognizable in order that his reference may enjoy the advantage of all the accumulated commentary and explanation linked to St. John of the Cross'
mystical philosophy. We can see this from the closeness
with which he makes them echo a translation of the saint's
own words:

    – In order to arrive at having pleasure in everything,
Desire to have pleasure in nothing...
    – In order to arrive at a knowledge of everything,
Desire to know nothing.
    – In order to arrive at that wherein thou hast no
      pleasure,
Thou must go by a way wherein thou hast no pleasure.
    – In order to arrive at that which thou knowest not,
Thou must go by a way that thou knowest not.
    – In order to arrive at that which thou possessest not,
Thou must go by a way that thou possessest not.
    – In order to arrive at that which thou art not,
Thou must go through that which thou art not.

This is clearly not defeatism or apathy. Nor is it a
philosophy of escape such as so many critics are constantly
seeing in Eliot's writings. To these, Agatha, in Eliot's
'Family Reunion' (Part II, Scene II), has already replied
in her answer to Amy's taunt - 'So you *will* run away,':

> In a world of fugitives
> The person taking the opposite direction
> Will appear to run away.

Stonier, in his review of 'East Coker,' writes that Eliot
'having abjured ecstasy, allows himself to fall into a mental trance.' What Eliot actually advocates is far from an
apathetic passivity. In 'Ash Wednesday' he prayed

> Teach us to care and not to care
> Teach us to sit still.

But 'to sit still' in the sense advocated by St. John as a
necessary step to spiritual purgation. For Eliot feels
with St. John of the Cross, that we must undergo not only
the mortification of the flesh by *The Ascent of Mount
Carmel* but also the trial of *The Dark Night of the Soul*,
before we can hope for that perfect union of the soul with
God in love, and for the divinization of all our faculties
described by St. John of the Cross in 'The Spiritual Canticle' and 'The Living Flame of Love.'
    Then in summing up his conclusions from the advocated
approach of St. John of the Cross, Eliot returns in the
last three lines of Section III to Heraclitus, 'The Dark'
- the unity of opposition, the harmony of strife:

> And what you do not know is the only thing you know
> And what you own is what you do not own
> And where you are is where you are not.

For among the Heraclitean fragments we read

> The unlike is joined together, and from differences
> results most beautiful harmony, and all things take
> place by strife. (XLVI)

It is this Heraclitean note combined with echoes of
the seventeenth century English metaphysical poets which
will characterize the entire following section of the
poem.

IV

There, in the opening lines, the poet sees Christ, with
His hands bleeding from the nail wounds, as the wounded
surgeon in a similar light to that in which Pascal sees
Him: 'Jesus suffers in His passions the torments which men
inflict on Him; but in His agony He suffers the torments He
inflicts on Himself.' ('Pensées,' No. 552) And at the same
time in these lines we have another echo of Heraclitus:

> The physicians, therefore, ... cutting and cauterizing,
> and in every way torturing the sick, complain that the
> patients do not pay them fitting reward for thus effect-
> ing these benefits - and sufferings. (LVIII)

The soul, according to St. John of the Cross, during
The Dark Night is 'under medical treatment for the recovery
of its health, which is God Himself.' The steel that questions the distempered part is God's love; for, as St. John
of the Cross describes it in the 'Living Flame of Love':
'...the soul will be conscious of an assault upon it made
by a seraph armed with a dart of most enkindled love,
which will pierce the soul...' Still the compassion of the
Surgeon is always evident. For the soul 'amidst these
gloomy and loving pains, is conscious of a certain com-
panionship and inward strength which attends upon it.'
('The Dark Night of the Soul')
'Our only health is our disease' since the soul must
suffer 'that it may become meet for the divine love.' The
constant care of God 'is not to please,' 'for as God sets
the soul in this dark night to the end that He may quench
and purge its sensual desire, He allows it not to find
attraction or sweetness in anything whatsoever.'
Furthermore, 'To be restored, our sickness must grow
worse' for only through the most complete suffering can we
hope for complete purgation.
Throughout all these stanzas we see the Heraclitean play
of opposites persevering. But an echo which this line
brings up gives us another key to the undercurrent thought
of this section: the vital need to put aside the blinding,
confining interests of the body and of the world. For
here, rhythm and figures both are clearly intended to recall those of Marvell's 'A Dialogue between the Soul and
the Body' in which the soul complains of its imprisonment
in the confining flesh:

Soul: O Who shall, from this Dungeon, raise
      A Soul inslav'd so many wayes? ...
      Here blinded with an Eye; and there

>   Deaf with the drumming of an Ear ...
>   Constrain'd not only to indure
>   Diseases, but what's worse, the Cure:
>   And ready oft the Port to gain
>   Am Shipwrackt into Health again.

'The whole earth is our hospital, endowed by the ruined
millionaire,' Adam, with original sin. As T.E. Hulme put
it in a passage quoted by T.S. Eliot in his introduction
to Baudelaire's 'Journaux Intimes,' 'in the light of these
absolute values, man himself is judged to be essentially
limited and imperfect. He is endowed with Original Sin.'

The cure is a fever cure - through the fever of love
which is kindled in burning away impurities until the
ascending chill will bring a calm similar to that which
will be brought into the world by

>   that destructive fire
> Which burns before the ice-cap reigns.

The purgation must grow from a purgation of the flesh to a
purgation of the mind.

>   The chill ascends from feet to knees,
>   The fever sings in mental wires.

We are reminded of the 'trilling wires of the blood' in
'Burnt Norton.' But here the experience has to do with
the spirit rather than with the flesh. And we remember
that Eliot feels that 'the great mistake made about Christianity is to suppose it primarily a religion and emotion
when it is primarily dogma and intellectual.' ('The Idea
of a Christian Society')

Suffering is the basis of our cure - a penitential
suffering and a thorough period of trial. We try constantly to blind ourselves to the need for humility and
penance with notions of the importance of man and with
materialistic emphases -

>   ...we like to think
>   That we are sound, substantial flesh and blood

- but at bottom we recognize the necessity of penance, and
the fact that even our own penance would be feeble without
the divine atonement made by Christ on our behalf. This
is the reason that we '...call this Friday good' - the day
on which the anniversary of Christ's sufferings is
observed. And just as we saw Eliot in 'Ash-Wednesday'
commemorating a victory over the temptation in the

wilderness and announcing his spiritual entrance upon a
penitential period, this Good Friday note in 'East Coker'
celebrates the culmination of suffering and purgation,
and an anticipation of the Resurrection to the light.

V

So now the poet feels, 'here I am, in the middle way,'
returning to his earlier echo of 'nel mezzo del cammin.'
He feels lost in the dark wood

...having had twenty years -
Twenty years largely wasted, the years of *l'entre deux
guerres* -
Trying to learn to use words.

He has come to feel with Pico della Mirandola, one of the
exemplars of his precursor, Sir Thomas Elyot, that:

We shall live for ever, not in the school of word-
catchers, but in the circle of the wise, where they
talk not of the mother of Andromache or of the sons of
Niobe, but of the deeper causes of things human and
divine; he who looks closely will see that even the
barbarians had intelligence not on the tongue, but in
the breast.

In 'Burnt Norton,' Eliot had already expressed a similar
sentiment:

Words move, music moves
Only in time; but that which is only living
Can only die. Words, after speech, reach
Into the silence.

But, in the opening chorus of 'The Rock,'

The endless cycle of idea and action,
Endless invention, endless experiment,
Brings knowledge of motion, but not of stillness;
Knowledge of speech, but not of silence;
Knowledge of words, and ignorance of the Word.

Again in 'Burnt Norton':

...Only by the form, the pattern,
Can words or music reach
The stillness, as a Chinese jar still
Moves perpetually in its stillness ...

Today the poet has come to realize that each venture
in 'trying to learn to use words' is merely

> ...a new beginning, a raid on the inarticulate
> With shabby equipment always deteriorating
> In the general mess of imprecision of feeling,
> Undisciplined squads of emotion.

He feels with Heraclitus that

> It is a weariness to labour at the same things and to
> be always beginning afresh. (LXXXII)

Emotion in Eliot's opinion is primarily a contributor
of confusion. In 'The Idea of a Christian Society' we read,
'It is not enthusiasm, but dogma, that differentiates a
Christian from a pagan society.' And Eliot feels with
T.E. Hulme, whom he quotes substantially in the closing
paragraph of his preface to Baudelaire's 'Journaux
Intimes,' that a man 'can only accomplish anything of
value by discipline - ethical and poetical. Order is thus
not merely negative, but creative and liberating. Insti-
tutions are necessary.' Emotion upsets order. The lack of
order, or discipline overwhelmed by emotion, only throws
us back 'into the general mess of imprecision of feeling.'
Whenever and wherever this occurs, according to Eliot,
ground is lost. What there is to conquer

> By strength and submission, has already been discovered
> Once or twice, or several times, by men whom one cannot
>   hope
> To emulate ...

Or in Heraclitus' words: 'Much learning does not teach one
to have understanding, else it would have taught Hesiod
and Pythagoras, and again Xenophanes and Hecataeus.' (LVI)

> There is only the fight to recover what has been lost
> And found and lost again and again: and now, under con-
>   ditions
> That seem unpropitious. But perhaps neither gain nor
>   loss.
> For us, there is only the trying. The rest is not our
>   business.

Humility outweighs individualism and material achievement.
In the end it is only 'the still point' of which 'Burnt
Norton' spoke which matters.

> ...there the dance is,
> But neither arrest nor movement. And do not call it
>   fixity.
> ...Except for the point, the still point,
> There would be no dance, and there is only the dance.
> I can only say, *there* we have been: but I cannot say
>   where.
> And I cannot say, how long, for that is to place it in
>   time.

With the opening line of the second half of Section V
we have a restatement of the main theme in a new wording

> Home is where one starts from.

But

> As we grow older
> The world becomes stranger, the pattern more compli-
>   cated
> Of dead and living. Not the intense moment
> Isolated, with no before and after,
> But a lifetime burning in every moment
> And not the lifetime of one man only
> But of old stones that cannot be deciphered.

We are assailed increasingly by distractions and interests
of the world about us, whereas

> Love is most nearly itself
> When here and now cease to matter.

'Old men ought to be explorers': they should not be satisfied with the world at hand, but be ready to 'put off the
old man and put on the new.' Whether we are

> Here or there does not matter

- for love, according to St. John of the Cross, 'is like a
fire, which ever ascends, hastening to be absorbed in the
centre of its sphere.' ('The Dark Night of the Soul')

> We must be still and still moving
> Into another intensity
> For a further union, a deeper communion.

As Pascal urged ('Pensées,' No. 524) 'there must be feelings of humility, not from nature, but from penitence, not
to rest in them, but to go on to greatness,' -

Through the dark cold and the empty desolation,
The wave cry, the wind cry, the vast waters
Of the petrel and the porpoise.

For, even now,

Dawn points, and another day
Prepares for heat and silence.   Out at sea the dawn
    wind
Wrinkles and slides.

'In the end is my beginning.'

Note

1 'New English Weekly' (21 March 1940), xvi, 325-8, was
   the first London appearance. It first appeared complete in the USA in 'Partisan Review' (New York) (May/
   June 1940), vii, 181-7.

121. ETHEL M. STEPHENSON, T.S. ELIOT AND THE LAY READER
(II), 'POETRY REVIEW'

March-April 1942, vol. xxxiii, 80-3

This is the second part of a two-part article. The first
part appears as No. 123. Both articles were incorporated
into a book, 'T.S. Eliot and the Lay Reader' (London,
1944).

West of 'Burnt Norton' I am placing 'East Coker' and 'The
Dry Salvages' and eastward all the earlier works. I put
'Burnt Norton' as the junction, because it was in this
poem, if you remember, that Mr. Eliot seems to have definitely established the art of duality within himself. He
is no longer dependent on stage properties, the off-sets
of choruses, an assumed listener or a Watson. He is working within a complete conception of constancy; and we are
told by our scientists that the only thing which is constant is change.
     That Eliot follows this law is clearly shown in

'East Coker':

    Houses rise and fall, crumble, are extended,
    Are removed, destroyed, restored, or in their place
    Is an open field or a factory or a by-pass.

Further on in the same poem:

[Quotes 'East Coker', V, CPP, p. 182, 'Home is where' to
'be deciphered'.]

    In this suggested thought we do not find a poet sud-
denly rearing a Dutch barn on four gaunt posts as a
vaunted challenge to God's changing skies! We find instead a workman with careful hands and brain who has
learned to weigh the values of a beautiful earth and
thoughtfully to place its stones in a form that some
future shall recognize as the dawning of a ciphered plan.
    The human race, with all its toxic vanities and noisy
effects turned blindly from any form of constructive living, must perform the miracle of passing through the eye
of a needle if it is ever to survive from its own thought-
less self-destruction. In this respect perhaps some of
the world's great philosophers and poets may provide the
real solution, for they tend always towards simplicity of
living, since the superfluous is the unconscious voice of
wasted energy which is required for learning.

[Quotes 'The Dry Salvages', V, CPP, p. 190, 'And right
action' to 'significant soil'.]

    The first of these articles was concentrated on Mr.
Eliot's deep-rooted awareness of balance. It was important to establish this emphasis, as it applies directly to
his style. As his thought balances so do his sentences,
not in the sense of Pope's rhymed couplets, with the
caesura so clearly marked that a line could be drawn down
the middle, but in musical phrases which are the complement of each other.
    Free verse is very far from being the scattered, in-
consequent structure which is put upon it through its misleading title. I have read many clever poems expressing
excellent and beautiful thoughts but the effect produced
by the total misinterpretation of the term free has not
been unlike playing a line of Bach, another of Chopin,
followed hot by Debussy and so on. The result, alas, is
a characterless hotch-potch which the merited subject is
unable to save from extinction.
    Let us pull on the surgeon's rubber gloves and select

from his glittering trays our scalpel and trephine and
have our patient 'Etherized upon a table!' No. 3 in the
Rock Choruses shows many examples of the balanced sentence
and word order as used by Eliot, because the work of choral
poetry has to be simple in purpose and therefore cruder in
form than the developed design given to a poem read by a
single voice. In being a little unfair to Pope I must
also add some unfairness to Eliot in order to underline
the evidence of balanced sentences. Many phrases begin
the same way and therefore cut a deep channel from which
attention cannot escape, -

      I have given you hands -
      I have given you speech -
      I have given you my Law -
      I have given you lips -
      I have given you hearts -
      I have given you power of choice -

The cumulative effect of this cardinal thinking provokes
a demand for the culmination of each upward thrust.
     When studying Eliot those people who know America fairly
well will realize that it becomes increasingly urgent to
read him as an American and not as an English poet. In
any nation it is always the thought behind the thought
that is racial. The appeals of all nations have been centralized in recent years in America, and as an immediate
result of this its people have developed a quadrilateral
way of thinking, from which they extract what they hope
will be the kernel. By doing this they avoid excessive
emotions of either hate or admiration and also that depressing ancestral ghost which binds a race to do what its
grandfathers did, whether what they did is suitable to
present situations or not. It is also wisdom to remember
that the American is never a hustler, except in non-
essentials. Over vital decisions he takes time to be
correct before starting out -

      There will be time to murder and create
      And time for all the works and days of hands
      That lift and drop a question on your plate.

This was never an Englishman's thought, or a Frenchman's

      Briques et tuiles
      O les charmants
      Petits asiles
      Pours les amants! (Verlaine)

Eliot's American descent (from Andrew Eliot of East Coker,
Somerset, who settled in Massachusetts, in the early seventeenth century) has had its influence on the action of his
style. We do not find the orthodox stress of metre, regardless of vowel length, or a standard pattern faithfully
performed from the initial stanza. We find instead musical chords, panoramic music, tidal music. We see the
'Minute Man of new England' with his alert awareness of
the freedom for which he fought, reiterated in the instinct
for poetic freedom for which Eliot also fought. It is this
difference behind the meaning of the same language which
makes it necessary when reading this poet, to read him in
American and not English. So to return to Eliot's traditional music with a different understanding - I quote from
a poem, 'Marina', which to my mind he has never surpassed
in beauty:

> What seas what shores what grey rocks and what
>   islands
> What water lapping the bow
> And scent of pine and the woodthrush singing through
>   the fog
> What images return
> O my daughter.

It is impossible to read this without the swell of the
ocean's tide, its receding and again its rise and fall.

> What is this face, less clear and clearer
> The pulse in the arm, less strong and stronger -
> Given or lent? more distant than stars and nearer than
>   the eye
> Whispers and small laughter between leaves and hurrying
>   feet
> Under sleep, where all the waters meet.

These last two lines hold the receding wave, threading
back through the pebbles which are the leaves of the
shore. Listen to its muted music, withdrawing to the
matrix, the source of its Being.
   At the risk of incurring the censorious epithet 'eulogy'
which is particularly active in this present period, when
no one must be appreciated, no one must *try* to do anything,
and no one must *want* to do anything, it would be right to
stress the sheer beauty that lies in the simplicity of
word order, building this poem. First consider its word
economy in relation to the purport of the subject, then
the direct application, also its liquid alliteration and
internal rhyming, creating an undertow of rhythm, which

with the balanced sentences presents one of the most
beautiful counterpoints Eliot has ever written.

These then are the main guides in reading this poet's
work. The other devices of symbol, imagery, paradox,
follow in 'The Waste Land'. Lastly Eliot's imagination is
his own. I can dissect the component parts of his method
and show you how it works, but the inspiration that gives
movement and life to the vibrant words is thankfully as
far beyond the surgeon's knife as the beat of the heart.

> The desert is not remote in southern topics,
> The desert is not only round the corner,
> The desert is squeezed in the tube-train next to you
> The desert is in the heart of your brother.

Aladdin's lamp achieved no greater demand than the task
performed in those four lines of inward vision.

'Burnt Norton'

First separate edition, London, 20 February 1941

122. ANDREWS WANNING, FROM CRITICISM AND PRINCIPLES:
POETRY OF THE QUARTER, 'SOUTHERN REVIEW'

Spring 1941, vol. vi, 796-8

Wanning (b. 1912) has taught at Yale, Harvard and Bard
College, New York. His criticism has appeared in 'Southern Review', 'Kenyon Review' and 'Partisan Review'.
    The essay by C.L. Barber referred to is T.S. Eliot
After Strange Gods, 'Southern Review' (Autumn 1940), vi,
387-416, reprinted in Unger, pp. 415-43.

Yeats and Eliot have made their forms current, and we do
not now need to read their present work (in Yeats' case
his last) without the illumination of their past. In the
case of 'East Coker' we can get from the past poems, and
particularly from 'Burnt Norton,' not merely an understanding of the technique, but a point of support for the
meaning. 'East Coker' (the name is taken from a revisited
village in England, the home of the Eliot family before
their American visitation) is not entirely a restatement of
of 'Burnt Norton,' but it is clearly derived from the
earlier poem. One passage in particular recalls 'Burnt
Norton,' and it is a passage which defines the poem:

    Whisper of running streams, and winter lightning.
    The wild thyme unseen and the wild strawberry,
    The laughter in the garden, echoed ecstasy
    Not lost, but requiring, pointing to the agony
    Of death and birth.

'East Coker' is about the agony of death and birth, but
about the agony as it may be resolved in the ecstasy in
the garden not lost, an ecstasy which is symbol for consciousness in the reality, the out-of-time pattern, the
eternal rhythm that makes possible

> ...a lifetime burning in every moment
> And not the lifetime of one man only
> But of old stones that cannot be deciphered.

More specifically it is about a man such as T.S. Eliot -
a man 'in the middle way, having had twenty years -
/ Twenty years largely wasted, the years of *l'entre deux
guerres*...' - attempting to compose himself for age and
death. The only wisdom he can hope to acquire, he finds,
is the wisdom of humility, the humility of not-hoping,
not-loving, not-thinking. Yet this humility is not to be
passive: faith remains to be captured:

> We must be still and still moving
> Into another intensity
> For a further union, a deeper communion ...

One must return, to know what is meant by the union and
the communion, to the ecstasy in the pattern out of time,
where 'the darkness shall be the light, and the stillness
the dancing.'
   The poem, plainly enough, resumes many of the themes of
'Burnt Norton,' but it resumes them with a difference. In
'Burnt Norton,' the subject is the state of being symbolized by the ecstasy in the garden; in 'East Coker' the
subject is more precisely the effort to attain that state
of being. The real fulfillment whose emotional quality
was so beautifully established in 'Burnt Norton' is now
merely suggested by reference back to the earlier poem;
the tone as a whole is not confident. The conditions
'seem unpropitious'; for us there is perhaps 'neither gain
nor loss ... only the trying.' 'East Coker' seems to be
Eliot's 'Ulysses,' though his quest is at least allegor-
ized in more spiritual terms than in Tennyson's poem. But
the parallels are striking: 'Old men ought to be explorers,' says Eliot. In each what is valuable is the trying,
not gain or loss; and in each there is a tone of forlorn-
ness, though the end proposed is a fulfillment.
   Because such a state is more typical of most of us than
is the fine poise of 'Burnt Norton,' 'East Coker' is no
doubt to be described as more accurately in tune with its
times. By any other criterion of which I have any knowledge, 'East Coker' seems to me inferior to the earlier

poem. In 'East Coker' there is much discussion of the
state of being which is fulfillment, but its emotional
value is suggested only by the reference to 'Burnt Norton.'
That value is needed in 'East Coker' to resolve the agony
of birth and death, and therefore the poem seems not to be
self-contained, to be dependent for its balance on a reference outside itself. Its diction, furthermore, lapses too
often from the constant tension of Eliot's best work.
There are long passages that seem matter of fact, appropriate rather to a critical essay:

> And so each venture
> Is a new beginning, a raid on the inarticulate
> With shappy equipment always deteriorating
> In the general mess of imprecision of feeling,
> Undisciplined squads of emotion.

This is nicely said, but it is inferior in immediacy to a
corresponding passage in 'Burnt Norton':

> Words strain,
> Crack and sometimes break, under the burden,
> Under the tension, slip, slide, perish,
> Decay with imprecision, will not stay in place,
> Will not stay still.

The same lines will illustrate a final difficulty. In
'Burnt Norton' the passage about the inadequacy of words
is structurally justified because it is itself, since
'words move only in time,' a symbol of the paradox in
man's approach to the 'still point of the moving world.'
It is equally symbolic that the poem conquers the strain
of words. But in 'East Coker,' where there are at least
two such long digressions, the passages interrupt the
basic pattern of the poem. Instead of being integral,
they seem instead to be at once an apology on the part of
Eliot for the difficulties of his communication, and
(after the manner of Harry in 'Family Reunion' so cogently
described by Mr. Barber) a device for the elimination of
the grosser world from his private contemplation. In the
end, it seems to me, the difficulties of words overcome
the poem.
     One can concisely qualify the two poems by borrowing
a distinction that Yeats made between two plays presented
by his Abbey company: 'Burnt Norton' is a poem of suggestion, 'East Coker' a poem of argument and explanation....

123. ETHEL M. STEPHENSON, T.S. ELIOT AND THE LAY READER
(I), 'POETRY REVIEW'

October 1941, vol. xxxii, 289-94

If the question is put 'For what audience does Mr. Eliot
write?' the answer would be emphatically None. Any
writer who has a background of such strength that he has
founded a 'school of poetry' is not dependent either on a
public's likes or dislikes and he is therefore writing for
an epoch and not a fashionable people.

The full strength of the literary world has been
launched for and against T.S. Eliot. Dive-bombers, tanks,
dreadnoughts of the intelligentsia have manoeuvred and
battled, yet it might not be wrong to say that the versa-
tile young parachutists have carried much of the day in
their support of this twentieth-century poet.

For the peers of literature this article attempts no
persuasion; they either approve or disapprove; and for
both attitudes there are doubtless water-tight arguments;
and in any case it holds good that 'to persuade a man
against his will, he is of the same opinion still.'

But there is a further field beyond the contentiousness
of supporters or opposers, and it belongs to the growing
community of the reading public. This public wants to
know what Mr. Eliot has achieved and how he blew the
desert sands that bared the heads of ostriches.

When contemplating the work of any poet, the first
question to put is a simple one - 'What has this writer
achieved?' And if we do not fly off at a tangent of
literary fear, the answer should be as full of simplicity
as the question.

If we exclude the sun's light, which is turned into
chlorophyl for food value, there would appear to be nothing
wrong with the old saying, 'There is nothing new!' That
means that nothing new comes in from the outside, but it
does not mean that there is not a vast amount of material
at our feet which we neither understand nor know how to
manipulate. We are constantly discovering new things, new
meanings, new uses for things that have been here since
the world began. In other words there is always a new
interpretation for 'oldnesses.'

We may vary little from our ancestors, but whereas they
raced a chaise from London to Brighton, we now race a
Typhoon Aeroplane. The practice of racing is still the
same, but its form has evolved with the circumstances and
development of man. So we have extracted the cognisance

that there are 'new channels for expressing known axioms
and that there are always new poets who will find some
jewel hitherto uncovered.'

When we meet T.S. Eliot to-day, it is at the junction
of 'Burnt Norton' and 'East Coker.' The 'Rock' poems and
so on, back through the 'Waste Land' to 'Mr. Prufrock,'
precede us. This most happily falls into line with Eliot's
natural inclination towards the contra-plex. Because he
began with 'Mr. Prufrock' and met us at 'Burnt Norton,' we
establish a contrary sequence of events by travelling from
'Burnt Norton' to 'Mr. Prufrock.'

To launch into a poet's most mature work first is not
easy. It is like going in at the deep end and struggling
to swim through to the shallow end; but this is not so
unwise as it would appear, since the time of exhaustion
comes when there is no longer need for effort.

In 'Burnt Norton' all Mr. Eliot's past work is present.
His magnet is visibly seen at work, drawing each steel
filing to its centralized thought.

The co-ordinate use made of garlic and sapphires (one a
common vegetable, the other a precious gem) both obtained
from the origin of earth, that also holds the iron ore,
which later becomes the axle-tree or carden-shaft of a
motor-car, is not accidental. It is a minute, careful
collection of images, in themselves motionless, but which
Eliot sets moving like a clock whose hands rotate with the
day and night. The contra-plex is again in use, - the em-
bedded iron, the pebbled sapphire, the stored garlic are
all capable of immense activity if they are transposed
into a different sphere of circumstance. This transposi-
tion of thought, this fusion of substance with abstract
conception and inversely the use of abstract conception
manoeuvred into substance causes the reader a temporary
sense of crushing contradictions. Actually the shuttle
carries the thought-thread industriously backwards and
forwards and by the thickness of thread above thread Eliot
collects the whole texture which is ultimately his poem.
Then it is that we find there has been no real contradiction at all, but a movement of equal strength in opposite
directions, like positive and negative electricity. It is
this perfect balance of oppositional thinking strength,
towards and away from actuality, that creates the rhythmic
rise and fall of his objective work. The quietness, the
restfulness of 'Burnt Norton' is encompassed by the articulate restraint with which the vast subjects of 'timelessness' and 'interchanging fantasy' with reality are organized and guided into the pen of human conception. As a
tree is chained in sphere by its roots, as a fish is restricted by water, so is the human being limited in action

by a few degrees of heat or cold. Eliot follows this
scientific channel closely. He does not hitch his wagon
to a star that drops him panting and exhausted in its
aftermath of despair, nor does he go down to the gloom of
Hades. He keeps steadfastly to the breathing plain
allotted to human life; he appreciates the narrow scope
within which we have our being, and by doing this he
achieves a scope of thinking far beyond the inflated courage of bombastic flags that wave Excelsior - so impossible
to reach.

What has Eliot achieved?

The delicate poise of thought flowing in two directions,
but in equal strength, the balance between those things
which we imagine possess the texture of reality and those
things that occur and have the texture of memory. Is there
any difference between the two? Don't they both belong to
the realm of conjure? One in possibility, the other as a
shadow of the past. Both are real to us, because no longer
reality.

It is impossible to know what *now* is; we are either
conjecturing it or remembering it. Therefore the actual
moment of *now* must be the pivoting neutral point of conscious living.

When Eliot widened the conception of the Imagistic movement into the dialectic dialogue, he had taken an important
step; but when his technique was so skilled that he maintained the essence of dialogue in monistic form he founded
a 'school.' In all Eliot's later work his thought is kept
in flux, neither by a Dr. Watson nor an oration. His mind
has ejected a yeast ball of fermenting thought in continu-
ous spontaneity.

Later we shall go back to examine the musical phrases;
dialogues and imageries that made it possible for Eliot to
think and write in dual direction. His subtle intergrada-
tions, his sensitiveness to form, his reasoned search for
an interpretive motive behind the necessity of living,
shows a poet both aware of his background and of what goal
he wishes to reach.

The actual words used are no more poetic than the single
notes of a common chord are music. But if we take the
whole chord or the complete musical phrase we have a perfect analogy of what Eliot strove to find and has achieved
through his panoramic conception of poetry.

Let us try out his music, listen to the cadence and its
answering falling sequence; the refinement of touch; the
restful beauty that is obtained through restrained direc-
tional thinking. There is no plunging, bracing or sword
rattling; no baroque intensity or bizarre coquetry with a
pretence of life, God or fashion. He reiterates the

'C Major of this life,' the dominant note of the majority
who live this earth-life, and he strives to probe what this
major activity fulfils.

First comes the concrete phrase passing into abstraction:

> Time present and time past
> Are both perhaps present in time future,
> And time future contained in time past.

There is no contradiction. The results of present experience become memories and upon the basis of this collective
past, the future with its past experience is founded.

Now follows the completion of the opening phrase, the
contra-plex, which takes the abstract into the conrete -

> Down the passage which we did not take
> Towards the door we never opened
> Into the rose-garden.

Then the final duality, the counterpoint movement in one
musical phrase,

> There they were, dignified, invisible.

Everyone's imagination contains dignified, concrete images
of loved people or things, who are out of reach, which are
beyond contact; invisible and yet so full of reality to
our inward knowledge:

> Go, go, go, said the bird; human kind
> Cannot bear very much reality.

There is no place for scoffing here. We who know what the
passing of life means, in the love for those who are no
longer with us, have experienced the overwhelming crush of
their real yet invisible presence. Human kind cannot bear
very much reality. Again if we were asked to explain the
present, could we illustrate it with greater skill than
this:

> At the still point of the turning world. Neither flesh
>   nor fleshless:
> Neither from nor towards; at the still point, there the
>   dance is,
> But neither arrest nor movement. And do not call it
>   fixity.

Now come back to the narrow strata of our capacity of
living:

[Quotes 'Burnt Norton', II, CPP, p. 173, 'Time past'
to 'Be remembered'.]

Life is aware of its consciousness of having lived, only
through its recollection of the events which occurred.
The events are influenced by all that preceded them. It
is no use to bare our breasts to the stars, to dare them
to fail to drag our waggon. We have to find out what we
and the past 'we' did, which fumbled with a future and
gave it its oncoming shape. Our past is neither forgiven
nor forgotten, it goes along with us. 'The sins of the
fathers shall be visited unto the third and fourth generation.' Is there a braver, cleaner answer than this, to
those who would seek an escape from their deeds?

Eliot has not swept a rainbow paintbrush across an
exotic heaven; he has used the ingredient of concentrated
thought, the iron key with which each one is supplied to
solve the meaning of life and by reasoning find the door
and the key-hole which will let us through to a possible
Garden of Eden, - to something that lies in a better
category than this present destructive retribution. And
so Eliot's penultimate phrase is 'In my end is my beginning.'

'The Dry Salvages'

London, 4 September 1941

124. J.P. HOGAN, ELIOT'S LATER VERSE, 'ADELPHI'

January–March 1942, vol. xviii, 54-8

In the last war Wilfred Owen prefaced his poems with a disclaimer: 'Above all this book is not concerned with Poetry.
The subject of it is War, and the Pity of War. The Poetry
is in the Pity.' In 'East Coker' Eliot makes a similar
disclaimer:

[Quotes CPP, p. 179, 'That was a way' to 'does not
matter'.]

   Later in the poem we hear more of the 'intolerable
wrestle':

[Quotes CPP, p. 182, 'Twenty years largely wasted' to
'disposed to say it'.]

   Eliot has something to say; he is desperately anxious
to say it clearly and precisely. This is the poetry of an
honest man. But 'the poetry does not matter.' The poetry
matters only to the poets who are not poets, who have
nothing to say. To Owen, in the urgency of what he had to
say, the poetry did not matter. To Eliot, in an equal
urgency, the poetry does not matter.

         You say I am repeating
   Something I have said before. I shall say it again.
   Shall I say it again?

He does say it again. We shall see what he says later.

This poem, like every great poem, tells us clearly what
we already know vaguely and diffusely. Above all it demonstrates that genius in word and idiom does not make a poet.
What counts first is an inner urgency, the having something to say; and what counts second is the genius to say
it in the only words in which it can be said. But the second is dependent on the first; for in the saying is the
intolerable wrestle; and you suffer the intolerable wrestle
only if you have something to say; and you have something
to say only if you are moved by an inner urgency. Eliot's
work as a whole is a living testimony to this. With him
the intolerable wrestle has been threefold: with experience, which is the source of poetry; with the meaning of
experience; and with the words necessary to utter that
meaning.

But even that is too glib; it is not as simple as that:

[Quotes 'East Coker', II, CPP, p. 179, 'There is, it
seems' to 'all we have been'.]

The knowledge derived from experience forms a pattern, or
a varying series of patterns, which is philosophy. Philosophy falsifies. Truth is ephemeral, relative, never
absolute. 'Do not nail the pansy (*pensée*) down.' (D.H.
Lawrence). Truth is a shifting sand, and what is true today may not be true tomorrow. Poetry, being always quick
and deriving direct from specific, concrete experience,
and not from the knowledge derived from experience, is a
prophylactic against hebetude. Poetry compels honesty,
cannot lie. To be honest needs an intolerable struggle;
and to be honest about your honesty, to make an ever-new
beginning,

>   a raid on the inarticulate
>   With shabby equipment always deteriorating
>   In the general mess of imprecision of feeling,
>   Undisciplined squads of emotion,

needs a second struggle.

But this poem is only secondarily (or thirdly or
fourthly) a record of the struggle of creation in words.
Primarily it is an act of creation. It is about experience; it is about the meaning of experience; about the
meaninglessness of giving experience a fixed meaning; and
about the struggle with words.

All of which sounds as though the thing were a night-
mare of abstractions. On the contrary, it is clear, quick,
humble and poignantly beautiful. No word jars, or merely
skims precision, or is redundant. Its wisdom is as

concentrated as that of Lao-tzu. One would say that it derived from the 'Tao-tê-ching' if Eliot had not gone to elaborate pains (in 'After Strange Gods') to dissociate himself from the East and its works.

There are two planes of experience, two planes of suffering. There is the blind, dumb-ox suffering of the unaware; and the conscious suffering of those to whom the miseries of the unaware are misery and will not let them rest.

> Old stone to new building, old timber to new fires,
> Old fires to ashes, and ashes to the earth
> Which is already flesh, fur and faeces,
> Bone of man and beast, cornstalk and leaf.

Eliot, the conscious man, the man moved by an inner urgency, writes not out of a subjective suffering but out of an objective awareness of suffering, of birth and copulation and death, of change and decay, of the ebb and flow of earth's givings and takings.

Then there is Time. You will remember 'Prufrock':

> Time for you and time for me,
> And time yet for a hundred indecisions,
> And for a hundred visions and revisions,
> Before the taking of a toast and tea.

But now the note is deeper:

> there is a time for building
> And a time for living and for generation
> And a time for the wind to break the loosened pane
> And to shake the wainscot where the field-mouse trots
> And to shake the tattered arras woven with a silent
>   motto.

But the time for living and generation is not our time; ours is a time of waiting:

> there is yet faith
> But the faith and the love and the hope
>   are all in the waiting.

It is hard to wait, hard not to hope for the wrong thing, hard not to love the wrong thing, hard to do nothing about anything, hard to be humble, and to wait, always to wait - even 'without thought, for you are not ready for thought.' But there is meaning in this; it is too insistent throughout the poem not to be the very kernel of

Eliot's meaning:

[Quotes 'East Coker', III, CPP, p. 181, 'Shall I say it again?' to 'where you are not'.]

   Experience, then, does not enable us to eliminate our ignorance, but to realise its extent. The acquiring of wisdom is the process of realising, in ever-widening circles, the extent of our ignorance and of learning to be humble, of learning to wait. Is this the New Testament? Or the Tao? Or both?
   The poem closes with a gleam of promise, a moment's pallid sunlight on a stormy day:

> We must be still and still moving
> Into another intensity
> For a further union, a deeper communion
> Through the dark cold and the empty desolation,
> The wave cry, the wind cry, the vast waters
> Of the petrel and the porpoise. In my end is my
>   beginning.

   In 'The Dry Salvages' the theme of Time is continued. But first there is a breathing space. 'The wave cry, the wind cry' evokes memory of the rocky coast of Massachusetts, the scene probably of Eliot's boyhood.
   Ezra Pound has written:

> It is said that Flaubert taught de Maupassant to write. When de Maupassant returned from a walk Flaubert would ask him to describe someone, say a concierge whom they would both pass in their next walk, and to describe the person so that Flaubert would recognise, say, the concierge and not mistake her for some other concierge and not the one de Maupassant had described.

Pound then asks his hypothetical pupil to describe a tree - without mentioning the name of the tree (larch, pine, &c.) so that the reader will not mistake it for the description of some other kind of tree.
   That is the quality of pure poetry; it describes, reveals, *things*. Adulterated poetry expresses subjective *ideas*. 'The Dry Salvages' is full of *things*: a river, a stretch of rocky coast, a whistling buoy. It is so easy to spill ideas, so hard to tell people about things: a tree, a concierge, a whistling buoy. Tremendous humility is needed to do it - the humility of the novelist but more concentrated; for the novelist, with unlimited space and all the perils of prose, is apt to give you his *idea* of

of the rooms, houses, people, furniture he describes.

> You are not the same people who left that station
> Or who will arrive at any terminus,
> While *the narrowing rails slide together behind you;*
> And on the deck of the drumming liner
> Watching *the furrow that widens behind you* ...

The precision of observation in the lines italicised, that objective realisation of *things*, is what Shakespeare achieved in songs like 'When icicles hang by the wall,' &c. We *see* the narrowing rails and the widening furrow as Herrick, for example, makes us feel Julia's silks and hear them swish as she moves.

But where Eliot's especial genius comes in is that he extends the finite, sensible quality of things into what was hitherto the domain of ideas. Time, the protagonist of these poems, becomes as objectively perceived, almost, one might say, as real and finite an entity as his brown river and whistling buoy.

[Quotes 'The Dry Salvages', I, CPP, p. 185, 'And under the oppression' to 'is never ending'.]

But once again 'the poetry does not matter.' What matter are the moments of happiness, 'the sudden illumination,' and the approach to its meaning. 'Burnt Norton' opened with:

> Time present and time past
> Are both perhaps present in time future,
> And time future contained in time past.

The difficulties of the earlier poem are now clarified and resolved:

> It seems, as one becomes older,
> That the past has another pattern, and ceases to be a
>   mere sequence -
> Or even development: the latter a partial fallacy
> Encouraged by superficial notions of evolution
> Which becomes, in the popular mind, a means of dis-
>   owning the past....

But the past cannot be disowned:

> People change, and smile: but the agony abides.
> Time the destroyer is time the preserver....
> You cannot face it steadily, but this thing is sure,
> That time is no healer: the patient is no longer here.

Nor does the future lie before us; what lies before us
is the struggle to give meaning to the past:

> We had the experience but missed the meaning,
> And approach to the meaning restores the experience
> In a different form, beyond any meaning
> We can assign to happiness.

The lesson of 'East Coker,' of infinite humility and
patience, is reinforced:

[Quotes 'The Dry Salvages', V, CPP, pp. 189-90, 'Men's
curiosity' to 'and self-surrender'.]

This is the poetry of silence and stillness and waiting
and endless humility. To hear it read aloud is to feel as
though one were listening to a silence, as sometimes one
listens to a silence in Beethoven. But the dark cold and
the empty desolation are terrifying; one could wish one
had been born into a time of living and generation.
Indeed, so far as one is able, one hangs on to that world,
that other time, that warmth of living and contact and
togetherness and humanity.

One hangs on to it, I say, as far as one is able. But
we cannot have it both ways. If this poetry speaks to
our condition, if Eliot's is the adult voice of our generation, if his words, his meaning, so painfully brought
forth, represent the highest we know, then we must accept
what he says, we must abide by it and face what it implies.

His may be the saddest poetry ever written, but it is
not egoistic or inhuman or didactic. He speaks disinter-
estedly and objectively. Rarely does the first person
singular occur; and when it does it is de-personalised,
remote, as though Eliot had given himself a power of
attorney to speak on his own behalf. It is remote, not
intimate, not autobiographical nor autopsychographical.
He speaks as a man who has transcended the limitations of
the ego, who has denuded himself of personality.

Personality is the disease of our time. Personality is
what Churchill has, what the commercial traveller has,
what every comic-cuts of a policeman, parson or postman
has. Personality is the condition of the unhumble vacant;
one is reminded of Thackeray on one of the Georges: 'You
take off one waistcoat and find another underneath. You
take off that and find a third. And when you have taken
off all the waistcoats you find - nothing.' We are the
hollow men - with a sugary coating of personality. Hence:

> The only wisdom we can hope to acquire
> Is the wisdom of humility: humility is endless.

Eliot, by example, gives a final quietus to 'self-expression.' Of course it will go on, that noisy habit; but it will be a survival, as redundant as Wilde and the Nineties. We learn from Eliot that it is better to be silent than to say nothing.

There is introversion and there is egoism; humility and the assertiveness of the extravert. It is presumption to point to the evil in others, to try to transform the world. Let us be content to try to transform the evil in ourselves. To go deep into ourselves is to be introvert. To be fearlessly introvert, to have the courage not to be eternally justifying ourselves in extravert action, is to avoid egoism. Rilke told the Young Poet to go down deep into himself; he said it time and time again, because he knew that self-awareness is the first condition of other-awareness, which is imagination.

In Eliot's later work we pass beyond the world of ideas and ideals, of abstractions and absolutes, and enter the green kingdom within where no evil is done as a means to good, where there is no clamour of righteousness in pro-test against evil. Here one suffers consciously, not blindly, and asks for no insurance policy, no endowment of happiness in return for a premium of anguish.

But the kingdom within is not fenced off, is not proof against the assaults of time and experience, confusion and coincidence, events and interludes and waste. Here is no permanent pattern wrested from disorder; one does not digest only tabloids of spiritual essences; here, just as elsewhere, there is the roughage and the unassimilable. The kingdom within is not a monastic seclusion; for the deeper you penetrate your within-ness the more you are in, though not necessarily of, the outer tumult. Remember always - may I quote it again?

[Quotes 'East Coker', II, CPP, p. 179, 'There is, it seems' to 'all we have been'.]

Every moment, mark you. In the kingdom within, where we are liberated from the folly of action and competing and contending, there is no stasis but a new and different and terrible experiencing. This, this above all, is the con-dition of 'a further union, a deeper communion.' There is no short cut.

125. MURIEL BRADBROOK, THE LYRIC AND DRAMATIC IN THE
LATEST VERSE OF T.S. ELIOT, 'THEOLOGY'

February 1942, vol. xliv, 81-90

Muriel Bradbrook (b. 1908), a distinguished British
scholar, has written a number of studies of Eliot, most
particularly 'T.S. Eliot' (London and New York, 1950),
which surveys his career as a whole up to that date.

All Eliot's latest verse treats of an antinomy of Time and
Eternity. The flash of insight is familiar in many poets
- Shakespeare, Wordsworth, Blake, Yeats - perhaps isolated
in its own felt intuitive value. With his view that the
work of the poet is to 'connect', and form new wholes from,
disparate experiences, Eliot relates this supreme private
moment with the Christian doctrine of Eternity, springing
from the fact of the Resurrection and embodied in the
Sacrament of the Eucharist. The result is no theory of
time, in the philosophical sense, but a series of value
judgments. Time theories in modern science and philosophy
are no more destructive of the doctrine of Eternity than
Copernicus' cosmology was of the Christian interpretation
of the universe; for miracles of illumination, if not universal, are yet so general that, if they were delusions,
the nature and reason of the delusion would still require
explanation.
     The personal quality of the experience is preserved by
Eliot in that all his later poems are dramatic in form:
'Ash-Wednesday' was also written in the first person, but
the experience was not projected in so dramatic a fashion.
'Coriolan' and 'Marina' are typical of his new method,
in their vividness - partly dependent, of course, on the
Shakespearean reference - and their contrasting varieties
of satire and introspection: the one gives a picture of
power politics which perhaps seemed exaggerated when it
was written but is now generally accepted; the key to the
other is given by its motto, 'Quis hic locus, quae regio,
quae mundi plaga?', taken from Seneca's 'Hercules Furens',
at that moment when the hero emerges from hell into the
light of day. (a) The setting of the granite foggy shore
with its islands is taken from Eliot's own childhood; it
appears also at the end of 'Ash-Wednesday' and in 'The
Dry Salvages'. If 'Ash-Wednesday' is Eliot's 'Purgatorio',
'Marina' is his 'Paradiso', a glimpse of beatitude in
which the mortal world of sensuous beauty falls away.

By this grace, dissolved in place ...

and in its place comes a vision:

What is this face, less clear and clearer?
The pulse in the arm, less strong and stronger?
Given or lent? more distant than stars and nearer
    than the eye.

Marina, she who was lost and is found again, is here
identified with a very personal recollection, which is
also to reappear later. (b)

Whispers and small laughter between leaves and hurry-
    ing feet
Under sleep, where all the waters meet.

The power of the poem lies in its rhythm, which com-
bines a choric repetition, bolder than the chiming echoes
of 'Ash-Wednesday' and looking forward to that of the
plays, with a delicate, hesitant movement, depicting the
wonder of the recognition, at the moment when the beatific
vision reveals itself as something also known and familiar:

Those who sharpen the tooth of the dog, (c) meaning
Death;
Those who glitter with the glory of the hummingbird,
    meaning
Death...
Are become unsubstantial, reduced by the wind,
A breath of pine and the woodsong fog....
I made this, I have forgotten
And remember
The rigging weak and the canvas rotten
Between one June and another September
Made this, unconscious, half-knowing, unknown, my
    own....

These two contrasted moods are also in another way the
basis of 'Coriolan', the tramp of the death-filled
triumph,

Stone, bronze, stone, steel, stone, oak-leaves,
    horses' heels
Over the paving

and the momentary gleam of security which appears, however, only as a mirage to the doomed hero:

O hidden under the dove's wing, hidden in the turtle's
    breast, (d)
Under the palm tree at noon, under the running water
At the still point of the turning world. O hidden.

A combination of intimacy and detachment is here
applied, not to personal connexions, as in the early
poems, or to a contemplation of society, as in 'The Waste
Land', or to inward states, as in 'Ash-Wednesday', but to
all three simultaneously. It is a new adjustment, which
can be seen by comparing the end of 'A Game at Chess' in
'The Waste Land' (the pub. scene) with the end of 'Triumphal March' ('Coriolan', I), where the triviality and
incompetence of modern life for the city worker are suddenly presented as part of a deeper disease, and 'Please
will you give us a light?' becomes a cry for grace.

In these poems are freely mixed symbols from the
modern world: the catalogue of armaments and magnates in
'Coriolan', the Massachusetts shore in 'Marina'. Eliot
here anticipates 'Murder in the Cathedral' in giving a
truly Shakespearean mixture of ancient and modern, the
better to create a Mirror, not for Magistrates, but for
Everyman. The wheel of Fortune, identified with the
turning earth, and so with times and seasons, also
appears, in the lines quoted above; it was to become one
of the main images in his treatment of the problem of Time
and Eternity.

In 'Murder in the Cathedral' and the new sequence,
Eliot is attempting to picture the vision of Eternity with
its results in Time; miracles of Incarnation. (e) In the
play he uses the medieval setting because it helps his
purpose, since the medieval categories of thought and
organization are those he finds most suitable; yet the
Tempters, and the Knights, who are the Tempters' embodiments, are rightly played as modern figures. The play
demonstrates

                    The critical moment
That is always now and here. Even now, in sordid
    particulars
The eternal design may appear. (Part II, Scene I, p. 55.)

In 'East Coker', the Elizabethan forbears of Mr Eliot are
'faded out' into the Second World War. In 'Burnt Norton',
the 'moment in the rose garden', in 'The Dry Salvages',
the 'fog in the fir tree', stand for 'the point of the
intersection of the timeless with time', the study of
which is 'an occupation for the saint' and the saint
alone; in Thomas such a saint is depicted. The words of

the Women of Canterbury were not only the comment on the
fore-ordained assassination, they were the most adequate
poetic statement of the feeling of foreboding that culminated in Munich, and its conscious shame:

> We do not wish anything to happen.
> Seven years we have lived quietly,
> Succeeded in avoiding notice,
> Living and partly living....
> But now a great fear is upon us, a fear not of one but
>   of many,
> A fear like birth and death, when we see birth and
>   death alone
> In a void apart....
> O Thomas our Lord, leave us and leave us be, in our
>   humble and tarnished frame of existence, leave us:
>   do not ask us
> To stand to the doom on the house, the doom on the
>   Archbishop, the doom on the world....
> ...the small folk drawn into the pattern of fate, the
>   small folk who live among small things....

and in the final chorus:

> Forgive us, O Lord; we acknowledge ourselves as types
>   of the common man,
> Of men and women who shut the door and sit by the
>   fire....

In 'The Dry Salvages', the Massachusetts coast of Eliot's
childhood fuses with his present sense of the Battle of
the Atlantic, and both with their religious context. The
abrupt colloquialisms in a poetic setting, the sudden
switches of rhythm are the 'objective correlatives', the
vehicle of this fusion:

> Pray for all those who are in ships, those
> Whose business has to do with fish, and
> Those concerned in every lawful traffic
> And those who conduct them.
>   ('The Dry Salvages', IV.)

These patterns of times and seasons embody the feeling
made explicit in 'East Coker':

[Quotes 'East Coker', V, CPP, p. 182, 'Home is where' to
'of one man only'.] (f)

The prayer to the Virgin, the penultimate section of 'The

Dry Salvages', is, like the lament for the drowned
Phoenician Sailor in 'The Waste Land', the symbolic centre
of the poem. It is immediately followed by a loose-
flowing satiric section denouncing that old enemy of
Eliot, the Fortune Teller, dealer in past and future. The
conclusion introduces a new rhythm, heavy yet unemphatic,
with a triple-stressed line, a prosaic but not colloquial
vocabulary, considerable repetition and reiteration. The
whole gives an effect of steady, even power, of a massively
representative utterance:

[Quotes 'The Dry Salvages', V, CPP, p. 190, 'For most of
us, this is' to 'significant soil'.]

Compared with 'Ash-Wednesday', 'Murder in the Cathedral'
and the new sequence have both a new variety and a new
monotony. Phrases are repeated from poem to poem;
experiences which are recognizably related if not the same
reappear in different contexts. The preoccupation with
time and the rejection of time:

> Those to whom nothing has ever happened
> Cannot understand the unimportance of events ...
> Love is most nearly itself
> When here and now cease to matter ...

perhaps suggests Yeats or Wyndham Lewis as well as St
Augustine. (g) Eliot observes, sometimes defiantly and
sometimes dejectedly, that he is repetitive; but in re-
counting such types of experience there is no alternative
to monotony, as writers from widely different times and
places are agreed:

>   You say I am repeating
> Something I have said before. I shall say it again ...
> And what there is to conquer
> By strength and submission, has already been discovered
> Once or twice, or several times, by men whom one cannot
>   hope
> To emulate - but there is no competition....
>   ('East Coker', III, V.)

Monotony is inevitable in the attempt constantly to evalu-
ate the experiences of time by the experience of eternity.
Herein Eliot's preoccupation with time differs from that
of Lewis, and also of Proust and Joyce - though not from
Yeats; moreover, the experience of eternity is acknowledged ineffable in terms of time:

> I can only say, *there* we have been; but I cannot say
>   where.
> And I cannot say, how long, for that is to place
>   it in time.
>
> ('Burnt Norton', II.)

The *via negativa* of purgation, detachment, and illumination is either understood or not understood. The reader
at this point either grasps what Eliot is saying or he
does not; no half-understanding is possible:

> Absolute detachment from all creatures is the best
> and highest virtue. Higher than love, humility or
> mercy.... Such motionless detachment makes a man
> supremely Godlike. For that God is God is due to His
> motionless detachment, and it is from this detachment
> that He gets His simplicity and His immutability. To
> be empty of creatures is to be full of God, and to
> be full of creatures is to be empty of God....
>   What, then, I ask, is the object of this absolute
> detachment? I answer that it is neither this nor that.
> It is absolutely nothing, for it is the culminating
> point where God can do precisely as He will. - Meister
> Eckhardt, 'Works', I, p. 340 (trans. C. de B. Evans).

To quote a writer who is *not* used by Eliot is to show more
clearly the common ground of the experience:

> I said to my soul, be still and wait without hope
> For hope would be hope for the wrong thing; wait with-
>   out love
> For love would be love of the wrong thing; there is yet
>   faith
> But the faith and the hope and the love are all in the
>   waiting.
>
> ('East Coker', III.)

Some unfortunate observed that this is 'the most gloomy
verse Mr Eliot has given us'. Well might Eliot say that
states of beatitude are farther from what the world understands by cheerfulness than are states of damnation!
    Yet with this uncompromising renunciation Eliot
achieves a new flexibility and freedom. *Cantat vacuus*.
The image of what things felt like at the beginning of the
war ('As in a theatre the lights are extinguished for the
scene to be changed...'), the personal reflections on
poetry in 'East Coker' II and V, the satiric yet agonized
pictures of the general situation ('O dark dark dark...',
'The wounded surgeon plies the steel...'), establish a

connexion between past and future, between different modes
of being in an evaluative sense, which is the main purpose of this later verse. The poems are a whole, yet they
combine epigrammatic lines (e.g., 'the general mess of imprecision of feeling') (h) with a readiness in the two
satiric sections mentioned to draw equally upon 'Samson
Agonistes' and Mr Auden. Eliot has regained his old co-
ordinating power, ordered from a new point of view.

The whole development shows itself in changes in the
nature of the poetic 'I'. Dramatic monologue is an early
form with Eliot - e.g., 'Prufrock', 'Portrait of a Lady',
'Gerontion'. All of these are impressionistic, dependent
on the 'colouring' of a particular and limited point of
view, which is at the same time subjected to self-satire
and self-criticism. The degree of projection for the
writer and the reader is a ticklish question - it is, e.g.,
at least as much as in 'Bishop Blougram's Apology' - and
the satire does not check but reinforce it, being the most
'sympathetic' part. 'A friendliness, as of dwarfs shaking
hands, was in the air.' The main emotional effect is in
the nature of a by-product ('not a turning loose of emotion but an escape from emotion').

In 'The Waste Land' the 'negative emotions' are stronger: tedium, accidia, and the frozen pity born of fore-
knowledge and impotence to avert calamity ('And I, Tiresias, have foresuffered all'). Often the 'I' seems indeterminate, but nearer to a personal 'I' than to Tiresias
- e.g., in Section V. The vision is broken, shifting,
held together by the negative emotions which pervade it.
Some minor figures are dramatized satirically - they are
all women.

In 'The Hollow Men' the 'I' becomes 'we', for in the
sheer pain of that experience any sense of personality has
lapsed; the opening section announces it. The 'we' is an
indeterminate suffering consciousness, not people. 'Ash-
Wednesday' is written from a collected personality; the
'I' is clear, not as a person, but as a will, and parts of
the poem are addresses or prayers. The rhythm, a sure
index, is less nerveless, and has a taut power. In the
later dramatic monologues the 'I' is almost neutral: the
old man, the spectator, the stony public figure, no longer
tormented by self-satire or insecurity, but by exhaustion
and weariness of the flesh. No longer is the tempter the
satiric Mephistopheles, debunking all impulses in terms of
their origins, but the vehicle of a weltschmertz. In 'The
Rock', as in 'Coriolan', the country of 'The Waste Land'
reappears, not for satire but for judgment, with a faint
chorus of 'the unemployed' behind it:

> In the land of lobelias and tennis flannels
> The rabbit shall burrow and the thorn revisit,
> The nettle shall flourish on the gravel court....
> It is hard for those who have never known persecution
> And who have never known a Christian
> To believe these tales of Christian persecution....
> It is hard for those who live near a Police Station
> To believe in the triumph of violence....
>   ('The Rock', III, V; 'Poems', pp. 166, 170.)

This is a foreshadowing of the speech of Thomas to the Tempters. 'Murder in the Cathedral' has only two voices - that of Thomas and that of the Women of Canterbury. The Knights, Tempters and Priests are significant only in relation to the others. And the Chorus and Thomas perhaps only represent the two voices of Everyman: human frailty conscious of its failure, and human frailty conscious of its power. The theme is the old one: renunciation, purgation, perfection of the will, the *via negativa*. This is the whole duty of man. Thomas must not even crave the glory of being a martyr:

> The last temptation is the greatest treason:
> To do the right deed for the wrong reason.
>   ('Murder in the Cathedral', Part I, *ad fin.*, p. 44.)

Illumination, grace, the 'wink of bliss', can only so be obtained; to hope to obtain it is to be defeated at the outset:

> I say to you, *make perfect your will:*
> I say, take no thought of the harvest
> But only of proper sowing.
>   ('The Rock', I; 'Poems', p. 159.)

Or, as 'East Coker' puts it, 'For us, there is only the trying. The rest is not our business' (Section V).

For the world, or those who would 'settle all the inconvenient saints, apostles, martyrs in a kind of Whipsnade', there is in 'Murder in the Cathedral' the unsparing lash which has made Mr Eliot appear splenetic, not only to the enlightened Pagan, but also to his fellow Christians. (i) The Church is unpopular because 'she is tender where they would be hard, and hard where they like to be soft'. The Knights, who come from the land of lobelias and tennis flannels, as well as from Aquitaine, are completely condemned. 'Go, lost souls.' 'Murder in the Cathedral' shows one of those moments, 'in and out of time', when a saint is created, a moment in the pattern of

time which has a significance beyond time. Though a
successful drama, it is from the point of conflicting
'I's' a very simple one.
    'The Family Reunion' is Mr Eliot's worst failure. The
only real characters are the Furies, and they do not speak.
The other characters are simulacra, epiphenomena; the work
is a transitional piece, perhaps of more importance to the
writer than to the public. In the new sequence the satire
which was still perceptible in 'Murder in the Cathedral'
has almost completely faded; the world, in so far as it
enters, is mortal, temporal and therefore incomplete, but
neither hostile nor malignant. There is more stability
and a new refreshment not only in 'the moment in the rose
garden', but in the ordinary beauty of the Somerset village, the Massachusetts coast. The 'I' is occasionally
discursive, commentary, annotative ('East Coker', II, V;
'The Dry Salvages', II); sometimes absent altogether, as
in the beautiful sestines of 'The Dry Salvages':

    Where is there an end of it, the soundless wailing,
    The silent withering of autumn flowers? ...

Now Eliot has written for himself a body of work upon
which he can draw, and if there is danger in the repetition of his own themes, the present difficulties of any
writer justify the risk, even were it not inevitable in
his material. He is, too, well aware of the risks:

    One has only learnt to get the better of words
    For the thing one no longer has to say, or the way in
        which
    One is no longer disposed to say it.
                              ('East Coker', V.)

Formulation means supersession. What can be stated has
been isolated from the rest of the mind and is no longer
part of its growing tissue. It has suffered parturition.
Nevertheless it provides something from which to start
out again. In an age when traditions are so broken, the
poet quickly makes his own tradition, which, if he is
only a minor poet, amounts to a few tricks and mannerisms
upon which he ever after plays variations; men of thirty
today are as helplessly living on their own past work as
Wordsworth was at eighty. Eliot's work shows that power
to change, and yet to incorporate the work which has been
done, which marks a true writer; each separate work fits
into the pattern of the whole 'oeuvre'. The whole is
greater than the parts. Eliot, like Herbert, demands to be
read extensively.

Notes

a It is interesting to compare this poem with D.H. Lawrence's pseudo-Christian 'Ship of Death'.
b Cf. 'Burnt Norton', Section I:

      They were behind us, reflected in the pool.
      Go, said the bird, for the leaves were full of
          children,
      Hidden excitedly, containing laughter.

c Cf. 'The Rock', VI; 'Poems', p. 170:

      Men! polish your teeth on rising and retiring ...
      You polish the tooth of the dog....

d Coriolanus to Virgilia:

      What is thy curtsey worth, or those dove's eyes
      That can make men foresworn?

e 'Burnt Norton' is Norton House, Aston Subedge, Gloucestershire. The house was burnt down and rebuilt in the
   sixteenth century, hence its name. It now houses
   evacuated school children.
      East Coker is the Somerset village where the Eliots
   lived before emigrating to America. The poem was
   written for Good Friday, 1940, and appeared in the 'New
   English Weekly'. 'The Dry Salvages' appeared in this
   paper also, February 27, 1941. A fourth poem will complete the sequence. 'The Dry Salvages' are a group of
   islands off the north-east coast of Cape Ann, Massachusetts, with a bell-buoy. The name is presumably a
   corruption of 'les trois sauvages'. *Salvages* rhymes to
   assauges.
f Cf. the 'moments' of 'La Figlia Che Piange' and the
   Hyacinth Girl in 'The Waste Land', Section I.
g *E.g.*, the Crazy Jane and Mad Tom Poems in 'The Tower'
   and 'The Winding Stair', 'Time and Western Man', the
   'Confessions', Book XI.
h Cf. 'The Rock', IX; 'Poems', p. 178:

      Out of the slimy mud of words, the sleet and hail of
          verbal imprecisions;

   and 'Burnt Norton', VI:

      Words strain ... decay with imprecision, will not
          stay in place.

i E.g., he has been accused of being very illiberal towards D.H. Lawrence, and Mr C.S. Lewis, on the other
   hand, has rebuked him for his attitude towards 'the
   land of lobelias and tennis flannels'. Perhaps Mr
   Lewis forgot that this land belonged to 'decent *godless*
   people'.

126. ROLFE HUMPHRIES, SALVATION FROM SAND IN SALT,
'POETRY'

March 1942, vol. lix, 338-9

This review contains a reference to an essay by Van Wyck
Brooks, What is Primary Literature?, in 'Opinions of
Oliver Allston' (New York, 1941), pp. 218-27, reprinted in
Unger, pp. 114-19, which attacks Eliot's ideas on tradi-
tion as 'phantasmal' and self-created. Brooks's tone is
jocular and philistine.

The cadences of this new poem by T.S. Eliot rise, lapse,
and fold themselves under like the swells of a great grey
sea in still grey weather. The tide of emotion withdraws,
leaving the margin littered with curious excrescences of
prose; it comes flooding in again, deep and full. Against
the beat of the clanging bell of the final annunciation,
the poem moves, and is moving and beautiful.
     Some questions might be raised - and I venture them
with the diffidence of a novice - concerning Eliot's devotional attitude, and the extent to which it is conducive
to a great spiritual and religious poetry. How much of
him is Catholic; how much Oriental? Does his earlier
satirical manner disguise, and thereby attest, his sense
of temptation, or has he always been frightfully bored,
really, with the pomp and vanity of this wicked world, the
pride and sinful lusts of the flesh? In what he has written of past and present, it has usually been to contrast
the glory of the former with the sordidness of the latter;
or, more subtly, to use the latter to suggest that the
former, too, was hollow and false. But however it may be
with the temporal world, 'seared with trade; bleared,
smeared with toil,' is not the divine glory constant and
permanent? 'The world is charged with the grandeur of

469 T.S. Eliot: The Critical Heritage

God: it will flame out, like shining from shook foil.'
But you would never learn this from Eliot.

There is a difference between a lifetime's death in
love, and a lifetime love of death. The ardor must precede the selflessness; the self be made before it is
surrendered; otherwise what is given God is nothing. And
is God truly praised when His perfect greyness is made to
reflect only the greyness of a world resigned from lack of
interest? can one seek salvation in an ocean of salt,
fleeing damnation in the Waste Land?

'We had the experience,' writes Eliot, 'but missed the
meaning.' The sudden illumination was all too rare; the
moments of agony permanent, 'with such permanence as time
has.' And time is no healer.

[Quotes 'The Dry Salvages', V, CPP, p. 190, 'For most of
us, there is' to 'While the music lasts' and 'For most of
us, this is' to 'significant soil'.]

In that this is honest, humble, and beautiful poetry it
serves God's praise. But in that it has, with the agony
and the virtue of patience, the faithlessness and leaden
echo of despair, it is a Lenten praise: 'O why are we so
haggard at the heart, so care-coiled, so fagged, so
fashed, so cogged, so cumbered?'

I hope that the remarks above will not be so miscon-
strued as to place me in the camp of Mr. Van Wyck Brooks.

127. HELEN GARDNER, A STUDY OF ELIOT'S MORE RECENT POETRY

1942

This essay, entitled The Recent Poetry of T.S. Eliot,
first appeared in 'New Writing and Daylight' (London,
1942, pp. 84-96). It was later expanded for 'Penguin New
Writing', no. 29 (1946), and for 'T.S. Eliot: A Study of
His Writings by Several Hands', edited by B. Rajan (1947).
It was also the origin of 'The Art of T.S. Eliot' (London,
1949).

Dame Helen Gardner (b. 1908), Emeritus Professor of English Literature, Oxford University, has published a number of important studies of Eliot, including 'The Art of
T.S. Eliot' (1949), 'T.S. Eliot and the English Poetic
Tradition' (1965) and 'The Composition of "Four Quartets"'

(1978).   She gave the T.S. Eliot Memorial Lectures at the
University of Kent at Canterbury in 1968.

Criticism has two main functions, interpretation and valuation, and they are usually carried on simultaneously.
But with a living poet valuation often has to wait on
interpretation. Mr. Eliot is acknowledged to be an important poet by all critics of standing, but reviews of his
latest poems and comments on 'The Family Reunion' suggest
that many of his readers find it very difficult to follow
his thought. Partly this is due to ignorance of the tradition in which he writes, partly to a false dichotomy between his earlier and his later work; partly it seems due
at times to careless reading. When we find a poet and
critic of high reputation declaring, that in 'The Family
Reunion' Agatha tells Harry, 'who has just returned from a
cruise on which he pushed his wife overboard, that his
mother murdered his father,' (a) and adding the irrelevant
information, quite unsupported by the text, that Agatha is
an Anglo-Catholic, it seems time that praise of Mr.
Eliot's poetry, or criticism of its relevance or non-
relevance to modern life, should give place to the attempt
to understand it.

   Mr. Eliot has always been courteous to his critics, not
merely suffering them gladly, but sometimes giving them
gentle commendation, and he has invited the impertinence
of interpretation by his statement, that 'what a poem
means is as much what it means to others as what it means
to its author.' The best kind of interpretation is that
supplied by an author's other works, and this is particularly true of Mr. Eliot, since he constantly repeats himself, as he himself owns, -

                  You say I am repeating
      Something I have said before. I shall say it again.
      Shall I say it again?

His poetry is extraordinarily self-consistent, and there
is almost nothing that he has published that does not
form part of his poetic personality. One of the results
of this integrity is that his later work interprets his
earlier, as much as his earlier work does his later; so
that criticism of 'The Waste Land' to-day is modified by
'Ash-Wednesday,' and 'Ash-Wednesday' is easier to understand after reading 'East Coker.' This commentary will
try to interpret his last three poems by his other works
and by the reading that seems to lie behind them.

The structure of the poems is seen very clearly when
they are read together, and can be recognized as being
essentially the same as the structure of 'The Waste Land.'
With all four works before us, the form appears far more
rigid than we should suspect from each separate poem.   In
fact, Mr. Eliot has invented for himself a kind of poetic
equivalent of 'sonata form,' containing what are best described as five 'movements,' each with an inner necessary
structure, and capable of the symphonic richness of 'The
Waste Land,' or the chamber-music beauties of 'Burnt
Norton.'   The five movements suggest the five acts of the
drama, and the poems are built on a dialectical basis,
employing deliberate reversals and contrasts in matter
and style.   This form seems perfectly adapted to its
creator's way of feeling and thinking: to his desire to
submit to the poetic discipline of strict law, and to his
desire to find a form which gives him the greatest possible liberty in the development of a flexible, dramatic
verse, and the greatest freedom in 'violently yoking together heterogeneous ideas.'   The combination of an extreme apparent freedom with a great inner strictness
corresponds to the necessities of his temperament.
    The first movement in each of the three poems consists
of statement and counter-statement in a resolved blank
verse.   This must not be pressed too hardly, for in 'East
Coker' the first movement falls into four parts, the
statement and its contradiction being repeated, while in
'The Dry Salvages' the metaphors of river and sea are
more absolutely opposed than are the two paragraphs of ·
'Burnt Norton.'   But on the whole the opening movement is
built on contradictions which it is the business of the
poem to reconcile.   The second movement shows the most
striking similarities from poem to poem.   It opens with a
highly 'poetical' lyric passage - octosyllabics, rhyming
irregularly in 'Burnt Norton' and 'East Coker' and a simplified sestina in 'The Dry Salvages.'   This is immediately followed by an extremely colloquial passage, in
which the idea which had been treated in metaphor and
symbol in the first half of the movement is expanded, and
given personal application, in a free conversational manner and in a loose blank verse.   The third movement is the
core of each poem, out of which reconciliation grows: it
is an exploration, with a twist, of the ideas of the first
two movements, the twist being usually the point of the
poem. (b)   For instance, the shift in the emotions aroused
by the word *darkness* is the essential point of 'East Coker.'
The fourth movement is in all three poems a lyric.   The
fifth is again in two parts, but the change in manner and
metre is slighter than in the second movement, and it is

reversed. Here the colloquial passage comes first, and
then, without a feeling of sharp break, the rhythm
tightens and the manner becomes graver for a kind of falling close. The whole movement recapitulates the themes
of the poem, with personal and topical applications, and
makes a resolution of the discords of the first.

'The Waste Land,' if one allows for its much wider
scope, dramatic method, and hosts of characters, follows
the same pattern. 'The Burial of the Dead' contains far
more than two statements, but formally it is a series of
contrasts of feeling towards persons and experiences. 'A
Game of Chess' opens with the elaborate description, in
ornate style, of the lady at her dressing-table, which
contrasts violently, though not in its theme, with the
talk of the women in the public-house. 'The Fire Sermon,'
the poem's heart, with its suffocating intensity, has
moments when the oppression lifts, and a feeling of release and purification floods in. This twist is given by
the evocations of another world: 'Et O ces voix d'enfants,
chantant dans la coupole!', the 'inexplicable splendours
of Ionian white and gold,' the 'white towers,' and the
mingled emotions aroused by the word *burning*, for we
remember not only St. Paul's use of it to express the torment of desire, but also the brand plucked out, and the
fire of the 'Purgatorio.' The reference to the Buddha,
the 'collocation of western and eastern asceticism,' to
which attention is drawn in the notes, anticipates the use
of the 'Bhagavadgita' in 'The Dry Salvages.' The fourth
section is as always a brief lyric, and the fifth, while
being naturally far more complex than the final movements
of the later poems, fulfils the same function of resolution. Most people would agree today, in the light of Mr.
Eliot's later work, that the original critics of 'The
Waste Land' misread it, not recognizing it as an 'Inferno'
which looked towards a 'Purgatorio.' Finding in it 'the
disillusion of a generation,' they failed to see in it
what its treatment of history should have shown them, the
disillusion of those in every generation, 'qui se haïss-
ent, et qui cherchent un être véritablement aimable.'

'Burnt Norton,' 'East Coker' and 'The Dry Salvages' are
poems on one theme, or rather on different aspects of the
same theme, and they are closely linked with 'The Family
Reunion,' which is a dramatic treatment of the subject.
The theme can be variously defined, since we are speaking
of poetry, not of philosophy or theology. It might be
called the relation of time to eternity, or the meaning of
history, or the redemption of time and the world of man.
'The Family Reunion' emphasizes the idea of redemption,
for Harry is seeking salvation and release from his sense

of guilt. As he flies from the pursuing Eumenides, he is
a man fleeing from the eternal, turning his back upon it to
immerse himself in futile movement; when he recognizes them
and accepts their summons, they become 'bright angels' and
the ministers of his purgation. But this recognition
springs out of his discovery of the past, his own and that
of his family. As Agatha talks to him and tells him of
his parents' unhappiness and sin, he at last understands
the meaning of his own unhappy childhood and of his own
marriage. He becomes then 'the consciousness of his unhappy family' and so can make expiation. (c)

The close connection of 'The Family Reunion' with these
poems will become apparent in the course of the discussion, but the same themes had appeared in Mr. Eliot's
poetry before. They are made fully explicit in the
choruses of 'The Rock,' which contrast the determined and
endless motion of the world of time with the stillness of
eternity, and celebrate the union of time and eternity in

> a moment in and out of time,
> A moment not out of time, but in time, in what we call
>   history; transecting, bisecting the world of time, a
>   moment in time, but not like a moment of time,
> A moment in time, but time was made through that moment,
>   for without the meaning there is no time, and that
>   moment of time gave the meaning.

The same pre-occupation with time is present in 'Ash-
Wednesday.' In the fourth section the cry is heard,
'Redeem the time.' It is a common sundial motto and is
as appropriate there in a garden poem, as the memory of
the phrase is at the opening of 'Burnt Norton.' The problem of history and the time process is one of the great
themes of 'The Waste Land,' where it is mingled with the
desire for cosmic and personal salvation. No poem has ever
shown a greater sense of the pressure of the past upon the
present and of its existence in the present.

The problem of the time process and its meaning is
handled in these three poems under different natural
images and metaphors. All three poems have place-names
for titles; two of them are connected with Eliot family
history and it is possible the third is also. East Coker
is the Somerset village from which, in the seventeenth
century, Andrew Eliot set out for the New World: the Dry
Salvages is a group of rocky islands off the coast of
Massachusetts, part of the landscape of the poet's childhood, and part of the new experience of his ancestors
after their journey across the seas. It is possible that
the Gloucestershire manor house, Burnt Norton, may have

been in some way connected with the Eliot family, or with the ancestors of the poet's mother. The starting point in all three poems is a landscape and the emotion and thought are bound up with a deeply felt sense of place.

'Burnt Norton' is a land-locked poem: its whole feeling is enclosed. It builds up, by suggestion, a house and formal garden. Its imagery is social and civilized, weighted with human history and culture. A formal garden is an admirable symbol for man's attempt to impose a pattern upon his experience and to discipline nature. The picture gradually given here is of shrubbery and alley-walk, rose-garden, low box-borders and pool, sunflowers in the borders, clematis hanging from the wall, and clipped yews. Within the house, there are dried rose-leaves in a bowl, and there are references to a Chinese jar and to the music of the violin. All this is human and civilized and the image used for reality is human too - the hidden laughter of children among the leaves of the garden. This garden imagery of 'Burnt Norton' is used at the climax of 'The Family Reunion,' in the dialogue between Harry and Agatha in the second scene of Part II. Agatha speaks there of looking 'through the little door, when the sun was shining on the rose garden.' It is a moment of escape from the endless walking 'down a concrete corridor,' or 'through the stone passages of an immense and empty hospital.' This moment of release from the deadening feeling of meaningless sequence - 'in and out, in an endless drift,' 'to and fro, dragging my feet' - into what is always present, the moment when, in Harry's phrase, 'the chain breaks' is the subject of 'Burnt Norton.' It is a moment which happens unexpectedly, as a grace, without the mind's preparing itself, or making any effort. The laughter of the children is a lovely surprise; 'sudden in a shaft of sunlight' comes 'the moment in and out of time.'

'Burnt Norton' does not suggest any dogma; its lyric movement, with its halting tentative rhythms, is purely natural in its theme and images. The subject of the poem is an experience for which theology provides an explanation and on which religion builds a discipline, the immediate apprehension of a timeless reality, felt in time and remembered in time, the sudden revelation of 'the one end, which is always present.' It is in the third section only that the poem suggests another way to the stillness at the heart of movement, by a deliberate descent into the world of perpetual solitude, the negative way. Christianity has found room in itself for both types of mystical experience, that which finds all nature a theophany, and that which feels the truth of Pascal's favourite text: 'Vere tu es Deus absconditus.' The way through the darkness is the subject of 'East Coker.'

'East Coker' is much less confined in its setting; its
background is a village and its environs, a landscape full
of human history, but history of a ruder, less cultivated
kind. It is set in a countryside where the sea is not far
off, and the sea-wind can be felt. The first movement
ends with a lightly touched reference to the sea; the sea
provides an image of overwhelming desolation at the close
of the second; and the final impulse of release and escape
is given by the image of 'the vast waters of the petrel
and the porpoise.' The village is seen in its setting of
open fields, and the manor house is felt as part of the
village, not a place private and walled-in. There is
reference to the rhythm of the seasons and the farm. The
metaphors used for reality are mostly non-human - the winter lightning, the wild strawberry, the whisper of running
streams: the images of desolation are the dark wood,
brambles and rocks.

In 'The Family Reunion,' when Harry has become fully
aware of the sin he has to expiate, he feels a sense of
happiness and exclaims, 'This is like an end'; to which
Agatha replies, 'And a beginning.' 'East Coker' plays
throughout with Mary Stuart's motto, 'In my end is my beginning,' inverting it to a statement of rigid determinism
at the opening, breaking it, and exploiting the various
meanings of the word *end*. The final use of the phrase
holds more than one meaning: *end* can mean death or the
purpose for which we were created. The opening statement
of the poem is determinist, and establishes by powerful
rhythm and repetition the cyclic view of life and history.
The life of man and of mankind and of the works of man is
shown to be on the pattern of the life of the earth; all
are an endlessly recurring succession of birth, growth,
decay, and death. (d) Contrasted, within the first movement, with the two statements of life as rhythm, pattern
and sequence, are two passages in which the idea of stillness and rest is given. There is first the picture of the
village sleeping in the hot silence of a late summer afternoon, and, at the close, the delicate hint of the breath-
less stillness of the dawn of a hot day. The notion of
pattern and repetition leads only to despair: 'Feet rising
and falling.' (This was Agatha's image for the sensation
of imprisonment in time.) 'Eating and drinking. Dung and
death.'

The lyrical passage with which the second movement
opens contradicts both the rigid order and the stillness
of the first. The idea of pattern is rejected, but so is
the idea of peace. The seasons are all disordered.
Spring thunder peals in November: the flowers of high

summer jostle those of spring and winter. There is war
too among the constellations, ending with the apocalyptic
vision of the end of the world, burnt out to an icy
cinder. But this romantic vision of chaos the poet rejects, for a plain, almost prosaic statement of the same
chaos in the life of the individual. There, too, we find
no ordered sequence, pattern or development. The metaphor
of autumnal serenity is false applied to man; experience
does not bring wisdom, nor old age peace. The time when
one knows never arrives, and the pattern is falsified by
every new moment. We are always in the dark wood, in
which Dante found himself in the middle of his life, the
wood 'where the straight way is lost.' As we try to hold
the past, it slips from us, engulfed in the darkness of
the present.

> The houses are all gone under the sea.
> The dancers are all gone under the hill.

The third movement opens with this idea of darkness,
with blind Samson's cry of anguish; but this anguish soon
turns to a sombre triumph. The darkness, in which we are
lost, swallows up and hides from us the base, the trivial
and the ignoble, the meaningless pomps and vanities of the
world. The poet rejoices in this victory of the dark in
the same way as the writers of the early seventeenth century rejoiced in the levelling power of death. But this
welcome to the darkness takes then another turn, and it is
welcomed not only because it obliterates, but also because
it reveals. Within the darkness is light; within the
stillness, movement and dancing; within the silence, sound.
  Mr. Eliot is here writing in the tradition of those
mystics who followed the negative way. It is a tradition
that goes back beyond Christianity to the Neo-Platonists,
who turned what had been a method of knowing - the dialectical method of arriving at truth by negations of the
false - into a method of arriving at experience of the
One. This doctrine of the ascent or descent ('the way up
is the way down') into union with reality, by successively
discarding ideas which would limit the one idea of Being,
found a natural metaphor in darkness and night. It was a
double-edged metaphor, since night expressed both the
obliteration of self and all created things, and also the
uncharacterized Reality, which was the object of contemplation. The anonymous English mystic who wrote in this
tradition in the fourteenth century used for his symbol a
cloud, and called his book 'The Cloud of Unknowing.' The
actual phrase *a cloud of unknowing* occurs in 'The Family
Reunion,' used too trivially I have always felt, and it is

worth while indicating this book here as a source for
'East Coker,' instead of giving the obvious reference to
Saint John of the Cross. The third movement ends with a
deliberately unpoetic, almost light-hearted, riddling,
paradoxical expansion of this idea of knowing by not knowing. It has a naïve, fairy-tale quality, like a child's
riddle-me-ree, or like the answers in folk stories, which
seem nonsense, but lead the hero to the truth.

The lyrical fourth movement also unites despair and
triumph, but now in the contemplation of human pain. If
to know you must know nothing, then to live you must die.
'East Coker' is far more concerned with the response made
to experience than 'Burnt Norton' is; and the experience
to which response has to be made is a tragic one, of loss
and deprivation and homelessness. The lyric, therefore,
is a poem on the Passion, translated into the metaphors of
a hospital, and possibly suggested by Sir Thomas Browne's
phrase, 'For this world, I count it not an Inn, but an
Hospital; a place not to live, but to dye in.' The Passion is thought of here not as a single historic event,
but as an eternal act perpetually operative in time, and
it is linked with the Eucharist. The grave heavy beat of
the lines, the rigid stanza form, the mood, the paradoxes,
the sense of tragic triumph, which the rhythm gives, make
this lyric very like an early Passion hymn:

> Salve ara, salve victima,
> de passionis gloria,
> qua vita mortem pertulit
> et morte vitam reddidit.

In the final movement, the feeling that every moment is a
new moment and a beginning, but that the past is alive in
the present, modifying it and being modified by it also,
is at first applied to the poet and the problems of expression and finally to the life of the individual. The
poem ends with the injunction to be 'still and still
moving,' that we may pass through the 'dark cold and empty
desolation' to the open waters of the sea, which men have
always regarded as a symbol of eternity. The close is
typical of the whole poem, at once terrifying and exalting.

'The Dry Salvages' has for its landscape the sea-coast
of New England; its dominant imagery is of rocks and the
sea. This landscape of his childhood Mr. Eliot had used
in the final section of 'Ash-Wednesday,' looking on it
there with longing, as on a world hard to renounce. Of
all three poems, 'The Dry Salvages' is the most beautifully integrated and marries most absolutely metaphor and
idea. The sea imagery runs through it with a freedom and

a power hardly equalled in Mr. Eliot's other poetry. (e)
He seems to expatiate freely here and be at ease in
nature.

The first movement is built on the contrast between
two metaphors, the river of life and the sea of life. The
river is an old metaphor for the life of man, and its
flow from source to mouth is linked here with the flow of
the seasons from spring to winter, and that of man's life
from birth to death. The river is a reminder of what we
should like to forget, our bondage to nature. Though it
can for a time be ignored, it can assert its power by
catastrophe as well as by its inevitable progress. 'The
river is within us'; we feel it in our pulses. The sea
is time of another kind, the time of history, what Bacon
meant when he spoke of 'the vast seas of time.' Individual man launches himself on this ocean of life and makes
his short voyage, one of countless similar voyages. 'The
sea is all about us.' This metaphor of the tossing seas
of history denies both the cyclic view of history, the
biological interpretation, which imposes on events the
rhythm of a succession of rivers, each culture being first
young and vigorous, then mature, and finally decayed and
outworn, and also the doctrine of human progress, which
finds in history an upward development. We have instead
a meaningless, perpetual flux, a repetition without a
pattern, to which each separate voyage adds nothing but
itself. But through the apparently incoherent restless-
ness of the sea, there is carried to our ears the rhythm
of the ground swell, different from the rhythm of the
river, which we hear in our heart-beats, coming from the
very depths of the ocean itself.

> And the ground swell, that is and was from the begin-
>   ning,
> Clangs
> The bell.

The reminiscence of the doxology gives us the implication
of the symbol of the ground swell, which makes itself felt
in our hearts by the bell. The bell sounds a warning and
a summons: it demands a response. Like the bell of the
Angelus it is a call to prayer, and a commemoration of the
mystery of the Incarnation; like the bell at the conse-
cration it is a call to worship and announces the presence
of Christ; like the tolling bell it reminds us of our
death, and calls us to die daily. (f)

The sestina, with which the second movement opens, is a
poem on these several annunciations. Under the metaphor
of fishermen setting out on their perilous voyages, over

'an ocean littered with wastage,' it pictures the lives of
individual men, the sum of which makes history. It finds
meaning in the process only in the union of the temporal
with the eternal, in annunciations: the calamitous annunciation of terror and danger, the last annunciation of
death, and the one Annunciation of history. The only *end*
to the flux of history is man's response to the eternal.
As in 'The Waste Land',' it is 'by the awful daring of a
moment's surrender' that we exist, by praying

> the hardly, barely prayable
> Prayer of the one Annunciation.

The meaningless monotony and pointless waste of living
finds its purpose in the Virgin's words, 'Be it unto me
according to thy word.'
     As in the other poems, the idea of the lyrical passage,
given in metaphor and symbol, is then translated into the
experience and idioms of every day. The past does not
die; the visitations, particularly the visitations of
anguish, are a perpetual experience, always recurring,
preserved in memory and time. The whole of this passage
reads like a commentary on the scene in 'The Family Reunion' in which Agatha explains the past to Harry. It
might have been written of Harry that he

> had the experience but missed the meaning
> And approach to the meaning restored the experience.

The pattern of the past does not make a sequence, for if
it did, we could disown the past and look to the future.
But we cannot disown the past, we carry it within us;
its significance is in the present and in us.
     The third movement takes up the idea of the future.
Mr. Eliot introduces here, as he had in 'The Waste Land,'
the scriptures of the East. He finds the same doctrine of
response to the present in the 'Bhagavadgita.' There
Arjuna is concerned with the problem of how man can act
without sin and Krishna replies to his doubts by insisting
on the necessity for disinterestedness. Man must not look
to the future or for the fruits of an action; he must live
as if there were no future, as if every moment were the
moment of death. The New Testament teaches a similar
carelessness for the morrow, which was echoed in 'The
Rock':

> I have said, take no thought of the harvest, but only
>   of the proper sowing.

Here the future is thought of as something that exists
only in the mind, as if it were already past, and the
metaphor of the travellers, more lightly touched in the
first two poems, is fully explored. First in the train,
and then on the ocean, the travellers fare forward, bearing their past within them, and their future also, and
yet in a real sense in a space between two lives. But to
divide time harshly into past, present and future, is to
divide ourselves:

> You are not the same people who left that station
> Or who will arrive at any terminus.

Personality has meaning only in the present, in what we
are. Our real destination is here; where we are going is
where we are. (g)
    The lyrical fourth movement is a prayer to Our Lady,
and its tender gravity and perfect fitness springs from
the union in the poem of idea and symbol. She is rightly
prayed to in a poem of the sea, because she is *Stella
Maris*, to whom the fishermen and their wives pray. She
appears also, at the lyric climax, as the handmaid of the
Lord, who made the great response to the message of the
angel, and as the mother of Christ, whose birth gives
meaning to time. She is also prayed to as *Mater Dolorosa*,
for this is a poem of sorrows, and the whole lyric takes
up the theme of the lovely melancholy sestina of the
second movement; it recalls the dangerous voyages, the
'ocean littered with wastage,' and over all

> the sound of the sea-bell's
> Perpetual angelus.

The fifth movement opens with a topical passage on the
themes of past and future, which men peer into for comfort
and guidance, turning to astrologers and fortune tellers,
for re-assurance about the future which they dread, like
the 'anxious worried women' of the first movement, or
turning to the past to explain the present.

> Men's curiosity searches past and future
> And clings to that dimension.

Opposed to this search into past and future is 'the occupation of the saint,' the attempt to apprehend 'the point
of intersection of the timeless with time.' For the ordinary man, who is not a saint, there are moments of
illumination, 'hints and guesses' upon which he founds his
life of 'prayer, observance, discipline, thought and

action.' In these apprehensions of the eternal, preserved in memory, and fruitful beyond the moment in which they were first felt, we find freedom from the tyranny of past and future, and cease to feel ourselves the helpless victims of natural forces. Because of this inner freedom, we can accept our temporal destiny and our bond with nature, the 'dung and death' to which 'our temporal reversion' must return. In the 'hint half-guessed, the gift half-understood,' we find the meaning of our own lives and the purpose of history. By this, time is redeemed and is seen to be no enemy; for in time the world was made, in time God was and is manifested, and, as Blake asserted in his 'Marriage of Heaven and Hell,' 'Eternity is in love with the productions of time.'

It is not the purpose of this essay to attempt a criticism of these poems, but only to lay the foundations for a critical appraisal. As long as critics feel the obscure uneasiness which an incompletely understood subject-matter gives, rational discussion of a poet's achievement is impossible. This irritation has for some time been apparent in much of the criticism of Mr. Eliot by the younger school of poets and critics, who owe so much to his earlier work and have learned a great deal of their technique from him. It is hoped that some demonstration of the essential continuity of his work may help to dissipate prejudice, and that to hazard an interpretation, even though it be a faulty one, may be the first step towards a proper critique. When Mr. Eliot's thought is understood, it can be accepted and can take the same place in the discussion of his poetic merits as scholasticism takes in the criticism of Dante, or Toryism in the criticism of Dryden.

Notes

a It is quite clear from the text of the play that Harry's belief that he murdered his wife is an obsession, which is 'true in a different sense' (p. 104), and Agatha's information, which assists him to consciousness of the family curse, is that his father, just before he was born, was plotting to murder his mother. It is this complex of hatred and despair which makes up the history of the doomed family. Harry becomes at last aware of it and by recognizing the sin begins to expiate it.

b In all three poems, at this point, the image of passengers in a train is introduced. The 'place of disaffection,' with 'men and bits of paper whirled by the cold wind,' in 'Burnt Norton,' is surely the London Tube.

c It is probable that the close of the play owes something to Bazin's 'Life of Charles de Foucauld.' It is
   impossible for anyone who has read this book not to be
   reminded of it when Harry speaks of

>   the worship in the desert, the thirst
>   and deprivation,
>   A stony sanctuary and a primitive altar,
>   The heat of the sun and the icy vigil,
>   A care over lives of humble poeple.

   Mr. Eliot spoke of this book on the wireless early last
   year.
d It is possibly in order to assert this continuity of
   human experience, and also because this is a poem concerned with his ancestry that Mr. Eliot weaves into
   this first movement phrases from Sir Thomas Elyot's
   praise of dancing in 'The Governour' (1531); but the
   transition from modern to archaic English is not very
   skilfully managed, and, even when the source of the
   passage is recognised, I think there remains a feeling
   of strangeness and irrelevance.
e Mr. Henry Reed, to whom I am indebted for much sympathetic and illuminating criticism, and without whose
   encouragement this article would not have been written,
   has pointed out to me a passage in Herman Melville's
   'Redburn,' from which some of the sea imagery of 'The
   Dry Salvages' may derive. The voice of Mr. Eliot's
   sea-bell is certainly very like the sound of the Liver-
   pool bell-buoy, which Redburn heard as he sailed into
   the Mersey.
f The image of the sea-bell and the figures of the Eumenides in 'The Family Reunion' seem to me to hold the
   same meaning. Both are visitations of the divine,
   messengers from eternity, terrifying till accepted.
g It is worth noting that the phrase

>   this thing is sure
>   That time is no healer: the patient is no longer
>   here,

   echoes Pascal, while contradicting him: 'Le temps
   guérit les douleurs et les querelles, parce qu'on
   change, on n'est plus la même personne. Ni l'offensant,
   ni l'offensé, ne sont plus eux-mêmes' ('Pensées,' II,
   122) (1) Earlier in the same section Pascal had
   asserted the persistence of personality: 'Tout ce qui
   se perfectionne par progrès périt aussi par progrès,
   tout ce qui a été faible ne peut jamais être

absolument fort. On a beau dire: *il est crû, il est changé*; il est aussi le même; (88). (2) A reading of the 'Pensées' would be a good general introduction to any study of Mr. Eliot.

1   'Time heals griefs and quarrels, for we change and are no longer the same person. Neither the offender nor the offended are any more themselves.'

2   'All that is made perfect by progress perishes also by progress. All that has been weak can never become absolutely strong. We say in vain. "He has grown, he has changed"; he is also the same.' From the Everyman Library translation (1931), introduced by Eliot.

128. GEORGE ORWELL, POINTS OF VIEW: T.S. ELIOT, 'POETRY LONDON'

October-November 1942, vol. ii, 56-9

George Orwell (pseudonym for Eric Arthur Blair) (1903-50), novelist and social critic, contributed regularly to the leading periodicals of the day. One of his most famous works, 'Nineteen Eighty-Four' (1949), was re-issued in 1965 with an introduction by Stephen Spender.
    This item has been reprinted in 'Little Reviews Anthology', edited by Denys Val Baker (London, 1943), and 'Collected Essays, Journalism and Letters of George Orwell', volume 2 (London, 1968).

There is very little in Eliot's later work that makes any deep impression on me. That is a confession of something lacking in myself, but it is not, as it may appear at first sight, a reason for simply shutting up and saying no more, since the change in my own reaction probably points to some external change which is worth investigating.
    I know a respectable quantity of Eliot's earlier work by heart. I did not sit down and learn it, it simply stuck in my mind as any passage of verse is liable to do when it has really rung the bell. Sometimes after only one reading it is possible to remember the whole of a poem of, say, twenty or thirty lines, the act of memory being partly an act of reconstruction. But as for these three latest poems, I suppose I have read each of them two or

three times since they were published, and how much do I
verbally remember? 'Time and the bell have buried the
day,' 'At the still point of the turning world,' 'The
vast waters of the petrel and the porpoise,' and bits of
the passage beginning 'O dark dark dark. They all go into
the dark.' (I don't count 'In my end is my beginning,'
which is a quotation). That is about all that sticks in my
head of its own accord. Now one cannot take this as proving that 'Burnt Norton' and the rest are worse than the
more memorable early poems, and one might even take it
as proving the contrary, since it is arguable that that
which lodges itself most easily in the mind is the obvious
and even the vulgar. But it is clear that something has
departed, some kind of current has been switched off, the
later verse does not *contain* the earlier, even if it is
claimed as an improvement upon it. I think one is justified in epxlaining this by a deterioration in Mr. Eliot's
subject-matter. Before going any further, here are a
couple of extracts, just near enough to one another in
meaning to be comparable. The first is the concluding
passage of 'The Dry Salvages':

[Quotes CPP, p. 190, 'And right action' to 'significant
soil'.]

Here is an extract from a much earlier poem:

[Quotes 'Whispers of Immortality', stanzas 2 and 4, CPP,
p. 52.]

   The two passages will bear comparison since they both
deal with the same subject, namely death. The first of
them follows upon a longer passage in which it is explained, first of all, that scientific research is all nonsense, a childish superstition on the same level as
fortune-telling, and then that the only people ever likely
to reach an understanding of the universe are saints, the
rest of us being reduced to 'hints and guesses.' The keynote of the closing passage is 'resignation.' There is a
'meaning' in life and also in death; unfortunately we don't
know what it is, but the fact that it exists should be a
comfort to us as we push up the crocuses, or whatever it
is that grows under the yew trees in country churchyards.
But now look at the other two stanzas I have quoted.
Though fathered on to somebody else, they probably express
what Mr. Eliot himself felt about death at that time, at
least in certain moods. They are not voicing resignation.
On the contrary, they are voicing the pagan attitude towards death, the belief in the next world as a shadowy
place full of thin, squeaking ghosts, envious of the living, the belief that however bad life may be, death is
worse. This conception of death seems to have been general

in antiquity, and in a sense it is general now. 'The
anguish of the marrow, the ague of the skeleton,' Horace's
famous ode 'Eheu fugaces,' and Bloom's unuttered thoughts
during Paddy Dignam's funeral, are all very much of a
muchness. So long as man regards himself as an individual, his attitude towards death must be one of simple
resentment. And however unsatisfactory this may be, if
it is intensely felt it is more likely to produce good
literature than a religious faith which is not really *felt*
at all, but merely accepted against the emotional grain.
So far as they can be compared, the two passages I have
quoted seem to me to bear this out. I do not think it is
questionable that the second of them is superior as verse,
and also more intense in feeling, in spite of a tinge of
burlesque.

What are these three poems, 'Burnt Norton' and the
rest, 'about'? It is not so easy to say what they are
about, but what they appear on the surface to be about is
certain localities in England and America with which Mr.
Eliot has ancestral connections. Mixed up with this is a
rather gloomy musing upon the nature and purpose of life,
with the rather indefinite conclusion I have mentioned
above. Life has a 'meaning,' but it is not a meaning one
feels inclined to grow lyrical about; there is faith, but
not much hope, and certainly no enthusiasm. Now the
subject-matter of Mr. Eliot's early poems was very different from this. They were not hopeful, but neither were
they depressed or depressing. If one wants to deal in
antitheses, one might say that the later poems express
a melancholy faith and the earlier ones a glowing despair.
They were based on the dilemma of modern man, who despairs of life and does not want to be dead, and on top of
this they expressed the horror of an over-civilised intellectual confronted with the ugliness and spiritual emptiness of the machine age. Instead of 'not too far from the
yew-tree' the keynote was 'weeping, weeping multitudes',
or perhaps 'the broken fingernails of dirty hands.'
Naturally these poems were denounced as 'decadent' when
they first appeared, the attacks only being called off
when it was perceived that Eliot's political and social
tendencies were reactionary. There was, however, a sense
in which the charge of 'decadence' could be justified.
Clearly these poems were an end-product, the last gasp of
a cultural tradition, poems which spoke only for the cultivated third-generation rentier, for people able to feel
and criticise but no longer able to act. E.M. Forster
praised 'Prufrock' on its first appearance because 'it
sang of people who were ineffectual and weak' and because
it was 'innocent of public spirit' (this was during the
other war, when public spirit was a good deal more ram-
pant than it is now). The qualities by which any society

which is to last longer than a generation actually has to
be sustained - industry, courage, patriotism, frugality,
philoprogenitiveness - obviously could not find any place
in Eliot's early poems. There was only room for rentier
values, the values of people too civilised to work, fight
or even reproduce themselves. But that was the price
that had to be paid, at any rate at that time, for writing
a poem worth reading. The mood of lassitude, irony, disbelief, disgust, and not the sort of beefy enthusiasm
demanded by the Squires and Herberts, was what sensitive
people actually felt. It is fashionable to say that in
verse only the words count and the 'meaning' is irrelevant,
but in fact every poem contains a prose-meaning, and when
the poem is any good it is a meaning which the poet
urgently wishes to express. All art is to some extent
propaganda. 'Prufrock' is an expression of futility, but
it is also a poem of wonderful vitality and power, culminating in a sort of rocket-burst in the closing stanzas:

[Quotes CPP, p. 17, 'I have seen them' to 'and we drown'.]

There is nothing like that in the later poems, although
the rentier despair on which these lines are founded has
been consciously dropped.
     But the trouble is that conscious futility is some-
thing only for the young. One cannot go on 'despairing of
life' into a ripe old age. One cannot go on and on being
'decadent,' since decadence means falling and one can only
be said to be falling if one is going to reach the bottom
reasonably soon. Sooner or later one is obliged to adopt
a positive attitude towards life and society. It would be
putting it too crudely to say that every poet in our time
must either die young, enter the Catholic Church, or join
the Communist Party, but in fact the escape from the
consciousness of futility is along those general lines.
There are other deaths besides physical death, and there
are other sects and creeds besides the Catholic Church and
the Communist Party, but it remains true that after a
certain age one must either stop writing or dedicate oneself to some purpose not wholly aesthetic. Such a dedication necessarily means a break with the past:

[Quotes 'East Coker', V, CPP, p. 182, 'every attempt' to
'squads of emotion'.]

Eliot's escape from individualism was into the Church, the
Anglican Church as it happened. One ought not to assume
that the gloomy Pétainism to which he now appears to have
given himself over was the unavoidable result of his

conversion. The Anglo-Catholic movement does not impose
any political 'line' on its followers, and a reactionary
or austro-fascist tendency had always been apparent in his
work, especially his prose writings. In theory it is still
possible to be an orthodox religious believer without
being intellectually crippled in the process, but it is
far from easy, and in practice books by orthodox believers
usually show the same cramped, blinkered outlook as books
by orthodox Stalinists or others who are mentally unfree.
The reason is that the Christian churches still demand
assent to doctrines which no one seriously believes in.
The most obvious case is the immortality of the soul. The
various 'proofs' of personal immortality which can be
advanced by Christian apologists are psychologically of no
importance; what matters, psychologically, is that hardly
anyone nowadays *feels* himself to be immortal. The next
world may be in some sense 'believed in' but it has not
anywhere near the same actuality in people's minds as it
had a few centuries ago. Compare for instance the gloomy
mumblings of these three poems with 'Jerusalem my Happy
Home': the comparison is not altogether pointless. In the
second case you have a man to whom the next world is as
real as this one. It is true that his vision of it is
incredibly vulgar - a choir practice in a jeweller's shop
- but he believes in what he is saying and his belief
gives vitality to his words. In the other case you have a
man who does not really *feel* his faith, but merely assents
to it for complex reasons. It does not in itself give him
any fresh literary impulse. At a certain stage he feels
the need for a 'purpose,' and he wants a 'purpose' which
is reactionary and not progressive; the immediately available refuge is the Church, which demands intellectual
absurdities of its members; so his work becomes a continu-
ous nibbling round those absurdities, an attempt to make
them acceptable to himself. The Church has not now any
living imagery, any new vocabulary to offer:

> The rest
> Is prayer, observance, discipline, thought and
>   action.

Perhaps what we need is prayer, observance, etc., but you
do not make a line of poetry by stringing those words together. Mr. Eliot speaks also of

>   the intolerable wrestle
> With words and meanings. The poetry does
>   not matter.

I do not know, but I should imagine that the struggle
with meanings would have loomed smaller, and the poetry
would have seemed to matter more, if he could have found
his way to some creed which did not start off by forcing
one to believe the incredible.

There is no saying whether Mr. Eliot's development
could have been much other than it has been. All writers
who are any good develop throughout life, and the general
direction of their development is determined. It is
absurd to attack Eliot, as some left-wing critics have
done, for being a 'reactionary' and to imagine that he
might have used his gifts in the cause of democracy and
Socialism. Obviously a scepticism about democracy and a
disbelief in 'progress' are an integral part of him;
without them he could not have written a line of his works.
But it is arguable that he would have done better to go
much further in the direction implied in his famous
'Anglo-Catholic and Royalist' declaration. He could not
have developed into a Socialist, but he might have
developed into the last apologist of aristocracy.

Neither feudalism nor indeed Fascism is necessarily
deadly to poets, though both are to prose writers. The
thing that is really deadly to both is Conservatism of
the half-hearted modern kind.

It is at least imaginable that if Eliot had followed
wholeheartedly the anti-democratic, anti-perfectionist
strain in himself he might have struck a new vein comparable to his earlier one. But the negative, Pétainism
which turns its eyes to the past, accepts defeat, writes
off earthly happiness as impossible, mumbles about prayer
and repentance and thinks it a spiritual advance to see
life as 'a pattern of living worms in the guts of the
women of Canterbury' - that, surely, is the least hopeful
road a poet could take.

129. KATHLEEN RAINE, POINTS OF VIEW: ANOTHER READING,
'POETRY LONDON'

October-November 1942, vol. ii, 59-62

Raine (b. 1908), an English poet and critic, has written
on Blake and Coleridge as visionary poets, and in her
1976 Warton Lecture she drew Eliot into that company.
Speaking of the impact made by Eliot's poetry on her and

others of her generation in the late 1920s, she says:
'We did not read his poems in any perspective at all:
rather we were in them, ourselves figures in the sad pro-
cession of Eliot's London, that "unreal city" in whose unreality lay its terrible reality.' See Waste Land, Holy
Land, 'Proceedings of the British Academy' (1976), lxii,
379-97.

The item reprinted here is a reply to Orwell (No. 128).

I

I have been asked to write on Mr. Eliot's three latest
poems, because my point of view at once differs from that
of Mr. Orwell, and expresses the point of view of many of
my generation. I admire Mr. Orwell's article in certain
limited respects. He avoids the more obvious pitfalls, in
applying political, rational, non-poetic standards, to
poetry. Mr. Orwell does not fall into the error that Com-
munists usually make in such cases, of failing to see that
a problem exists that is not stated in terms of dialectical materialism. My point is, that Mr. Orwell has fallen
into the error of which he accuses Mr. Eliot - that of
pursuing a line of thought that has become a dead end; of
accepting certain statements about the universe as final
that are, like all knowledge, provisional.

Mr. Orwell does not misrepresent Mr. Eliot when he
quotes him as saying that 'the only people ever likely to
reach an understanding of the universe are saints, the
rest of us being reduced to "hints and guesses".' Nor is
he wrong when he says that 'so long as man regards himself as an individual, his attitude to death must be one
of simple resentment.' But one cannot accept Mr. Orwell's
conclusions. Who, then, does understand the universe?
About the individual resenting death, St. Paul himself
could not have stated more concisely the point of the
Christian attack on the self-loving ego. But man does
not necessarily, as Mr. Orwell implies, think of himself
first and foremost as an individual. Freud, in his concept of the *id*, the death-instincts, and indeed, the unconscious mind altogether suggests that many doors open
out of that individual entity. James Joyce has drawn a
picture of the mind of man, that has little of the individual contour about it. A world inside us presents a
landscape as impersonal, vast, and beyond our reach and
knowledge, as does that which opens on the other, the
outer side, of our senses. Picasso, too, has stripped
the contours from the object and the individual, and

presented us with an image of man liberated from himself,
that gives life a scope that explodes like a balloon the
individual pigmy, and his squeaking ghost.

Those two artists - and Mr. Eliot is a third - have
been quicker in the uptake of the new sciences than those
who, like Mr. Orwell, stand firmly by the values that were
solid before Einstein; before biochemistry, before modern
physics, genetics, psychology; Joyce, Picasso and the
cubists, tore down the old limits drawn, not by nature but
by habits of thought and language, and put up others that
have made the world look very different. We live not only
at the end of a decadent materialist age; but at the beginning of a new period - one in which the concern of humanity
will be with values more than with facts. For the circum-
navigation of the material sciences has been completed.
There are no more Eldorados of science. In essence, we
know what is in the material universe, as we know the con-
tinents and the islands of the earth. Science has long
held, for our imagination, that world of fantastic promise
that wishful thinking will always substitute for true
values. Some health and wealth science may indeed give,
as South America yielded gold and potatoes. But it will
not teach us values; and those must come, now as at any
other period of civilisation, from the human spirit.

Like Mr. Orwell, my point of view is limited. Perhaps
I am overlooking more than I know in omitting to consider
deeply Mr. Eliot's political importance - the sources and
the implications of the Anglo-Catholic Royalist position,
without which, Mr. Orwell perhaps rightly says, Mr. Eliot
could not have written a line of his work. But whatever
point I may be missing, Mr. Orwell misses another - that
Mr. Eliot is a poet not a political pamphleteer. If poets
are 'the unacknowledged legislators of the world' it is
by virtue of their poetry, and not of their legislation.
Who now cares whether Dante was a Guelf or a Ghibelline?
Or even whether Milton was a Royalist or a Cromwellian?
Mr. Eliot has been a movement, as well as a poet, and Mr.
Orwell has seen the movement and missed the poetry - but
it is not the movement that remains, but the poetry. Whoever wins the class or any other war will inherit Mr.
Eliot's poetry, when his politics concern only the histor-
ian. Poetry is an approach to the world, as science and
religion is, and a poet is something more than the total
of his poems. A poem is not written in a day but in a
lifetime. Mr. Orwell has stood still in the Waste Land,
and he expects to find that Mr. Eliot is also still there.
But the poet is saying something more, 'mumbling about
prayer and repentance' Mr. Orwell calls it. But what if
Mr. Eliot is in advance of his juniors? Never, so far as

I know, has the work of a poet been more clearly stated
than in 'East Coker.' Indeed it is one of the main themes
of the poem.

[Quotes CPP, p. 179, 'That was a way' to 'does not
matter'.]

and again

[Quotes CPP, p. 182, 'So here I am' to 'on the inarticulate'.]

Let every poet lay these words to heart. 'A raid on the
inarticulate' is the work of all poetry, and that work
carries poets into strange places.

[Quotes CPP, p. 181, 'You must go by a way wherein' to
' dispossession'.]

The raid on the inarticulate means, of course, much
more than the problem of language. Mr. Eliot's three new
poems are concerned with the greatest issue of all - man's
place in eternity. His discovery, or re-discovery will be
an influence, during the next poetic generation, as potent
as was that of the Waste Land on the last.

                              II

'East Coker' is a stern and dark, but not a tragic
poem. Its darkness is the darkness of Dante's hell, or
purgatory, that implies the light and the love of paradise.
An implicit acceptance of the inherent rightness of the
laws that decree also death, darkness, and change, sus-
tains the poem. It is written by a poet who believes that
man is a spiritual being. No-one who does not see what
this means can see that assertions like these are positive:

    The only wisdom we can hope to acquire
    Is the wisdom of humility: humility is endless.

or

    I said to my soul, be still, and wait without hope
    For hope would be hope for the wrong thing; wait without
        love
    For love would be love of the wrong thing; there is yet
        faith

But the faith and the love and the hope are all in the
    waiting.

There is Mr. Orwell's pagan hell of squeaking ghosts,
too:

O dark dark dark. They all go into the dark,
The vacant interstellar spaces, the vacant into the
    vacant,
The captains, merchant bankers, eminent men of letters -

but for Mr. Eliot, that is a part of the divine plan, not
the whole. Mr. Eliot is trying to rediscover that divine
plan, ' under conditions that seem unpropitious.' For
those poets who follow him, the conditions are less unpropitious - for they include Mr. Eliot's work.
  'Burnt Norton,' the second of the three, is a less
sombre poem. Its theme is time. The poem is full of
moving and beautiful images of the temporal world - the
rose-garden, the pool, the leaves, children, birds,
laughter.

[Quotes CPP, p. 171, 'Shall we follow?' to 'first world'.]

This world is the lovely illusion woven by time -

[Quotes CPP, p. 172, 'Go, go, go' to 'always present.']

That ever-present end is love.

[Quotes CPP, p. 175, 'Love is itself' to 'limitation.']

  Of that love, 'Burnt Norton' contains one of the most
profound and wonderful descriptions ever written, beginning with the already often quoted lines:

At the still point of the turning world.
    Neither flesh nor fleshless;
Neither from nor towards; at the still point,
    there the dance is.

  The theme of 'The Dry Salvages' is the greater part of
life, that is not ourselves. For 'The river is within us,
the sea is all about us.' The sea and its rhythm measures
'time not our time' and on that sea we are travellers.

[Quotes CPP, pp. 189-90, 'Man's curiosity' to 'death in
love'.]

Mr. Eliot is not a saint nor a theologian, but a poet.
Yet a poet at his best, is a saint of his own medium, and
performs a miracle in his work. These poems are revolutionary is a sense that transcends the mere use of words.
They are a re-assessment of life. Mr. Orwell's evaluation
reminds me of the comment that Coleridge made of some
critics of Wordsworth who belittled him - I quote, as
seems to be the general war-time habit, from memory - that
the poet strode so far ahead of his critics, that he was
diminished in their eyes, by the distance between them.

Perhaps I have given the impression that Mr. Eliot is
concerned with spiritual values that refer to another life,
and not to this one. But he writes of what is most human.
I can speak only for myself, but I find that what Mr. Eliot
writes about love is nearer the heart's mark than anything
that Stephen Spender - to name one of the better poets
who speak the language of my generation - has written on
that theme. Yet no one, I think, regards Mr. Eliot as a
poet of love primarily. My point is that Mr. Eliot is a
passionate and human man, and speaks the language of humanity, and that language is not a simple one. But is it less
human to be great, wise, and many-sided; than to be immat-
ure, ignorant, and falsely simplified? Is the worst more
human than the best? The Christian believes that the best
is accessible to the worst, and the highest to the hum-
blest human soul. Mr. Eliot's consistent adherence to the
highest values of Christianity, and the inheritance of
civilisation, shows a deeper respect for the ordinary man
than any facile simplification that Mr. Orwell, the B.B.C.,
or the Mass Observers offer to a public that they at heart
despise.

130. A CORRESPONDENT INTERVENES, 'POETRY LONDON'

February-March 1943, vol. ii, 61

Irene Browne, a reader of the magazine, wrote in to medi-
ate between Orwell and Raine.

Dear Sir, - Mr. Orwell is a dangerous man to admire, and I
do so (who can resist his pungent metaphor?) with reserva-
tions. His literary function is the valuable one of

provocation, but provocation only serves its purpose when
it provokes revision of thought - it is useless if it
arouses only a violent emotional reaction.

In his criticism of Mr. Eliot's poems in the last issue
of 'Poetry London,' Mr. Orwell displays more honesty than
sense, for if he had studied this journal he would have
realised that he was falling into the ranks of Eliot
enthusiasts. I am not inferring that I disapprove of
enthusiasm, which is a positive quality of particular
value to a democracy, but I deprecate the tendency of
enthusiasts to blind themselves to the shortcomings of
their idol and to regard criticism and, even more unfortunately, the merits of another school of thought, as heretical and fit only for oblivion.

If Mr. Orwell was aware of this and wrote his article
with explosive intent he gets his answer from Miss Raine.

Poor Miss Raine! In her rush to defend Mr. Eliot she
could scarcely contain her fury with Mr. Orwell. She is at
a disadvantage, too, in the prose medium and I turned with
a sigh from the lucidity of Mr. Orwell to Miss Raine's obscurity of thought. One of the critic's chief tools, said
Mr. Eliot, in 1923, is analysis, but Miss Raine reads this
as amplification, with little elucidation and with little
attempt to justify her statements.

Mr. Orwell's contention is that Mr. Eliot has degener-
ated from being a great poet of futility to a futile poet.
This, surely, is a trifle arbitrary - after all, Mr. Eliot
was a great poet before he was an Anglo-Catholic, and he
is still an important poet despite himself.

Miss Raine goes to the opposite extreme and attempts to
convince us that Mr. Eliot's later work contains a new and
important message for our embryo poets. In the 1920's Mr.
Eliot was reshaping our poetic heritage and shaping the
future. Is it not rather a lot to expect of one man that
he should exercise two profound influences during his lifetime? It is a disservice to Mr. Eliot to push his work
beyond its natural, and very great, value.

This new influence of which Miss Raine speaks is Mr.
Eliot's concern with man's place in eternity; but I think
it is more with Mr. Eliot's place in eternity that he is
concerned, and his approach is too gloomy and sectarian to
have the profundity which commands adherents.

When Miss Raine says: 'If poets are "the unacknowledged
legislators of the world" it is by virtue of their poetry
and not of their legislation' she is attempting to divide
the indivisible. Poetic form is the means toward the
philosophic end: if the end is narrow the poetry suffers,
and if the poetry is poor the philosophy is cramped. Form
and content are one and their division an unnatural

distinction of use only to the analyst.

It is also important to remind Miss Raine that it is
the philosophy of a poet that regulates the interest he
arouses. Rudyard Kipling, Wordsworth's moral poems, and
John Donne are sufficient examples.

Miss Raine should not pretend to herself that Mr. Eliot
is not tired of his raids upon the inarticulate. We are
only undefeated, he says, because we have gone on trying.
Mr. Eliot will continue to try because he is afraid of
defeat, a fear so potent that it has led him to take out
an Anglo-Catholic insurance policy.

I am not decrying Mr. Eliot's work. But poems reflect
ourselves and we should be careful that we see a clear
reflection and do not regard the mirror as our servant, to
tell us only what we wish to hear or to be beaten if we do
not approve.

I should like to contrast with the conclusion of 'The
Dry Salvages' the following lines from another great poet:

> For, however they dream they are scattered,
> Our bones cannot help reassembling themselves
> Into their philosophic cities to hold
> The knowledge they cannot get out of,
> And neither a Spring nor a War can ever
>
> So condition his ears as to keep the Song
> That is not a sorrow from the invisible twin:
>   O what weeps is the love that hears, an
>   Accident occurring in his substance.

Yours truly,
Irene Brown.

'Little Gidding'

London, 1 December 1942

131. UNSIGNED REVIEW, MIDWINTER SPRING, 'TIMES LITERARY SUPPLEMENT'

19 December 1942, no. 2133, 622

Mr. Nicholas Ferrar and the 'Protestant Nunnery' he founded at Little Gidding had presumably something to do with the title of Mr. Eliot's new poem, and perhaps he is the stranger met in the waning dusk, the 'dead master'

> Whom I had known, forgotten, half recalled
> > Both one and many; in the brown baked features
> > The eyes of a familiar compound ghost
> Both intimate and unidentifiable.

But the title of this poem, as of its three predecessors, is allusive and, to the reader at least, of little importance. Its essential theme, however, and its tone will be familiar enough to readers of those earlier poems. The first line strikes the basic note,

> Midwinter spring is its own season.

It is the second spring of possible regeneration, when the fires of Nature's first spring have died in the hearth, upon which Mr. Eliot meditates and of which, when the rhythm of his brooding mounts to a pitch of greater intensity, he sings. Here is the clear-eyed borderline between middle-aged disillusion and the achievement of a new and true illusion. 'Let me disclose the gifts reserved for age,' he writes,

496

[Quotes 'Little Gidding', II, CPP, pp. 194-5, 'To set a
crown' to 'like a dancer'.]

'Unless restored' - that is the burden of the poem. The
ageing and the old must 'become renewed, transfigured, in
another pattern.' All shall be well then, and Love, 'the
intolerable shirt of flame,' which human power cannot remove, is the means.

> The only hope, or else despair
>   Lies in the choice of pyre or pyre -
>   To be redeemed from fire by fire.

Mr. Eliot's expression of this theme is, at its best, impressive, because he realizes to the full how hard and
costly the choice between the two fires is. But while this
gives a tension to his utterance and a winter starkness to
his imagery, which heightens the sense of a second spring
breaking in the concluding lines, it also tends to reduce
the music of poetry to the dry discourse of the moralist
and the intellectual. His characteristic and recurrent
use of the paradox, too, is almost becoming a trick. Even
when it defines truly enough the intrinsic identity of
opposites, as in the lines,

> What we call the beginning is often the end
> And to make an end is to make a beginning,

it is dangerously near to the trite. Mr. Eliot has stood
so long between the two pyres, intellectually and morally
aware of the meaning of the redemption of one by the other,
that we cannot help wishing he could take, as a poet, an
imaginative step forward. For, to quote two lines of his
poem,

> Last year's words belong to last year's language
> And next year's words await another voice.

132. ROBERT SPEAIGHT, A REVIEW, 'TABLET'

19 December 1942, vol. clxxx, 302-3

Speaight (1904-76), actor and writer, appeared as Becket
in the first production of 'Murder in the Cathedral'. In

his autobiography, 'The Property Basket' (1970), he shows
how important Eliot was for him in the 1920s: '[Eliot's]
broad acceptance of orthodoxy had shown that it was more
than a refuge and a "rock of ages" - for it was from this
rock that the life-giving waters would flow.' It is clear
that Speaight's conversion to Roman Catholicism (he was
received in 1930 by Father D'Arcy) was heavily influenced
by Eliot's thought and example.

This is the fourth and last of Mr. Eliot's new series of
poems, and its publication gives the reviewer an opportunity to assess with rather more certainty than has hitherto been possible, the qualities of the poet's later work.
There is a type of critic, lofty in brow and very small
in sympathy, whose appreciation of Mr. Eliot stops short
with 'The Waste Land.' I cannot pretend to have much
patience with this exclusiveness. Mr. Eliot's verse is
not, I agree, of a uniform intensity and merit. No good
poet's ever was. But it all proceeds from the same
accuracy and integrity of vision which set upon 'The Hollow Men,' let us say, the unmistakable mark of permanence.
Mr. Eliot refuses to falsify his own personality, or to
borrow the accents of other men. He will hesitate in a
periphrasis rather than steal a short cut to the truth.
He will perambulate around his subject rather than fail it
by an impulsive approach. Above all, he is ever seeking,
within the limits imposed by a severe sincerity of purpose, to do something new with words; to fit them in an
original pattern to the shape of an original thought.
  Judged by this test, the series of which 'Little Gidding' is the last appears extraordinarily impressive.
There are no other English poems quite like these. They
come within the category of Christian verse, and here
their mood and emphasis are unique. The intersection of
Eternity and time; the necessary asceticism; the drawing
onward through the Dark Night to the knowledge of the
Divine Love; the certain, sober hope - these themes are
all, within a varying framework of imagery and reference,
interwoven with each other. Each poem is personal. Each
is the utterance of a poet wrestling with the validity of
words; doubting sometimes the instruments of his art, as
he approaches the Truth that the tongue cannot utter, nor
the heart conceive. The poet is not merely singing - he
is saving his soul; and he is putting the salvation before
the song. It is by these renunciations, when they are
necessary, that the highest art is, paradoxically,
achieved. For the poet, no less than other men, must lose

his soul before he can find it.

'Little Gidding' is like its predecessors in shape. It
has the movement and the divisions of a quartet. The free
verse, written with a careful ear for assonance, alliteration, repetition, and interior rhyme, is varied by passages in rhyme and in unrhymed *terza rima*. The grand abstractions of Mr. Eliot's thought are clothed in the
tissue of time and place. Readers of 'John Inglesant'
will remember Little Gidding as the home of Nicholas
Ferrar and his Anglican community; as a place where
'prayer has become valid.' And from this terra firma of
English earth in the seventeenth century, the poet ranges
back to Juliana of Norwich with her refrain:-

All shall be well and
All manner of thing shall be well.

and to 'The Cloud of Unknowing' with 'the drawing of this
Love and the voice of this Calling.' The tragic figure of
Charles I is the image of every man confronting his doom;
the scaffold and the 'illegible tombstone' are essentially
one destination. The reflections of Mr. Eliot's maturity
are perhaps echoed in part by the second figure in the
poem. This is the dead master of words with whom the poet

Treads the pavement in a dead patrol

during an air-raid, and who

Faded on the blowing of the horn.

A correspondent suggests Milton to me here, but I think
the following lines rather recall the desperate epigrams
of the later Yeats, struggling with an invincible vitality.

...the cold friction of expiring sense
Without enchantment, offering no promise
But bitter tastelessness of shadow fruit
As body and soul begin to fall asunder.

And then, appropriately enough, the shadow of Yeats is
crossed by the shadow of Swift.

...the conscious impotence of rage
At human folly, and the laceration
Of laughter at what ceases to amuse.

The reception of Mr. Eliot's central meaning does not,
however, depend on picking up this kind of clue. His

purpose is clear. 'The refining of fire by fire,' and
'the purification of the motive in the ground of our
beseeching' - this is the teaching of all the mystics; in
particular, of St. John of the Cross, whom Mr. Eliot so
clearly echoed in 'East Coker.' It is the burden of all
the poet's later verse, expressed with an increasing
beauty and precision. Many competent judges will assess
this work by literary standards, but only those who are
prepared to accept the fundamental doctrines of Christian
asceticism at a moment when they have never been more unpopular, will receive the profound thought to which the
poetry so rigorously conforms.

133. LUKE TURNER, O.P., A REVIEW, 'BLACKFRIARS'

February 1943, vol. xxiv, supplement xii-xiv

Turner (b. 1914) worked on the staff of 'Blackfriars' from
1936 to 1947.

Reviewing the later poetry of T.S. Eliot before the publication of 'Little Gidding', a distinguished critic
wrote: 'It should by now be impossible to doubt that he is
among the greatest poets of the English language.' (1)
The new poem decisively supports that judgment. It shows
the development of the new poetic phase upon which Mr
Eliot's work entered in the experimental period following
'Ash-Wednesday'. Shorter poems like 'Marina', indeed, are
among the loveliest and most satisfying pieces Mr Eliot
has written; but they stand alone, poetically: they do
not offer resources capable of technical advance to the
length of a major poem. 'Burnt Norton' was regarded
variously as the beginning of Mr Eliot's decline and as
the greatest poem he had made. In the light of subsequent
publications, it seems clear that 'Burnt Norton' was, in
fact, a transitional piece, and that only now can it be
placed; and if the judgment quoted above be accurate,
'Burnt Norton' was an important moment in the history of
English verse.
    A sympathetic understanding of Mr Eliot's poetry seems
to demand an acceptance of two principles which he himself
has often enunciated: that the poetry which was adequate

for one moment and one set of circumstances can never be
valid for any other; and that 'for us, anything that can
be said as well in prose can be said better in prose.
And a great deal, in the way of meaning, belongs to prose
rather than to poetry.' Once it has been recognised that
poetry does not seek to communicate prose meanings, the
fact that Mr Eliot is writing poetry, and striving for the
new poetry in the new experience should render unnecessary
repetition of the charge of obscurity, which had some relevance in the 'twenties, before the technique of his writing became generally known. Standards of criticism, if
true, are objective; but they have to be applied, and
applied in relation to the intention of the writer and the
particular task he is attempting. And here, as in all his
later poetry, Mr Eliot is attempting something not only
more difficult but more important than in his earlier work.
'The Waste Land' is a very great poem, in which a range of
experience is controlled and organized into poetic language of a pressure which has not often, if at all, been
attained in English since the seventeenth century. Yet the
problem of communication in 'Ash-Wednesday' is a greater
one, arising from the utter complexity of the Simplicity
with which it is concerned. And since those poems were
written, the problems of language have not grown less
acute: the work has to be done again, 'the intolerable
wrestle with words and meanings' has to be undertaken each
time a new poem is begun; and the sequence of poems from
'Burnt Norton' to 'Little Gidding' constitute a truly
noble effort to overcome the supreme difficulties of expressing, in a dying language and at a most unpropitious
time, the relations of man with God. The difficulty is
the measure of the achievement.

Like all Mr Eliot's principal poems, 'Little Gidding'
is not simple, and engages the problem on more than one
level. He has never been concerned with the mystery of
time, simply; and certainly not in the way in which Proust
was concerned with it: that problem is there, but as an
aspect of a deeper problem: the relations of God and the
world, of the significance of human grasp and endeavour in
relation to the still point which is their constant, uni-
fying centre, yet also their apparent negation and the
denial of their validity. In particular, there is the
relation of language to the shifting of experience; and
this, for the poet, raises questions which have to be overcome: mastered and not only stated. The whole of this sequence of poems has been concerned with these things; but
'Little Gidding', which recalls 'Burnt Norton' in technique and fulfils that poem on a higher level, is free
from those detailed failures of language, and therefore of

sensibility, which could not be overlooked in the two previous pieces. Indeed, 'Little Gidding' is a magnificent
completion of a task that might have been thought beyond
the powers of a community of poets; and since the death of
Yeats (who lived and worked in a wholly different tradition) and the poetic death of Ezra Pound in the 'Cantos',
Mr. Eliot has been without the support of any poet of
stature comparable with his own. Yet here he adds to his
already great achievement with a poem of a strength and
generosity beside which all other contemporary verse seems
'as straw'.

Note

1 F.R. Leavis, Eliot's Later Poetry, 'Scrutiny' (Summer
   1942), xi, 71.

134. EDWIN MUIR, 'LITTLE GIDDING', 'NEW STATESMAN'

20 February 1943, n.s., vol. xxv, 128

The theme which Mr. Eliot treats in this poem - as in the
three poems preceding it - is very difficult to state except in the form in which he has stated it; the vocabulary
we are accustomed to use about time lacks the fitting
terms; they have either fallen out of use or not yet come
into currency. These poems contain probably the most
essential and intimate poetry that Mr. Eliot has written,
yet to those who accept the modern conception of time,
the conception of development or evolution, it may easily
appear remote and tenuous. For it goes beyond the idea
of development and concentrates its main attention neither
on the past nor on the future, finding no ultimate meaning
in the one or ultimate hope in the other. It is concerned
with

     a moment in and out of time ...

     ...transecting, bisecting the world of time, a
     moment in time, but not like a moment of time,
     A moment in time, but time was made through that
         moment, for without the meaning there is no time,
         and that moment of time gave the meaning.

When Mr. Eliot has to state the theme of his later poetry
with such scholastic precision, there is little hope of
paraphrasing it. But roughly, and inaccurately, it may be
described as that state of human experience which is existence, not change, a state without which our life would
be meaningless to us, yet which is embodied in the texture
of change, so that it appears as a contradiction only to
be described by posing a sequence of contradictions. To
ring changes on these, to speak of

    the still point of the turning world,

or of the communication of the dead as

    tongued with fire beyond the language of the living,

or of the intersection of the timeless moment as

    England and nowhere. Never and always

may appear to some people merely a remote and abstruse
game. But it is not only remote and abstruse; it is also
intimate. Whether Mr. Eliot has been influenced in the
form he has chosen for those poems by Beethoven's last
quartets, as has often been said, I do not know, but they
certainly resemble the quartets in this combination of
remoteness and intimacy, a strange but harmonious combination. They are remote because they pass beyond time as we
ordinarily conceive it, and intimate because they go to
the hidden heart of human experience and touch

    the still point where the dance is.

    Their curious quality may be described in another way
by saying that they are both very intimate and impersonal.
The man who has experienced, questioned, inquired does not
appear at all except as a deliberately dramatised figure
seen like any other figure, a part of the machinery of the
poem, as in the second section of 'Little Gidding.' This
impersonality by its insistence occasionally produces difficulties, as in the fine introduction to the present
poem:

[Quotes CPP, p. 191, 'When the short day' to 'dark time of
the year'.]

Something more was needed, one feels, to make us accept
the descent of the pentecostal fire on the generalised
spectator, in spite of the beauty of the intense winter

mood evoked to prepare for it. But this is an incidental
criticism, for the impersonality itself is an essential
part of the dignity and beauty of the poem.

Those who accept Mr. Eliot's conception of time and of
life will be more profoundly moved by this poem than those
who do not, though such assent is not required for an
understanding and enjoyment of it. 'Little Gidding' is in
five movements. The first is introductory and sets the
theme. The second is a sort of leavetaking, with a remote
echo of 'The Waste Land'; the versification in this section is superb. In the next movement Mr. Eliot reaches the
resolution of the poem (and of all four poems). Beginning
with a passage on the use of memory, which is

> For liberation - not less of love but expanding
> Of love beyond desire, and so liberation
> From the future as well as the past,

he goes on to assert that

> All shall be well, and
> All manner of thing shall be well,

an affirmation caught up in the song in the next section,
which has much the same resemblance to a simple lyric
as the *alla danza tedesca* movement in the B flat major
quartet has to a simple dance. The fifth movement, like
the third, is reflective, playing for the last time with
the paradox of the timeless moment:

> Every phrase and every sentence is an end and a
>   beginning,
> Every poem an epitaph ...

> The moment of the rose and the moment of the yew-tree
> Are of equal duration ...

> And the end of all our exploring
> Will be to arrive where we started
> And know the place for the first time.

The mood of still intensity which runs through the poem
deepens towards the end:

> All manner of thing shall be well
> When the tongues of flame are in-folded
> Into the crowned knot of fire
> And the fire and the rose are one.

This poem, like its three predecessors, is filled with statements which are both statements of a paradox and statements of the things in which Mr. Eliot believes. Readers who go to the poems for their poetry cannot be expected to accept all that Mr. Eliot believes; but it will be hard for them to question the accuracy and force with which the paradox is stated, in a sustained concentration of thought, feeling and imagination, or to doubt that these four poems are the most original contribution to poetry that has been made in our time.

135. JAMES KIRKUP, ELIOT, 'POETRY LONDON'

February-March 1943, vol. ix, 52-5

'East Coker' was a natural sequel to 'Burnt Norton,' and 'The Dry Salvages' seemed to indicate a culmination in the poet's thought. The final poem of the series is a re-examination of what has been said already in the three previous poems, though the implications of 'East Coker' seem, in 'Little Gidding,' to predominate.

The 'humility' which was the theme of 'East Coker' (and which now seems to have been too conscious for real humility, which might not bear thinking about at all) pervades 'Little Gidding.' Here, humility, though never mentioned, is actual humility, a realising of personal limitations, a natural and uncomplaining relaxation of body and gesture into the simplicity of universal amplification.

The process of dying, disintegration and re-integration through death into life and into renewed dying, the *perpetuum mobile* of death, is one which affects all things, and which all things must accept. And this is the only significance in being alive.

>   ...what you thought you came for
> Is only a shell, a husk of meaning
> From which the purpose breaks only when it is fulfilled
> If at all.

The question, why should such a process exist, is beyond the scope of the poem, as it is beyond the scope of living things: though it can be answered by the dead, and the answer is given to all who are fulfilled by death:

And what the dead had no speech for, when living,
They can tell you, being dead: the communication
Of the dead is tongued with fire beyond the language
    of the living.

Death comes through air, fire and water, and through
earth; and it is the 'death of hope and despair,' both
being invalid before what ultimately denies them. In the
impressive dialogue which follows between what may be
called the poet's past-self and present-self (though the
distinctions of time are too narrow here, at 'the intersection of the timeless moment'), we learn how the more
spiritual part of life, our thoughts and theories, are
swept away with the body's prolonged withdrawal. The
past-self says:

        I am not eager to rehearse
    My thought and theory which you have forgotten.
    These things have served their purpose: let them be.

The word, speech, poetry, are finished and removed, and
on their resurrection they, like the physical body, have
suffered change and passed into the possession of others:

    For last year's words belong to last year's language
    And next year's words await another voice.

And so in living, he who is alive is confronted with
death in the form of memory; with the places, the objects
and the words which were part of a phase in a process, and
belonged formerly to a world remote and similar:

    But, as the passage now presents no hindrance
        To the spirit unappeased and peregrine
        Between two worlds become much like each other,
    So I find words I never thought to speak
        In streets I never thought I should revisit
        When I left my body on a distant shore.

And 'as body and soul begin to fall asunder,' the
fruits of having lived, the 'crown upon your lifetime's
effort,' viewed in the light of necessity, become, with
the collapse and scattering of all things done, no more
than tasteless shadows; and he who is dying sees for a
moment the futility of isolating life from the rest of
the process, and is incapable of remedying his own past
folly, which he will endorse again and again in the process of existence:

> ...the rending pain of re-enactment
>   Of all that you have done, and been ...

The pain for a while is removed and the spirit restored
by the 'refining fire' of being dead,

> where you must move in measure, like a dancer.

This last passage from the second section of the poem
shows us the necessity, in the face of an overwhelming
process, for faith of some sort, a faith which exists only
in what may be the most insignificant phase of a consummation. Of the faith, if any, we entertain between life and
life we can know nothing.
The deathlike condition of indifference exists between
attachment to, and detachment from, 'self and from things
and from persons.' Yet even love of a country or history
or freedom, all of which are never indifferent, are
eventually submerged in the indifference of death. It is
perhaps here that the humility implicit in the whole poem
becomes most clear:

>   See, now they vanish,
> The faces and places, with the self which, as it could,
>   loved them,
> To become renewed, transfigured, in another pattern.

This humility is essentially optimistic, for it pre-
supposes a condition of simplicity in which the supreme
and unfailing process can be accepted:

> All shall be well, and
> All manner of thing shall be well ...

for ultimately the faces and places and the self will re-
emerge, changed, but restored and unimpaired. And here
the poet asks why we should celebrate certain great men
'of peculiar genius' more than those who are actually
dying. For all thoughts and theories vanish, all policies
and governments and parties are ultimately nullified and
united in a common pattern:

[Quotes 'Little Gidding', III, CPP, p. 196, 'We cannot
revive old factions' to 'a single party'.]

In death, those who were great and fortunate bequeath to
us their spirit and their body: the rest leave us the
symbol of their defeat, which also has value. And all
shall be well, by dying and living, by faith and the

refining power of prayer:

> By the purification of the motive
> In the ground of our beseeching.

There can be no beginning and no ending as far as life
is concerned. What are called the beginning and the end
are one, separated only by the concessions of time. To
call death an end and birth a beginning is to live mis-
takenly, for in an existence where every action is a step
towards death, death is the perpetual starting-point, the
birth from which all things proceed:

> ...and that is where we start.
> We die with the dying:
> See, they depart, and we go with them.
> We are born with the dead:
> See, they return, and bring us with them.

The passage of time in what is 'a pattern of timeless
moments' can only be a sentimental fiction. In pure time,
the 'unimaginable Zero summer,'

> The moment of the rose and the moment of the yew-tree
> Are of equal duration.

Within and beyond this is the mystical power of Love and
the soul to sustain us, as we proceed through boundless
explorations and re-discoveries,

> When the last of earth left to discover
> Is that which was the beginning.

And it is with humility,

> A condition of complete simplicity
> (Costing not less than everything)

that we proceed to our consummation,

> When the tongues of flame are in-folded
> Into the crowned knot of fire
> And the fire and the rose are one.

Mr. Eliot's language, imagery and treatment of his theme
are familiar. The dust, ashes, the roses, the children in
the apple-tree, the garden and the bird-echo at the end of
the poem, from 'Burnt Norton':

> Quick now, here, now, always ...

and, used in a more mystical way, the words fire, flame,
rose, tongue, beginning, end; and the dance which in 'East
Coker' seemed to symbolise death is now the real dance of
death. The life-death paradox is one which is especially
fitted to the poet's incantational style, and this poem
presents us with a true fusion of form and content. As in
'East Coker,' the poet attempts a short analysis of the
business of writing poetry, and fuses it successfully with
the theme of the poem:

> (The common word exact without vulgarity,
> The formal word precise but not pedantic,
> The complete consort dancing together)
> Every phrase and every sentence is an end and a begin-
>   ning,
> Every poem an epitaph.

The whole is a deeply musical and studied pattern of words.
And as a background to the principal theme, there is a
vaguely apocalyptic contemporary landscape:

> Water and fire deride
> The sacrifice that we denied.
> Water and fire shall rot
> The marred foundations we forgot,
> Of sanctuary and choir.

and:

>   In the disfigured street
> He left me, with a kind of valediction,
> And faded on the blowing of the horn.

The meaning of the poem, related to recent events,
becomes even more terrible, as we watch helplessly and
with the 'conscious impotence of rage' our own disintegration, and the folly of those who still strive to 'revive
old factions,' 'restore old policies or follow an antique
drum.' The references to the 'dove,' too, are capable of
translation into other terms, as in the lovely fourth
part:

> The dove descending breaks the air
> With flame of incandescent terror
> Of which the tongues declare
> The one discharge from sin and error.

and in the lines preceding the dialogue:

> After the dark dove with the flickering tongue
>   Had passed below the horizon of his homing....

though to concentrate on one explicit meaning would be to
make poetry unsuitable and useless. The association of
dove with aeroplane, and the actual statements of collapse
in various parts of the poem with contemporary ruins
should be no more in the reader's mind than an undercurrent giving strength and direction to the poem's main
flow.

136. MURIEL BRADBROOK, REVIEW, 'THEOLOGY'

March 1943, vol. xlvi, 58-62

> Whatever we inherit from the fortunate
> We have taken from the defeated
> What they had to leave us - a symbol:
> A symbol perfected in death.

Perhaps one of the best examples of the symbol of
defeat perfected in death is Bossuet's text in the Oraison
Funèbre on Marie Thérèse, Queen of Louis XIV. An unfortunate nonentity, overshadowed by his mistresses, Louis
mourned her with 'she never gave me a moment's trouble.'
And Bossuet chose for his text 'A lamb without stain.'
She was an ineffectual, good, simple woman, whose significance could not be seen till her death, when the completed
pattern of a life of patience emerged: the pathos that it
would have been insulting to dwell on in her life placed
her far above the splendid court, and should have shamed
them all.
    'Little Gidding' is symbolic in this fundamental sense:
not through complication of overlaid meanings, but through
a refinement of discipline issuing in consummation:

> A condition of complete simplicity
> (Costing not less than everything)....

Much of the material is familiar from earlier poems, but
it is used in a new way. Though this poem completes the
series beginning with 'Burnt Norton,' there is a

distinctive tone and accent, and a distinctive quality in
the vocabulary. The note of striving and seeking is replaced by certitude. At first, the verse strikes toneless
and cold compared with, e.g., the 'wounded surgeon' passage in 'East Coker'; but on re-reading, the peculiar precision defining with the particularity of a frost, the
colourless clarity which is the last reward of disciplined
integrity, penetrates at a deeper level - the level of
'the terrible crystal,' of the final chorus of Milton's
'Samson.'

The poem is in five sections: two contrasted visions, a
meditative passage, an apocalyptic lyric, and a conclusion.

The first twenty lines are prelude and epitome: the
dazzle of frosty mid-winter noon is the paradox of the
nadir, 'suspended in time between pole and tropic', a midwinter spring, 'but not in time's covenant.' That strange
consolation found only at the centre of loss is here mar-
vellously rendered in terms of the frosty blossoming of
the hedges. And this experience is also the central experience of Christian life. Mr Eliot has never concerned himself in his poetry with dogma, but with experience: not
with the Truth, but the Way. He has invoked not the creed
but the liturgy, not the theologian but the contemplative.
And in Little Gidding, which emerges as the end of the
journey, it was a way of life that was practised. Here are
no questions of intellectual concepts, but of a mode of
living:

You are not here to verify,
Instruct yourself, or inform curiosity
Or carry report. You are here to kneel
Where prayer has been valid.

'I believe in the communion of saints' is dramatized,
where the dead speak to the living, and there is the
'intersection of the timeless moment.' (It is an article
of the Christian belief which must to the non-Christian
appear not so much unacceptable as meaningless.) The poet
stands here in the relation to the theologian that the
love-poet does to the psychologist: he presents and defines an experience both highly personal - as to everyone
there is a personal and unique apprehension given - and
also genuinely representative (a) And whilst the religious apprehension is given directly, as experience, the
relating and placing, the very highly organized integra-
tion, is a matter of the secular context, whether that be
daily living or the language of philosophy.

For Eliot does on occasion use philosophy for poetic
ends. Christianity is the main vehicle by which European
thought has harnessed philosophy to work directly on the

refinement of daily living. And it is in the work of
great Christian writers, of Dante, Pascal, (b) the company
of seventeenth-century mystics and divines who are echoed
so subtly throughout the poem, that the delicate art of
interpretation is achieved - as Eliot says, not by indifference, not theoretically, but with the full incarnation
of the Here and Now, the precision of sensitive life.

The second section gives in dead, echoing monotone the
vision of London under fire. Death, suffering, the sense
of emptiness and shock that follow a vast catastrophe are
not directly invoked: they are *suggested* in terms of a
rhythm heavy, yet somehow also serene:

> Ash on an old man's sleeve
> Is all the ash the burnt roses leave.
> Dust in the air suspended
> Marks the place where a story ended....

The strange stillness of bereavement hangs over these
stanzas and over the suspended cadences of the dawn scene,
(c) where in the blitzed street the form of the 'familiar
compound ghost' drifts with the dawn wind, a poet came
from purgatory to revisit a world not dissimilar:

> After the dark dove with the flickering tongue
> Had passed below the horizon of his homing.

(These lines do not seem to me very happy. The conceit
has too fabricated an air and its purpose in pointing forward to the fourth section is too obtrusive.)

The ghost states in words quite glacial in their precision the special sufferings reserved for poets in their
age:

> First, the cold friction of expiring sense....
> And last, the rending pain of re-enactment
> Of all that you have done, and been....

With a final word, recalling that particular dead master,
Arnaut Daniel, whose phrases Eliot has used so often, he
speaks of the suffering spirit as being restored by
'refining fire'; and so, like Hamlet's father, 'faded on
the blowing of the horn.'

The third section relates these visions of the past
and the present, Little Gidding and the blitz, prayer and
the craft of verse. They are related through that detachment (d) which alone perceives the pattern binding them.
Eliot begins by defining detachment, as distinct from
attachment and indifference. Memory is the servant of

detachment, liberating the spirit through co-ordinating
its experiences:

>   Not less of love, but expanding
>   Of love beyond desire, and so liberation
>   From the future as well as the past.

(A significant variation upon the praise of detachment in
'East Coker': 'I said to my soul, be still, and wait without
hope....')
   So if history is seen detachedly, 'history may be freedom.' And though the past as it was embodied at Little
Gidding cannot be revived, we inherit from both victors and
vanquished in those wars. So, too, in turn, if we achieve
detachment by the purification of the motive behind our
petitions and prayers, we may transmit our best to others:

>   And all shall be well and
>   All manner of thing shall be well
>   By the purification of the motive
>   In the ground of our beseeching.

The fourth section - two short rhyming verses - is the
poem's focus. It is an apocalyptic vision in which the
descent of the Spirit in tongues of flame is blazoned upon
a field of fire which is at once burning London, the shirt
of flame and deifying funeral pyre of a dying Herakles,
and the purgatorial fire of Arnaut Daniel. The fire of
agony is seen, as all see it in moments of insight, as
Hopkins' nun saw it in 'The Wreck of The Deutschland,' as
the flame of that Person to whom Love is appropriated as
His title.

[Quotes CPP, p. 196, 'Who then devised' to 'fire or fire'.]

   The ringing vowels, a's and i's, which clang over the
tolling o's, both excite and bind the feeling which flows
up from the complex images resolved in the symbol of fire.
As a technical performance it is astonishing. But there
is no sense of its being merely a technical performance:
nor is 'the incandescent terror' merely emotional. It is
a triumph of a more elemental kind: all that is not sensuous is spiritual, and the sensuous is completely informed
as the vehicle of the spiritual:

>   A condition of complete simplicity
>   (Costing not less than everything)....

The conclusion recalls old themes: it is a conclusion

to the whole series. The seamless web, only perceived
when it is completed; the pattern of words, of lives, of
events in history - these have all been illustrated in the
preceding sections and in the preceding poems. 'History,'
says Eliot, 'is a pattern of timeless moments' - the significant moments which redeem it from being a succession
of events, and give life to a nation or a civilization.(e)
In the life of a person, his self-discipline may lead him
back to his earliest intimations, and Man himself return
to the primal garden, when the fire becomes a crown, the
thorn a rose, and purgation blends into beatitude.

It will be seen that the theme of this poem is related
to the earlier verse and yet that the certainty, the finality of precision is new. The measure of the suffering,
which is given in spiritual terms - there are no atrocity
close-ups, there is not even a suggestion of any delimited
event - is the measure of the integrity and the power
needed to present it. 'Little Gidding' provides both a
standard and a tool for inner reflection on the times. It
was a great opportunity worthily met.

Notes

a   The poet, whether of religion or of love, conveys an
    experience to those who have not directly had it, by
    relating it to what they do know. There is a sense in
    which he who has not known love is handicapped in read-
    ing 'Songs and Sonets' more than in reading Freud: yet
    the poems are also an *éducation sentimentale*. Simi-
    larly, a non-Christian may in reading Christian verse
    get very much nearer to what it feels like to be a
    Christian than he could otherwise do.
b   How far 'Le Mémorial' is behind 'Little Gidding' is
    perhaps unsafe to speculate. It is certainly highly
    relevant.
c   Readers of Eliot will be reminded here of 'The Waste
    Land,' as in the preceding section of 'A Song for
    Simeon.'
d   In 'Theology' for February 1942, I dwelt at some length
    upon Eliot's use of this theme: see The Latest Verse
    of T.S. Eliot, *loc cit*.
e   Cf. the definition by Eliot of tradition in Tradition
    and the Individual Talent ('Selected Essays,' 1932).

137. D.W. HARDING, WE HAVE NOT REACHED CONCLUSION,
'SCRUTINY'

Spring 1943, vol. xi, 216-19

This review was reprinted in 'The Importance of Scrutiny',
edited by Eric Bentley (New York, 1948), pp. 269-73.
   The following two items arise out of Harding's review.
R.N. Higinbotham (No. 138) objects to Harding's account as
being too favourable towards Eliot, while F.R. Leavis
(No. 139) comes to Harding's defence. The whole debate
has been reprinted in 'T.S. Eliot: "Four Quartets"', a
Casebook edited by Bernard Bergonzi (London, 1969),
pp. 64-80.

The opening of the poem speaks of renewed life of unimaginable splendour, seen in promise amidst the cold decline of
age. It offers no revival of life-processes; it is a
spring time, 'But not in time's covenant'. If this 'midwinter spring' has such blooms as the snow on hedges,

   Where is the summer, the unimaginable
   Zero summer?

With the sun blazing on the ice, the idea of pentecostal
fire, of central importance in the poem, comes in for the
first time, an intense, blinding promise of life and (as
later passages show) almost unbearable.
   The church of Little Gidding introduces another theme
of the poem. Anchored in time and space, but for some
people serving as the world's end where they can fulfil a
purpose outside time and space, it gives contact with
spiritual concerns through earthly and human things.
   A third theme, important for the whole poem, is also
stated in the first section: that the present is able
to take up, and even give added meaning to, the values of
the past. Here too the pentecostal idea comes in:

   And what the dead had no speech for, when living,
   They can tell you, being dead: the communication
   Of the dead is tongued with fire beyond the language
      of the living.

   Section II can be regarded as the *logical* starting
point of the whole poem. It deals with the desolation of

death and the futility of life for those who have had no
conviction of spiritual values in their life's work.
First come three sharply organized riming stanzas to
evoke, by image and idea but without literal statement,
our sense of the hopeless death of air, earth, fire and
water, seen not only as the elements of man's existence
but as the means of his destruction and dismissal.   The
tone having been set by these stanzas, there opens a narrative passage describing the dreary bitterness in which
a life of literary culture can end if it has brought no
sense of spiritual values.   The life presented is one,
such as Mr. Eliot's own, of effort after clear speech and
exact thought, and the passage amounts to a shuddering
'There but for the grace of God go I'.   It reveals more
clearly than ever the articles in the 'Criterion' did,
years ago, what it was in 'humanism' that Mr. Eliot re-
coiled from so violently.   What the humanist's ghost sees
in his life are futility, isolation, and guilt on account
of his self-assertive prowess - 'Which once you took for
exercise of virtue' - and the measure of aggression
against others which that must bring.

The verse in this narrative passage, with its regular
measure and insistent alliteration, so effective for com-
bining the macabre with the urbane and dreary, is a way
to indicate and a way to control the pressure of urgent
misery and self-disgust.   The motive power of this passage,
as of so much of Mr. Eliot's earlier poetry, is repulsion.
But in the poem as a whole the other motive force is dominant: there is a movement of feeling and conviction out-
wards, reaching towards what attracts.   The other parts of
the poem can be viewed as working out an alternative to
the prospect of life presented in this narrative.

Section III sees the foundation for such an alternative
in the contact with spiritual values, especially as they
appear in the tradition of the past.   Detachment (distinguished from indifference) allows us to use both our own
past and the historical past in such a way as to draw on
their present spiritual significance for us without en-
tangling us in regressive yearning for a pattern which no
longer is:

> History may be servitude,
> History may be freedom. See, now they vanish,
> The faces and places, with the self which, as it could,
>   loved them,
> To become renewed, transfigured, in another pattern.

Once we accept the significance of the spiritual motives
and intentions of the past, even the factions connected

with the church and community of Little Gidding leave us
an inheritance; we can be at one with the whole past,
including the sinning and defeated past, for its people
were spiritually alive,

> All touched by a common genius,
> United in the strife which divided them.

But the humanist's fate cannot be escaped in so gentle
and placid a way; a more formidable ordeal is waiting.   In
contrast to the leisurely meditation of section III, the
fourth section is a forceful passage, close-knit with
rime, and incisive. Its theme is the terrifying fierce-
ness of the pentecostal experience, the dove bringing fire.
This is not the fire of expiation, such as the humanist
had to suffer. It is the consuming experience of love,
the surrender to a spiritual principle beyond us, and the
only alternative to consuming ourselves with the miserable
fires of sin and error. This pentecostal ordeal must be
met before the blinding promise seen in 'midwinter spring'
can be accepted.

The final section develops the idea that every experience is integrated with all the others, so that the ful-
ness of exploration means a return, with better understanding, to the point where you started. The theme has
already been foreshadowed in section III where detachment
is seen to give liberation from the future as well as the
past, so that neither past nor future has any fascination
of a kind that could breed in us a reluctance to accept
the present fully.

The tyranny of sequence and duration in life is thus
reduced. Time-processes are viewed as aspects of a pattern which can be grasped in its entirety at any one of
its moments:

> The moment of the rose and the moment of the yew-tree
> Are of equal duration.

One effect of this view of time and experience is to rob
the moment of death of any over-significance we may have
given it. For the humanist of section II life trails off
just because it can't manage to endure. For the man
convinced of spiritual values life is a coherent pattern
in which the ending has its due place and, because it is
part of a pattern, itself leads into the beginning. An
over-strong terror of death is often one expression of
the fear of living, for death is one of the life-processes
that seem too terrifying to be borne. In examining one
means of becoming reconciled to death, Mr. Eliot can show

us life too made bearable, unfrightening, positively
inviting:

> With the drawing of this Love and the voice of this
>   Calling
>
>> We shall not cease from exploration
>> And the end of all our exploring
>> Will be to arrive where we started
>> And know the place for the first time.

Here is the clearest expression of a motive force other
than repulsion. Its dominance makes this poem - to put it
very simply - far happier than most of Mr. Eliot's.

Being reconciled to death and the conditions of life
restores the golden age of unfearful natural living and
lets you safely, without regression, recapture the wonder
and easy rightness of certain moments, especially in early
childhood:

[Quotes 'Little Gidding', V, CPP, pp. 197-8, 'At the
source' to 'not less than everything)'.]

The whole of this last section suggests a serene and
revitalized return from meditation to one's part in active
living. It includes a re-affirmation of that concern with
speech which has made up so much of Mr. Eliot's work and
which could have been the bitter futility that it is for
the ghostly humanist. The re-affirming passage (introduced as a simile to suggest the integrated patterning of
all living experience) is an example of amazing condensation, of most comprehensive thinking given the air of
leisured speech - not conversation but the considered
speech of a man talking to a small group who are going to
listen for a time without replying. It is one example of
the intellectual quality of this poem. In most of Mr.
Eliot's poems the intellectual materials which abound are
used emotionally. In much of this poem they are used
intellectually, in literal statement which is to be understood literally (for instance, the opening of section
III). How such statements become poetry is a question
outside the range of this review. To my mind they do,
triumphantly, and for me it ranks among the major good
fortunes of our time that so superb a poet is writing.

138. R.N. HIGINBOTHAM'S OBJECTIONS TO HARDING'S REVIEW,
'SCRUTINY'

Summer 1943, vol. xi, 259-61

R.N. Higinbotham is a pseudonym.

The Editors have received the following communication:

> La vostra nominanza è color d'erba,
>   che viene e va, e quei la discolora,
>   per cui ell'esce della terra acerba.

The review of 'Little Gidding' in the last number of
'Scrutiny' was an exposition, almost a paraphrase, but
hardly a criticism, and crossed, I think, the line which
separates the 'abeyance of the critical function' from its
favourable exercise. Surely any reviewer should suspect
his reactions when he can find nothing better to say than
what his poet has already said better? Perhaps the last
paragraph represented a hasty concession to the necessity
of making some objective remark about the work. But even
here, alas, the question raised was 'outside the range of
this review'. That gives me a pretext to codify some disturbing impressions - not faked up *ad hoc* - about Mr.
Eliot's recent verse.
    Mr. Harding drew a distinction between the emotional
and the intellectual use of intellectual material. One
between emotional and intellectual material, each used
intellectually, is more illuminating. Mr. Eliot used to
contemplate the conditions, of mind or affairs, which he
wished to represent, from the outside, personifying such
of himself as was relevant in some as it were dramatic
character. He then represented what he saw by consciously
assembling fragments of it intense enough to express all
he left out. In this way he created poems both evocative
and passionate. But at least since 'Burnt Norton' he has
stopped being satisfied with the mere representation of
conditions in isolation. He now finds them only properly
understood or indeed significant when placed in a framework of more important and permanent truth. This is a
natural development from earlier work obsessed by the
meaninglessness of autonomous mood. But the significance
of such qualifications of a condition can only be properly
apprehended intellectually, syllogistically. Certainly

they can be suffused with emotion, but the raw material is
plain, logical argument. Now Mr. Eliot's general method,
of assembling intense fragments, has not changed. Since,
however, many aspects of the conditions as he has come to
represent them are thus intellectual, many of his fragments
also must be intellectual. Furthermore they must be sufficiently powerful to stand the pressure generated by the
emotional fragments.

His only hope of fulfilling this last necessity would
be to feel what he thinks as intensely as he feels what he
feels. Then the intellectual material would go about with
him as constantly as the emotional and, like that, would
pick up the diverse associations and occurrences which
somehow make poetry. With certain exceptions, however, it
has not done so. It lacks body, is thin. As for method,
there is sometimes the crass, palpable expression of it
which Mr. Harding notes at the beginning of section III of
'Little Gidding'. In themselves such parts escape both
censure and praise, except in so far as one may be interested in the skilful arrangement of unimportant rhythms
and Mr. Eliot's personal re-distribution of emphasis among
familiar arguments. But he is seldom so uncompromising
with the blatancy of direct statement. Usually he resorts
to symbols. But, since his intellectual material is not
felt enough to be constantly with him and with the whole
of him, it has insufficient background and body to produce
spontaneous symbols. His symbols have to be thought up
and clapped on. Again it is a matter of opinion: I myself
cannot believe that these recurrent children in foliage,
this silent music, these still dances, these gardens,
these roses and yews which have their moments, these
flames, that eternal wild thyme unseen and the useful, the
universally adaptable, the good old sea, which figures so
largely in the similes of our island race, are genuine and
necessary expressions of a meaning. They are not existent
enough and they are too uniform. They are a poeticising
device, a private code, whose cyphers are often determined
by the obsolete emotional associations attached to certain
words in poetic convention. Kings at nightfall, for instance, really mean nothing; 'king' is a nice, emotive
word; so is 'nightfall': that's all, that's all, that's
all. Premiers at question-time would be more moving.
Kings now can only impinge forcefully on a mind which is
playing literary chess. Mr. Eliot has even succumbed to
the unselfconscious use of old phrases like 'the world's
end'; of clichés like 'the enigma of the fever chart',
'transient beauty', 'worshippers of the machine'. Nothing
is gained by such paraphrasing. The original meaning's

effect is not widened but confined, forced into the compass of a stock-response. Often the meaning is lost;
often it does not seem worth finding. Secondary effects
of this artificiality are preciousness, disappearance of
verbal evocativeness, vagueness and a continual groping
after the elusive, with the one authentic word slipping
through the enunciation. Finally the straining after
effect causes an occasional portentousness, as though
Mr. Eliot were promulgating, rather than writing, verse:
see the opening of sections I and V of 'The Dry Salvages'.

The melancholy of the failure is in the contrast with
the successes. The most noteworthy success is the second
part of section II of 'Little Gidding', applied to which
Mr. Harding's praises are accurate. There are others:
'Burnt Norton', most of section III, section IV; 'East
Coker', most of section I, section II; 'The Dry Salvages',
section II and section IV. They are all seen or felt;
they are vivid, real, not existing in an impossible rose-
shot, children-tinkled haze. Their material, in fact, is
emotional, whereas the failures, as I have tried to show,
are in attempts to use intellectual material.

The unevenness and lack of homogeneity in these four
poems from 'Burnt Norton' onwards are therefore the result
of disequilibrium in the author's feelings. If Mr.
Eliot's achievements were not so great and his seriousness not beyond question I should use the term 'insin-
cerity' to describe the general effect.

139. F.R. LEAVIS REPLIES TO HIGINBOTHAM, 'SCRUTINY'

Summer 1943, vol. xi, 261-7

Leavis (1895-1978) was the foremost critic of his generation in England. Eliot's work was one of his major preoccupations, from 'New Bearings in English Poetry' (1932)
to 'The Living Principle' (1975). An excellent introduction to Leavis's life and work is Edward Greenwood's pamphlet, 'F.R. Leavis', written for the British Council and
published in 1978.

Mr. Higinbotham disagrees with D.W. Harding's critical
estimate of 'Little Gidding': that is what he means when,

522   T.S. Eliot: The Critical Heritage

ironically quoting me, he speaks of an 'abeyance of the
critical function'. And his manner of expressing his dis-
agreement commits him, I think, to an indefensibly
restricted view of the ways in which that function may be
performed. 'Surely', he asks, 'any reviewer should suspect his reactions when he can find nothing better to say
than what his poet has already said better?' To bring out
how much better the poet has said it is, of course, the
whole point and the conscious critical purpose of Harding's elucidation, and that such elucidation has its
essential part in the critical function where 'Little
Gidding' and the companion poems are concerned Mr.
Higinbotham's own criticism serves, I think, to bring out,
though the service this time is unintentional. (And Mr.
Higinbotham's views on Eliot, as a friend remarked to me,
are probably shared by many people).

A value-judgment can't, we all know, be demonstratively
enforced; the critic can only attempt to help other readers to an approach by which, freed from inappropriate
expectations and preconceptions and adverted as to the
kind of thing they have in front of them, they will be
able to *take* the poem - take it for what it is: the judging goes with the taking. Mr. Higinbotham finds the meaning of 'Little Gidding' so obvious that he can't believe
(one gathers) that any reader a critic need bother about
will be grateful for such an elucidation as Harding's, and
this alone would lead us to doubt the grounds of Mr.
Higinbotham's confidence ('what the poet has already said
better') that he understands well enough what the poet has
said. He goes on, of course, to complain that Harding
leaves unanswered, having raised it, an important question
about the working of the poem. And it is true that if
Harding had been able to find the time, and had claimed
the space, to elaborate that account of the working which
the elucidation demands for its completion, his readers
(or most of them) would have found even more cause for
gratitude. But the reviewer of an interesting and complex
work doesn't, in proposing for his review a limited scope,
need to plead the pressure of war-time employments.
There have been before in 'Scrutiny' relevant discussions
of Eliot's poetic methods, and no one who has read Harding's examination of 'Burnt Norton' in his review of 'Collected Poems 1909-1935' (see 'Scrutiny' for September,
1936) is likely to suppose that when he pronounced the
question about Eliot's use of intellectual materials to be
'outside the range' of his review of 'Little Gidding' it
was because of any uncertainty as to how he would proceed
to answer it.

Unfortunately he hasn't been able to contribute to this

number of 'Scrutiny' at all, and has had reluctantly to
renounce the opportunity offered by Mr. Higinbotham's
letter of going further with the discussion of 'Little
Gidding' and of the problems it raises. I myself have had
no chance of discussing things with him; he hasn't seen my
comments on Mr. Higinbotham's criticism of Eliot's poetry,
or been consulted about them, and what follows must be
taken as coming from me, and me alone.

Mr. Higinbotham, offering to correct and supplement
Harding, gives his own account of the relation between the
'intellectual material' and the 'emotional' in these late
poems of Eliot's. I am bound to say that in so doing he
seems to me to show a complete failure to recognize the
kind of organization the poems present, and an accompany-
ing failure to appreciate the distinctive genius of the
poet. Early in the first paragraph of his argument (the
second of the letter) he pulls us up with: 'But at least
since "Burnt Norton" he has stopped being satisfied with
the mere representation of conditions in isolation'. It
seems quite plain from the general context that we are not
to take 'at least' as meant to qualify seriously the implication that up to 'Burnt Norton' the poet *was* satisfied
with such mere representation. This implication will, I
know, have surprised others as much as it surprised me.
For some account of the way in which, from the first of
the 'Ash-Wednesday' sequence onwards, Eliot's poems, so
far from being preoccupied with 'conditions in isolation'
or 'autonomous mood', are preoccupied with establishing,
in a constructive exploration of experience, the apprehension of a reality in relation to which life in time has
what meaning it can be made to yield, I may perhaps be
allowed to refer back to 'Scrutiny' for Summer last year.
What Mr. Higinbotham is constating is the notable presence
in 'Burnt Norton' of 'intellectual materials' used, as the
review of 'Little Gidding' puts it, intellectually. He
thinks that any going beyond 'the mere representation of
conditions in isolation' must depend upon such a presence
— 'But the significance of such qualifications of a condition can only be properly apprehended intellectually,
syllogistically'.

In taking over Harding's phrase, 'intellectual materials', Mr. Higinbotham, unconsciously and significantly,
gives its meaning a shift into another plane. Harding, in
talking of 'materials', is thinking, not of something behind the text, but of what lies on the page before us, to
be taken up by us, in the re-creative process of reading,
into the organism of the realized poem. For Mr. Higinbotham the 'materials' are what we deduce to be behind the
text, they are in Mr. Eliot and are what he tries, with

very incomplete success, to make poetry out of. Or perhaps, it would be better to say that they are what were,
on a kind of inner workman's bench, *before* him. A con-
comitant of this shift is the curious account we are
offered of the relation between the two postulated kinds
of 'material', the emotional and the intellectual ('each
used intellectually'). The passage quoted in my last
paragraph continues:

> Certainly they can be suffused with emotion, but the
> raw material is plain, logical argument. Now Mr.
> Eliot's general method, of assembling intense frag-
> ments, has not changed. Since, however, many aspects
> of the conditions as he has come to represent them are
> thus intellectual, many of his fragments also must be
> intellectual. Furthermore they must be sufficiently
> powerful to stand the pressure generated by the emo-
> tional fragments.

In this way Mr. Higinbotham faces the poet with a very
difficult - in fact, an insoluble - problem. Here are the
two different stuffs, the separate rolls or sheets (so to
speak), from which fragments have to be selected to go
into the poem. The emotional stuff is 'live' - poetically
active, and the fragments carry with them into the poem a
charge derived from the context from which they have been
taken. In this way, though in itself non-poetical, the
intellect (for clearly we have to explain the 'intellec-
tuality' of 'emotional and intellectual material, each
used intellectually' by correlating it with the 'consciously assembled' of the sentence I am on the point of
quoting) can work to poetic effect - 'He then represented
what he saw by consciously assembling fragments of it
intense enough to express all he left out. In this way he
created poems both evocative and passionate'. But what
can the intellect do with the intellectual stuff, the
chosen fragments of which can carry from their context, of
its nature poetically inert, no charge with them?
Just how Mr. Higinbotham conceives of this intellectual
stuff, this 'raw material' of 'plain, logical argument', I
can't figure to myself convincingly. Nor do I understand
the relation between thinking and feeling implied here:

> His only hope of fulfilling this last necessity
> [that the intellectual fragments should be 'sufficiently
> powerful to stand the pressure generated by the emo-
> tional fragments'] would be to feel what he thinks as
> intensely as he feels what he feels. Then the intel-
> lectual material would go about with him as constantly

as the emotional, and, like that, would pick up the
diverse associations which somehow make poetry.

For the essential argument makes 'thinking' a matter pertaining to an abstract realm that is insulated from concrete experience, though the intellect is somehow able,
across the insulating boundaries, to take cognizance of
'conditions' outside, and place them 'in a framework of
more important and permanent truth' - a framework the
significance of which, one gathers, 'can only be properly
apprehended intellectually, syllogistically'.

I shouldn't myself like to have to try and explain to a
psychologist or a philosopher my own notions about the
relations between 'thinking' and 'feeling', but my acquaintance with poetry as a literary critic is enough to convince me that I am justified in pronouncing Mr. Higinbotham's account, in so far as one can gather it, inadequate to the facts. A literary critic can hardly fail to
have given a great deal of attention to the problems
raised by those two terms, 'thinking' and 'feeling', in
company. He certainly can't have failed to do so if he
has grappled with Eliot's later poetry, for there the
poet's essential preoccupations entail, inseparably, a
conscious preoccupation with those problems.

But the problem of inducing intellectual material to
'pick up the diverse associations and occurrences that
somehow make poetry', so that fragments can go duly
charged into the poem with a chance of holding their own
against emotional fragments, coming from an emotional context, was provided by Mr. Higinbotham. It is only if you
suppose the poet to have been faced with it that you can
judge him to have been beaten by it. The passages that
Harding instances as exemplifying intellectual materials
used intellectually are (I concur in his judgment) poetry
because of their context, the poem as a whole - or rather,
the sequence as a whole; because, that is, they belong to
a vital organization. When Harding says the materials are
used intellectually his appositional clause makes quite
plain what he means: 'in literal statement which is to be
understood literally'. That is, they demand to be taken
as if we were for the moment reading a prose treatise,
moral or philosophical. As if - but they have a force and
a life that no treatise could have given them. Their context, instead of being one of statement and argument, is
one that evokes concretely the living experience from
which they emerge as the index and summary. We don't feel
them as a matter of abstract thinking about or of; the
presence in them of the concrete they focus and transmit
is too immediate and commanding - if, that is, we have

understood the organization and made ourselves capable
of taking the poem. What in fact this poetry renders concretely is the exploratory process in which experience is
ordered into significance - a process a good deal more inward and organically complex than that envisaged by Mr.
Higinbotham as being operated by the intellect on 'conditions in isolation' ('He now finds them only properly
understood or indeed significant when placed in a framework
of more important and permanent truth'). The way in
which, in this poetry, intellectual formulation emerges
from the experiential matrix clearly has general bearings,
and a literary critic can't help believing that those
whose business is with intellectual formulation, and those
- pyschologists or philosophers - whose business is to be
interested in the nature of thought, must, if they achieve
the approach, find themselves notably indebted to the
genius of the poet.

Failing to achieve the approach Mr. Higinbotham finds,
not only that the passages of intellectual material are
'thin' and 'lack body', but that, since this material not
being felt enough by the poet, 'has insufficient background and body to produce spontaneous symbols', his
'symbols have to be thought up and clapped on'. In this
way a large proportion of the other-than-intellectual
material is dismissed as not 'genuine and necessary
expression of a meaning':

> They are not existent enough and they are too uni-
> form. They are a poeticizing device, a private code,
> whose cyphers are often determined by the obsolete
> emotional associations attached to certain words in
> poetic convention. Kings at nightfall, for instance,
> really mean nothing; 'king' is a nice, emotive word;
> so is 'nightfall': that's all, that's all, that's all.
> Premiers at question-time would be more moving.

This illustration brings home pretty forcibly with what
insistence Mr. Higinbotham reads the poem as an assemblage
of fragments. He not only misses the wider and more recondite organization; he ignores the connexions that for
any reader, one would have thought, lie obvious on the
page in view. Here is the phrase he objects to restored
to its immediate context:

[Quotes 'Little Gidding', III, CPP, pp. 195-6, 'If I
think, again' to 'than the dying?']

The 'place', explicitly enough, is Little Gidding. The
associated 'people', plainly, are of the seventeenth

century, and so, equally plainly, are the figures in the
rest of the sentence, and that one of them should be a
king can surely be more naturally and convincingly explained than by invoking a blind need in the poet to
clutch at a worn poetical property. These are particular
figures of the past that have lodged in the poet's imagination - historic figures very relevant to the theme of the
poem. And it will have been noted that the whole 'If I
think' passage leads up to the question:

> Why should we celebrate
> These dead men more than the dying?

Even if for a reader who can't take the passage in its
place in the whole organization the question has nothing
like its due force, the explicit intention as given locally
makes Mr. Higinbotham's reaction look odd:

> It is not to ring the bell backward
> Nor is it an incantation
> To summon the spectre of a Rose. etc.

For the reader who has, from 'Burnt Norton' on, taken the
essential organization and development, the question has
behind it that mercilessly resourceful process by which
human and historic time is de-realized into a dismaying
relativity and his habit-confident sense of present and
past and reality routed - the process so disturbingly
furthered, in 'The Dry Salvages', by that symbolic and
evocative use of the sea to which Mr. Higinbotham (in what
looks to me like mere petulance) objects. Possessed by
this consciousness of evanescence and insignificance, of
not-being, why indeed should we celebrate these dead men
more than the living (the 'dying') - why should we
attribute to them more reality?

The force of the positive answer indicated by Harding
is conditioned by the effect of the negative or solvent
process. I can imagine it's being said that it depends
upon it too much - that the poet creates a vacuum which
the duly 'conditioned' reader is drawn in to fill too
readily with the hints provided. But from the outset a
positive creative process has accompanied the sapping,
unsettling and dissolving - a process any account of
which must be mainly an enlargement of Harding's account
of the 'creation of concepts' in 'Burnt Norton'. I won't
attempt such an enlargement here, or recapitulate what I
offered last year in the Summer 'Scrutiny'. I will
merely suggest that Mr. Higinbotham ponders the relations
in 'Burnt Norton' between the proposition,

> Time past and time future
> What might have been and what has been
> Point to one end, which is always present,

the imagery of 'our first world', 'reality', 'the still
point', 'the dance', 'consciousness', 'the form' and 'the
pattern', and tries to grasp what kind of co-operation
between all these (and a great deal else) is *intended* - a
co-operation of which we are given a kind of clinching
résumé in the closing section, with its culminating

> Quick now, here, now, always -.

That he has not really tried is sufficiently shown, I
think, by his dismissing 'transient beauty' in section III
as a *cliché* - a reaction as betrayingly arbitrary as his
reaction to 'kings at nightfall'. And what would he substitute for 'world's end' in 'Little Gidding'? Does he
perhaps think that 'end of the world' means the same
thing? If Eliot is to be judged guilty of a weakness for
clichés, then no poet who ever wrote can escape conviction. Of course, what we have here is not criticism, but
a patent expression of that curiously strong feeling which
pervades the note as a whole. I remarked on this feeling
to a friend to whom I showed the note and he replied: 'I
think a possible explanation is that he's one of the many
people who like their poetry miserable. The passages he
notes for praise bear this out. After all, Eliot's
earlier work was bound to have a strong appeal for
[people who go to poetry to indulge their sense of
grievance against things], and I can see that they would
feel it is a final outrage if *he* started turning happy on
them'.
I ask Mr. Higinbotham to believe that it is with my eye
on the 'many people' that I quote this. In the general
bearing of his comment my friend was certainly right, and
the point he makes is an important one; it calls attention
to another aspect of the difficulty of Eliot's later
poetry. This poetry is difficult by reason of the discipline of self-knowledge and readjustment it imposes. To
deal with one's miseries in the manner indicated above is
comparatively easy, and it offers by way of satisfaction
(at various possible levels) a sense of superiority and a
licence for a measure of self-congratulation. It involves
too the temptation to protect oneself from effort with
sanctioned and respectable *clichés* of feeling and attitude.
Eliot's later poetry exacts of the reader who proposes to
feel that he has mastered it a far more difficult emotional and moral readjustment.

Such in fact is the demand under this head made by
'Little Gidding' that few readers will be quick to feel
that they are in a position to render anything like a
final account of what, for them, the poem is and does.
Harding's account seems to me admirable - admirable in
positive definition and admirable in its patent awareness
of the problems of concrete determination it leaves the
assenting reader with. A critical account of any poetry
can only point, or draw a line round. It must always be
left to each reader to grasp for himself what is concretely presented. In the case of 'Little Gidding' the
grasping must be a matter, not only of much attentive re-
reading of the whole sequence, but of meditation and disciplined self-searching. That what we are offered is worth
these, and in what general ways, ought, I think, to be
plain to any qualified reader of poetry who has seriously
attempted the approach. But he will be a rare reader who
does not go on feeling that he must re-read the whole, and
question his experience, again and yet again. 'Detachment
(distinguished from indifference)' - yes, one in a sense
known well enough what one ought to have there, though the
having will clearly be more than a matter of reading a poem
attentively. 'For the man convinced of spiritual values
life is a coherent pattern in which the ending has its due
place and because it is part of a pattern, itself leads
into the beginning': 'the present is able to take up, and
even give added meaning to, the values of the past': - just
what corresponding to these phrases one actually grasps is
a question that, in the stock-taking with which a reading
tries to complete itself, leads one back again and again to
a re-reading. The poetry and the question - the questions
- have to be lived with.

140. JAMES JOHNSON SWEENEY, 'LITTLE GIDDING': INTRODUCTORY
TO A READING, 'POETRY'

July 1943, vol. lxii, 214-23

'*Qua* work of art,' Eliot wrote in an early paper on
'Hamlet,' 'the work of art cannot be interpreted; there is
nothing to interpret; we can only criticize it according
to standards, in comparison to other works of art; and for
interpretation the chief task is the presentation of relevant historical facts which the reader is not assumed to

know.' There is no definitive 'interpretation' possible
for any poem worthy of the name. A poet should aim, as
Eliot says in his essay introductory to 'A Choice of
Kipling's Verse,' 'at making something which shall first
of all *be*, something which in consequence will have the
capability of exciting, within a limited range, a considerable variety of responses from different readers'.

To *be*, in Eliot's sense, a poem must have form, or
better, structure. As he says, 'the poem may begin to
shape itself in fragments of musical rhythm, and its
structure will first appear in terms of something analogous to musical form.' This is the first feature of a
poem to win the reader's or listener's interest. It is
in part 'a language of enticement' - a way of expressing
what one has to say in a manner that will hold the reader
and persuade him to examine the statement. In fact,
according to Eliot, certain poets even find it expedient
to occupy their conscious minds primarily 'with the
cratsman's problems, leaving the deeper meaning to emerge,
if there, from a lower level' - either direct to the
intelligence or indirectly by suggestion. But we must
never lose sight of the fact that 'music of verse is inseparable from the meanings and associations of words.'

It is not the poet's part to offer recommendations
toward a reading of his work. By so doing he would limit
its suggestive power. But for a critical approach to an
unfamiliar poem, after our first, immediate response, a
consideration of its meaning is essential - that is to
say, an examination of its fundamental reference points
and its allusive materials. This is one sound way to
reach the structural skeleton of a poem. The skeleton by
itself has no life - no value '*qua* work of art'; nor can
such a skeleton ever be outlined clearly. With the true
poet, the interplay of thought and the words that express
it attain the condition of a dance, valuable to watch in
itself. A dancer in his movements does not *do* anything
or *go* anywhere. In Paul Valéry's words"

> Si le sens et le son (ou si le fond et la forme) se
> peuvent aisément dissocier, le poeme se *décompose*.
> Conséquence capitale: les 'idées' qui figurent dans
> une oeuvre poétique n'y jouent pas le même rôle, ne
> sont pas du tout des *valeurs de même espèce*, que les
> 'idées' de la prose.

('If the sense and the sound, or if content and form, can
be easily separated, the poem disintegrates. Chief consequence: the 'ideas' which figure in a poetic expression
do not play the same role there, are not at all values of

the same sort, as ideas in prose.')

For poets such as Eliot, however, there must be some
basic schema of 'meaning' - a scaffolding to support their
structures as they build them, an armature around which
their materials may take form. Intentional associations
give definition and stability to their expressions through
which unintentional suggestions and associations prolifer-
ate to give them their textures of detail. And only by a
chart of 'meaning' can the reader find his bearings among
the incidental details of a poem so as to be able to judge
the author's organization of them. The working out of
such a chart will, and should, differ with every reader.
But its delineation is a necessary step in any intelligent
reading after our initial sensory response to a poem. And
with a true poem such a schema need not in any way limit
the freedom or variety of response to the details which in
their individual ambiguities and in the multiple interactions constitute the essence of poetic expression.

The publication of 'Little Gidding,' the fourth and
concluding section of T.S. Eliot's sequence initiated by
'Burnt Norton' in 1935, puts us finally in a position to
approach the poem as a whole. While each part, as it
appeared, seemed quite able to stand by itself, the publication of an additional section threw a fresh light on
certain points of significance, or qualities undiscerned
in the previous ones. At the same time certain themes
and ideas of the first three sections continued to run
parallel without achieving any finality or resolution.
The contrast of time and eternity; the anomaly of esteem-
ing temporal values in the face of eternal values -
appearances in the face of reality; the need for a renunciation of worldly desire for supernatural - the renunciation of 'the rose' for 'the Rose'; and the constant
stress on the omnipresence of pain, change and disillusionment. Sin and suffering were evidently natural to our
world. The situation was persistently restated in each
new section. Finally in 'Little Gidding' we find the
philosophical key to the whole sequence in the famous
words of Dame Julian of Norwich 'the devout ankress' of
the fourteenth century;

Synne is behovabil, but al shal be wel & al shal be
    wel and al manner of thyng shal be wele.

Or as Eliot, in accordance with various modernizations,
adapts it, in 'Little Gidding':

Sin is Behovely, but

> All shall be well, and
> All manner of thing shall be well.

Sin is inevitable, unescapable - 'behovely' in the four-
teenth-century use. But 'Adam's sin was the most harm
that was ever done.' For this Christ made the 'glorious
Satisfaction.' And in Dame Julian's words: 'this Amends-
making is more pleasing to God and more worshipful, without comparison, than ever was the sin of Adam harmful.'
As E.I. Watkin says in 'The English Way': 'She sees sin as
God's scourge for our discipline. It humbles us and in-
creases our knowledge of His Love. For redeemed humanity
sin is also an occasion of greater good. "Sin is behovely," that is, it has its part in the Divine economy of
good.... God will bestow on redeemed mankind a better
gift than we should have enjoyed had man never fallen.'
   Christ, the second Adam, won redemption for man through
His Incarnation, 'that central paradox of Christian theology' - in the union of the Divine and the human, of Eternity and time. By this the User imparted virtue to the
instrument; the Final Cause operating through subsidiary
causes bestowed value on them, with the result that if a
man follows a route such as that indicated by St. John of
the Cross in 'The Ascent of Mount Carmel,' through 'The
Dark Night of the Soul,' in spite of sin and evil he may
yet know 'The Living Flame of Love.'

> And all shall be well and
> All manner of things shall be well
> When the tongues of flame ...

- that is, the love of God - the Pentecostal tongues which
are universally comprehensible by the spirit - 'are in-
folded,' with an echo of St. John of the Cross' Spiritual
Canticle -

> Into the crowned knot of fire

'And the fire' (love) 'and the rose' (desire) 'are one,'
as in the last canto of the 'Paradiso', when St. Bernard
discloses to Dante the Mystical Rose of divine union.
   Renunciation, humility - a recognition of the true
Reality behind appearance, of the Timeless beyond the
temporal - is the only way. And this by God's grace will,
in the words of the anonymous author of 'The Cloud of Unknowing', 'at the last help thee to knit the ghostly knot
of burning love betwixt thee and thy God, in ghostly one-
head and accordance of will.'

The theme of 'Little Gidding is love - the renunciation of temporal interests for a loving contemplation of
God. The title gives the lead at once. Little Gidding is
a small village in Huntingdonshire in England. There, in
the early part of the seventeenth century existed the only
house dedicated to the contemplative life within the Anglican Church. Nicholas Ferrar, its founder, was a man of
conspicuous talents. After an education at Clare Hall,
Cambridge, and several years of travel on the Continent,
he became actively connected with the Virginia Company.
When this Company was deprived of its patent in 1623
Ferrar turned his attention to politics and was elected to
Parliament. He was well on his way to a brilliant career
when suddenly, awakened by a miraculous preservation from
death in the Alps, he renounced the world and adopted a
life of obscurity and poverty in which he and his family
dedicated themselves wholly to God.
    In the opening lines of this last Quartet we have an
echo of the figurative associations of physical and spiritual seasons which introduced the 'Waste Land':

    April is the cruellest month, breeding
    Lilacs out of the dead land, mixing
    Memory and desire, stirring
    Dull roots with spring rain.

But here the image has primarily to do with light, spiritual and physical: 'A Vision of Spring in Winter' - Swinburne's 'ghost arisen of May before the May.' And in view
of the seventeenth-century associations of the poem's
title, this introductory emphasis on light at once recalls
the contrast of natural and supernatural light in Crashaw's 'Ode on the Epiphany' and its exploration of the
mysticism of the *via negativa* of 'the right ey'd Areo-
pagite.' For Richard Crashaw was one of Ferrar's close
friends. And the pseudo-Dionysius may be said to be a
fundamental inspiration of both Dame Julian and the
anonymous author of 'The Cloud' as well as the whole Vic-
torine tradition of contemplation.
    The experience of a bright day in a dark season for
Eliot is the particular through which he sets about to
suggest the universal. Like 'Midwinter Spring,' the
'eternal brightness of God' 'is its own season,' sempiternal - 'Suspended in time,' eternally present. It is
a promise

    ...of the new season.

In 'Murder in the Cathedral' the Tempter offered Thomas

Becket a promise of temporal pleasures to come in almost the same words.

> Spring has come in winter. Snow in the branches
> Shall float sweet as blossoms. Ice along the ditches
> Mirror the sunlight. Love in the orchard
> Send the sap shooting.

But here we have it as an analogue to an intimation of Divine Love, the ultimate reality of the universe. Just as the brief winter sun flames the ice with

> A glare that is blindness in the early afternoon

so God may 'send out a beam of ghostly light, piercing this cloud of unknowing that is between thee and Him.' ('The Cloud of Unknowing.') And such a sudden beam of enlightenment or intuition may leave us dazzled like the three kings in Crashaw's 'Ode on the Epiphany' - by

> A Darkness made of too much day.

In such a foretaste of Eternity, a promise of the Divine summer, sense is put aside: 'there is no earth smell,' - no interest in living things: this is the spring promise of a season outside Time. Similarly on a spring day in winter we may see the hedgerow

> blanched with transitory blossom
> Of snow ...
> ... neither budding nor fading
> Not in the scheme of generation.

Through the grace of God, a

> ...glow more intense than blaze of branch, or brazier,
> Stirs the dumb spirit: ...

This is God's love. And as we read in 'The Cloud of Unknowing,' there is 'a devout stirring of love that is continually wrought in his (man's) will, not by himself, but by the hand of Almighty God.' 'There occurs that most delicate touch of the Beloved, which the soul feels at times, even when least expecting it and which sets the heart on fire with love, as if a spark had fallen upon it and made it burn. Then the will in an instant, like one aroused from sleep, burns with the fire of love, longs for God, praises Him and the sweetness of love.' (St. John of the Cross: 'The Spiritual Canticle' XXV, 5.)

These stirrings are movements of grace. Still it is
the constant burden of 'The Cloud' and its companion
'Epistle of Privy Counsel' that they are a work in which
the will, or the soul, is industriously operating: 'a
naked intent stretching unto God,' 'a longing desire ever-
more working.' Or as Eliot says in quoting directly from
'The Cloud' (Chapter II) in the concluding section of
'Little Gidding,'

> With the drawing of this Love and the voice of this
>   Calling

> We shall not cease from exploration ...

'Contemplation is a great and a "perfect" state of
prayer. To arrive at it, sanctifying or habitual grace is
not enough; faith, hope and charity are not enough; there
is also required that touch of the finger of God's right
hand, and that quick response of the soul thereto, which
imply the active operation of the seven great gifts of the
Holy Ghost.' When the Holy Ghost descended on the
apostles after Christ's resurrection, 'suddenly there came
a sound from heaven as of a mighty wind coming.' (Acts of
the Apostles II, 1-2.) But the gifts of the Holy Ghost
come to the simple Christian informally:

> No wind, but pentecostal fire.

And 'it is the gifts of the Holy Spirit which pour on the
soul that exquisite and subtle light, that rapture of
attention, that spiritual sensibility, as if new senses
had been given us, which combine to elevate ordinary
meditation and affection into contemplation.' (Bishop
Hedley: 'Prayer and Contemplation,' quoted by Abbot
Butler, 'Western Mysticism.')
    According to the Neoplatonic school of Christian
writers, which included among others St. Augustine, the
pseudo-Dionysius, Meister Eckhart, Dame Julian, the
author of 'The Cloud of Unknowing,' and St. John of the
Cross, 'God so transcends as really to be unlike any
created thing.' (Philip H. Wicksteed: 'Dante and
Aquinas.') Any assertion as to God cannot possibly have
more than a partial or relative truth. To assert that
God is this or that would imply some limitation or exclu-
sion and so qualify His all-embracing Being or Super-
Being. 'We may indeed say with actual, not only relative,
truth that God is in-visible, that He is in-finite, in-
comprehensible, un-moved, for these are negatives and say
not what He is, but what He is not. Since you cannot

assert God to be this or that thing, or indeed any "quid" whatever, it follows that He is nothing (*nihil or nihil-um*).' (Wicksteed: *op. cit.*)

As a consequence of this belief, Dionysius the Areo-pagite and his followers in the *via negativa* 'taught that the return of the soul to God (its end and its beginning) is effected by successive denials and abstractions: the initiate must leave behind all things both in the sensible and in the intelligible worlds. Only in this way will he enter that darkness of nescience that is truly mystical, - the "Divine darkness" which surrounds God, the absolute Nothing which is above all existence and all reason,' that unimaginable summer beyond sense, that inapprehensible

Zero summer.

141. JOHN SHAND, AROUND 'LITTLE GIDDING', 'NINETEENTH CENTURY'

September 1944, vol. cxxxvi, 120-32

Shand wrote occasionally for the 'Criterion'.

> Obscurity in affection of words and indigested con-
> ceits, is pedantical and childish; but where it
> shroudeth itself in the heart of his subject, uttered
> with fitness of figure and expressive epithets, with
> that darkness will I still labour to be shadowed.
>   Chapman's Dedication of his Translation of
>   Ovid's 'Banquet of Sense.'

Poetry is not to be enjoyed, nor perhaps recognised as poetry, by careless readers; and pleasure and understanding grow only with acquaintance. We must labour to appreciate 'fitness of figure and expressive epithets,' and to illuminate 'that darkness' in which meaning may be shadowed. So far we may go with the old poet's proud statement. But is not his faintly arrogant tone a confession of conscious weakness? Surely poetry should create immediate joy? How may pleasure be increased and understanding deepened if at first reading of a poem there is more to bewilder than to enjoy? The question is raised by

all 'difficult' poetry, such as that of Chapman, who
several times announced that he wrote not for the vulgar;
that art was sacred and for the few. So he laboured to be
shadowed with that darkness of which he boasts, and
succeeded; and succeeded sometimes in deepening that darkness with the very obscurity he objects to. As a result
he was not and is not read by the many who, for instance,
read Shakespeare. Art is always for the few; and 'few'
and 'many' are relative terms; but 'many' is correctly
applied to the number of Shakespeare's readers in contrast
to the 'few' who read Chapman, excellent poet though he
be.

    Much of to-day's poetry - much of the little I have
read - seems to be shrouded by both kinds of that obscurity mentioned by Chapman: it suffers from 'affection of
words and indigested conceits,' and it appears to be written in cipher or in a private shorthand which is to be
decoded, if at all, only with fasting and prayer. Mr.
T.S. Eliot's poetry, for example. But one would say un-
hesitatingly that he is a true poet. It is a trifle late
to applaud Mr. Eliot's poetic gift, which by some has long
been recognised; one can hear the titter of amused laughter at one's effrontery; but better late than never - and
the author of 'Little Gidding' will not despise a sincere
if tardy compliment extracted from a prejudiced reader by
the beauty of his last published poem. What was it in
'Little Gidding' that so delighted one that anticipated
dislike became surprised admiration? First, the tone
moved a responsive sympathy. Parts of the poem 'meant'
nothing, one's understanding could not grasp what the
poet was saying - and this is still true after repeated
readings, though the area of one's perplexity has been
lessened; but one felt positive that the thought and emotion of the poem were such as a merely clever mind could
not conceive nor mean language express; and the poet's
choice and order of words were undeniably beautiful. The
surface was calm; but what intensity lay beneath, what
balanced forces had produced that profound stillness? It
seemed possible that what was 'difficult' in the poem was
caused by an inevitable compression of statement as well
as by a conscious condensation. Mr. Eliot has remarked
that the chief use of the 'meaning' of a poem, in the
ordinary sense, may be

    to satisfy one habit of the reader, to keep his mind
    diverted and quiet, while the poem does its work upon
    him.... But the minds of all poets do not work that
    way; some of them, assuming that there are other minds
    like their own, become impatient of this 'meaning'

which seems superfluous, and perceive possibilities of
intensity through its elimination....

In short, as Chapman neatly phrased it:

Beauty, like fire, compress'd more strength receives.

But what pleased one in 'Little Gidding,' what persuaded one to extract as much pleasure as further study
could produce, were those very sequences which kept the
mind diverted and quiet. For instance, the description of
a bright winter's day in the country, with which the poem
opens: a clear image, intensely seen and sharply reflected, though shadowed with thought, of one of those joyous
intervals of 'midwinter spring' when:

The brief sun flames the ice, on pond and ditches,
In windless cold that is the heart's heat,
Reflecting in a watery mirror
A glare that is blindness in the early afternoon.

Who reads the whole of this opening sequence must
surely confess that this is something at once old and new;
it is what we have all seen and felt but is here seen and
felt freshly. The reader may puzzle unsuccessfully over
some lines, such as the alliterative second line:

Sempiternal though sodden towards sundown.

or he may succeed, later, in explaining other lines, such
as 'cold that is the heart's heat' by remembering that
extreme cold and extreme heat can produce like effects,
such as wounding with burns. But whether the reader
succeeds or fails in his attempts to reduce certain lines
or sequences of lines in this poem to a rational meaning,
he must admit that the poet *appears* to be saying precisely
what he means. There is nothing vague or loose about his
sentence structure, and his language on the whole is
simple, and it is always correct. Mr. Eliot, of course,
is aware of his virtues; as he remarks in the poem
itself:

[Quotes CPP, p. 197, 'every word is' to 'not pedantic'.]

We may easily and profitably test his claim. As an
example of his use of common words one might choose:

[Quotes CPP, p. 197, 'any action' to 'equal duration'.]

These are simple words, as simple as those used by the
early translators of the Bible; only one word might give
the unlearned pause: illegible. The rhythm has an intricate grace, flowing easily with the thought and feeling.
Occasionally, the 'formal' words may hinder for a moment
the literate. For example:

Sin is Behovely

'Behovely' is not to be found in most dictionaries, but
obviously it derives from 'behove.' 'Sin is behovely' one
takes to mean that sin is something imposed on us, it is
what, being what we are, we must commit; it is what we
cannot escape or avoid; and since one word telescopes all
this meaning into three syllables it is neither pedantic
nor ostentatious; and its rarity rouses the mind to
attend to the commonplace: Man is born to sin.
A passage in the poem that also gave immediate delight
at first perusal is where the poem addresses 'a familiar
compound ghost' of himself - a phrase perhaps derived from
Shakespeare's 'affable, familiar ghost'. (a) Here the
poet achieves an extraordinarily felicitous marriage of
sense and emotion, of meaning and music. Sense and feeling
are sombre and sad, and are expressed with solemn,
melancholy bitterness. For example, these lines:

[Quotes 'Little Gidding', II, CPP, pp. 194-5, 'Since our
concern' to 'like a dancer"'.]

What one can be sure of after reading such verse as
this is that it is an individual and contemporary variation on a traditional theme and of a traditional form -
that is to say, that it expresses in a manner peculiar
to one what has been thought and felt by many; and that it
is blank verse which, while it would doubtless please
readers of any period since blank verse was written, is
unmistakably stamped to-day's and Mr. Eliot's. But after
noting, as of technical interest, that the diction is
never below the standard set by himself, and that throughout the passage there is a strict alternation of eleven
with ten syllables, one reflected, after enjoying these
lines, that the whole poem, and perhaps other poems by
Mr. Eliot, would yield a comprehensive pleasure. But as
I read the poems collected between 1909 and 1935 there was
so little to 'divert,' so much to bewilder, that I gave up
puzzling over what seemed a concatenation of apparently
significant but (to me) unintelligible statements which
'moved in measure.' Only some of the later poems seemed
to 'belong' to the writer of 'Little Gidding.' 'Burnt

Norton,' I could see, is spiritually and verbally related
to 'Little Gidding.' There is relation in the tone, the
thought, the feeling, the rhythm, the images or symbols,
the words. There is one line in 'Little Gidding' that is
repeated from the earlier poem:

> Quick now, here, now, always -

One observed this repetition while noting that the laughter of children hidden among leaves and the half-heard
sound of distant water are significant images to the poet.
In the first section of 'Burnt Norton':

> Go, said the bird, for the leaves were full of children,
> Hidden excitedly, containing laughter.

And in the conclusion of the same poem, which has the same
exquisite phrasing and delicate modulation as the conclusion of 'Little Gidding':

[Quotes 'Burnt Norton', V, CPP, p. 176, 'Sudden in a shaft,
to 'now, always - '.]

And in 'Little Gidding':

[Quotes 'Little Gidding', V, CPP, pp. 197-8, 'Through the
unknown' to 'now, always -'.]

And in 'The Family Reunion':

[Quotes 'The Family Reunion', I, ii, CPP, p. 309, 'you
seem' to 'Between two storms'.]

    Enough of these resemblances. Naturally, they are to
be found in the work of every poet, but are more quickly
noticed when the body of the work is not large. There
are, in these later poems, also passages that 'divert' the
mind of the reader while the poem does its work upon him
- or, as I would put it, vulgarly, there are passages
that to the common reader make sense. Anyone who enjoys
reading poetry should find pleasure in these lines from
'The Dry Salvages':

[Quotes 'The Dry Salvages', I, CPP, p. 185, 'The sea howl'
to 'and the seagull'.]

The poet's note explains that a 'groaner' is a whistling
buoy. Who that has been close to the sea, in a small
fishing boat, for instance, but has felt the menace and

heard the caress of waves breaking on water? The poet
then takes another 'sea-voice,' that of the bell-buoy
rolling in the swell, for more detailed treatment; and
there is pleasure in noting the technical skill with which
he embraces all of it in the compass of a sentence:

[Quotes 'The Dry Salvages', I, CPP, p. 185, 'And under the
oppression' to 'The bell'.]

When one reads such verse one is persuaded to read the
'difficult' parts with more attention, as any reader of
Mr. Eliot's critical essays, sensible that he is a man of
character and intellect and learning who has something to
say about literature and can say it clearly, is convinced
that his poetry, however 'difficult,' cannot be merely ingenious foolery designed to tickle the sophisticated and
to enrage the innocent. But as these remarks are at least
as much a personal confession of inadequate comprehension
of Mr. Eliot's poetry as an attempt to discover the 'meaning' of the particular poem under discussion, I feel bound
to state that the poetry that has fascinated me since
childhood, the only poetry with which I can truly say I am
familiar and about which I have read all that the better
critics have had to say, never presented the initial
obstacles to enjoyment and understanding that are found
in Mr. Eliot's poetry. Of Shakespeare's poetry my enjoyment and understanding have grown as I have grown - of
course, always within the limits of that unstretchable
tether to which one is tied by the measure of one's own
capability to grow. Of his poetry I can truly say that I
never had to take pains to enjoy and to understand, though
I have taken pains to increase my enjoyment and understanding. Perhaps one explanation is that Shakespeare
wrote the bulk of his poetry in plays; and the first rule
for a play is that it must 'mean' something to all sorts
of audience, including the least intelligent and the least
sensitive. Plot, action, characters, speech, all must be
immediately intelligible on the surface, whatever profun-
dities and obscurities lie below. 'Easy Shakespeare' is a
correct label for our greatest poet, in spite of the
libraries of comment and interpretation that prove what
depths are under that easiness as well as what mountains
of artificial difficulties scholars and pundits may raise
above it. But with much of Mr. Eliot's poetry I seem to
be reading some alien language, though the turns of speech
and the grammar are English. In various instances, however, after repeated readings, the meaning suddenly became
clear, and I realised humbly, that these seeming obscurities had been plain enough perhaps to one of quicker mind.

For some time I puzzled myself with the three rhymed
stanzas which open the second 'movement' of 'Little
Gidding.' Over and over again, I read:

[Quotes 'Little Gidding', II, CPP, p. 192, 'Ash on' to
'death of air'.]

The lines were beautiful, but what did they mean? I
tried to associate the final lines of each stanza:

This is the death of air.
This is the death of earth.
This is the death of water and fire.

with the theory of Heraclitus that (as Montaigne puts it)
'the death of fire is the generation of air, and the death
of air the generation of water.' Then I remembered
Hamlet's:

Imperious Caesar, dead and turn'd to clay
Might stop a hole to keep the wind away.

Of course, it was much the same thought as Mr. Eliot's.
He was saying, was he not? that the air is full of par-
ticles, which once belonged to living things. The second
stanza then partly explained itself to my dull understanding: The poet, having observed that the air itself is a
grave, points to that place of burial, that hole in the
earth, in which the human dust now suspended in the air
was once reverently covered, and from which it arose -
'earth to earth, ashes to ashes, dust to dust.' Then, at
last, I was able to connect these thoughtful rhymes with
the blank verse sequence that follows. The last stanza,
'Water and fire succeed The town, the pasture and the
weed,' surely referred to death *from* the air? The poet's
dialogue with the 'compound ghost,' which had hitherto
been framed in a setting vague and mysterious to me, was
seen to be taking place after the 'interminable night' of
a bombing raid, as he walked the pavement 'between three
districts whence the smoke arose.' The 'dark dove with
the flickering tongue' was (so it seemed to me) a poetical
expression for an aeroplane, and the 'blowing of the
horn,' which sounded 'in the disfigured street,' was the
note of the siren sounding the 'raiders passed' signal.
    Literary allusion is often a clue to Mr. Eliot's
verses, but the anxious reader must be well acquainted
with several modern languages as well as the classic
literatures if he would be certain that he has not lost
the trail of meaning. But I doubt, even when one has

traced such allusions, and can prove they have been consciously used, whether they are useful aids to interpretation.   In these lines from 'Burnt Norton,' for instance,
my knowledge of Chapman's poetry was sufficient to trace
various thefts from that poet; but this did not really
help me to fathom the meaning, which is perhaps clear
enough without a knowledge of Chapman to a more subtle
mind?

[Quotes 'Burnt Norton', II, CPP, p. 172, 'Garlic and' to
'among the stars'.]

   The punctuation carefully follows the printed text.
One dimly apprehends that there lies a meaning here, significant thought, but one cannot feel sure one has caught
it.   The fact, then, that the second line is derived from
a line in one of Chapman's plays does not help interpretation, especially when one does not understand Chapman's
line.   Certainly it seems odd that in these fifteen lines
there are at least two other concealed quotations from the
same poet.   You will find the unusual 'inveterate scars'
in Chapman's translation of the second of 'Petrarch's
Seven Penitential Psalms,' and in the same psalm is the
image of the boar below upon a soddened floor in contrast
with what is fair and light above:

   Raze, lord, my sins' inveterate scars.

   As clear as silver, seas shall roar
   Descending to that noisome sink
   Where every hour hell's horrid Boar
Lies plunged, and drown'd, and doth his vomits drink.

This is clear enough.   That these lines of Chapman
were consciously or unconsciously in Mr. Eliot's mind cannot well be doubted.   There is also an association, at
least to my mind, of the lines:

   Ascend to summer in the tree
   We move above the moving tree
   In light upon the figured lead.

with Marvell's clearer image and sweeter melody:

   Here at the fountain's sliding foot
   Or at some fruit-tree's mossy root,
   Casting the body's vest aside
   My soul into the boughs does glide;
   There, like a bird, it sits and sings,

> Then whets and claps its silver wings,
> And, till prepared for longer flight,
> Waves in its plumes the various light.

With these 'clues' to Mr Eliot's lines, do we see what
he 'means' more clearly? Perhaps the poet intends to suggest that the most precious and the least valued things
(whether garlic is the one or sapphires are the other
depends upon the point of view) derive from the same common mud; that the pulsation of animal blood is in related
rhythm to the movement of the stars and the rise of sap in
the vegetable creation; and that if the mind can grasp
this it can reconcile itself to all manifestations of
life, and to the universe. But perhaps the poet 'means'
something quite different, or would repudiate any rational
interpretation. He may have written these lines in a
state of enchanted delirium, or, recollecting such a
state, he may be trying to reproduce its emotional effect
upon the reader.

But it is time to approach 'Little Gidding' a little
nearer by asking: Why is the poem so called? There is no
note of explanation, and not much in the text to guide the
reader. One may find pleasure and interest in the poem,
as I hope I have clearly suggested, without knowing the
answer. Nevertheless, the poem is called 'Little Gidding';
there are delicately allusive references to the following
facts: Little Gidding is somewhere in England where there
is a chapel off the beaten track which was once visited
by a king and which the poet has visited for some special
reason. That is enough to rouse curiosity but not to
satisfy it. We must, then, make further inquiry, if only
because we feel that by doing so puzzling lines may become intelligible. But how long would the search exact
from the reader? Would he ever find an answer without good
luck or extraordinary pains? I cannot say because I was
given some of the necessary information by Mr. Desmond
MacCarthy, whose tribute to 'Little Gidding' persuaded me
to read it. He wrote:

> Little Gidding is, of course, the name of a lonely
> spot not far from Peterborough, where Nicholas Ferrar
> and his few followers in the reign of Charles I built
> a small plain chapel in which to worship undisturbed.
> Readers of history (or of 'John Inglesant') will recall
> that they were fervent Anglo-Catholics. Their chapel
> now stands in empty fields, near a few old farm build-
> ings. It is often visited by those who revere it for
> its associations....

I question only the critic's polite 'of course.' Why
give such useful information if it be not necessary.   It
is not to be taken for granted in a criticism; and I doubt
whether the poet may take it for granted.   So learned a
critic and poet as Dr. Johnson said of poetry: 'Every
piece ought to contain in itself whatever is necessary to
make it intelligible.'   Given even such a small clue as
Ferrar's name, and our interest in Mr. Eliot's poem may
induce us to find some relevant facts about Ferrar in
various books of reference. We may read, perhaps for the
first time, Shorthouse's well-known novel, in which
Ferrar and his household are seen in ideal light, radiant
with sanctity and good works. We may read 'The Ferrar
Papers,' a volume of the family documents and papers which
may have been the source of Mr. Eliot's interest in the
subject, and in which, with a little trouble, we may discover how very much the monastic austerity of life at Gidding was disliked by an ordinary piece of Eve's flesh who
was unlucky enough to marry one of the saints - John,
Nicholas Ferrar's brother, and with what comic speed she
fled to London when her husband's death released her. -
But not to digress, if Johnson's critical rule be sound,
it is surely a defect in 'Little Gidding' that there is so
little in the poem, and not even a prefatory note, to help
us discover why it is so called. Some explanation, a few
facts to mollify our ignorance, would prevent readers from
being needlessly puzzled by various lines in a poem which,
in its statement of religious and philosophical ideas, is
not in any case easy to comprehend.
   For example:
When it is known, to quote the preface to 'The Ferrar
Papers,' that Nicholas Ferrar 'holds a distinguished place
in the annals of the Church of England,' and that 'in
singleness of vision and completeness of achievement he
stands as the most original genius in the Church during
the vital period of her post-Reformation history'; when it
is known that the holy community he formed had its ridiculous aspect - they would gravely discuss, for instance,
whether a mother should kiss her own child, or whether a
coffin was not a more suitable garment for an ascetic to
wear even than a shroud; when it is known that Charles I
visited Gidding in secret one night just before he surrendered himself to the Scottish army; and that the Puri-
tans in power regarded these Catholic Protestants at Gidding as virtually Papists, and dispersed them, so that
some fled to the Continent, but all remained spiritually
if not physically united when so many of their countrymen
were engaged in fratricidal strife; when we remember, however vaguely, that the Civil War was as much a religious

as a civil commotion, and that not only Strafford and his
royal master but also Archbishop Laud went to the block,
whereas the Puritan Milton died in his bed; and when we
remember that the Anglo-Catholic or High Church party is
still opposed by Puritan opinion in this country - then
we begin to understand why Mr. Eliot writes, of Ferrar's
chapel:

[Quotes 'Little Gidding', III, CPP, pp. 195-6, 'If I think,
again' to 'than the dying?' and 'We cannot restore' to
'a single party'.]

When it is known that Ferrar is to-day a spiritual
influence in the Anglican Church, and that the chapel he
built, in which he and his followers prayed day and night,
still stands near farm buildings in rural solitude, and
is visited, not for its historical interest or architect-
ural beauty by gaping tourists, but only by the devout because of its saintly memories, and because Ferrar died and
was buried there - then one begins to appreciate the significance of such lines as:

It would be the same, when you leave the rough road
And turn behind the pig-sty to the dull facade
And the tombstone. And what you thought you came for
Is only a shell, a husk of meaning
From which the purpose breaks only when it is fulfilled
If at all ...
                    ...You are not here to verify,
Instruct yourself, or inform curiosity
Or carry report. You are here to kneel
Where prayer has been valid.

Without knowing the few facts one has here gathered and
set down, how could any reader hope to understand what the
poet is saying? Knowing them, how can he fail to enjoy
the skill with which the poet uses them? I say nothing of
the verbal beauty of any of these extracts, which I take
to be evident to any sensitive reader. Nor does it seem
necessary to point out such literary allusions as

Of no immediate kin or kindness

in which most will recognise Hamlet's:

A little more than kin and less than kind.

Thus one might go on, trying to elucidate the text. I
would submit that in perusing poems of this author,

Johnson's observation on the metaphysical poets seems
peculiarly apt:

> The mind is exercised either by recollection or
> inquiry; either something already learned is to be re-
> trieved, or something new is to be examined. If their
> greatness seldom elevates, their acuteness often sur-
> prises; if the imagination is not always gratified, at
> least the powers of reflection and comparison are em-
> ployed....

But how, one may humbly ask, how is a reader to 're-
trieve something' he has never learned? Alas, these poets
disregard the unlearned. If you are not a scholar, they
will not speak with you. The reader who knows the legend
of the shirt of Nessus will inevitably peruse with more
interest lines which must be without meaning to those ignorant of the legend or to those - perhaps not a few - who
do not as they read catch the allusion:

> Who then devised the torment? Love.
> Love is the unfamiliar Name
> Behind the hands that wove
> The intolerable shirt of flame
> Which human power cannot remove....

Johnson's remarks on the metaphysical poets seem
appropriate because his verdict, which on the whole was
against them, cannot be questioned on the ground that he
was ignorant of what they were trying to do: he was at
least as learned as they; and another reason to quote
Johnson is that the situation created for the common
reader by the poetry of Mr. Eliot and by other contemporary poets, closely resembles, it seems to me, the situation described by Johnson in his 'Life of Cowley':

> ...About the beginning of the seventeenth century
> appeared a race of writers that may be termed the
> *metaphysical poets*. The metaphysical poets were men
> of learning, and to show their learning was their
> whole endeavour ... their learning instructs, and their
> subtlety surprises; but the reader commonly thinks his
> improvement dearly bought, and though he sometimes
> admires, is seldom pleased.

Mr. Eliot may confidently be described as a poet who is
excited by metaphysical ideas. The idea of time, for
example, is one that seems to haunt him. At whatever he
is looking, on whatever subject his thoughts are fixed, at

his back he seems always to hear:

Time's winged chariot hurrying near,

and to see before him:

Deserts of vast eternity.

Time as a measure: time as that 'timeless moment' which is
eternity. Time that may be 'out of joint,' time that
'delves deep parallels in beauty's brow,' clock time, geo-
logical or stellar time: time as God's time, which is no
time, and so passes out of the confines of language. Thus
when, in 'Little Gidding,' the poet writes:

                        A people without history
   Is not redeemed from time, for history is a pattern
   Of timeless moments,

we may, if we choose, pause to inquire how a moment, which
is a measure of time, may properly be described as timeless? We may, if we choose, say that here the poet strains
the language into ambiguity, though we may confess that
what we feel he means is almost inexpressible. To approach
Mr. Eliot's ideas of time, and to sympathise with his preoccupation, it may be helpful to remember certain Greek
philosophers through the medium of some sentences in
Florio's translation of Montaigne's great essay, An Apolo-
gie of Raimond Sebond:

   The Stoicks affirme, there is no present time, and
   that which we call present, is but conjoyning and
   assembling of future time and past.

In much the same words, Mr. Eliot writes in 'Burnt Norton':

   Time present and time past
   Are both perhaps present in time future,
   And time future contained in time past.
   If all time is eternally present
   All time is unredeemable.

Or, as he puts it more ornately, if less clearly, in 'The
Dry Salvages':

   That the future is a faded song, a Royal Rose, or a
      lavender spray
   Of wistful regret for those who are not yet here to
      regret,

> Pressed between the yellow leaves of a book that has
>   never been opened.
> And the way up is the way down, the way forward is the
>   way back.

And in 'Little Gidding' the contrast between the word, and
the meaning of time, as we commonly use it, and this
philosophic conception of time, is neatly telescoped into
the couplet:

> Here, the intersection of the timeless moment
> Is England and nowhere. Never and always.

The contrast is again presented in:

> What we call the beginning is often the end
> And to make an end is to make a beginning.
> The end is where we start from.

And a few lines later the poet finds what seems to me to
be his most beautiful expression of the contrast:

> The moment of the rose and the moment of the yew-tree
> Are of equal duration.

As Montaigne, who is quoting the Greek, observes:

> But then what is it, that is indeed? That which is
> eternall, that is to say, that which never had birth,
> nor ever shall have end; and to which no time can
> bring change or alteration. For time is a fleeting
> thing, and which appeareth as in a shadow, with the
> matter ever gliding, alwaies fluent, without ever being
> stable or permanent; to whom rightly belong these
> termes, *Before* and *After*: and it *Hath Beene*, or *Shall
> Be*. Which at first time doth manifestly show, that it
> [Time] is not a thing which is; for, it were a great
> sottishnesse, and apparent false-hood, to say, that
> that is which is not yet in being, or that already hath
> ceased from being. And concerning these words, *Pre-
> sent, Instant, Even Now,* by which it seemes, that
> especially we uphold and principally ground the intel-
> ligence of time; reason discovering the same, doth
> forthwith destroy it: for presently it severeth it a
> sunder and divideth it into future and past time, as
> willing to see it necessarily parted in two.'

A better explanation of Mr. Eliot's poetical musings
upon the mystery of time could not, perhaps, easily be

found; and its seems probable that he has indeed read this
essay of Montaigne's with some attention. A poet who
engages himself and his readers in such questions is
obviously to be called a metaphysical poet, and, as
Johnson said of such poets:

> To write on their plan, it was at least necessary to
> read and think. No man could be born a metaphysical
> poet, nor assume the dignity of a writer, by descrip-
> tions copied from descriptions, by imitations borrowed
> from imitations, by traditional imagery, and hereditary
> similes, by readiness of rhyme, and volubility of
> syllables.

In brief, no poetasters may hope to exhibit their feeble or
synthetic talents in such a difficult and laborious poetry.
The triflers and the earnest mediocrities and the specious
writers should confine themselves to conventional forms.
This may be true, on the whole; but we may justly suspect
that in a form of writing in which what is genuine is not
easy to understand, what is not genuine will be written in
the hope to deceive. No kind of poetry is proof against
the mockery of imitation; and the merely clever may surely
be as emptily ingenious in metaphysical poetry as they may
be sweetly vacuous in lyric poetry. Indeed, Johnson admits
as much when he remarks of Cowley and his school that:
'When their reputation was high, they had undoubtedly more
imitators than time has left behind.'
    That a true metaphysical poet should be also a man of
learning perhaps follows of course. Of Mr. Eliot, as of
Cowley, it may be said, 'without any encomiastic fervour,'
that he brings 'to his poetic labours a mind replete with
learning, and that his pages are embellished with all the
ornaments that books could supply.' He earned the degree
of Doctor of Literature at one famous university, and he
was accorded the honour of that title by three other universities. He is a man of languages, and 'hath a mint of
phrases in his brain' from the ancient and modern European
literatures. To an unlearned reader, the perusal of such
a poem as 'The Waste Land' suggests that the author, as
Moth irreverently said, has 'been at a great feast of
languages, and stolen the scraps.' In this poem, according
to his own notes, Mr. Eliot quotes from or makes allusion
to the following: Ezekiel, Ecclesiastes, Sappho, Virgil,
Buddha, an Upanishad, Dante, Baudelaire, Shakespeare,
various other Elizabethan dramatists, St. Augustine,
Marvell, Verlaine, 'Tristan und Isolde,' and other authors
and subjects, including Frazer's 'The Golden Bough.' And
in addition to this immense library of reference attached

to a short poem, the author recommends the inquisitive
reader to study J.L. Weston's book on the Grail Legend,
'From Ritual to Romance,' as this work 'will elucidate the
difficulties of the poem much better than my notes will
do,' - that is, of course, if the reader considers 'such
elucidation worth the trouble.'

It may justly be said of Mr. Eliot, then, that he is a
man of learning who 'shows' his learning. In 'The Waste
Land,' and similar poems, therefore, his subtlety cannot
surprise, his learning cannot instruct, without the erec-
tion of a formidable apparatus of investigation, if then;
and the reader, as the great critic said of Cowley, and as
Mr. Eliot hints of Mr. Eliot's poem, may think 'his
improvement dearly bought.' In a fit of temper, caused
doubtless by an unpleasant feeling of inferiority, the unlearned and the impatient may well be tempted to dismiss
all such poetry as a new kind of complicated cross-word
puzzle. A poet may write poetry in this way because he
cannot help it, or with the conscious intention to give
its meaning only to those who deserve to know it, or
deliberately to mystify every reader; in any case, he knows
he must thereby confine what pleasure there may be in his
poetry to a small circle. But we who are outside the
circle may remind ourselves that to write for a coterie is
sooner or later to write for a coterie within a coterie;
and that the tendency of the very erudite and the super-
subtle is to grow so refinedly subtle and so heavy with
erudition that the audience at last reached - or declined
to - is single and singular, the author himself at last
being the only person able to understand what he is saying.
To exclude the common reader is to exclude posterity. For
we are to remember, to make a final quotation from Johnson,
that 'by the commonsense of readers, uncorrupted by literary prejudices, after all the refinements of subtilty and
the dogmatism of learning, must be finally decided all
claims to poetical honours.'

Note

a   Sonnet 86. Believed to refer to Chapman.

'Four Quartets'

New York, 11 May 1943; London, 31 October 1944

142. CHARLES WILLIAMS, A DIALOGUE ON MR. ELIOT'S POEM,
'DUBLIN REVIEW'

April 1943, vol. ccvii, 114-22

Williams (1886-1945), novelist, essayist and playwright,
worked for the Oxford University Press. Eliot admired his
work and wrote an introduction to his novel, 'All Hallows'
Eve' (1948). Eliot also wrote the unsigned obituary for
Williams in 'The Times' (17 May 1945), 7.

This dialogue is a consideration of the four poems
which make up 'Four Quartets', though they had not yet
been published as one work.

It is (said Eugenio, as he laid down 'Little Gidding') a
most difficult poem to read aloud with a proper sensitiveness.

Nay, sir (answered Nicobar, in a youthful kindness of
condescension), I protest you have done nobly, and Mr.
Eliot, did he know, were indebted to you. A precise judge
could not complain of anything beyond, here and there,
somewhat of a greater rhetorical emphasis than the poem
requires.

A fine thing, Nicobar (said Sophonisba, a little
sharply), if you are to complain of rhetoric. It was you
who, when you did us the kindness to read 'The Dry Salvages', seemed to attempt all the sounds of the sea.

Nicobar: Nay, madam (said he), I did but speak impar-
tially. You are to consider that this last poem peculiarly removes itself from mortality, and is more like the

cry of a strange bird flying over that sea from a coast
beyond it than anything in the sea itself. But I ask
Eugenio's pardon if I have wronged him.

Sophonisba: What say you, Celia?

Celia had seemed in a study all this while, and now at
first she said only:

Celia: Let us draw the curtains. There may be birds
from beyond another sea tonight whose rhetoric would be
less quiet than Nicobar approves. (And when this had been
done, she went on.) But in truth, though I do not think
Eugenio could have managed better, yet I am partly of
Nicobar's mind.

At this they both smiled and flushed a little, being
young and greatly affecting each other's person and judgement. But Sophonisba said:

Sophonisba: I do not know what you would have. Do you
suppose one can express the soul by a monotone?

Celia: If Eugenio will pardon me, and I very well know
that none of us three could more properly have satisfied
the ear than he, I will say only that soliloquies from the
heart's cloister are ever the most difficult poems to read
aloud - perhaps because they have in them something which
contains a greater urgency even than poetry, but which is
not poetry, or at least troubles us as if it were not.
And while I listened to Eugenio, I was almost ashamed, as
if I were eavesdropping, outside the door, to the murmurs
of the prayers of some saint within.

Sophonisba: That is all very well, Celia, but you are
to consider that Mr. Eliot would not wish to be taken for
a saint, and if he has published his poem he has himself
most certainly opened the door, so that we shall do him a
double wrong to embarrass him with such comparisons.

Nicobar: Why, true, Sophonisba, but look at what you
are saying. A poet may produce, _per accidens_, an effect
different from his purpose, and it would be hard to refuse
to recognize an accent of the soul for fear of overprais-
ing his own. There are examples of it in English verse.
No one, to be sure, would call Patmore a saint, yet I have
felt sometimes in the Odes which he wrote of Psyche that I
was intruding on a holy dispute for which I was not fit.
Eugenio may perhaps tell us his mind now without thinking
that Celia and I are to discredit his reading.

Eugenio: Nay, I hope we are all too wise to suppose
that either verse or reading of verse is to be left free
from judgement. And I think, if Celia will pardon me,
that her modesty does but make her the fitter listener.
It is said _He that hath ears, let him hear_, and the undertones of our lord the Spirit are permissible for such intimate ears.

Sophonisba: Well, I think you are all making a great
pother about a simple thing -
Celia: ⎫
Nicobar: ⎭   A simple thing! O Sophonisba!

Sophonisba: - and for my part, if we are to talk so, it
was more a sermon than a prayer, and I will rather thank
Mr. Eliot for an edifying instruction than pretend he has
gone out of his pulpit into his oratory. I have heard my
mother read as good an exhortation by the great Mr. Donne
on a Sunday afternoon. But you young people do not read
Donne.

Nicobar: Not read Donne! He was my pocket companion
for long enough.

Sophonisba: Until Hopkins came in, I warrant. Poetry
goes more by fashion than by favour. But some of your
elders were familiar with ancient poets before we were
taught them by Mr. Eliot's camp-followers. We had heard,
too, of those exhortations, which of late are sieved in a
pretty cullender of critical taste, so as to let through
the dust of literature and keep out the gold nuggets of
the soul. Only here it is strangely the dust which is
prized and the nuggets thrown away.

Celia: Dear madam, we have heard you before now on your
Dean. Would it please you to return to Mr. Eliot?

Sophonisba: Ay, child, you must ever have the new manners. You will be talking of him one day as I do now of
Donne; nay, I have heard that some younger than you - to
think of it! - speak of him already as of yesterday's
load; and even those who were once his partisans suppose
him to have flown off into hiding and clapped-to his
wings in a church for want of other resting-place.

Eugenio: It is one of the strange diseases of our age -
yours and mine, Sophonisba, for these young ones are clear
of it - that so positive a mind should have been counted a
negative. Those who supposed him disillusioned spoke perhaps wiser than they knew, for he stood from the beginning
on a bare solidity. Few poets change much - and he less
than some, except indeed in language. How did he put it?
Reach me the poem, Nicobar.

[Quotes 'East Coker', V, CPP, p. 182, 'Trying to learn'
to 'on the inarticulate'.]

Poets, more than most, have their 'ends in their beginnings', their 'beginnings in their ends'. Only by running
very hard, as the Red Queen in Mr. Carroll's tale saw, can
they so much as stay where they are.

Celia: Is that moment, the moment of running and
remaining, what he talks of in those passages of 'Burnt
Norton'? As

...say that the end precedes the beginning,
And the end and the beginning were always there
Before the beginning and after the end.

Eugenio: The co-existence of the end and the beginning
in the work of poets is perhaps an image of something
more, and more general. Few poets have been able to go
all their distance; in any who have won to an end, and not
to a mere breaking-off, we may be aware that there is but
one thing said. I would not prophesy how noble or how
lasting a poet Mr. Eliot may prove to be, but, lesser or
greater, he is one who will have gone, it seems, all his
distance. I speak only of his art.
  Celia: Might you not speak of more?
  Eugenio: No, I would not dare it even of you with whom
I have had some close acquaintance, though I take pleasure
to think so privately. Nicobar may indeed write you a
poem – and he justly – admiring your spirit's perseverance,
for at his age such things are a joyous courtesy. But at
mine I do you the more honour to recognize your serious
duty and the necessity of your zeal. Or say I have talked
with the apparition in our poet's fourth poem.
  Sophonisba: Do you think, Eugenio, that that is the
finest passage?
  Eugenio: It is, perhaps, for reasons, the most sustained
towards fineness. And you?
  Sophonisba: I am no true judge of greatness. But I love
better the opening of 'East Coker' – the lane and the dancing round the bonfire and 'the time of the seasons and the
constellations'. And the fourth movement of the other
poem, 'The Dry Salvages,' which begins 'Lady, whose shrine
stands on the promontory'.
  Nicobar: It is lovely. And you, Celia?
  Celia: I do not very well know. I think it is the manner of incantation in each poem that I love best, and if
Eugenio says that the last is the greatest I shall easily
believe him. But for myself I think I love the other best,
'Burnt Norton,' and all the birds and children, the
flowers and sunflower, the footfalls echoing

Down the passage which we did not take
Towards the door we never opened
Into the rose-garden.

Do not, dear madam, smile at me so tenderly. I am more
than content not to have taken it. I have known more.

                    After the kingfisher's wing
Has answered light to light, and is silent, the light
  is still

At the still point of the turning world.

Nicobar: Celia!
Celia: O Nicobar!
Nicobar: But when he says

That which is only living
Can only die –

may we say that only that which does not live, as we mean
living, will not die? Is everything else only 'the loud
voice of the disconsolate chimera'? How ridiculous and
how right a phrase! Eugenio?

Eugenio: I would answer you if I were not afraid. But
suppose that I am one of the foolish elders he talks of?
Might I not, affirming it, offer you merely 'a recipe for
deceit'? It is your poem as much as mine.

Celia: I do not think you would deceive us unless we
chose, and it would not then be for want of warning. He
has taught us not to rely only on process. Read again,
Nicobar; there, look!

Nicobar:

We are only undeceived
Of that which, deceiving, can no longer harm.

Sophonisba: It is a terrible saying.
Celia: I do not think it so terrible – even if it were
true. But I am not quite sure that it is true, so long as
one remembers that other saying – where is it? – about the
action in the mind at the moment of death being that which
should fructify in the lives of others, 'and the time of
death is every moment'.

Sophonisba: We are quoting our way through the poem.
Eugenio: It is the only valid way unless we were master-
critics. Or poets whose own poems might answer his.

Celia: Mr. Eliot's little body may by now be aweary of
the great world of poets who do.

Nicobar: But, Eugenio, if we quote here and there and
out of place, do we not alter the whole order, and make
the poem something different than it was? I could even
play tricks with Celia's only Wordsworth so.

Eugenio: We can only remember to return always to the
original; in that end is our beginning and in that beginning our end. We must alter our order back again. For it
is true we must say after every critic, however good, that

There is only the fight to recover what has been lost.

Nicobar: It will be a merry world in the grand art of poetry when every critic remembers that and so welcomes his next successor, and unloves his own particular. I cannot say that I see much business of the kind on foot at present.

Sophonisba: You said, Eugenio, that every poet who covered all his distance has said only one thing. Tell us, if you will, what you think Mr. Eliot has said.

Eugenio: I see it was a great rashness, and I must prepare to welcome you three my successors. But if you will have it in a poor phrase - that you can only be a thing by becoming it.

Celia: May I remind you, Eugenio, that he has been called a learned, difficult, and obscure poet?

Eugenio: With reason - and even now with reason. I am not to remind you that the simplest things are obscure to most men and difficult to all. I have known Nicobar once or twice expect a short cut, a metamorphosis as quick as Arachne's, or as a more heavenly could I but think of a comparison. Virtue and wisdom may sit with us at our feasts and walk with us on our roads; they may even smile upon us so intimately that we take them for our very hearts' masters, but all time is between them and us unless we have given ourselves to the change, and always the change. We may otherwise find on our death-day how alien they are; or if before, when we are old enough to know our harvest only deceit,

> only the knowledge of dead secrets
> Useless in the darkness into which we peer.

I must alter the case to apply the words; he wrote 'they peered'. Old men are like poets; few go the whole distance. It was Bunyan, I think, who set a slumbering-ground far beyond battles and martyrdoms; but the vigil must be for one knows not what.

[Quotes 'East Coker', III, CPP, p. 180, 'I said to my soul, be still, and wait' to 'the dancing'.]

Celia: The stillness is the dancing. Movement is all within the stillness, that is true, and that is the difference between such a moment and all else. 'Love is itself unmoving'. Is that 'the redemption of time'?

Eugenio: What will you tell her, Sophonisba?

Sophonisba: I am not as oracular as you. But I know that the greatest moments are those whose movement is within them - yes, even all our little bodily movements.

Nicobar: 'The last apparent refuge, the safe shelter'.

Those moments are not shelters, because of the interior
dance.
   Sophonisba: Love is not a shelter.
   Nicobar: You spoke, Eugenio, of the apparition in the
fourth poem, or rather in the fourth part of the whole
poem. Will you not discourse to us on it at more length?
   Eugenio: I could say little that would make it more
effective, and I might be too apt to catch the sad note
of exposition, than which I can imagine nothing our poet -
poeta nostra - would more dislike. We have not spoken of
his allusions, which (if one knows them) enlarge his poem
from within. But there is one here we must not altogether
pass. 'What! are *you* here?' - there is only one place in
all Christendom where that cry was heard, and that was out
of Christendom. Do you remember, Nicobar?
   Nicobar: I had forgotten - till now. '*Siete voi qui,
Ser Brunetto*?' But why is the baked countenance of Brunetto Latini remembered here?
   Eugenio: There is fire in the distance here - in 'three
districts', as in that other place it fell from the dark
skies; and here it is the time of 'the recurrent end of
the unending', much as the torments of Dante's hell in each
moment become again recurrently unending. But we were not
perhaps meant too closely to hunt out comparisons; or if,
I am not the one to do it. Let us observe only how that
terrible remembrance accentuates the cry, and how the dialogue between the poet and the apparition,

            a familiar compound ghost
     Both intimate and unidentifiable,

however different, is awfully undershaken by the Italian.
The whole passage, correctly or incorrectly - or I will
say wisely or unwisely - seems to me full of infernal
reminiscence, though the English poet is ostensibly speaking of time ending here and not of time unending there -
and yet his words reverberate through the monotonous funnel of hell; indeed, the funnel is here. Listen:

[Quotes 'Little Gidding', II, CPP, pp. 194-5, 'Since our
concern' to 'blowing of the horn'.]

Is not that a proper summary of the dark journey from
Styx to Judecca? And is there anywhere a greater word for
the deepening yet monotonous perpetuity of the lost than

     From wrong to wrong the exasperated spirit
     Proceeds?

Sophonisba: I have seen it said somewhere that the last line - 'And faded on the blowing of the horn' - has a relevance to 'Hamlet' - 'It faded on the crowing of the cock'.

Eugenio: It may well be so, for there has been a reference to the 'refining fire' of that purgatory in which the ghost of the elder Hamlet dwelled. But you are also to remember that, below the sand where Brunetto Latini ran, there was indeed a horn:

Ma io senti' sonare un alto corno.

And on that sounding Dante saw Nimrod, who held the horn and had destroyed speech, and the other giants and the last pit.

Sophonisba: You would say that that is what Mr. Eliot had in mind?

Eugenio: I would not take upon me to assert it. But I do not conceive that a mind pre-eminently stored with such learning is likely to have been unaware of such clear propinquities of meaning.

Nicobar: I remember your saying once, Eugenio, that this poet had, as it were, one moment which he put in many different lights, and I remember also that you compared the Eternal Footman in 'Prufrock' to the Dweller on the Threshold in a more ancient myth -

Sophonisba: What moment?

Eugenio: Alas, I have said so much that I do not clearly remember.

Celia: But I do. There was no particular kind of moment; it was then a moment in itself - any moment of time. And you quoted a line about the inability 'to force the moment to its crisis'. And I think, Eugenio, you rather hinted that you were waiting for Mr. Eliot to do so.

Eugenio: I hope, with a greater shyness than you seem to give me. But if -

Celia: Sir, you were as courteous as ever.

Eugenio: It is yours to keep me so. But 'force' for this poetry is too violent a word. It seems that there is a change; for now this crisis is within the moment. Most poets begin with man in a situation; presently man is himself the situation; that is, in them, not an increase of knowledge but a mounting power of style. That is true of poetry, and more than poetry. The grace of time is to turn time to grace.

If all time is eternally present
All time is unredeemable.

And again,

> The hint half guessed, the gift half understood, is
>   Incarnation.

Sophonisba: *The* Incarnation?
Eugenio: Do not let us say more than he. Our pious
meditations may take what hints they choose, but let us
keep them separate from our poetic. We wrong the poetry
else, and we do not much help religion. Say only,

> With the drawing of this Love and the voice of this
>   Calling.

Celia: And all else only 'the loud voice of the disconsolate chimera'.
Eugenio: Either that or the end of his 'Ash-Wednesday'
- 'And let my cry come unto thee'. Leave it; we shall not
end better than with those two lines.
Celia: Shall we go, Nicobar? Good night, Sophonisba;
good night, Eugenio; and may the wish not be the voice of
the chimera, but come with the cry where the cry comes.
Good night again, and blessings.

143. HORACE GREGORY, FARE FORWARD, VOYAGERS, 'NEW YORK
TIMES BOOK REVIEW'

16 May 1943, 2

It has been said in certain quarters, thoughtlessly, I
think, that the years of the present World War have
failed to produce memorable poetry, and it has been implied that poetry in some mysterious way has failed to
live up to great occasions. With Mr. T.S. Eliot's 'Four
Quartets' before me I wish to modify the gloomy accusa-
tion that the better poets of our time have been
'irresponsible' or have failed to realize the seriousness
of living through a difficult hour. For the past twenty
years distinguished writers in England and in the United
States have been aware of the potential existence of
another world war, and they have warned their readers of
its hidden forces long before its actual events took
place, and in that sense most of the best poetry written
in the present generation continues to be 'war poetry.'

It has been Mr. Eliot's destiny to anticipate, without
seeming overtly prophetic, the mutations of feeling which
have taken place within the past twenty years, and his
perceptions have given him the right to speak with more
than merely personal authority when he writes the following statement into his 'Four Quartets'.

> So here I am, in the middle way, having had twenty
>   years –
> Twenty years largely wasted, the years of *l'entre deux
>   guerres.*

One recalls his 'Difficulties of a Statesman,' written
long before the Munich pact; one remembers its notes of
warning, its moments of satire, and its devotional spirit,
for Mr. Eliot has held to the promises he gave his readers
in 'Ash-Wednesday,' and has continued his progress through
the choruses of 'The Rock,' through the scenes of 'Murder
in the Cathedral,' and, most impressive of all, in his
present collection of four poems, each bearing a place-
name, 'Burnt Norton,' 'East Coker,' 'The Dry Salvages' and
'Little Gidding.'
     To us who read his 'Four Quartets,' what do the place-
names mean? They mean as much, let us say, as 'Tintern
Abbey' meant to readers of Wordsworth's early poetry; it
is enough to know that the place-name is rich in emotional
associations for the poet and whether or not the emotion
conveyed to the reader is genuine in quality. We may recognize East Coker as being on a guidebook route from
London to Exeter, with beautiful churches near by and
ancient factory yards, or The Dry Salvages as a small
group of rocks off our North Atlantic Coast, or, perhaps
more significantly, Little Gidding as an Anglican retreat,
the scene of Nicholas Ferrar's 'Protestant nunnery,' which
has been so memorably described in J.H. Shorthouse's
finely tempered historical romance, 'John Inglesant.' But
these recognitions may be used as the content of footnotes
merely to the four poems; one may photograph each place
with anxious care, and yet not feel the emotion that the
quartets with the melodic or lyrical interludes convey.
The poems must be read for the quality of their emotion
and its meaning – and I think I am not wrong when I say
that the 'Four Quartets' (without being in the least Words-
worthian) represent the best poetry of their kind since
Wordsworth wrote 'The Prelude.'
     One remembers that 'The Prelude' was somewhat portent-
ously subtitled 'Or Growth of a Poet's Mind: An Autobiographical Poem,' and though it is almost needless to say
that Mr. Eliot's 'Four Quartets' are not intended to

sustain so weighty and so pretentious a claim upon the
reader's interest in the philosophy of poetic composition,
it is true that Mr. Eliot's new book contains a recapitulation of very nearly everything he has written since 'The
Waste Land' made its controversial appearance in the
'Dial' in 1922. I think it can be said that there is
nothing more dangerous than the attempt of a highly respected and gifted poet to imitate himself, to improve
upon his original impulses and their expression - yet this
is precisely what Mr. Eliot has done in the writing of his
'Four Quartets,' and he has succeeded where many another
poet has lapsed into mere repetitiousness or dullness. In
'Burnt Norton' (which, by the way, was the last of his
poems in his 'Collected Poems, 1909-1935' and is reprinted
here as the first of the four quartets), he greatly enriched the devotional premises of 'Ash-Wednesday': and
with the completion of 'Little Gidding' we now know that
the earlier poem was the first in a new vehicle of expression for Mr. Eliot's characteristic themes. And among
them, not the least important is:

     Seek only there
     Where the grey light meets the green air
     The hermit's chapel, the pilgrim's prayer.

However closely certain passages in the new poems may
seem to echo the choruses of 'The Rock' and of 'Murder in
the Cathedral,' or lines within the last scene of 'The
Family Reunion,' Mr. Eliot's quartets convey an impression
of a newly awakened insight and of a control that seldom
fails to delight the mind and eye and ear. Let us take
the concluding passage of the third section of 'The Dry
Salvages,' with its emotional temper reawakening the dis-
courses between Krishna and Arjuna of the 'Bhagavadgita';
and if one is so inclined, one may read a timely meaning
into the cadences of what seems a timeless utterance:

[Quotes 'The Dry Salvages', III, CPP, p. 188, 'O voyagers'
to 'forward, voyagers']

And we might well say that this is Mr. Eliot's mature
and deeply affirmative answer to his 'Death by Water'
passage in 'The Waste Land.' More important than these
considerations is the beauty of the new statement and its
depth of feeling, for I happen to believe that the value
of Mr. Eliot's sensibilities has been vastly underrated in
favor of paying further tribute to his ingenuity and his
acknowledged scholarship. His work is of a character that
gives a pedant unholy delight in searching out its sources,

and while such labors are not without their rewards, they
tend to become irrelevant to the poetic gift which endows
the following lyric from 'Little Gidding' with such brilliantly inspired felicity:

[Quotes 'Little Gidding', IV, CPP, p. 196, 'The dove' to
'either fire or fire'.]

   I submit this quotation as one of the finest lyrics
written in our time; and for those who wish to take heart
as against others who are convinced that poetry was among
the early casualties of the present war, I strongly recommend a reading of Mr. T.S. Eliot's 'Four Quartets.'

144. MALCOLM COWLEY, BEYOND POETRY, 'NEW REPUBLIC'

7 June 1943, vol. cviii, 767-8

T.S. Eliot's 'Four Quartets' is one of those rare books
that can be enjoyed without being understood. I have
heard people of good judgment praising it and, in the same
breath, confessing that they didn't know what the poet
intended to say. Apparently he gave them a few noble
visions and a general impression of austerity, learning,
goodness and even saintliness. Reading the book for the
first time, I remembered the Swedenborgian sermons to
which I half-listened every Sunday morning during my boyhood; I didn't grasp their meaning, but I knew that Bishop
Pendleton was a good man and a scholar, and I went home to
dinner with a pleasurable feeling of elevation.
   Perhaps that is the best way of approaching 'Four
Quartets.' But if the reader insists on understanding as
well as admiring the book, he might begin with the article
on mysticism in the 'Encyclopedia Britannica'; or better
still by turning to the third chapter of Aldous Huxley's
'Gray Eminence,' which is perhaps the simplest statement
of the mystical way. If the nearest library has the
spring, 1941, issue of the 'Southern Review,' he might
also read the essay on 'East Coker' by James Johnson
Sweeney, who is a profound student and Scotland Yard
inspector of Eliot's later work.
   Even after this preparation, there are points that may
still escape the reader. My own difficulties began with
the second word of the title: why are these poems called

quartets? They seem to be spoken in a single voice, that
of the author, and each of them is divided into five
parts instead of four. The title of the first poem is
equally mysterious, considering that the three others have
now been explained by the author or his critics. East
Coker is supposed to be the birthplace of Sir Thomas
Elyot, author of 'The Boke Named the Gouvernour,' as well
as being the original home of the Eliot family as a whole.
It is therefore an appropriate title for a poem that is a
mixture of history and autobiography. The Dry Salvages -
pronounced to rhyme with 'assuages' - is a small group of
rocks, with a beacon, off the Massachusetts coast; and the
name is set above a poem that deals with the river of time
and the sea of timelessness. Little Gidding was the site
of an Anglican monastic community that Eliot might have
joined, if he had lived in the seventeenth century. But
what about Burnt Norton, which F.O. Matthiessen says (1)
is a manor in Gloucestershire? What is its connection
with a poem describing an ecstatic vision? No matter how
much he explains, and how many points his critics elucidate, Eliot always leaves us with unanswered questions.
Reading his poems is a little like working over a cross-
word puzzle that will never be completely solved.

But there can be no doubt concerning his general purpose in 'Four Quartets.' The book deals with mysticism
in its dictionary definition - that is, with the belief in
the possibility of union with the divine nature, and the
description of methods by which that moment of union may
be achieved. It belongs to the mystical tradition that
goes back to Vedic days, that was carried to the West by
the Neo-Platonists, that was introduced to Christianity
by the pseudo-Dionysius in the fifth century, that was
Latinized by Scotus Erigena four centuries later, that
was continued during the Middle Ages by a whole band of
saints and heretics - French, German, Spanish and English
- that declined in the days of the Enlightenment, and that
is now being revived in our own time of troubles. Eliot's
principal source is St. John of the Cross, the Spanish
mystic who died in 1591, but he also borrowed largely from
the 'Bhagavadgita' and, I am told, from the anchoret Dame
Julian of Norwich, who wrote 'XVI Revelations of Divine
Love' and died in 1443 at the age of a hundred. He might
have borrowed from many other sources without destroying
the unity of his work, for the mystical tradition has
changed very little from age to age or from nation to
nation. Eliot is not trying to remake that tradition, but
simply to recapture it. Even his obscurity is a convention often followed by mystical writers. He says at one
point:

> There is only the fight to recover what has been lost
> And found and lost again and again: and now, under
>   conditions
> That seem unpropitious.

What has been found and lost again is the intuition of
pure being, the timeless moment of union with the divine.
In order to recover it, two difficult steps must be taken.
The first is to achieve the good life by means of what
Eliot describes as 'prayer, observance, discipline,
thought and action' - in other words, the practices that
used to be demanded of every pious Christian. The second
step should be taken only by those who intend to follow
the mystic or contemplative life. It consists in a rigor-
ous attempt to empty the mind of all passions, fancies,
analytical ideas and mere distractions, while directing
one's thoughts solely toward union with God. The process
is described at length in the third section of 'East
Coker,' and more briefly in 'Burnt Norton':

[Quotes 'Burnt Norton', III, CPP, p. 174, 'Descend lower'
to 'world of spirit'.]

The reward that the mystic receives for leading the
good life and for divesting himself of selfhood is the
ecstatic sense of oneness with the divine nature. Eliot
describes this ecstasy in many different fashions. Sometimes it is the moment when 'the light is still at the
still point of the turning world,' and sometimes 'the
point of intersection of the timeless with time.' Again
it may be 'the release from action and suffering,' or 'a
condition of complete simplicity (costing not less than
everything),' or else a 'music heard so deeply that it is
not heard at all, but you are the music while the music
lasts.' However described, it is for Eliot the central
experience of a lifetime; and he even suggests that history itself is a pattern composed of these timeless
moments -

> When the tongues of flame are in-folded
> Into the crowned knot of fire
> And the fire and the rose are one.

I am not qualified to pass on the truth or value of the
moral system that Eliot is expounding. Theologians might
say that, like all mystics, he is running a grave danger
of heresy. Even a layman feels that Eliot's new faith,
instead of being Catholic or Anglo-Catholic, has a moral
atmosphere that is a curious mixture of Calvinism and

Buddhism: it is Calvinist and even New England Congrega-
tional in its finely drawn scruples; it is Buddhist in its
utter rejection of the world. More interesting to most
readers is the fact that Eliot's preoccupation with the
contemplative life seems to be carrying him into an abstract sphere beyond the limits of poetry.

It is true that he is still extremely interested in the
use of language - in finding 'the common word exact without vulgarity, the formal word precise but not pedantic.'
He is interested in putting words together into a pattern
which, like a Chinese jar, 'still moves perpetually in its
stillness.' The pattern of Eliot's verse has never been
more skillful and intricate than it is in 'Four Quartets.'
But the music of poetry, its sense of everyday life and the
images with which it recaptures the floating world - all
these are matters beneath the notice of a man bent on
union with the ineffable. He is even trying to put them
out of his mind, by the contemplative process that leads to
'desiccation of the world of sense, evacuation of the world
of fancy' - in short, to the total destruction of all the
world where poetry is accustomed to dwell. There is one
point at which he reveals his weariness over the business
of writing verse. After a lyric that repeats several
themes from 'The Waste Land,' he says prosaically:

> That was a way of putting it - not very satisfactory:
> A periphrastic study in a worn-out poetical fashion,
> Leaving one still with the intolerable wrestle
> With words and meanings. The poetry does not matter.

Wrestling with words and meanings, he thereupon writes
a blank-verse passage that would have read much better if
it had been printed as ordinary prose. Indeed, much of
'Four Quartets' is on this same level of bare, abstract
and sometimes hermetic expression; it seems to belong in
some handbook of mystical philosophy. Much of it, on the
other hand, is the sort of poetry that Eliot writes at his
best, and the book includes some of his finest lyrics.
But one feels that he now writes good poetry by habit or
by a talent he is unable to suppress, rather than by intention. He is almost like a skillful bridge player who
has abandoned cards as a frivolous occupation, but who
sometimes forgets himself and plays a perfect hand.

Note

1 Eliot's Quartets, 'Kenyon Review' (Spring 1943), v, 161-
   78. Reprinted in 'The Achievement of T.S. Eliot' (1947).

145. DELMORE SCHWARTZ, ANYWHERE OUT OF THE WORLD,
'NATION' (NEW YORK)

24 July 1943, vol. clvii, 102-3

Schwartz (1914-66), an American poet and critic, wrote an
important essay on Eliot's general position, entitled The
Literary Dictatorship of T.S. Eliot, 'Partisan Review'
(February 1949), xvi, 119-37. The essay was reprinted in
'Literary Opinion in America', volume II, edited by M.D.
Zabel (1968), pp. 573-87.

Any work by T.S. Eliot is bound to be interesting in a
complicated way. But this new work compels, in me at
least, a greater complexity of impression than any other
of Eliot's works. I speak thus of my own feeling because
I know how differently, and with what unmixed admiration,
many other readers have greeted these new poems. Yet at
the tenth reading I have the same mixed feeling, and this
after having tried to force in myself the delight of those
who find these poems just what they should be throughout.
    Two extended passages, a sestina made more difficult
and extraordinary by rhyme and a miraculous exercise in
the idiom and method of 'The Divine Comedy,' are equal,
at least from the standpoint of technique, to any modern
poetry. Throughout these poems there is also the invention of new rhythms, of unimagined possibilities in the
movement of language, which has always marked Eliot. He
is perhaps more original and inventive in rhythm than any
other poet in English.
    But when this is said, the weakness of other long
passages is underscored. These passages are of two kinds.
In one, the poet uses conventional forms in an effort to
write the kind of lyric which is traditional to English
poetry, and here what is to me the inadequacy comes
chiefly from the choice of image and phrase: the earth as
a hospital 'endowed by the ruined millionaire' lacks the
permanent surprise, shock, and uniqueness of - to use the
used instance, permanently fresh- 'April is the cruellest
month.' Then too the images seem *made*, self-imitative,
forced; they have the look of the artificial, and when
they are intended as emblematic or established symbols,
they look merely decorative.
    The other kind of unsuccessful passage is composed of
blocks of long lines very close to the rhythm of prose,

like much of 'The Family Reunion,' and deliberately
direct, matter of fact, and prosaic. Nothing is more
important to modern poetry than such a use of the prosaic
for its poetic quality, for nothing else can give the
poet the thickness, the particularity, the full actuality
of modern experience, which will justify his avowed emotions and beliefs. The prosaic versification here is so
much better than the same kind of thing in 'The Family Reunion,' partly because of a greater use of overflow, that
it may mark a stage in the mastery of a new style. But in
itself, it remains weak and wrong, not only in the trite-
ness of the phrasing -'we have gone on trying,' for
example - but in the effort, self-consciousness, and fal-
sity of tone. If one hears a man *trying* to be modest,
sincere, or frank, and if one hears the trying, rather
than the modesty, sincerity, or frankness as such, one has
an analogy for what is wrong with these passages both as
language and as emotion:

[Quotes 'East Coker', V, CPP, p. 182, 'So here I am' to
'to say it'.]

It is not enough, in a poem, to say 'I am unhappy' or 'I
have failed'; and especially in the poetry of direct statement the commonplace or colloquial statement must be
lifted up to a new light, by one device or another, so
that it is not merely itself, but something penetrated and
understood as a symbol. The touchstones for this profound
usage are Laforgue, Marianne Moore, William Carlos Williams
- and Eliot himself, but not in these poems. And then the
choice of instances in these passages, 'fruit, periodicals, business letters,' 'even a very good dinner,' marks
a like relaxation of the poet's sensibility, one which
suggests that he is at such times echoing the idiom he
himself discovered. Too much is often made of the sheer
texture of the language, when modern poetry is examined;
but here it is not merely a matter of texture: the crucial
instant of insight is betrayed by the language. Thus, at
one important moment one gets such a weak play and shift
with the meaning of a phrase as 'Not fare well, But fare
forward, voyagers,' when in 'Ash-Wednesday,' at a like
moment, the poem rose to such a phrase as 'Teach me to
care, and not to care.'
However, there can be no doubt about the satisfaction
and the success to be found in the modified sestina, the
Dantesque interview, and the organized movement of the
poems. Especially the encounter with a dead master just
before morning in London in war time strikes one with such
astonishment and admiration that some grand rhetorical

statement seems proper; so that, as Cocteau declared of
the motion pictures, 'At last the theater has an air-
plane!' one wishes to say, 'At last Dante has been translated into English and into modern life.' This is literally true in that Eliot has accomplished the effect of
terza rima in English by alternating masculine and feminine endings without rhyme, thus evading the comparative
poverty of rhyme in English and thus instructing future
translators and poets. But the renovation of Dante is
more than a matter of versification:

[Quotes 'Little Gidding', II, CPP, p. 193, 'Over the
asphalt' to 'some dead master'.]

And the organized movement of the four poems makes the
title of quartets denote more than the stock analogy of
music with poetry. Perhaps late quartets would be still
more exact, for as in those of Beethoven, the movement
from part to part goes from a passage lyrical, quick,
joyous, and exalted; to a passage suddenly slow, turned
in upon itself by variation or repetition of the same
thought, hovering over divided parts of the same symbol or
idea; harsh, flat, discursive, and tortuous; and then once
more quickened to certainty, difficult conviction, and the
explicit declaration and direct chant of belief.
The belief, made clear by the use of phrases and doctrines in the 'Bhagavadgita,' Heraclitus, and St. John of
the Cross, is that the only meaningful event in history is
the Incarnation, and all else - 'the moment in the rose-
garden,' the place of one's forbears, the practice of
poetry, and the whole of one's life - illusory, deceptive,
empty, vain, and without meaning except in relation to the
Incarnation. Seen in that light, everything still remains
false and of little worth, except as a phase to be endured.
All that is natural and merely human contradicts itself,
love is not love, time is not time, the end of life is the
beginning of life, exaltation and despair are the same
thing, all desire, effort, and action must be transformed
into passages of patient waiting - 'waiting without hope'
- to be wholly disengaged from everything in this life.
Here, as in Eliot's poetry from the start, what declares
itself above all is an obsessing desire to be free from
'birth, copulation, and death,' to be 'divested of the
love of created things,' to be utterly out of the world.
This rejection and renunciation are dominant to such an
extent that the affirmation of belief seems only lyrical
after-thought. The Incarnation is present for the sake
of the rejection of this life, not the renunciation because of the Incarnation. And this suggests once more

that Buddhism is perhaps a doctrine just as well suited as
Christianity to the poet's mind; perhaps better suited,
since the doctrine of reincarnation in some form of natural
life becomes true and inexhaustible damnation, given
Eliot's vision. To say this is to recognize that the
poet's hatred and rejection of this life is something beyond any belief whatever. It must have some personal and
private source, but it exists for all readers both as a
profound criticism of life and as a necessary phase in the
life of the spirit. If there is a phase superior to it, as
most Christians, at least, must suppose (how different is
the Christianity of St. Francis or Aquinas), the rejection
and renunciation which Eliot celebrates is prior and not to
be evaded, if one is to be in the full sense a human being.
To see that this is true, one has only to remember such
very different actualities as the moral disillusionment of
our time and the present war; and in literature, such
wholly different authors as Céline and Rilke, for 'The
Duino Elegies' have a close resemblance to these poems, and
these poems, however different in subject matter from
Céline's exhaustion of cynicism and despair, are also a
journey to the end of the night, inadequate only when the
journey is discussed and commended, and not endured.

146. PAUL GOODMAN, T.S. ELIOT: THE POET OF PURGATORY,
'NEW LEADER'

14 August 1943, 3, 7

Goodman (1911-72), an American poet, novelist and essayist, was a prolific writer of experimental literature. He
taught in 1950 at Black Mountain College, though before
Charles Olson took up permanent residence there.

This poem of personal experience and historical experience, and the experience of eternity, is excellent. So
far above the poems that appear these days that one has
almost a duty to ally himself with the poet against the
average, and write nothing but praise. Easy to do; for on
the one hand Eliot has for a long time had no poetic
faults, of excess or lapse, of writing beyond what he
knows or of merely repeating himself; he writes what he

is, for better or worse. And on the other hand, this poem
has glorious new perfections. In the diction always a
subtle edge of irony and paradox, but an edge even more
subtilely and beautifully blunted in the interest of the
humility that is his theme. And a wonderful conversational use of meters far from the iambic pentameters in
which we others have learned to think at our ease. And a
thought everywhere so central and self-known that he can go
off at liberty yet never divagate, for we are always close
to the heart of it. And a symbolism that, more in keeping
with his genius, has returned to great overall metaphors
and place-names, renouncing the factitious detailed symbolism of his earlier period -

   A way of putting it - not very satisfactory:
   A periphrastic study in a worn-out poetical fashion.

(I do not mean, of course, the high Symbolism that he
never attained, and which is precisely sensuous creation
itself.)
   Yet Eliot is not one of the colossal poets whose truth
and attitude we spontaneously advocate, or if we dissent
we feel nevertheless that their creating will loom against
(and tomorrow overwhelm!) our doubt; thus it is always
relevant to ask if what he says is binding. Or to put
this another way - for I am not speaking of the compulsion
of philosophy, but of spiritual energy and salvation one
might say that Eliot is everywhere, but especially in this
poem, the poet of Purgatory; and we may ask if there *can*
be a great poet of Purgatory; a great poet not *always*
attended by some angel of Paradise. But he says, referr-
ing to the central theme of this poem,

[Quotes 'The Dry Salvages', V, CPP, pp. 189-90, 'to
apprehend' to 'death in love' and 'For most of us' to
'distraction fit'.]

   In the nature of the case this is the poet whose voice
has a famous 'dying fall.' But would one not expect that
as a poet, not a saint, he could not possibly fail to have
an abiding confidence - a confidence not, of course, in
his propositions, but in his ability to make something in
the medium, the gift ('given and taken') of the Creator
Spirit?
   Or to put it still another way, looking at what he
says, we see more clearly here than elsewhere why Eliot is
not a Christian poet; how his Christianity is sapped by
Indian ideas; and yet he does not have the Indian wisdom
either.

What he says - I think it can be synopsized without
distortion - is that time, past present or future, is loss
of the soul; that practical desire, action, suffering,
inner and outer compulsion, are an endless round; salvation is in the release from these, in abstention from
motion, abiding at the still point of the turning world,
and this is love; and yet, and this is the capital point,
it is only through experience in time, and returning on
that experience completed to perceive its pattern, that
the timeless may be grasped, for 'only through time time
is conquered,' and 'a people without history is not redeemed from time, for history is a pattern of timeless
moments'; and therefore, for 'a further union, a deeper
communion' we must have courage to start on the round
again, 'we must be still and still moving,' 'old men
ought to be explorers,' our destiny is to fare forward,
'not fare well but fare forward' -

> We shall not cease from exploration
> And the end of all our exploring
> Will be to arrive where we started
> And know the place for the first time.

The perfection of the earthly paradise of youth is the
rose, and of the purification of desire is the refining
fire; and in the timeless, 'the fire and the rose are one.'

What a relief this noble doctrine is after the wasteland
of Anglicanism and new Humanism!   Is it not ironic to
come on precisely the doctrine of Lessing, 'fare forward,'
that used to be singled out for contempt as a cult of
experience!   And it is even delightful to find T.S. Eliot
coming to a kind of antinomianism - 'all shall be well,
all manner of thing shall be well' - for obviously sin
also is a venture to fare forward on.   And it is moving to
hear the poet (in the face of the world-wide catastrophe)
speak autobiographically for the first time, and point to
his

> twenty years largely wasted, the years of
>   l'entre deux guerres.

But the doctrine is false.   We may theologically take time
as a loss and an endless return if we also take it as an
illusion; for then there is also prescribed a discipline
of ridding ourselves physically of the illusion, an even
certain and controllable way of attaining salvation for
those who know the science.   (This is the Indian way.)
But on the contrary, if time is real, as the poem has it,

it is impossible for it to be hopeless, for time is the
theatre of creation, of creative acts, virtues and
miracles, given by grace; not that the sequence of time
is a progress, for new evil also abounds, but that God
willing it is full of glories, future as well as past. If
faith can move mountains, then the man of faith does move
them not only to act out his faith (like Thomas in the
'Murder'), but with confidence that their *motion* will do
God's work. If pressed, Eliot's despair of material events
and his confidence in only the emerging pattern (or in mere
meditation on the emerging pattern) would conclude, I
think, in denying the Creation itself. (But salvation is
in the resources of creative nature, and the hidden God is
not an object of experience.)

> The faith and the love and the hope are all in the
>   waiting.

Yes, if like Milton in the sonnet one knows that 'thou-
sands at His bidding speed, and post o'er land and ocean
without rest'; or at least that they could do so, given
the right inspiration. But *No*, if one imagines that in
any case it will make no difference, or will make a difference only in the contemplation of essences, for one essence
is as eternal as another and then why consent to fare forward (and do worse).
  Even so! the poet is right to torment himself and not to
make a commitment where in fact he does not believe. Yet
perhaps the divine commitments are simple things after all,
and all that is easiest is best. I wonder if he did not
experience this when he composed the beautiful cadences of
these 'Quartets.'

147. JOHN GOULD FLETCHER, POEMS IN COUNTERPOINT, 'POETRY'

October 1943, vol. lxiii, 44-8

Fletcher (1886-1950), an American poet and writer, published his autobiography, 'Life is My Song', in 1927. He
remembered Eliot for his charm and for his tolerance as
editor of the 'Criterion', but disapproved of his
Anglicanism.

The great beauty of T.S. Eliot's latest book - and it is a
long time since there has been a book of poetry in which
the form and the matter seem so appropriate to each other
- need not blind anyone to the fact that in each poem of
this series, Eliot is dealing with a theme not frequently
tackled in modern poetry: the theme of the relation of a
supernaturally revealed religion to man, and the question
of what man, temporal and accidental as he is, can make of
this revelation. The intellectual scheme of each poem in
the series represents a further stage in the poet's search
for personal adjustment to a set of values already given
him by the creed he has embraced; and it is this set of
fixed and unalterable values, as given by such Catholic
mystics as Saint John of the Cross and Dame Julian of
Norwich, that form the framework on which the personal
quests of the poet for values that transcend his local and
temporal circumstances are set up. The question of the
meaning of the whole series has already been ably discussed by James Johnson Sweeney in an article in the July
issue of 'Poetry,' and need not be further dealt with at
this point. What I wish to stress is the relation of the
content to the form and the degree in which the form com-
bines with the content to produce that 'willing suspension
of disbelief' which is so characteristic of poetry.

The title 'Four Quartets' suggests immediately a musical
structure, something on the lines of my own 'Symphonies' or
'Elegies' or Conrad Aiken's 'Preludes.' And it is in this
respect that I find Eliot's achievement most impressive.
This is the work of a better poet than the Eliot who wrote
either 'The Waste Land' or 'Ash Wednesday.' Where the
themes of 'The Waste Land' were in brutal juxtaposition,
and violently clashed with each other - few poems ever
written have been so lacking in transition passages, in
progress from detail to detail as this one - and where the
main theme of the latter (the abandonment of temporal
love) carried with it details that did not immediately
convince one as being appropriate to their purpose, the
relation of detail to the main structure here is nothing
short of masterly. The 'Four Quartets,' in their use of
leit motifs and variation, in the contrapuntal effect, are
the work of a theologically-minded poet determined to ex-
plore difficult ground, the ground of the technical analo-
gies between poetry and music. They are by intention and
accomplishment musical poems.

But what is a musical poem? Eliot himself has supplied
the answer, in a lecture, The Music of Poetry, which was
reprinted as an essay in the 'Partisan Review' for
November-December, 1942; an essay which I think might have
served admirably as an introduction to the 'Quartets'

themselves, inasmuch as it offers the best possible explanation of them on the technical side. As he points out
in this essay, it is quite common among poets for 'a poem,
or a passage of a poem - to realize itself first as a particular rhythm before it reaches expression in words.' In
other words, the way a poem should sound as rhythm usually
presents itself to a poet before the actual words of the
poem are set down. Poets are people who go about with
tunes in their heads: and whether the tunes employed be
those of Mallarmé or Eliot, or of Kipling and Robert Tristram Coffin, makes all the difference.

The other sense in which the analogy of music holds
good for poetry is in the question of structure. The free
verse revolution in poetry, coming in English-speaking
countries between 1908 and 1914, had as its aim the bringing of poetry back to the rhythm of conversational speech
and the renewal of poetic structure in that idiom. As
Eliot says in the essay to which I have already referred,
'It was a revolt against dead form, and a preparation for
new form, or a renewal of the old; it was an insistence
upon the inner unity which is unique to every poem,
against the outer unity which is typical.' Structure, however, must always be a preoccupation of every important
poet, whatever the form employed; and the liberation
preached by the free versifiers - resulting in much bad
prose and some good verse - has seemed most intelligently
applied when new devices, bearing a considerable analogy
to music, have enforced form on what might have been otherwise formless. These devices are, roughly, the setting of
the theme of a poem in several different and contrasting
rhythms (for example sad and humorous); the juxtaposition
in the same poem of passages of high lyric intensity with
others of conversational comment; the repetition of leading themes with variation; the amplification in sound-
intensity possible between the open and closed quality of
vowel sounds; and finally, the effect of contrapuntal
recapitulation possible to sustain by returning to one's
leading statements. All these devices have their analo-
gies in music; and it is because Eliot is not only aware
of them, but employs them with the utmost skill, that one
takes pleasure in his work as a poet.

Is this the only reason why, as a poet, he remains so
important today? So far as I am concerned, it is. I do
not share his scheme of beliefs, which are familiar to
anyone who has read deeply in the Catholic mystics; I am
appalled by any method of salvation which implies the
emptying out of all human sensation in favor of a demand
for a miracle:

Only the hardly, barely prayable
Prayer of the one Annunciation.

The negative way to salvation, as recommended by the
orthodox, seems to me largely valueless in the present
crisis. Rather is it important for most men, who have
either lost God or never found Him in the existing
churches, to build up God again through the operation of
the sense of human solidarity. The ideal of man, rather
than of race or creed, the proof of human character
through suffering and endurance, the achievement of something resembling a moral conscience - it is for these
things we should strive again today, as never before. The
Little Giddings of this world can shed little light on the
problem that has come upon this age with renewed force -
the problem of creating, while we fight for it, a true
democracy. To solve that problem we have to start, not
with God as defined by the theologians, but with man, and
his relationship towards his fellows. Modern science,
though it may help towards a solution, cannot provide one.
There is, be it remembered, a mysticism implicit in democracy - a system of beliefs possibly not worked out with
the clarity of detail of the medieval schoolmen, but declaring just as surely as Dame Julian of Norwich that
'All shall be well and all manner of thing shall be well.'

148. LOUIS UNTERMEYER, A REVIEW, 'YALE REVIEW'

December 1943, vol. xxxiii, 348-9

This is taken from a longer review of new poetry.

The title of Eliot's later poems, 'Four Quartets,' was
certain to provoke, and already has provoked, comparisons
with Beethoven's later quartets in intention as well as
accomplishment. Towards the end, Beethoven fashioned a
music to reach beyond music; in his fifties, Eliot employs mind to stretch beyond mind. The result is an intricate paradox: 'Four Quartets' is both simpler and subtler than anything Eliot has written since 'The Waste Land.'
The language is more direct, sometimes even prosaic; the
allusions are much less remote and recondite; the

connectives are clear. But the meanings are more complex
than ever, and the frame which encloses them is decep-
tively patterned. Structurally 'Four Quartets' is magnificent; it unfolds design after design. Some of the patterns are obvious: the series of fours; the mixed symbolism of the four seasons and the four elements, air, earth,
water, and fire; the dexterous alternation of unrhymed
slow passages and rapidly rhymed lyrics; the turn of the
theme with minute variations.

But the best of the four-part poem disguises its
effects. Never has a poet used repetition more skilfully
and persuasively; never have variations been so insinuat-
ing. Here Eliot's chief preoccupations are the sense of
time and timelessness, the involution of life, and the
difficulty of communication. It is not a narrow interpretation of the poet's art that leads Eliot to complain
of the years lost in learning how to use language - 'the
intolerable wrestle with words and meanings' - the old
attempts, the new starts, and the failures 'because one
has only learnt to get the better of words for the things
one no longer has to say, or the way in which one is no
longer disposed to say it.' And so, says Eliot, each venture

    Is a new beginning, a raid on the inarticulate,
    With shabby equipment always deteriorating
    In the general mess of imprecision of feeling,
    Undisciplined squads of emotion.

The accent of 'Four Quartets' is grave, sometimes sadly
nostalgic, but it is by no means lugubrious. The music as
well as the meaning is solemn, and it will not be to
everyone's taste. Eliot's counterpoint of private experience and impersonal mysticism is not easy to follow. But
few will question the beauty of the communication; few
will doubt the perfection of the poet's art....

149. REGINALD SNELL, T.S. ELIOT AND THE ENGLISH POETIC
TRADITION, 'NEW ENGLISH WEEKLY'

14 December 1944, vol. xxvi, 77-8

A few weeks later a letter from Eliot appeared in the
'New English Weekly' (25 January 1945), xxvi, 112, drawing

attention to an error in the text of 'The Dry Salvages'.

The four poems (three of them, as faithful readers of the
'New English Weekly' will be proud to recall, first
printed in the pages of this journal) which together constitute one of the most important poetic achievements of
our time, have now appeared in a single volume, where they
may be - as they always deserved to be - considered as a
literary unity. A note speaks of 'improvements of phrase
and construction,' but the only significant alteration
from the pamphlet form of the poems, apart from the substitution of 'and' for 'or' in one place, and a semi-
colon for a full stop in another, is the appearance of the
word 'appeasing' instead of 'reconciling,' in connection
with 'forgotten wars' - a risky change, considering the
emotional overtones to which the newer word now gives
rise. The title is a good one: this is the chamber music
of poetry, the wholly mature work of a most distinguished
craftsman, and the poetic diction is as civilised, as
grave and pure as good late Haydn. Each poem consists of
five 'movements,' the fourth being much shorter than the
others, and lyrical in form; themes are stated and restated, in the manner of music, inside each separate quartet, and certain phrases are common to them all. Their
total length roughly doubles that of 'The Waste Land.'
   It would be tempting to let the critic in Eliot review
the poems himself; the thing could be done, easily
enough, from that admirable essay of his, Tradition and
the Individual Talent, which appeared in 1917. For these
poems represent precisely the achievement of that true
traditionalism which he there describes. Such prose
quotations as follow in this article are all taken from
that essay. What a remarkable, and what an exciting,
development has taken place in Eliot's writing between
those early poems of urbane disgust, diffident, private,
mannered and in the best sense decadent (they were the
final statement of the *kind* of poetry that had preceded
them, and were of course immensely competent technically),
and these latest poems which are bone and flesh of the
English tradition! In one sense, no doubt, nobody but
Eliot could have written them, but in another, it does not
matter much who did write them - they are part of the
whole body of English poetry. 'Prufrock' and 'Poems 1920'
were first-rate minor poetry, and intensely individual;
'The Waste Land' and 'The Hollow Men' were already major
poetry, but still individual; 'Ash-Wednesday' and the
Ariel poems were recognizably the poetry of the later

Eliot, whose work has reached universality and, in losing individuality, has found it (the same law obtains in artistic creation as in spiritual life). As he himself wrote, if we appreciate a poet without a prejudice in favour of individuality, in the sense of divergence from the main stream of tradition, 'we shall often find that not only the best, but the most individual parts of his work may be those in which the dead poets, his ancestors, assert their immortality most vigorously.' Much of the significance of the early poems was esoteric - that array of notes to 'The Waste Land' (an average of one to every eight lines of the poem) was most of it necessary; but the 'Four Quartets,' though parts of them are at least as conventionally 'difficult,' are in no need of notes. If a reader does not catch every literary allusion as such (and few readers are likely to), it is no great matter. He will certainly enjoy the poetry more if he is familiar with some, at any rate, of the books that the poet has loved and made part of himself (though few people would probably care to challenge him over Elizabethan drama- tists, seventeenth century divines, Seneca's plays, the Upanishads and a good many other things), but he will not necessarily understand it any better. The echoes from other writers are here truly organic, and the poems are not personal reflexions garnished with choice morsels from other men's books - they are a cut from the joint of Eng- lish poetry, and Eliot has wielded the knife. He has be- come wholly and effortlessly aware 'of the mind of Europe - the mind of his own country - a mind which [a writer] learns in time to be much more important than his own private mind.' Of all living poets, he has the strong- est historical sense, which is 'nearly indispensable to anyone who would continue to be a poet beyond his twenty- fifth year.' Some of his early work has been reproached, and justly, for its too heavy load of erudition; it may be true that 'a poet ought to know as much as will not en- croach upon his necessary receptivity and necessary lazi- ness,' but one cannot quite forgive those early explana- tory notes - a poem should no more need them than a string quartet does. The notes were necessary before, but are no longer. The gazetteer will tell anyone who is interested that East Coker is a village of 1360 acres in Somerset, with a population of 798, and that Burnt Norton is not to be found on the map (he will probably conclude that the poet has named it after the Harvard critic who shares his name); but neither this knowledge, nor a familiarity with Nicholas Ferrar's community at Little Gidding (acr. 724, pop. 39 - and you really do 'turn behind the pig-sty' when you make pilgrimage to that remote and lovely spot,

'to kneel where prayer has been valid') and its connection with Charles I, is necessary for purely literary
appreciation of the poems. If such facts as these, and
many others, are known, they merely add extra and extra-
literary enjoyment.

The handling of the symbolism throughout the 'Quartets'
is superb. Eliot has reached the stage when he can quote
freely from other writings of his own as well as other
people's ('human kind cannot bear very much reality' had
already been said by his Becket); the corridor ('Gerontion'), the rose garden ('Ash-Wednesday'), the shaft of
sunlight ('Murder in the Cathedral'), the heard laughter
of children ('New Hampshire') - all these were used again
in that fine and underrated play 'The Family Reunion,' and
all of them occur more than once in these latest poems.
To them are now added the figure of the dance, and the
pattern (already important in 'Murder in the Cathedral'). The various metres and stanza forms throughout the
poems are, with the possible exception of the second section of 'The Dry Salvages,' handled in a masterly way.
There remains that special characteristic of Eliot's verse,
his continual protestations of inarticulateness. 'Prufrock' exclaimed nearly thirty years ago 'It is impossible
to say just what I mean,' and the poet has been repeating
the same thing, on and off, ever since - he says it, very
beautifully and with a skilful variety of phrasing that
carries its own denial, several times in these 'Quartets.'
It is becoming increasingly less true; the conversation
that was once, indeed, 'so nicely restricted to What Precisely and If and Perhaps and But' has lately assumed a
lovely lucidity. And it is difficult to see how his
almost Trollopian use of the propria persona is artistic-
ally justified, or what place there is for such phrases as
'I have said before' and 'You say I am repeating something
I have said before.' I shall say it again' in the work of
one who believes (how rightly!) that 'the progress of an
artist is a continual self sacrifice, a continual extinction of personality,' and has himself triumphantly
achieved the classical manner of writing that 'is not a
turning loose of emotion, but an escape from emotion ...
not the expression of personality, but an escape from
personality.'

It never does to ignore the quotations at the head of
his poems; the two fragments from Heraclitus printed at
the beginning of this book, pre-Christian words with
their profoundly Christian significance, form a fitting
introduction to these four magnificent poems - to 'Burnt
Norton' with its faultless opening and concluding sections about Time, and its resolute pursuit of the *via*

negationis to reach the 'still point of the turning
world' (the Grecian urn has here become a Chinese jar); to
'East Coker' with its brilliant use of a typographical
device to gain a particular poetical effect, its strong
and thoroughly characteristic chthonic sense, and the
lovely section about humility and the need for 'waiting
on' God; to 'The Dry Salvages' with its admirable opening
passage about the River (a new note in Eliot's verse is
heard here) and the further preoccupation with 'the un-
attended Moment' that alone brings perfect reconiliation;
and to 'Little Gidding,' certainly the finest poem of the
four, with its Dantesque second section, its further handling of the themes of renunciation and the intersections
of Time and the Timeless, above all perhaps the moving refrain from the thirteenth 'Shewing' of Julian of Norwich,
in which Our Lord tells her that 'synne is behovabil, but
al shal be wel and al shal be wel and al manner of thyng
shal be wele.' These nine-hundred-odd lines ask for constant re-reading, not so much because of their 'difficulties' (which are not really considerable) as because of
the astonishing richness of their poetic content, and for
a proper appreciation of their technical achievements.
They are a true part of the English poetic tradition.
They provide, also, the theme of a meditation, in which
the intellectual and emotional elements are admirably
balanced and mutually fortified, upon the mystery of the
Incarnation.

150. E.J. STORMAN, S.J., TIME AND MR. T.S. ELIOT,
'MEANJIN'

Winter 1944, vol. iii, 103-10

Father Storman (b. 1912) joined the Society of Jesus in
1934, and teaches at the United Theological Faculty of
Melbourne. His publications include studies both of Eliot
and of Dante, for example, Laforgue and Eliot, 'Essays in
French Literature', edited by J.R. Lawler (Western Australia Press, 1965), and 'Romance and Religion in "The Divine
Comedy"' (Melbourne, 1966).
    Father Storman asks that the following be appended to
his final footnote: 'Had I known at the time what a
"crowned knot" was in nautical terminology, I should have
developed my comment rather differently.'

Over the last seven years Mr. T.S. Eliot has been working
on a sequence of poems published separately as 'Burnt
Norton,' 'East Coker,' 'The Dry Salvages,' and 'Little
Gidding.' These have been recently brought together for
the first time in an American edition under the title
'Four Quartets.' Thus assembled they make a long meditation, interspersed with lyrics, on the conquest of time
and the meaning of history. This is the most considerable
thing Eliot has done, and is destined to be of importance
in the history of contemporary verse. A much larger
claim, however, might be made for it. Our literature is
not particularly rich in philosophic poetry of a high
order, but here at last is something that can live, as a
work of art, in the company of Dante and Lucretius.

It is one of the advantages of Mr. Eliot's work that he
has chosen a subject of peculiar significance for modern
times. The meaning of the time process has been occupying
European thought to an unprecedented degree in this century, as may be conveniently seen, for instance, from Mr.
Wyndham Lewis's polemical 'Time and Western Man.' Mr.
Eliot has the distinction of suggesting at various points
the thought of such diverse thinkers and general writers as
as Whitehead, Bergson, Christopher Dawson, Berdyaev,
Spengler, and, behind them, of a mixed company which includes Kierkegaard and Hegel, St. Augustine and Heraclitus. A number of these would, of course, prove inimical
to his central position, but he has the virtue of being
able to draw on those whom he does not follow for a method
of approach or an interesting mental perspective. Thus
unexpected windows open out from time to time within the
poem, not merely on the subject-matter, but on the history
of human thought about it.

The general scheme of 'Four Quartets' is suggested by
two Greek fragments from Heraclitus which preface 'Burnt
Norton.' One reminds us of the Heraclitean world of flux
with its cyclic interchange between the elements of earth,
water, air and fire, between the four seasons, and between
life and death. Alternation between these opposites can
be considered a 'way up' and a 'way down,' but, since the
process is cyclic, these are only two aspects of the same
movement. The other fragment concerns the remarkable
Heraclitean doctrine of the *logos* or Word. There is a
directive principle behind the cosmic flux, and of this
human intelligence, and, at a further remove, language,
are participations. Symbolism based on this doctrine
obviously lends itself to a Christian interpretation.
What Mr. Eliot has in fact done is to take the Heraclitean
formulas and penetrate them with Christian meaning without
quite obliterating their original import. It is possible

now to make out the chief structural principles. The poem
is in a double sense a 'harmony of opposites.' Not merely
are oppositions in the world of flux and time reconciled,
but the cosmic cycles of change and succession are harmonized with the permanence of eternity, repetitions within
the world process with the forward movement and ultimate
consummation of history. Each of the four poems deals with
the Heraclitean alternations, with an emphasis on one particular element and one particular season. In each there
is question either of the conquest of time through contact
with eternity in a 'timeless moment,' or of impregnating
time with significance by a prolongation and diffusion of
this experience. The synthesis of eternity and time is
treated as a consequence of the Incarnation of the Word,
and the finalism of history is taken in function of the
extension and fulfilment of that unique event.
    Such a scheme involves a dialectical movement of
thought and feeling which finds issue in a form analogous
to that of music, where contrasts can be harmonized and
resolved. The musical technique, already suggested by the
title, can be seen most obviously in the sudden variations
of movement and the complicated interweaving of themes.
Each poem is built up of five parts or movements, with
statement, counter-statement, and resolution chasing one
another throughout. A meditative movement, usually execu-
ted in long, loose-fibred lines of *vers libre*, is
succeeded by a lyric, which in its turn is followed within
the same movement by a further meditation. The third and
fifth movements are again meditative (the lines at the end
of the fifth being tautened into a shorter measure), while
in between them is a short fourth movement consisting entirely of a lyric. The first lyric deals with some aspect
of the Heraclitean rotation of elements, seasons, etc.,
viewed either as a resolving harmony, or, more usually, as
strife and disintegration. The second treats some form of
suffering or self-abnegation.

    'Burnt Norton' takes its title, so English reviewers
tell us, from a manor house in Gloucestershire, where Mr.
Eliot was staying for a time. There is a kind of oscilla-
tion between this manor, with its rose-garden, its yew-
trees, sunflower and clematis, and the 'gloomy hills of
London,' region of newspapers and dim trains. The time is
autumn, and the Heraclitean element most in prominence is
air ('the cold wind that blows before and after time').
The problem of the whole sequence, the 'redemption of
time,' is stated here in such a form as to seem insoluble.
In point of fact, however, the initial statement is only a
thesis which is to be met with an antithesis, and these

are assumed into a synthesis in 'East Coker,' and, more
triumphantly, in 'Little Gidding.'

The ancient Greek doctrine of the 'return of all
things,' based on a theory of the circular movement of
time, would seem to make freedom impossible, and, with it,
a significant pattern in history. The cosmic cycles hold
on their inexorable way, bringing change which is only
repetition. The present and future are contained in the
past, the past is repeated in the future. The present is
the momentary term of a deterministic process, and could
not have been otherwise:

> What might have been and what has been
> Point to one end, which is always present.

Here supervenes the first experience of what Mr. Eliot,
possibly borrowing a formula from Kierkegaard, calls the
'timeless moment.' This seems to be (for Mr. Eliot,
though not for the Dane) an imaginative and partly intellectual insight which reproduces on a lower plane some of
the conditions of mystical intuition. A sudden hint of
eternity is obtained, and the time process seems momentarily suspended. The 'timeless moment' is usually
associated with certain sensible images which seem to lead
up to it. It is -

> the moment in and out of time,
> The distraction fit, lost in a shaft of sunlight,
> The wild thyme unseen, or the winter lightning
> Or the waterfall, or music heard so deeply
> That it is not heard at all, but you are the music
> While the music lasts.

(*Cf.* 'Murder in the Cathedral,' first chorus: 'I have
seen these things in a shaft of sunlight.') In 'Burnt
Norton' the experience is given by way of an excursion
from actuality into a world of the 'might-have-been'
(symbolized by the rose-garden), where childhood is linked
with a past that was never realized. Insight comes in the
midst of the day-dream, but the moment may not last, for
'human kind cannot bear very much reality,' and the movement ends with a reassertion of the 'one end, which is
always present.' A shift, however, has occurred within
the meaning of the word 'end,' which now indicates primarily the goal or destiny of man, so that the verbal
repetition of the initial thesis constitutes in part a
real antithesis. Through a moment in time time itself has
been transcended, and the deterministic cosmic forces have
been conquered.

A meditation on this experience, in which the contact
between eternity and time is represented by 'the still
point of the turning world,' leads to a consideration of
the ascetic *via negativa*. Only by the 'noughting' of
soul and sense can one hope to approach the reality obscurely indicated in moments of insight. By contrast we
have a picture of the time-victims ('men and bits of
paper') in the London Tube:

> Only a flicker
> Over the strained time-ridden faces
> Distracted from distraction by distraction
> Filled with fancies and empty of meaning.

A beautiful 'Burnt Norton' lyric on the theme of renunciation leads to an analysis of language as an instrument for
the formulation of inarticulate experience, and this in
turn seems to provoke a repetition of the 'timeless
moment':

[Quotes 'Burnt Norton', V, CPP, p. 176, 'Sudden in' to
'before and after'.]

The redemption of time has only begun. Escape through
the timeless moment is not a final solution. The virtue
of that moment must be diffused through the time process,
since man must sooner or later return to the changing
world. The emphasis in 'East Coker' falls on the 'exploration' or forward movement in which man is once more caught
in the flux, but is already transforming it by contact
with eternity:

> We must be still and still moving
> Into another intensity
> For a further union, a deeper communion
> Through the dark cold and the empty desolation.

East Coker is the name of the village in Somersetshire
whence Mr. Eliot's ancestors sailed to the New World and
where he himself was later to live. The poem is of the
summer and the return of things to earth. Heraclitus had
observed that in a circle beginning and end are the same.
This gives rise to two complementary propositions with
which Mr. Eliot makes play: 'In my beginning is my end,'
'In my end is my beginning.' The application is, as
usual, both to human and subhuman forms of existence. Not
merely 'bone of man and beast, cornstalk and leaf,' but
the stone and timber of houses go back to earth. In their

beginning is their end. 'On a Summer midnight,' the peasants of the past are resurrected in the fields by the village, and dance again round the fire. The rhythm of their dancing is one with the rhythm of the seasons and constellations, of life and death, and so, involved in the cyclic turning, these ghosts go back to earth:

>   Feet rising and falling.
> Eating and drinking. Dung and death.

(It is interesting to note that the sense of the past, which Mr. Eliot wishes here to evoke, is accentuated by literary reminiscences of the Book of Ecclesiastes, of the fifteenth century Sir Thomas Elyot - a rather too esoteric reference, of Lucretius, Book V, and perhaps of Hardy's Wessex novels.)

Half way through the poem the darkness of death is used to suggest the 'Dark Night of the Soul' of the Spanish mystic St. John of the Cross, and, since this night is the way to spiritual light, the other aspect of the time process comes into play: 'In the end is my beginning.' Here we are to think of the doomed Mary Queen of Scots (it may be remembered that the well-known device on her handkerchief read: 'En ma fin est mon commencement'), and of such dicta as 'He that will lose his life shall save it.' The solidarity between individual suffering and the redemptive Passion of Christ is then brought out in a curious and felicitous lyric in which stanzas of four-beat measure are ravelled up by final alexandrines. By the end of the poem the various levels of meaning contained within 'In my end is my beginning' have been worked out, and hope has arisen out of many kinds of death.

With 'The Dry Salvages' we move to the New England coast of America, the home of Mr. Eliot's youth. We are told in a note that the title derives from a 'small group of islands' (perhaps once called 'Les Trois Sauvages') 'off the N.E. coast of Cape Ann, Massachusetts.' Here we have to do with winter and the conquering sea. We are back in the world of flux and time with a vengeance. But the bell which tosses on the sea near the islands, 'rung by unhurried ground swell,' does more than measure time; it sounds an annunciation, which, while being a warning, a herald of pain, is finally also an angelus, and we are reminded of the Virgin's shrine on the promontory. (a) Annunciation and Incarnation, acceptance of the ravages wrought by cosmic change and consequent transformation of time, become indissolubly linked. (At this point, it may be remarked, Mr. Eliot touches on the central thought of

Gerard Manley Hopkins' 'Wreck of the Deutschland.') With
release effected in the soul, we can resign ourselves to
the operation of the cosmic cycles on the body:

    We, content at the last
    If our temporal reversion nourish
    (Not too far from the yew-tree)
    The life of significant soil.

'Little Gidding' is likely to become the most popular
portion of Mr. Eliot's work, as the thought content is not
as difficult as elsewhere, and the poetic quality can be
very readily experienced. Here, for the first time, the
poet of 'Infernos' and 'Purgatorios' ('The Waste Land,'
'The Hollow Men'; 'Ash-Wednesday,' 'The Family Reunion')
attempts a 'Paradiso.' The torturing history of time
turns out after all to be a 'Divina Commedia,' a story
with a happy ending. The triumph of fire in the periodic
general conflagration of the Heraclitean scheme is
assumed into the final consummation of history by love
through the fulfilment of the Incarnation. But this is
to anticipate. The time is the depth of winter, but it is
a winter that suggests the spring. Snow in the hedgerows
seems like hawthorn blossom, and the 'brief sun flames the
ice, on ponds and ditches.' It is 'midwinter spring,'
however, chiefly in virtue of the heart's heat, and, at
the same time, since the bloom is 'neither budding nor
fading,' 'not in the scheme of generation,' it is an
augury of a summer beyond sense. It is characteristic of
Mr. Eliot that he refuses to round off his scheme by giving us spring pure and simple: any 'Paradiso' he has to
offer us will be no easy apocalypse, but 'a tremor of
bliss, a wink of heaven' out of the midst of travail.
    Little Gidding, it may be remembered, was the home of a
community established by Nicholas Ferrar in the seventeenth century. The poet Crashaw, among the better known,
lived there for a while. It is a place in which the sense
of the past is strong: memories of 'a broken king' 'at
nightfall' (Charles I, who once came riding into Little
Gidding), and, by association, of 'one who died blind and
quiet' (presumably Milton), and of the various factions of
the seventeenth century, are in the air. One of the chief
constitutive elements in this, as in the preceding three
poems, is an awareness of the organic continuity of history, of 'the past gnawing into the present.' Mr. Eliot,
in fact, has his own version of that excellent saying:
'neminem vere vivere diem praesentem nisi dierum praeter-
itorum memorem.' Memory is used to view individual

experience, whether of happiness or pain, as of a piece
with the past experience of the race: the perspective
widens as we look back, so that we come to transcend the
limitations of self-interest and live in the general pattern of history. Our lifetime is -

> not the experience of one life only
> But of many generations ('The Dry Salvages')

> not the lifetime of one man only
> But of old stones that cannot be deciphered ('East
>   Coker').

History, however, is not only of the past, but very
emphatically of the present: it is war-time, and 'History
is now and England.' We move from Little Gidding to London, the London of the air-raids. A 'Dark dove with the
flickering tongue' (a fighter-plane, which, while spitting
death like a serpent, is, in a mysterious secondary sense,
also an instrument of peace), has 'passed below the horizon of his homing,' and the shrapnel still falls. In the
darkness before the dawn the poet falls in with a 'familiar compound ghost' (cf. the 'affable familiar ghost' of
Shakespeare, Sonnet 86), who, when addressed in the language of Dante's 'Inferno,' is resolved into Dante himself. A consummate section of terza rima (with masculine
and feminine endings as the connecting principle instead
of rime) gives the message of the master of language, a
message which is in substance that of the conclusion of
'Purgatorio' xxvi (where rehabilitation is effected by
willing endurance of the 'refining fire'). Then, with
dawn breaking in the bomb-shattered street, the visitation
ceases -

> He left me, with a kind of valediction
> And faded on the blowing of the horn. (b)

The last part of 'Little Gidding' is dominated by Dame
Julian of Norwich, the mystic of an optimism snatched from
the fire of pain. Looking over the course of her own
suffering, and over the tangle of human history, Julian
was able to say: 'Love was his meaning.' Mr. Eliot, in
his most perfect lyric, with 'flame of incandescent
terror' breaking from the sky (the fighter passing into
the Holy Ghost) can conclude:

[Quotes 'Little Gidding', IV, CPP, p. 196, 'Who then
devised' to 'fire or fire'.]

It is the medieval, too, who supplies the refrain,
'And all shall be well,' with which Mr. Eliot finally
brings together the chief themes of his poem in a piece of
remarkable symbolism:

> And all shall be well and
> All manner of things shall be well
> When the tongues of flame are in-folded
> Into the crowned knot of fire
> And the fire and the rose are one. (c)

This is the consummation of history, for the individual,
the race, the material universe. Time and change find
their issue in redemption.

So much for a general account of 'Four Quartets.' The
work has, I believe, been sometimes misinterpreted as it
appeared in its separate parts, and so there is some point
in calling attention to the main movement of its thought.
But it is important primarily as a poem, and I am aware
that I have hardly begun to speak about that.

Notes

a The explicit statement of the theme in Section IV (a
   free-verse lyric) is 'doubled' by an extremely sensitive line-movement in which the sad clamour and subsi-
   dence of the sea-bell is made to melt into the pealing
   of an angelus. The two sound-effects are heard, as it
   were, on distinct but related auditory levels.
b This is perhaps the most obvious instance of Mr. Eliot's
   skill in suggesting a background of reference. The
   ghost of Hamlet's father, it may be recalled, 'faded on
   the crowing of the cock.' One thinks, too, of the
   'horns of elfland faintly blowing,' and then remembers
   that the horn here is probably an air-raid siren.
c Such symbolism represents Mr. Eliot's device for com-
   bining great complexity of meaning with the utmost
   simplicity and economy of statement. The reader who
   sinks sympathetically into the mood of 'Little Gidding'
   will find that the symbols readily release sufficient
   meaning for a genuine aesthetic enjoyment. Total comprehension, however, may make considerable demands on
   one's background of reading, and is obviously not
   always necessary or even desirable. Those interested
   in such elucidation may find something in the following
   suggestions.
      The 'tongues of flame,' on one level, are the fire

of suffering (the spurts of flame from an enemy
fighter), and, on another, Pentecostal fire. The
'knot,' for the individual, is the 'burning knot of
ghostly love' of the 14th century mystical treatise,
'The Cloud of Unknowing' (c. 47). In the cosmological
sense it is the 'nodo' of Dante, 'Paradiso' xxxiii, 91
(*i.e.*, the 'complex' of the universe). It is also a
Marian symbol, as may be seen from Henry Vaughan's poem,
'The Knot.' The 'fire,' as well as being an 'incen-
dium amoris' for the individual, is also the Heraclitean and Stoic *ekpyrosis*, or universal conflagration, but
more particularly represents the consummation of the
world at the end of time according to St. Paul and the
early Greek theologians. (*Cf.*, *e.g.*, Eph. I, 10, with
I Pet. iv, 12-14; II Pet. iii, 5-13; and perhaps Origen
on the 'anakastastasis.') The 'crown' (for the individual) recalls an earlier line of 'Little Gidding':
'to set a crown upon your lifetime's effort' (echoing
'finis coronat opus') as well as Apoc. (Rev.) ii, 10.
Cosmologically, 'crown' is probably suggested by the
Greek word used by St. Paul of the recapitulation of
the universe (the 'bringing-to-a-head' of all things in
Christ). The Alexandrian Greeks are also possibly in
the background. The Marian meaning will emerge from a
comparison of Vaughan's poem with the coronation in
Dante, 'Par.' xxiii (v, particularly, l. 119, 'la coro-
nata fiamma'). The 'rose' is not merely the rose of
youth and joy ('Burnt Norton'), but the Rosa Mystica of
Catholic liturgy, and the 'multifoliate rose' (the
'candida rosa,' 'gran fior ... di molte foglie') made
up by the assembly of the redeemed in Dante, 'Par.'
xxxi-ii.

This exegesis will perhaps not seem excessive if it
is remembered that the manifold of experience which the
poem attempts to communicate takes in literature as
well as life, and is at once intellectual and emotional.

'The Cocktail Party'

First produced at the Edinburgh Festival, 22-7 August 1949;
first edition, London, 9 March 1950;
first American edition, New York, 10 March 1950

151. I.H., MR. T.S. ELIOT'S NEW PLAY, 'MANCHESTER GUARDIAN'

23 August 1949, 3

EDINBURGH, MONDAY NIGHT

More than a comedy, Mr. T.S. Eliot's new play, 'The Cocktail Party,' which was given its first performance here
this evening, is as clear a definition of comedy itself as
has been seen; and in search of its immediate ancestry one
must go, strange though it may seem, to neither 'The
Family Reunion' nor to 'Murder in the Cathedral' - nor,
for that matter, save in theatrical technique, to any
comedy ancient or modern - but to the 'Four Quartets,'
that long meditative poem in four parts.

This play is largely a dialectical expression in theatrical terms of that sombre poem; but, lest there be misunderstanding, it should be said that this play pays its
way very well as a play. Mr. Eliot has coated a bitter
pill with much success. The main characters are a barrister (Robert Flemyng) and his wife (Ursula Jeans), a young
novelist (Donald Houston), and a young woman poet (Irene
Worth), four persons engaged in diagonal adultery, and a
strange figure, played finely by Alec Guinness, who is all
at once Tiresias, the voice of conscience, and a psychiatrist of that ideal sort who causes the patient to cure
himself. The barrister and his wife are, ostensibly
through the agency of this person, brought to realise one
another's isolation, and so through this realisation they
reach eventual reconciliation; the young novelist also in
the end realises that other people are not merely projec-
tions of his own desire; but the young woman poet dies in
desperate circumstances - the result, however, of her own
conscious choice.

591

The play begins with a cocktail party and it ends with
one. At the first the protagonists are ignorant; at the
second, having recognised the tragic nature of existence,
they realise, in spite of the news of the young woman's
death, that they must make the best of a bad job - that
is, get on with the cocktail party. They have had their
vision. Dr. Edith Sitwell once wrote of life as a play
conducted on a match-boarding stretched over hell; and
this is a comedy in that it insists that the play must continue - on the match-boarding. It is, that is to say,
only a fraction of a millimetre from tragedy. Hear how
the phrases recur: 'The same isolation.' 'We must make the
best of a bad job.' 'An awareness of solitude.' 'A sense
of sin.' 'The kind of face that arises from despair.'
'Go in peace; work out your salvation with diligence.'

If this seems a queer sort of comedy, let me quote the
words of Julia (Cathleen Nesbitt), a woman gloriously of
the world of necessary convention and perhaps the greatest
character in the play: 'You think I'm a silly old woman -
but I'm very serious really.' The core of the play is
this, that her words might quite easily be reversed: 'You
think I'm a serious old woman - but I'm very silly really.'
Eliot's difficult, extremely precise, and stoical thought
has never been expressed with more clarity, and the result
is remarkable.

152. PETER RUSSELL, A NOTE ON T.S. ELIOT'S NEW PLAY,
'NINE'

Autumn 1949, vol. i, 28-9

Russell (b. 1921), an English poet and critic, was founder-
editor of 'Nine'. The first issue, from which this review
is taken, opened with an encouraging message from Eliot.

A note on a play which has neither been published nor
widely presented on the stage, is no place to attempt a
general appraisal. In spite of difficulties encountered
by both audience and newspaper critics, the play was an
outstanding success. Considering the fact that the actors
neither knew their parts well nor even professed to 'understand' them, only strengthens one's conviction that 'The

Cocktail Party' will take its place with others of Mr.
Eliot's works, among the great achievements of our time.

Let us consider the factor in the play which baffled so
many people - namely, the contrast between its apparently
frivolous humour and its earnest contemplative philosophy.
It would be almost a platitude to say that most good works
of art act on the receptive mind at several simultaneous
levels. Dante even defined four of these 'levels' of
appeal in his 'Commedia'. Mr. Eliot's poetry is no exception to this principle yet it was a long time before his
method was accepted by more than a very small number of
serious readers. One of the main reasons for this appears
to have been the extreme diversity of the 'levels' in his
verse. A common seriousness of purpose appeared to be the
property of Dante's four levels and this was easy to
appreciate. Accordingly, it is through his later and
apparently more homogeneous verse, namely the 'Four Quartets', that wide recognition has come to Mr. Eliot. On
the other hand it is possible to see a similar unity in
the contrasts of 'The Waste Land' and 'Sweeney Agonistes',
and there is no reason to be surprised that the author of
these is the same poet who 'sits writing verses upon cats
that speak'. Few critics have mentioned the relevance of
Edward Lear, and this is perhaps symptomatic of the age we
live in, for we tend to be specialists not only in our
work but also in our leisure. The brilliant literary
critic of, say, the Queen Anne period is happy if not
proud to be quite unable to tell the difference between
Bach and Handel, and content never to have heard one note
of Vivaldi, Couperin or Rameau. Mr. Eliot has been
sneered at as 'academic' both by the most academic of
critics, like Dr. Leavis, and the most individual, like
Ezra Pound, but be that as it may, he has always had an
all-round grasp of the 'situation'. Eminently gifted for
an academic career of outstanding success, Mr. Eliot has
chosen the harder way, and kept not only the element of
novitas in his vision, but also the *diversitas*. In this
century few 'academics' have been strong enough to do
this.

It is not surprising, therefore, that the critics of the
play have divided into two parties, each baffled. One lot
felt it had had an evening of wit and fun worthy of Oscar
Wilde, or at least of Noel Coward in his better moments,
but found the play clouded by gloomy Hamlet-like soliloquies, private jokes, and subversive Christian propaganda.
The other lot laughed too - they could not help it, for
the play is an extremely witty one - but they were really
waiting for the recurring old shiver of recognition when
Mr. Eliot's 'real message' came through. Probably both

factions were scandalized by the surprising identity of
the 'guardians'. These latter appeared, in fact, to be
quite ordinary people, who, happening to have accepted
entirely their lot on earth, have become agents of Divine
Providence. Undoubtedly people were shocked by the almost
inhuman levity of the description (in the last act) of the
death of Celia, the society-girl, who became a missionary
nurse among savages. This was indeed melodramatic (more
like the work of Charles Williams than of T.S. Eliot), but
once granted that what happened had to happen, there can
in the intelligent Christian mind, be neither surprise nor
censure for the mature sophisticated attitude of the
teller of the story. He is a serious and responsible
character. He understands. The honest pagan mind, I
think, would also react in this sensible way. Naturally
the unoriented humanistic pseudo-Christian reacts with all
the petty rage of extreme sentimentality.

The play was cut considerably it seems, and no doubt
revision could make certain events and circumstances
clearer, but even as it was acted, it was an uncommonly
good theatrical piece. The curiously moving and obviously
effective moral philosophy of 'wait, and reflect' is as
much an integral part of the play as the farcical reversals and surprises. Contrary to common opinion, Mr.
Eliot's style and method has produced a play which is very
near to life as we suffer it to-day.

153. DESMOND SHAWE-TAYLOR, FROM A REVIEW OF THE EDINBURGH
FESTIVAL PRODUCTION, 'NEW STATESMAN'

3 September 1949, vol. xxxviii, 243

Shawe-Taylor (b. 1907) was music critic of the 'New Statesman' from 1945 to 1958.

A masked ball and a cocktail party, with Verdi and Mr.
Eliot, respectively, as our hosts: these have been the outstanding diversions of the first week at Edinburgh. They
were not so dissimilar as you might suppose: one culminated
in murder, the other in martyrdom, and both contrived to
introduce a good deal of light relief along the tragic
path.

'The Cocktail Party,' unlike Mr. Eliot's two earlier
plays, is on the surface a specimen of contemporary
dramatic style, as it is understood in Shaftesbury
Avenue. The curtain rises on the usual stylish flat, with
a white telephone, a Marie Laurencin, and a group of
rather exasperated people determined to make the party go.
The host, we begin to perceive, is also anxious to make
the party go - in another sense; but when at last they depart, he persuades one of them to stay, a stranger to whom
he can blurt out the embarrassing truth which he has tried
to conceal from the rest: his wife has left him, and the
guests we have seen are merely those who couldn't be
reached and put off. A first-rate situation, and what
follows is better still. The hitherto obscure and taci-
turn guest comes to life with a bang, takes command of the
situation, and pours out a stream of sardonic and paradoxical home-truths to the egotistical husband; finally,
like Mr. Bridie's lady, he bursts into song. The spirit
of early Shaw hovers deliciously in the air; the wit
sparkles and we begin to feel pleasantly sure that everything will be turned inside out and upside down in the
second act.
     So it is. The obscure guest is revealed as the eminent
Sir Henry Harcourt-Reilly, of Harley Street; the two most
tiresome of the guests turn out to be his assistants,
almost his spies. The party-givers (the husband who is incapable of loving, and the wife who can never inspire
love) are shown the truth about themselves, and persuaded
to make the best of it. Making the best of it, says Sir
Henry (and here for the first time we detect the accents
of the lay preacher), making the best of a bad job is
what we all have to do - all except the very few who are
potential saints. One of these also comes to his consulting room: a girl who has just seen the bottom fall out
of her ideal of romantic love. It is she who chooses the
via crucis which leads from Sir Henry's mysterious 'sanatorium' to literal crucifixion, accompanied by revolting
details, at the hands of fanatical natives. When the news
reaches another cocktail party, two years after the first,
everyone shudders, except Sir Henry, who smiles his in-
scrutable smile. It was an issue which he had more or
less foreseen.
     No less inscrutable must be the author's smile. He has
written a dazzling light comedy which is also a tract for
the times; and the audience, who lap up the surface cream,
don't know what to make of the depths, while suspecting
that they must be more interesting than milk. Will the
author help them? Only, a very, very little. When Sir
Henry, accustomed to pronounce a priest-like benediction

on his departing patients, remarks, 'I do not understand
what I myself am saying,' a slight ripple of mirth went
round the audience. Pressed by one of the characters for
an explanation of his philosophy, he quotes Shelley:

>   Ere Babylon was dust,
> The Magus Zoroaster, my dead child,
> Met his own image walking in the garden,
> That apparition, sole of men, he saw.

In short, know yourself; choose; come to terms with your
insignificance, or - if you happen to be one of the
saintly few - face the full consequences of your choice.

If the moral, as I attempt to put it, sounds rather thin
and milky, it is doubtless my fault - one which deeper
acquaintance with this fascinating play might mend. But
there is something about it which chills me: perhaps the
lack of delight in the rich variety of human nature. Mr.
Eliot's characters are admirably amusing puppets, he
manipulates them as cunningly as the magician in 'Petrou-
chka,' but, like the host at his own party, he seems incapable of love: of warmth towards the particular, as
opposed to a diffused benevolence. The muddy adorable
substance of life as it is lived seems curiously far from
this fragile community, and I find something faintly repellent in the quiet smiles and antiseptic wisdom of Sir
Henry and his two pals. Considered as moral teachers and
'guardians' (a key-word of the play), they suggest a group
of infinitely superior Buchmanite leaders, out of the
Upper Sixth instead of the usual Lower Fourth; but considered simply and solely as theatrical figures they are
superb, just as the whole play is a superbly contrived
conversation piece - lively, often cynical, sometimes
profound. The verse is perceptible only as a gentle
rhythmic pulse, and the language is almost that of life
except for the substitution of 'was not' for 'wasn't,'
etc., which gives a pleasant stiffening to the dialogue.
The play is capitally produced by E. Martin Browne, and
finely acted by Robert Flemyng, Irene Worth, Ursula Jeans,
Donald Houston, Cathleen Nesbitt and Alec Guinness. Mr.
Guinness lends an extraordinary sort of comic authority to
Sir Henry: with his long quizzical face, his sardonic
humour and his impressive delivery, he conveys (am I wrong
who never saw the Great Man?) something of the magnetism
of another Sir Henry.

154. ROBERT SPEAIGHT, A REVIEW, 'TABLET'

3 September 1949, vol. cxciv, 154-5

'The Cocktail Party,' presented last week at the Edinburgh
Festival, is the most advanced and original point yet
reached in Mr. Eliot's dramatic writing. Yet of his three
plays this one will surely prove the most accessible to
the ordinary playgoer. 'Murder in the Cathedral' pre-
supposed a certain familiarity with Christian dogma and
liturgy, and a readiness to accept a poetry which never
concealed its metrical diversity. In 'The Family Reunion'
the Greek Eumenides were made the messengers of grace; and
although 'The Family Reunion' marked a long step forward
in theatrical technique, and although Mr. Eliot had discovered a verse form suitable for a contemporary subject
and setting, the play moved a little stiffly and its climax of conversion was not dramatically realized. It was
the actor rather than the dramatist, who had to sharpen
the play to its point in the great dualogue between Agatha
and Harry. But in 'The Cocktail Party' there is little
impediment for anyone who is not tone-deaf to the supernatural. It is a profound and subtle play, with multiple
layers of meaning and an intricate symbolism. But the
poetry, more loquative than the poetry of 'The Family
Reunion,' is precise and lucid; and the design is clear.
    In the play's centre are four people whose lives have
become entangled. Edward, a middle-ageing barrister, whose
wife, Lavinia, has just left him, and who has for some time
been in love with Celia; Peter, his friend, who is also in
love with Celia; Celia, who loves Edward; and Lavinia, who
loves Peter but knows herself to be unloved by him. It is
a familiar mixture, but it is not the mixture as before.
Around this central group are two friends, Julia, a grey-
haired, good-natured society chatterbox, with Alex, a
bright young man about town, and a third figure, unidentified at first, whom they have introduced to the Cocktail
Party which opens the play.   This is a well-known psychiatrist, Sir Henry Harcourt-Reilly, and his purpose is
to set these frustrated lives in order. In the first act
the pattern of personal relationships unfolds itself. In
the second, Lavinia returns to a husband who surprisingly
wants to take her back, although he has not yet learned
to love her; and Celia says good-bye to a lover whom she
had thought to marry but has now mysteriously outgrown.
In the third act the scene shifts to Sir Henry's
consulting-room. The psychiatrist, whom both Edward and

Lavinia have been persuaded to see, neither of them knowing that he is their unidentified friend of the Cocktail
Party, confronts husband and wife with each other and
sends them back, not to the ecstasies and illusions of
romantic love, but to what is still 'in a world of lunacy,
violence, stupidity, greed ... a good life.' From now on
they will be

> ...contented with the morning that separates
> And with the evening that brings together
> For casual talk before the fire
> Two people who know they do not understand each other,
> Breeding children whom they do not understand
> And who will never understand them.

The scene that follows is the finest passage in the
play. Celia comes in and we presently realize that here
is a soul capable of subsisting on the glaciers of the
spiritual life. Though she does not yet know it herself,
she is a contemplative. This development has been subtly
prepared for us, in her previous scene with Edward. At a
loss to explain her own reaction at his desire to have
Lavinia back – she is humiliated but surprised at her
capacity to survive humiliation – she is aware of a state
of mind for which Edward was not mainly responsible.

> It no longer seems worth while to speak to anyone.

Now, confronted with the surgery of a consulting-room
which is also a confessional, she can articulate her sense
of sin. This is not a remorse for anything she has done,
not a conventional consciousness of immorality, it is a
sense, rather,

> of emptiness, of failure
> Towards someone, or something, outside of myself;
> And I feel I must ... atone.

She is coming, also, to a new understanding of love –

> a vibration of delight
> Without desire, for desire is fulfilled
> In the delight of loving.

And so Sir Henry sends her to the Special Sanatorium,
which is reserved for those who, by suffering greatly
themselves, can teach others that without suffering there
is neither salvation nor significance. Celia is on the
threshold of the intolerable discovery – that only

sanctity makes sense. Supported by the 'faith that
issues from despair,' she does not even know where she is
going.

> The destination cannot be described;
> You will know very little until you get there;
> You will journey blind. But the way leads towards
>   possession
> Of what you have sought for in the wrong place.

For Celia, who is pre-eminently a lover, there can be no
turning back.

> I couldn't give anyone the kind of love -
> I wish I could! - which belongs to *that* life.

Her nuptials are to be elsewhere; and as she goes, Sir
Henry with Alex and Julia, who have contrived all these
consultations and listened to them from the next room,
pour out three glasses of sherry, and, breaking for the
first time into formal verse, implore protection on her
journey.

In the fourth act Edward and Lavinia are giving another
cocktail party. Among the guests are Sir Henry and Julia;
Alex, returned from Africa, where he had been sitting on a
Royal Commission; and Peter, arrived from Hollywood, where
he has made good as a script writer, and eager to claim
Celia as the film actress which he believes her to be.
Then Alex explains that he cannot have Celia - because
Celia is dead. She had joined a nursing order of nuns and
been crucified by natives in a village which Alex had
visited. He had seen her body decomposed and devoured by
ants. This revelation, so dreadful and so uplifting, is
achieved with extraordinary skill. The rattling of
glasses and banter of conversation is suddenly arrested -
and we are not embarrassed. Here, as elsewhere, Mr. Eliot
is helped by his actors; no one puts a foot or an inflec-
tion wrong. The play ends with Sir Henry explaining why
Celia's death had been a happy one, and with him, Julia
and Alex going off to another party.

The play is a masterpiece of theatrical contrivance.
In the first act the trivial interventions of Julia and
Alex, which seem an interruption of serious emotional
business, prepare us for their critical intervention
later. (Perhaps the Guardian Angels, whom they so
amusingly symbolize, are more familiar than we guess.)
The dramatist focuses his light, first upon Edward, who
is our old friend J. Alfred Prufrock, and then upon Celia,
who is already living the experience of the 'Four

Quartets.' Thus the play resumes, in its unstressed
fashion, the long journey that Mr. Eliot has travelled.
The loneliness of Gerontion is in Edward's definition of
his dilemma:-

    Hell is oneself,
    Hell is alone, the other figures in it
    Merely projections. There is nothing to escape from
    And nothing to escape to. One is always alone.

This is the other side of the Sartrian image which was
dramatized in 'Huis Clos.' The Lenten reminders of 'Ash-
Wednesday' are in Sir Henry's parting words to the reconciled couple:-

    Go in peace. And work out your salvation with
        diligence.

Just as the realism and humility of the 'Quartets' are in
his subsequent observation:-

    The best of a bad job is all any of us make of it.
        Except, of course, the saints.

    The gesture with which Mr. Alec Guinness took out his
watch on these last words was perhaps the most imaginative
moment in a magnificent performance. Sir Henry might so
easily have become an ethical bore, sugaring his pills
with whimsy. But with Mr. Guinness we are worlds away
from ethics; this is the confessional and the choice is
between the loss of personality and the love of God.
Miss Irene Worth suggested, in a moving and vibrant study,
the whole of Celia's capacity for sacred and profane love;
Miss Ursula Jeans, with no sacrifice of natural charm,
made Lavinia naturally unlovable, but yet made us realize,
in the last act, how grace was doing its work; Mr. Robert
Flemyng, young in years for Edward, gave us the authentic
sag of middle age and a twinge of the Existentialist
agony; and Miss Cathleen Nesbitt conducted Julia with both
judgment and wit along the realistic and symbolic levels.
This superb ensemble of English acting was so well
directed by Mr. Martin Browne that you didn't notice it.
But then Mr. Browne has been Mr. Eliot's theatrical *eminence grise* since the days of 'Murder in the Cathedral' -
and earlier. Author, actors and audience should be grateful that he has assisted into life a play which is among
the rare masterpieces of the modern stage.

155. WILLIAM CARLOS WILLIAMS, IT'S ABOUT 'YOUR LIFE AND
MINE, DARLING', 'NEW YORK POST'

12 March 1950, M18

'The Cocktail Party' is a very thrilling play which in the
reading moved me deeply. The lines begin with capitals so
that you see at once that it is all intended as verse.
Those who hear the play and have not read it will not know
that. I think definitely though that they will feel it to
be verse - without knowing and without offense. To me
this would be a very considerable achievement on the part
of Mr. Eliot.
Verse by its arrangement of them attempts to do something above the literal meaning of the words. It attempts
to erect a structure of meaning that raises the literal
meaning to moral heights, a moral that goes back to the
state itself - if we knew.
I don't think that Mr. Eliot's lines quite do that. It
is a bare sort of verse, verse cut down to pure numbers,
to pure counting on a very elementary basis. I must say
though that I don't know what other kind of verse could
have been used to the purpose. It fits the very simple
story, the very plain everyday sort of story that Mr. Eliot
has chosen for his effects; a quadrangular affair of husband and wife with their complementary partners in illicit
love.
The whole parade of events, very quiet events, that make
make up the play is illumined by revelations of the
character of a girl named Celia as she goes calmly to her
destruction - which casts a sunset glow over all the final
scenes. I think this is, on or off the stage, Mr. Eliot's
most moving character. As the tremendous emotional climax
approaches you might expect the verse to quicken and gain
an increased closeness of emotional texture. It doesn't.
As a matter of fact this reticence enhances the tragic
effect. The poet has kept a close rein on the texture of
the verse quite as ordinary speech would have it. This is
in the English character and in character too with the
later Eliot. He has come down to his audience with
humility and, I believe, success.
The cocktail party, on the stage, with which the play
begins and ends, not the same cocktail party but a cocktail
party B.C. and A.D. you might say, is, darling, your life
and mine. And there are two ways out - and it was very
kind of Mr. Eliot to have provided them - the way of the
Chamberlaynes and Celia's way. Without Celia and her

heroism (a strange new note in Mr. Eliot's poems) the day-
to-day solution by homely honesty could not have emerged
quite as brilliantly as it did. But it was kind, I repeat,
for Mr. Eliot to offer the poor married ones an escape
also.

The final toast is to Lavinia's Aunt, invented by
Edward, the husband, for his own convenience - the imagination, the lie, the poem itself that occasionally serves to
waken us from a sleep troubled by violent dreams.

I shall say no more, I do not want to spoil the fun.

156. E.M. FORSTER, MR. ELIOT'S 'COMEDY', 'LISTENER'

23 March 1950, vol. xliii, 533

Forster (1879-1970), novelist and critic, was associated
with the Bloomsbury Group, though he was never one of its
central figures. His greatest novel is 'A Passage to
India' (1924), after which he wrote no more novels. He
did, however, continue to publish biographies and collec-
tions of his essays. This review was reprinted in one
such collection, 'Two Cheers for Democracy' (London,
1951), pp. 268-70.

A comedy where one of the characters is crucified on an
ant-hill is not comic in the usual sense of the word, and
readers of 'The Cocktail Party' will do well to arm themselves against difficulties. On the stage, those difficulties may diminish: the play was well received when it was
produced at the Edinburgh Festival last year, and it is
having a tremendous success in New York. The faces and
voices and clothes of the characters may help to establish
a perspective which is unobtainable through words.

Where does the mere reader find himself? In an
operating-theatre - a spiritual one. He has realised in
the first act that something is wrong with some of the
characters, perhaps with all of them; they chatter miser-
ably and endlessly and drink unprofitably, and Lavinia,
the wife who should be helping Edward her husband to throw
the party has just deserted him. In the second act the
reader gets a dramatic surprise - his big laugh, if the
phrase be permissible. He discovers that three of the

worthless guests were really doctors, who were mingling
with their unsuspecting patients in order to gather information about them. Surgeon-in-chief is Sir Henry
Harcourt-Reilly, previously an anonymous buffoon and now
enthroned in his consulting room. With him work Julia,
previously mistaken for an ill-natured feckless old
woman, and Alex, mistaken for a globe-trotter with
pseudo-connections which turn out to be genuine. The
patients arrive. Edward and Lavinia are confronted with
one another, to their mutual indignation, and the similar-
ity of their cases emphasised. They are refused any
spectacular cure. They are followed by Celia, the girl
with whom Edward has intrigued. Celia's position is different, is unique. She has a sense of sin - not for anything specific, but a general sense, and she desires to
'atone'. A way is pointed out to her, and accepted by
her, no fee is charged her, and she is assigned to a
'sanitorium' the outcome of which no one can foresee, not
even the experts. A fourth patient is expected, but he
is too much immersed in worldliness, and does not come.
The act ends in a solemn and touching libation to the
safety of Celia. It has become clear to the reader that
he is actually in the presence of the Church, which is
directing its children, through its priesthood, on their
appropriate paths.

   In the third act he learns what has happened. Edward
and Lavinia are reconciled, are living together happily
and civilly in their old flat, and are about to throw yet
another cocktail party. It is the best they can achieve.
Their quarrel was not important, nor is their reconciliation. The worldly young man has become still more worldly.
As for Celia, we hear that she has chosen the path of
Devotion and Dedication, has become a nurse and a nun, and
has perished agonisingly amongst savages. Her sufferings
are dwelt on, are indeed gloated over, and no doubt this
is consonant with Mr. Eliot's religious outlook and with
his 'comedy'. But aesthetically the sufferings disturb
the reader and distract him. The Christian ethic of
atonement, which has been impending over his head since
the end of the second act, comes down with too sudden a
bump. He hears the doctor-priests analysing the successful martyrdom as they sip their drinks, and he wonders.

   The difficulties of 'The Cocktail Party' do not extend
to its diction. It is most beautifully and lucidly
written. Mr. Eliot can do whatever he likes with the
English language. This time he has selected a demure
chatty verse-form which seems to be like prose, but it is
full of turns and subtle echoes, and always open for the
emotional intensity he occasionally needs. On the stage,

such diction may well carry all before it, and, reinforced
by the sound stage-craft, may place affairs in a less
puzzling perspective.

157. FROM AN UNSIGNED REVIEW, ENTERTAINMENT AND REALITY,
'TIMES LITERARY SUPPLEMENT'

31 March 1950, no. 2513, 198

If it were no more than an academic experiment in verse
drama, 'The Cocktail Party,' simply by virtue of its
technical accomplishment, would demand attention alike
from Mr. Eliot's fellow experimentalists and from all who
are convinced that the present theatrical forms badly need
to be refreshed with a new kind of energy. But the comedy,
to judge from its reception at the Edinburgh Festival and
in New York, succeeds on the stage; and to win just this
kind of success is the main object of the experiment.
    It seeks to show in practice how well founded is the
theory that verse can deal with the dramatic material that
is of most immediate interest to the ordinary playgoing
public. The appeal is not to a small circle of initiates,
but to the main body of theatrical pleasure-seekers who
hold very reasonably that the primary business of dramatic
entertainments is to entertain. It has yet to be known
what the verdict of London will be, but potential patrons
- many of whom will scarcely trouble to read the text -
may be assured that the author has in this instance
shown as much respect for what Shaftesbury Avenue is supposed to want as for his own sense of reality.
    The characters are the men and women of drawing-room
comedy. To that convention belong all the perplexities,
conflicts and misunderstandings in which they are involved.
The cocktail party chatter, light, easy, amusing, is gaily
decorated with the sprightly extravagances that make in
the theatre an effect of wit. The action moves from first
to last with smoothness and speed, and at least two of the
three acts have a continuing tension. It is true that the
reality to which the characters ultimately conform is the
author's own and may not win anything like general acceptance, may indeed excite the active hostility of those who
have a more affectionate regard for the vagaries of human
character than Mr. Eliot permits himself. But then the
validity of Mr. Eliot's spiritual convictions is always

open to debate. To debate it in connexion with 'The Cocktail Party' is to cloud a question of more moment to the
theatre: does the comedy issue its idiosyncratic challenge
in good dramatic terms?

It is relevant to the dramatic values of the piece to
point out that by the end of the second act the main
crises have been virtually resolved. The third act is no
more than an epilogue describing how the persons involved
in the crises have fared. When the husband and wife - he
a man who finds himself incapable of loving, she a woman
who finds that no man can love her - have been brought to
accept their limitations they have made their dramatic
choice. They have faced the reality of their own little-
ness and, abandoning their fixed attitudes, have agreed
to regard the common sense of isolation not as a reason
for loathing each other but as the bond which holds them
together. Their decision to make the best of a bad job
is dramatic; what in practice they make of it is not of
much dramatic importance. So it is with the heroine, a
cocktail-drinking girl who has the courage to face her own
truth. The scene in which she bares her spiritual misgivings and strivings in the Harley Street consulting room
is superbly charged with energy. Tension is controlled by
verse which makes its transitions between the prosaic and
the poetic with unfaltering certainty and the utmost
smoothness. It is perhaps the finest scene in modern
poetic drama. Celia Coplestone chooses the hard, the
terrifying way to fulfilment, and having made the choice,
she becomes a character fulfilled. The third act reports
that she has died a martyr in the most horrible way imaginable, but the fact adds nothing, dramatically speaking,
to our knowledge of her as a woman capable of making the
hard choice. Mr. Eliot uses the third act to moralize the
crises which have been resolved and also to deepen the
shadows of a world behind the world which have flickered
disturbingly through the comedy. The Chamberlaynes are
shown in process of working out salvation according to
their limited means, and Celia's death is represented by
the doctor who has helped her to make the choice which led
to it as the happiest of deaths, that of a saint. 'She
did not suffer as ordinary people suffer?' asks Edward
Chamberlayne, clutching at easy comfort. 'She suffered
all that we should suffer in fear and pain and loathing,'
replies Sir Henry Harcourt-Reilly, 'She paid the highest
price in suffering. That is part of the design.' By
these means Mr. Eliot keeps interest alive through the
third act, but the play would be structurally stronger if
more were made of Peter Quilpe, a young film producer who
stands spiritually midway between the mediocrities and the

saints. He finds his own path to salvation, but it is a
dimly, even perfunctorily lighted path, and the chiaro-
scuro of the act could certainly afford him a few more
lamps.

Mr. Eliot has incurred easy smiles by saying that the
verse he uses in this play need not be recognized as
verse. Stage performance has made his meaning clear. The
purpose of the verse is not to paint scenery in the Elizabethan way, nor to make verbal patterns, nor to create
emotions in excess of the matter under discussion, but to
give the dialogue the finest possible precision and intensity. It avoids specifically poetic language, but it is,
even during the prosaic passages of the dialogue, preparing the ear of the auditor for scenes which have by imperceptible transitions reached a pitch of intensity needing
the compression of verse to sustain them. The auditor
need not notice the versification. He is meant only to be
aware of the higher charge of energy which has entered the
scene by means of the versification.

158. WILLIAM BARRETT, DRY LAND, DRY MARTINI, 'PARTISAN
REVIEW'

April 1950, vol. xvii, 354-9

Barrett (b. 1913), an American philosopher, was editor of
the 'Partisan Review' from 1946 to 1953. One of his best
known works is 'Irrational Man' (1958).

Among the many questions raised by T.S. Eliot's 'The Cocktail Party' the first and most immediate would seem to be
how far we can separate, even provisionally, the play and
its success from the author and his fame. The audience
did not appear to wish such separation, for one sensed in
its enthusiasm a certain self-congratulation that it was
able to enjoy what it felt it *ought* to enjoy, and had
feared, coming to the theater, it might not be able to
enjoy. The critics simply made this response articulate:
some were enthusiastic by the standards of Broadway;
nearly all were pleased with themselves that they were
not bored by what they had been told in advance was a play
in verse; some seemed to veil their real dissatisfaction
with the play for fear of self-exposure in attacking so

great a name. I labor these points at the start because I
have found, in talking with people who have seen the play,
a very curious ambiguity in its reception: on the one hand,
the play seems to have been carried to a critical and commercial success by the author's name, but on the other
hand seems to be finally approved of by the standards of
Broadway, which are hardly those of Eliot. For my own
part, I am unable to separate the play from its author;
and, this being the case, I must assimilate the play by
the standards that Eliot's other work invokes and often
satisfies, and measuring by such standards I find 'The
Cocktail Party' a disappointing work: thin and unconvinc-
ing as drama and weak as poetry - perhaps the weakest
poetry that Eliot has yet written.

The play, and very largely because of its success, does
throw a new light upon Eliot's old problem, his lifelong
obsession with the possibility of restoring the poetic
drama to the modern stage. 'Murder in the Cathedral' was
produced here by the WPA, (1) 'The Family Reunion,' so far
as I know, only by little theater groups, while 'The Cocktail Party' is now a Broadway hit! Eliot would seem then
to have solved his problem, at least for practical purposes; but the question is whether he has not succeeded by
so sugar-coating his pill that very little of the poetic
substance remains: whether, in short, he has so compromised
with the formal convention of verse in accordance with
which poetic drama ought to be written that the audience is
never shocked from its habitual habits of listening and can
receive this play as merely another version of the drawing-
room comedy. 'Isn't it wonderful!' a friend said to me as
we left the theater, 'It's poetry but you never know it.'
I am simple-minded enough to think that this must be a
very ambiguous compliment for the author even though he
seems to have calculated some such effect, according to his
own explanation of the theory behind the play:

The verse should be unnoticeable; the audience should
not be conscious of the difference from prose. The purpose of the verse should be to operate upon the auditor
unconsciously so that he shall think and feel in the
rhythms imposed by the poet without being aware of what
these rhythms are doing. All the time these rhythms
should be preparing the audience for the moments of intensity when the emotion of the character in the play
may be supposed to lift him from his ordinary discourse
- until the audience feels, not that the actors are
speaking verse, but that the characters of the play
have been liften into poetry.

This is very well put, and the strategy sounds good, but does 'The Cocktail Party' really lift its actors at any point to that level of intense or moving speech where the poetry is no longer hidden but open? In the last act, the leading character, the psychiatrist-priest Harcourt-Reilly, quotes some lines from Shelley, and the effect, to my ears at least, was like the sudden clear ringing of a bell, in comparison with which the rest of Eliot's play might very well have been written in prose. The reading of the play has confirmed this impression: the beat of the verse is so indefinite and uncertain, at times so limp and flat, that if one had not seen the play one could scarcely believe that the verse would sound even as well as it does from the stage. Eliot has been very lucky indeed to have, in this production by the Sherek Players, a performance of the play that could scarcely be improved upon, so that one feels there are no lurking places of drama or symbolism that might be brought out by any other and different staging. (I suspect that the play's success is in good part due to this excellence of performance, and particularly to the pleasure of hearing English well and naturally spoken, - a not too common experience for American playgoers.) In his earlier fragment 'Sweeney Agonistes' Eliot had not sought to transmute the formal convention of verse into something hardly distinguishable from prose, but had in fact insisted upon the convention with a starkness of rhythm and syncopation that makes this work, fragmentary as it is, his greatest achievement as a dramatic poet. A whole play in the style of 'Sweeney' would have been a much more considerable step toward the revival of poetic drama, but I doubt that such a play would ever reach Broadway, for it would demand an audience ready to accept a formal and stylized theater; and years ago Eliot himself in his Dialogue on Dramatic Poetry announced through one of the interlocutors that the search for a poetic drama valid for our time must be carried forward by small experimental theaters. But the question of the audience aside, what we would like to recall is Eliot's own repeated emphasis in his earlier critical writings that poetic drama to be valid must insist upon its convention, the form and stylization implicit in verse, and that the error of William Archer and the realistic theater was to believe that only the convention of prose was valid. 'The Cocktail Party' seems to parallel a tendency apparent in recent years in the production of Shakespeare, where the passages of blank verse are made to sound more 'natural' - i.e., acceptable to the audience - by being spoken as if they were prose, or at most some vaguely rhythmic free verse.

The present play demands comparison with 'Sweeney

Agonistes' on other grounds, for both deal, though [dif]-
ferent ways, with the sheer overwhelming fact of hu[man]
banality: in 'Sweeney' the crudity of the lower orders,
here the tedious chatter of the middle classes. The opening scenes attempt in fact to rework the same devices of
repetition that had been so successfully banal in the
earlier work, but they do not do so well here because they
lack the formal definiteness, the bare strident saxophone
note, of 'Sweeney.' One critic thought the opening scene
funnier than Noel Coward, but to my mind the garrulous
old harpy Julia Shuttlethwaite, who dominates the opening
conversation and whom Eliot wishes to depict as tedious,
was nothing less than that. To this general cocktail
atmosphere Eliot adds some typically modern ingredients:
the strained marriage of the Chamberlaynes, the separate
affairs of husband and wife (*mélange adultère de tous*),
the running away of the wife, and then the entrance of the
modern tinker of broken marriages, the psychiatrist. (All
these carefully calculated elements show a cunning intelligence at work, and it is not generally deficiency of
literary intelligence, but of creative vitality, that we
complain of in this play.) Against the background of
these banal furnishings Eliot wishes, of course, to
develop his own Christian themes, but right there the difficulties of incongruity begin, and we are asked, among
other things, to accept the astounding transformation in
the second act of the two fatuous cocktail figures, Julia
and Alex, into guardian angels with supernatural powers.
Eliot has set himself a formidable problem: How to make
the possibility of the saint meaningful against this background of cocktail chatter? The saint appears here in the
person of the young woman Celia Coplestone, who, when her
affair with Edward Chamberlayne breaks off, becomes a
missionary and is finally crucified by the natives of a
remote island. 'She will go far, that one,' the psychiatrist says of her as she sets off on her journey, but there
is little given us to back up this judgment and Celia
hardly stands out as very different from the other trivial
people at the party.

In a certain sense all these difficulties of incongruity are concentrated in the character of Harcourt-Reilly,
who as psychiatrist and priest seems to be somehow func-
tioning simultaneously on both the natural and supernatural levels. As a psychiatrist he performs the quite
unbelievable feat of bring the estranged Chamberlaynes
together by explaining that they are perfectly suited to
each other since the wife is unlovable and the husband incapable of loving. Chamberlayne, when he hears this, is
on the edge of a nervous breakdown, and it strikes me that

the only possible effect of these words would be to drive
him off the deep end. I was surprised that some of the
critics found the thought of the play difficult and obscure, when it is in fact simple and obvious: we must,
Eliot is saying, either make the best of a bad job - bear
with resignation the limitations and frustrations of daily
life - or follow the path of the saints; there are no other
alternatives. One does not quarrel with the alternatives
but with the fact that the Chamberlaynes, who are as boring and empty a couple as can be found only in the most
trivial stories of the 'New Yorker,' should represent the
fullness of natural life in contrast to the life of
sanctity. The psychiatrist hardly improves things by explaining this 'good life' of marriage:

[Quotes 'The Cocktail Party', II, CPP, p. 417, '(they)
Maintain themselves' to 'never understand them'.]

One can have a pretty vivid sense of the horrors of
marriage, as well as of the final isolation in which we
are all imprisoned, but still one gags at these lines as
representing the ultimate possibilities for human love.
What comes to my mind immediately is that great poem of
marriage, James Joyce's 'Finnegans Wake,' which knows all
the disgust and anguish of married life but also all its
dear dirty joys. The question is not so much that of
'understanding' but of opening oneself in love to another
person; human kind, as Eliot puts it, may not be able to
bear very much reality, but even the Chamberlaynes of this
world are capable of more than he allows them. Here we
must remember that Eliot, the last great product of the
Puritan mind, has never shown in his poetry any real belief in the possibility of human love. The moment of love
is presented always as the moment of withdrawal and renunciation, the awful daring of a moment's surrender, one of
'the things that other people have desired'; and consequently the beauty of the world is never present in the
fullness of joy, but always with that painful clutch at
the heart as at something taken away, lost, uncapturable.
No doubt, resignation is necessary to get through life at
all, and Freud himself stated that the aim of analytic
therapy was to enable the neurotic to bear the sufferings
inevitable in human life; but this is only half the picture, for the work of the analyst may also be to liberate
the patient for the positive joys that life can hold, even
perhaps for the possibility of love, and if the neurotic
were told that he is to be resigned only for resignation's
sake, it is very unlikely that he would have the strength
to go on.

I was surprised to read that one critic found in the
play the gaiety that Stendhal recommends for all art, for
it seems to me that at bottom the world of 'The Cocktail
Party' is the same empty world of 'Prufrock,' except that
37 years ago Eliot did not disguise his contempt for this
emptiness. So I feel at the heart of this play some
immense *tricherie*, or at least self-deception, for I can't
believe that Eliot takes the Chamberlaynes as seriously as
he pretends to. Here again, comparison with 'Sweeney
Agonistes' becomes instructive, for in this earlier fragment Eliot fully released all his hatred of human life
and really enjoyed himself in the raucous company of Doris,
Sweeney, Klipstein, and Krumpacker - in comparison with
whose vulgar vitality the characters at the cocktail party
are genteel skeletons. As a writer Eliot has never really
given us God's plenty: the qualities of his genius are not
robustness and richness, but precision, terseness, and
intensity; and the shadow which haunts these qualities is
a certain tendency to thinness and brittleness that here
in 'The Cocktail Party' has at last caught up with him.
   The public reception of this play points toward the
larger problem (that we can only mention briefly here)
arising from Eliot's present position in the world of
letters: the embarrassing and delicate situation of the
master at the height of his fame and influence at the very
moment when his creative powers and energy appear to be at
their lowest ebb. Many years ago now, it seems, we were
undergraduates, and Eliot's name was a secret and holy
conspiracy among us against our teachers of English literature and the tastes they taught. Since then we have seen
his influence spread abroad, and his figure become en-
trenched in the academy itself; this influence has been
immensely valuable, and it is hard to imagine what we
might be without it; but every influence is exclusive in
some directions, and so we have seen this one too become in
time stiff and rigid, and finally lend itself to academi-
cism. It would be, of course, unfair to blame a man for
all the things done in his name, but the character of this
influence, the doors of experience it closes, must be
pointed out, for we have, if we are to go on living, to
make way always for a new future. Perhaps every new literary generation has to begin by killing its father.

Note

1 Work Projects Administration (WPA): a former agency of
   the US government, created in 1935 by executive order of
   President Franklin D. Roosevelt to provide work for the

unemployed. Amongst other things, it sponsored many
arts and theatre projects.

159. BONAMY DOBRÉE, BOOKS AND WRITERS, 'SPECTATOR'

21 April 1950, vol. clxxxiv, 541

Dobrée (1891-1974) was Professor of English at the University of Leeds from 1936 until 1951. His publications
include 'The Lamp and the Lute' (1929), 'Modern Prose
Style' (1934) and 'The Early Eighteenth Century' (1959).

Mr. Eliot is, from all appearance, one of that class of
poets who work from the 'meaning' or intuition to the
symbol, what he has called 'the objective correlative,'
rather than from the spectacle of life to an 'imitation'
so shaped that some meaning will emerge from it, some
attitude be induced. It is for this reason, one supposes,
that his chief technical difficulty would seem to be the
fusing together of the various planes of reality, which
must co-exist to some degree in any play, and which with
him is a major problem, as it must be with any playwright
whose work is at the same time original and highly complex. The problem did not trouble the Elizabethans, who,
living in a pre-scientific age, were prepared to accept
the simultaneous presentation of various planes (as, say,
in 'The Tempest'): but it did trouble Ibsen, as it does
M. Sartre. To some extent the re-handling of an old myth
is a solution, as so many French playwrights including M.
Anouilh have found, and as Mr. Eliot did when he flirted
with one in 'The Family Reunion': but here, in his new
play, though his Furies have become Eumenides, or
Guardians, they are not ghostly characters, but, at the
same time as Guardians, men and women living in the world.
Strange vessels of the spirit indeed, to whom we shall
return.
His other technical problems Mr. Eliot seems finally to
have resolved. He never had much difficulty over dramatic
movement; the sense of it is in his blood: it shaped 'The
Waste Land' and gave form to 'Four Quartets': but to trans-
late this into stage terms was none the less an operation
needing experience, and Mr. Eliot stumbled a little in

'Murder in the Cathedral'; but afterwards there was no
hitch. His medium of speech was not so easily attained:
too heavily rhythmed in 'Sweeney,' uncertain and wavering
in 'The Rock,' it was nearly right in 'The Family Reunion,'
though there it occasionally swung off into a lyrical
movement which in the setting was a little disturbing,
though by itself, in the study, enchanting. Now, we feel
secure, Mr. Eliot has achieved his mastery: he has worked
out a form of speech suitable for an actor to say, and
actor-proof, cadenced enough to enable the stresses to
tell, flexible enough to be either portentous or light;
and while it is a universal medium it yet carries his own
individual rhythms. A third problem, still not quite
solved, perhaps, is how to get the important universalis-
ing statements made by the characters. The chorus simply
will not do today, as others together with Mr. Eliot have
discovered: it was cunningly disguised in 'The Family
Reunion': but here, though perhaps vestigial traces remain
in the libation scene at the end of the second act, the
effect is more that of ritual utterance among the Guardians than of a chorus. Indeed the Guardians throughout
carry the *sententiae*; but in so far as they are ordinary
people living in the everyday humdrum world, they do not
draw undue attention to the fact that they are doing so.
Here and there, however, they seem a little self-conscious
about it.

A comedy? What you think of that label will depend
upon your idea of comedy. In so far as comedy is concerned with man's relation to man, the goings-on of the
Chamberlayne-Quilpe group are certainly comic, indeed at
moments brilliant comedy with all the classical implications of the word: but in so far as tragedy deals with
man's relation to God, then the other group, and certainly
Celia Coplestone, belong to the world of tragedy. Yet, in
so far as they are humans - the outrageous society harri-
dan, the preposterously complacent psycho-analyst, the man
of the world, half-social half-business, the Guardians are
comic. You might even say that the chief Guardian, Reilly,
is a figure of hideous sardonic comedy, a kind of Sir
Epicure Mammon in another sphere; but I do not think Mr.
Eliot meant this. And if you object that the Celia scene
in Act II is of a grave and high beauty incompatible with
comedy, you may remind yourself that certain scenes of
'Le Misanthrope' also have this quality. All, of course,
depends on the attitude the play finally induces in you,
in which particular world you feel involved, and what you
think the play is really about.

And it is here, perhaps, that Mr. Eliot has not quite
conquered his medium: though he himself, it would seem,

can now move with perfect freedom within the form, it is
not quite clear in what direction he is expecting us to
move. There are, perhaps, too many meanings, and we may
come away regarding the play either as a comedy within a
thin outer shell of tragedy, or as a tragedy within a
thick casing of comedy. And the trouble, I think, is that
there are moments when we do not know what plane of reality we are supposed to be on: we sometimes feel that we
are being offered two or three planes at one time in one
person, especially at the transitions. What, at any given
moment we might ask, is Julia? A superannuated frippery,
a Lady Wishfort? Or a divine messenger? As a rule the
transitions, or the fusings, in the tone of the play itself
are admirable. There are, we may say, four planes. First,
the a-moral one of Sweeney: the conversation of the first
few moments might come directly from 'Sweeney Agonistes';
then, when the yet undiscovered Reilly after some witty
cynicisms says:

> But let me tell you, that to approach the stranger
> Is to invite the unexpected, release a new force,
> Or let the genie out of the bottle.
> It is to start a train of events
> Beyond your control....

we are on the plane of Agatha in 'The Family Reunion,' the
moral one. Later, when first Peter and then Celia speak
of the nature of reality, we are on a metaphysical plane:
finally, with the Guardians in session as Guardians, on
a transcendental one. And the main 'meaning' of the play
seems to be dual - moral and transcendental.

Yet the statement in either case is that every individual must find that place in life which suits him: it is
the old conception of degree in the chain of being, combined with a Stoic acceptance. 'Resign yourself to be the
fool you are,' Sir Henry Reilly tells Edward Chamberlayne.
To lead the humdrum life is itself good. Each and every
person is offered a choice and must make one, though it is
not very illuminating to be told that 'the right choice is
the choice you cannot but make,' though indeed a sense of
destiny runs faintly through the play. Celia, predestined
as we are later told, made a choice based on 'the kind of
faith that issues from despair,' and found crucifixion in
the vicinity of an ants' nest. Each person, in short,
gets what he hungers for. 'A Chacun Selon sa Faim,' such
is the title of a play by a young playwright, Mr. Jean
Mogin, now running at the Vieux Colombier, and that might
well be the subtitle of Mr. Eliot's play, for the themes
are not dissimilar, and in each play a young woman chooses

a path which leads, a little wilfully, to martyrdom.   But
there are so many fascinating themes in 'The Cocktail
Party,' the play is so rich, so amazingly complex, that
each person will gain from it what he can, or put in it
what he must: for, as Mr. Eliot himself has said, in a poem
of any complexity the poet himself is not aware of all the
possible meanings.

With a play of such original texture as this, it is
difficult to judge from however imaginative a reading what
it would be like to see on the stage.   That it is a tense
play which will hold an audience one would suspect; that
it does hold audiences through laughter is, I understand,
being proved by the event, though it is difficult to see
how the shock of Celia's crucifixion, and the theological
implications which will revolt more people than Lavinia
Chamberlayne, can in the final passages be resolved into
the apprehensions of comedy.   The forthcoming production in
London will enable one to put theories to the test.   Some
scenes, obviously, are intensely amusing; many of the quiet
ones are the highest Meredithian comedy.   The play is a
disturbing experience, and certainly nobody will lay the
book down - and it is to be suspected that nobody will come
away from seeing the play - without feeling that somewhere
some barb has pierced beneath the skin.   If he does not
feel that, he had better begin looking into himself: or
perhaps, on reflection, he had better not.

160. JOHN PETER, SIN AND SODA, 'SCRUTINY'

Spring 1950, vol. xvii, 61-6

Peter (b. 1921) teaches at the University of Victoria,
British Columbia.   He has written a number of pieces on
Eliot, the most widely known being that on 'The Waste
Land' ('Essays in Criticism' (July 1952), ii, 242-66) in
which he suggested that the protagonist was in love with
'a young man who soon afterwards met his death, it would
seem by drowning'.   For an account of Eliot's reaction and
threatened libel suit, see F.W. Bateson, Editorial Commentary, 'Essays in Criticism' (January 1969), xix, 1-5.   In
the Spring issue of the same year, Peter's original essay
was reprinted, together with Postscript (1969) defending
and expanding the argument.   (The same issue contains two
further essays, though not by Peter, on 'The Waste Land',

both in varying degrees critical of the poem.) Peter contributed quite regularly to 'Scrutiny' in its latter
years.

Though the play seems very much closer to 'Sejanus' than
to 'Every Man In His Humour' one cannot feel that it was
strange of Jonson to call 'Volpone' a comedy. Some such
description was usual on the title-pages of his times and
of the two chief he chose the least misleading. But when
Mr. Eliot calls his new play a comedy he seems to me to
be closer to the position of a Shakespeare calling 'Macbeth' a comedy on the strength of the Porter Scene. Only
the incidentals in the play are, in fact, comic and,
though on the stage they should be much more effective, on
paper they barely deserve the adjective. I suppose that
the more perspicacious readers will think of Dante and
accept the description in the very limited sense in which
it seems intended; the rest are likely, however, to yield
to the general chorus of the dramatic critics, to accept
the play as 'witty' and 'delightful', and to get little
further into it than the title might seem to tempt them to
get. If they find it unsatisfactory it will be on the
grounds that parts of it are dull and not because - what
is surely the real criterion for judgment - it is unsuccessful on the terms that it prescribes for itself.
    A good deal of the play, and particularly that part of
it that relates to Celia Coplestone, is a development of
the ideas handled in 'The Family Reunion', and the reader
will be well advised to discard any presuppositions which
the use of the term 'Comedy' may raise and to treat the
play with the same sobriety that he would bring to its
predecessor. Like 'The Family Reunion' it is an attempt
to discuss religious topics in theatrical terms and, again
like that play, it essays this discussion by using situations from modern life. Both plays, that is, attempt
something much more difficult than is attempted in 'Murder
in the Cathedral', where the remote historical setting
allows even the sceptical among the audience to concur in
the argument without, as it were, feeling themselves too
personally or immediately implicated in it. The difficulty in both the later plays is to effect the necessary
emotional synthesis between the world of ideas, of belief,
in which the topics discussed may be said to exist, and
the mundane world of taxis and boiled eggs which is the
milieu of the characters. This is not to suggest that
there is an inveterate hostility between these two worlds,
but rather to indicate how comparatively easily a

dramatist seeking to fuse them may be betrayed into, on
the one hand, bathos and, on the other, seemingly gratuitous lurches towards sublimity. I think that it is significant that the single (fairly long) quotation in 'The
Cocktail Party' should be a neo-Platonic passage from
'Prometheus Unbound':

> For know there are two worlds of life and death:
> One that which thou beholdest; but the other
> Is underneath the grave ...

That we should be given such lines seems to indicate that
the playwright is aware of the dichotomy in his material
and apprised of the difficulties inherent in his task. We
begin, then, by looking at the play to see whether it has
improved upon its predecessor in the handling of these
difficulties.

Two improvements can be at once perceived. In the first
place, because Sir Henry Harcourt-Reilly is made a professional consultant his analytical probings, comments and
advice are given a more than individual authority, and
seem far less queerly oracular than do the rather similar
speeches of Agatha in the earlier play. This is so, I
think, even when he ceases to speak as a doctor and reveals himself as a 'Guardian', intent upon the health of
the soul rather than that of the body. His authority
tends to pass over with him from the one rôle to the
other, and if we are responding naturally we shall tend
not to question it. In the second place the development
of Celia Coplestone (we might call her Harry Monchensey
in the guise of a young woman) is really only half the
play, the other half being concerned with the marital
difficulties between Edward and Lavinia Chamberlayne.
If not the most important part of the play this other
half is at least the most prominent and this has the
effect, not only of making the martyr seem more exceptional, more of a departure from the average (as she
surely should seem), but also of giving a more balanced
picture of religious experience than that given in 'The
Family Reunion'. The Chamberlaynes are shown as following
a religious development of their own which, while quite
different from it, is yet supplementary to that of Celia.
As Reilly says:

> Neither way is better.
> Both ways are necessary. It is also necessary
> To make a choice between them.

The impression is thus quite different from that given by

'The Family Reunion'. There we are left with the sense
that virtue is somehow the prerogative of a limited class
of 'sufferers', an esoteric quality to which more normal
persons cannot hope to attain; here on the other hand
martyrdom is only one of several varieties of religious
experience, and that one of the less common. To an audience composed (let us hope) of non-'sufferers' the latter
view is much more likely to recommend itself.

Another difference between the two plays is that there
are evidently intended to be no fundamentally bad or trivial characters in 'The Cocktail Party'. This may seem so
slight a point as hardly to be worth noticing but in fact
I think it is crucial. In life, I suppose, we are only
aware of virtue negatively, and through knowing the virtuous party for some time. Sobriety is consistent but un-
aggressive, abstaining from drunkenness, charity from
malice or unkindness, humility from arrogance or condescension, and so on. As soon as these qualities become
too positive or overt, as soon as we have a man who
ostentatiously refuses a drink or sententiously refuses
to criticize his neighbour, we have, not virtue, but
hypocrisy or priggishness. It is by their works that we
know the virtuous and not by their professions, and it
usually takes time before our knowledge ripens into any
sort of assurance. Now where a dramatist means to present
a virtuous character he has obviously to work in firmer
and more immediate stuff than this and it is understand-
able that he usually employs his own sort of negative
approach, by playing the character off against a number of
others who are palpably less virtuous. At times, indeed,
as in some of the Elizabethan and Jacobean plays, he is
content to work almost entirely in negative terms - that
is, through a cast of villains - and to allow his moral
positives to present themselves merely as implications or
inferences. Dramatically speaking, either of these
approaches has obvious advantages over the direct approach,
where the good characters have to be positively established as good, because they do not involve the characters
in description or suggestion of one another's goodness,
and so give rise to something more convincing than a dull
assortment of eulogies. 'Damn braces, bless relaxes',
said Blake: the relevance of this to drama should be self-
evident.

In this play Eliot is trying to present virtue directly,
without the traditional advantage of a contrast with its
opposite, and it seems to me that he is often perilously
close to relaxation of the kind I take Blake to have
meant. At the end of the play Edward is clearly on the
way to regeneration, his relations with Lavinia clearly

more unselfish, yet how is this presented? Partly, to be
sure, it is a matter of contrast with their previous
relationship. But the dramatist does not leave it there.
He goes on to give Edward a string of compliments and
'thoughtful' remarks that are as monotonous as they are un-
convincing - 'I hope you've not been worrying'. 'It's you
who should be tired'. 'I like the dress you're wearing'.
'You have a very practical mind'. 'You lie down now,
Lavinia'. Even if this is meant to suggest that Lavinia is
pregnant it is surely an unhappy way of drawing attention
to domestic harmony. Happiness in marriage would inhere in
far less definite particulars - a glance, a touch, a tone
of voice. Edward is, in fact, in a position analogous to
the ostentatious professor of virtue; he has himself to *show*
how virtuous he is, and we accordingly at once suspect that
he is only mimicking the real thing. This is not charity
but solicitude. Yet how else, granted the chosen approach,
could the point be made? Celia is another focus for this
sort of weakness, though she is at least removed off-stage
when her decision is complete. It is true that Alex's
laconic narration of her martyrdom is effective, true also
that the reactions of the other characters are at first
simple and convincing enough. But very soon they begin to
magnify her image into portentousness so that it cracks and
allows her validity as a symbol to drain away:

> I've only been interested in myself:
> And that isn't good enough for Celia.

> Do try to come to see us.
> You know, I think it would do us all good -
> You and me and Edward ... to talk about Celia.

> I cannot help the feeling
> That, in some way, my responsibility
> Is greater than that of a band of half-crazed savages.

It seems to me that the unprejudiced reader will find this
insistence almost as tiresome as the muscular Christianity
of the foreman in 'The Rock,' and will react away from
rather than towards the values sought to be embodied in the
martyr. His recollections of her pleasantly sensitive normality at the opening of the play will hinder him from seeing her in these large and cloudy terms, and he may even
feel that she would have merited more sympathetic attention
had she remained the woman she at first sight appears.
Skilful acting could doubtless conceal some of these weaknesses but the play is not to be called successful because
that is so.

It is not only to Celia, however, that this sort of jar, between an initial and a later character, is confined. Julia and Alex, who with Reilly make up the group of 'Guardians', have an even more striking metamorphosis from their initial selves. This is so palpable that it must be intentional, a sort of deliberate convention, and we are no doubt intended to take Edward's remark about 'the guardian' as a clue showing how to accept the convention:

> The self that wills - he is a feeble creature;
> He has to come to terms in the end
> With the obstinate, the tougher self; who does not
>   speak,
> Who never talks, who cannot argue;
> And who in some men may be the *guardian* ...

In the light of this the Julia and Alex of Acts Two and Three are presumably the inner selves of their analogues in Act One, and not real people at all. Yet the contrast between the selves in each case is almost wantonly exaggerated, and most readers or members of an audience must surely surely find it impossible to accept. Alex is at first vain ('I'm rather a famous cook') and suspicious ('Ah, so the aunt Really exists') and it would appear that he is also not above drinking half a bottle of Edward's champagne. As for Julia, she is vapid ('Lady Klootz'), avaricious ('Are there any prospects?'), featherbrained (see p. 18) and inquisitive, and vain enough to take umbrage when Reilly sings his song. To transform this figure into a 'Guardian' of such potency that she can condescend ('You must accept your limitations') even to her fellow-Guardian, the perspicacious Reilly, seems to me preposterous. Are we to infer that no matter how stupidly vicious people may be on the surface they can be spotless within? The human Julia's flippant mention of St. Anthony is scarcely sufficient to bridge the yawning void between herself and her *alter ego*, and in fact it is difficult to see how, given two such different quantities, it could be bridged.

Obviously, it will be retorted, Eliot has not tried to bridge it: why impugn him for not doing what it was no part of his intention to do? This is easily said but I do not think that in this instance it is a valid defence. The fact is, as I have pointed out, that there is already something of a tension between the two worlds handled in the play, and to make the contrast between the Julia of the real world and the Julia of the spiritual world so gross is only to increase that tension to a point at which the play begins to tear apart. Where the play should be forcing us to see the interdependence of the two worlds, forcing us to

admit that the spiritual underlies and informs the actual,
we get instead the impression that they are so distinct, so
little related, that to move from one to the other is like
putting on an impenetrable disguise. What, after all, besides the name, have these Julias in common? Could we
identify the one after being acquainted only with the
other? That the deliberate convention of 'inner selves'
should at first sight give an impression of simple inepti-
tude is thus not its chief defect. What is serious is that
in another way it is itself inept, and draws attention to a
material dichotomy which it was part of the business of the
dramatist to dissolve or remove. I have not seen the play
and I am aware that it might be argued that this contrast,
between the earlier and the later Julia, is less serious on
the stage. With a book one can turn back to the early
pages and make comparisons; but on the stage there is a
temporal progression which leaves us dependent on memory
and for this reason we may tend to accept the changed
figure more readily. The play's popularity may be evidence that the convention works better in the theatre than
the study, and I should be happy to believe that it does.
On the other hand there may be other reasons for its popularity, reasons more properly the province of the sociolo-
gist than of the critic. Even in the study do we, after
all, *need* to turn back to the early pages for the contrast
to be felt, and felt disturbingly?

These might be called structural criticisms. I should
like to conclude by observing that the flaccidity of the
verse does little to compensate for them. Some of Celia's
speeches to Reilly in Act Two are so inexplicit that one is
tempted to call them Eliotese. They seem to rely on certain concepts such as 'love' and 'shame' and 'aloneness'
(I use this barbarism because the state is clearly neither
loneliness nor solitude) yet they do nothing to make these
concepts real. This is at all events what seems to me to
be taking place in such a speech as Celia's on p. 123.
Again, at other times the verse is so obviously *not* verse
that to have printed it as such gives one much the same
pause as does the 'Comedy' of the title-page:

> Well, Peter, I'm awfully glad, for your sake,
> Though of course we ... I shall miss you;
> You know how I depended on you for concerts,
> And picture exhibitions - more than you realized.
> It *was* fun, wasn't it! But now you'll have a chance,
> I hope, to realize your ambitions.
> I shall miss you.

'Anyone who tries to write poetic drama, even today', Eliot

has written, 'should know that half of his energy must be exhausted in the effort to escape from the constricting toils of Shakespeare'. This was well said, and it is to his credit that in 'The Family Reunion' and, more particularly, 'Murder in the Cathedral' Eliot has written dramatic verse that is both verse and underivative. The impression left by 'The Cocktail Party', however, is rather that the 'constricting toils' have been, if that is possible, too thoroughly cast off. It is not that the dramatist here eschews Shakespeareanisms - no sane reader would throw that in his teeth - but that the verse is of so poor a quality as to make them unthinkable. Even a quotation from Shakespeare rather than Shelley would throw up its context in all too harsh a light. One seems to see the shade of William Archer smile ironically.

161. FROM AN UNSIGNED REVIEW, WRITING FOR THE THEATRE, 'TIMES LITERARY SUPPLEMENT'

25 August 1950, no. 2534, viii

The review opens with a consideration of Christopher Fry's 'The Lady's Not for Burning' (1949) and 'Venus Observed' (1950).

Certain it is that Mr. Fry's achievement as it stands is not substantial enough to support any very high hopes of a revolution of theatrical method. Mr. Eliot's achievement, on the other hand, has little that is tentative about it. He has not been borne to popular acclaim on the wings of luck and blind soaring genius, but simply as the result of solving a problem which he had very completely envisaged. He himself has described the problem. If poetic drama is to make itself at home again on the popular stage it has got to show that it can deal with what appears to be the most refractory material. It must pass beyond religious and historical subjects and find one in the perplexities, conflicts and misunderstandings of the men and women of to-day. The verse must not be Shakespearian and it must utter no lines not relevant to the situation, the mood and the dramatic action. Since the greater part of life consists of prosaic passages a verse play must have prosaic

passages. The need is for a kind of verse capable of both
the poetic and the prosaic. The transitions from one to
the other should be imperceptible.

The actors are speaking in the same rhythms, with the
same vocabulary, as before, and the change is felt, not
in awareness of versification, but in awareness of the
higher or lower charge of energy in the whole scene.

Mr. Eliot's planned advance to this ideal of stage language
began with 'Murder in the Cathedral', in which he was at
least not imitating Shakespeare; it proceeded to 'The
Family Reunion', in which he achieved a form of verse as
close as possible to modern conversation. But here he was
still employing poetic props which were not dramatic, and
for the drama itself he was depending too much upon the
literary association with Aeschylus. In 'The Cocktail
Party' he discarded alike the poetic props and the framework of classical drama. He told the kind of story which,
except for its underlying spiritual implications, is the
staple of fashionable entertainment in Shaftesbury Avenue,
and the verse he used for this purpose satisfied his own
theoretical requirement of strict relevance to the situation, the mood and the movement of the comedy. And largely
it fulfilled the general hope of a verse which should in
circumstances of modern social comedy say more than prose
could say in the same circumstances.

'The Cocktail Party' is obviously something more than a
successful play; it is the practical demonstration of a
patiently conceived theory of dramatic form, and as such
of high historical interest, even should its immediate
influence be small. However, there is reasonable hope in
the published plays of Mr. Ronald Duncan, Mr. Norman
Nicholson, Mrs. Anne Ridler, and other young poets whose
workshop is the Mercury Theatre that the new seed will not
fall on stony ground. It is not perhaps unjust to suggest
that the weakness common to this group of poet-dramatists
is that they are poets before they are dramatists. There
are those to say that Mr. Eliot has 'proved' the possibility of applying verse drama to modern life with a play
in which he carefully refrains from writing poetry. The
gibe implies a wilful misunderstanding of his general intention, which is not so much to find a new platform for
poetry as to provide the stage with dialogue of greater
expressiveness. It is true that his play is without passages to take the breath with lyric beauty; there is no
place in it for such passages. It is equally true that
there are passages to make the audience realize that what
they are hearing is not prose. But at such times they feel

624 T.S. Eliot: The Critical Heritage

it is perfectly natural for the characters to express their
thought with the precision and intensity only made possible
by the compression of verse; and that acceptance of the
language-convention is the justification of a method of
verse writing for the stage in which the poet remains subordinate to the dramatist. Perhaps the most useful lesson
which Mr. Eliot teaches his fellow poet-dramatists is the
poet's proper place in the theatre....

162. WILLIAM ARROWSMITH, NOTES ON ENGLISH VERSE DRAMA,
'HUDSON REVIEW'

Autumn 1950, vol. iii, 411-30

Arrowsmith (b. 1924), a Rhodes Scholar from 1948 to 1951,
was founding editor of the 'Hudson Review' from 1948 until
1960. He is known for his translations of Petronius,
Euripides and Aristophanes.

   ...in the perusal of this treatise, you shall find
   another kind of taste, and a doctrine of more profound
   consideration, which will disclose unto you the most
   glorious doctrine and dreadful mysteries, as well in
   what concerneth our religion, as matters of the public
   state.
                      - Rabelais, Prologue to 'Gargantua'

                              I

For depth, for richness, 'The Cocktail Party' is not what
we ordinarily call a 'popular' play; yet it has been
popular and has competed for some time with lesser plays
on the commercial stage. This popularity - much of it -
seems partly the accident of Eliot's having recently come
to be 'in fashion.' Nonetheless, I believe it was the
author's intention to write a play which could manage to
be profound at the same time it was popular (or, in Eliot's
terms, a play that was Christian at the same time that it
was secular in form). By such a play, I do not mean one
that is written for two separate audiences, one Christian
and the other secular, but a Christian play in secular

dress so constructed that it should be possible for a
neutral and intelligent (not 'intellectual') reader to
penetrate to the Christian interior from the secular surface. Such a play is possible only if Eliot's conviction
that we still live in a partially (even unconsciously)
Christian world is true; if not, the play must be, for our
time at least, a failure. It will also be a failure if it
permits any compromise of value; this is automatic since
the kind of play I think Eliot has in mind is a play which,
because it achieves its ends not by 'writing down,' but by
writing 'in depth,' in body, cannot compromise. The risks
of this method are enormous, - and so are the stakes
involved.

If we are to understand this method, it is essential
that we should understand what the play is about. One
thing the play is about is actual Christian life and the
dramatic creation of a possible Christian society; it is
this aspect of the play which has not been sufficiently
understood, especially in detail. And whether or not we
happen to share Mr. Eliot's religious views (I do not), it
is impossible to judge the play or its relevance to a possible theater until the play has been, to a point, understood.

II

Even a glance at the *dramatis personae* will show us that
there is more to the play than meets the eye. Remembering
the 'Guardians,' it is perhaps mere coincidence that both
Edward (ead-*ward*) and Alex (*alex*-andros) are etymologically
'guardians,' 'defenders.' Lavinia is, of course, an epo-
nym; but it is curious that in its classical locus, the
'Aeneid,' it is almost invariably accompanied by the appo-
sition, *coniunx*. Quilpe is too odd: it is merely an
archaic variant of the word 'whelp'; or, as we would say,
Quilpe is 'Peter the Pup' ('There is one for whom the
words cannot be spoken ... yet'). And, if you wish to
push things, *Coplestone* and *Shuttlethwaite* and *Chamberlayne* will all yield some kind of sense when broken up and
attached to their bearers. But all these are merely minor
means of richening a text; they are not, in themselves,
dramatically relevant or particularly revealing.

It is the name *Celia*, among the Christian names, that is
revealing. Offhand, one would guess that it came from
caelia and meant 'lady of heaven,' and this would be
appropriate although, in fact, the etymology is a false
one. But Celia is short for Cecilia, and the name Cecilia
is a Christian name because it was hallowed by the life of

St. Cecilia, Virgin and Martyr. Clearly, there is an
immediate resemblance between the saint and her namesake
of the play. But there is more to it than that. Consider
the full traditional meaning of the Christian name,
Cecilia. It is given at the beginning of the saint's life
in 'The Golden Legend' of De Voragine, Englished by
Caxton:

> Cecilia is as much to say as the lily of heaven, or a
> way to blind men. Or she is said of celo, that is
> heaven, and leos, that is people. She was a heavenly
> lily by cleanness of virginity, a way to blind men by
> information of example, heaven by devout contemplation,
> lia by busy operation, lacking blindness by shining of
> wisdom, and heaven of the people.

This etymology, too, is forced and false, but it is nonetheless operative: it is the meaning of the *Christian* name,
Cecilia, if you grant names to have meaning. But it is not
so much the *cael*-root (heavenly) as the *caec*-root (blind)
- turned by the martyrologist to 'lacking blindness' and
'a way to blind men' - that is immediately important. For
it is the related metaphors of sight and blindness, dark
and light, which are the major imagery of the play.
   Consider Edward's 'And what is the use of all your analysis / If I am to remain always in the dark?'; Julia's
'I must have left my glasses here, / and I simply can't
see a thing without them / ... But I'd know them, because
one lens is missing'; Reilly's 'And me bein' the One Eyed
Riley....'; Celia's 'I can see you at last as a human
being' followed by Edward's 'I'm completely in the dark';
Julia's 'You must have learned to look at people, Peter /
... That is, when you're not concerned with yourself / But
just being an eye'; or this little sequence:

Julia: Well, my dears, I shall see you very soon.
Edward: *When* shall we see you?
Julia: Did I say you'd see me?

And there are at least a dozen more such (unobtrusive)
visual metaphors. Finally, consider that Cecilia means
'lacking blindness' and that Celia is said to have gone
the 'way of illumination.'
   If, by metaphor, Edward and Lavinia (and Peter, and
Celia at first) are said to be, in their own words, 'completely in the dark,' and Celia soon goes the 'way of
illumination,' what are we to make of Reilly and Julia and
Alex? Julia is said to be 'very observant,' but she
cannot (she says) see without her glasses, and one lens is

missing: she is effectively blind in one eye, a literal
monocle. In response to her query, Reilly sings 'And me
bein' the One Eyed Riley.' Actually, Reilly's song is
Eliot's variant upon a well-known and thoroughly obscene
RAF song; but 'One Eyed' is, so far as I know, Eliot's own
invention and clearly applies to Reilly. We have then
three metaphorical conditions: blindness, half-sight, and
full vision, typified by Edward, Julia (and her partners),
and Celia, in that order. What, however, the half-sight
of Julia and Reilly means is to be found, like so much else
in 'The Cocktail Party,' in a proverb: *In the kingdom of
the blind the one-eyed man is king.* And there may be a
further gloss in this incident from 'The Golden Legend,'
under the life of St. Edward:

> Thirty days after his burying, there came to his tomb
> a man which had but one eye, leading after him six
> blind men, and each of them held other by the skirt.
> And they all devoutly prayed to God ... that they might
> have their sight... And anon as they had ended their
> prayers all they received perfectly their sight. And
> then each of them that had been blind looked fast on
> each other, and thought it a new world with them.

In any case, the passage should illustrate what the intent
of the imagery is: the parable of a *moral* miracle, the
recovery of sight.

If we understand Reilly and Julia (and Alex) as the
'one-eyed in the kingdom of the blind,' we should be able
to discover their true position in the play. Most criticism of the play has found the position of these 'Guardians' somewhat ambiguous. They have seemed to be, now
semi-divine, now entirely human, now mechanical abstractions for divided selves and, most often, an unresolved
mixture of saint and sinner. Most of these charges of
poor conceptualization have arisen, I think, because critics have made the mistake of taking the statements of any
character about another as literally true. Assent has
generally followed Edward's description of Julia as 'that
dreadful old woman,' and it has certainly been intended by
the dramatist that we should assent - to a point. Against
Edward's description of Julia, however, we have to balance
the more appreciative remarks of Celia and Peter. Nonetheless, Julia certainly *appears* to be a 'dreadful old
woman,' a frivolous busybody, throughout the first act;
she certainly *seems* to be radically different from the
Julia of Acts II and III. And it is this seeming difference which has led critics and audiences to suppose that
there is an impossible gulf between these two Julias;

that the early Julia is a fantastic distortion of the later
and more saintly Julia. In fact there should be no question of divinity, of or divided selves, or of an *unaccount-
able* change of character. (a) This emerges quite clearly
if we remember that Reilly, in his interview with Celia,
discloses that he was at the party 'at the instance of
Mrs. Shuttlethwaite.' As this line is spoken, the audience
should suddenly feel the scales drop from its eyes, should
see that it has been guilty, like Edward, of imposing its
own myth upon the characters. For if we think back, we
will remember that Julia has denied knowing Reilly ('Edward, who is that dreadful man?') when she clearly must
have known him well enough to invite him. Reilly can have
no purpose in lying to Celia about the manner of his coming to the party. It is Julia who is lying or, more
accurately, playing a part, and playing it well. So, for
that matter are Reilly and Alex playing parts, and it
should be clear that the part they are playing has something to do with their being 'Guardians.' In Act II, when
Reilly worries about Edward and Lavinia, 'stripped naked
to their souls,' Julia replies: 'Nonsense, Henry, *I* shall
keep an eye on them.' In fact, she has never kept her
(one) eye very much off them; it is this benevolent watching (shared with Alex) which makes her seem to both Edward
and the audience a professional busybody.

This illusion has been composed with great subtlety.
In the first place, Eliot has postponed our knowledge of
the kindly conspiracy of 'Guardians' and allowed us,
throughout Act I, to take our measure of Julia and her
fellow-conspirators from the eyes of purblind Edward and
Lavinia. Second, he has made a persuasive appeal to that
convention which seemed most likely to lull the audience's
suspicions. That convention is the slick comedy of marital misunderstanding with its rigid 'laugh' types: the
ubiquitous, tiresome Scot who 'knows everybody' (MacColgie
Gibbs) and the frivolous gossip and busybody (Mrs.
Shuttlethwaite). Against taking this convention too
literally, and against the tendency of the others (Edward,
Lavinia, Peter and Celia) to project a personality of
their own making upon each other, comes this warning:

> ...we die to each other daily.
> What we know of other people
> Is only our memory of the moments
> During which we knew them. And they have changed since
>   then.
> To pretend that they and we are the same
> Is a useful and convenient social convention
> Which must sometimes be broken. We must also remember
> That at every meeting we are meeting a stranger.

It is this which Edward and the others *and* the audience
have to learn: to *see* one another as 'strangers'; only
then can they learn, of themselves, 'the change that
comes / From seeing oneself through the eyes of other
people.' Celia learns it, painfully:

> ...I see another person,
> I see you as a person whom I never saw before.

The audience has to learn too, for it is involved in the
general blindness, as much 'in the dark' as Edward is.
The penalty for not *seeing* is to miss the rest of the play,
as well as the meaning of the play. We have to see that
the real Julia, the real Alex, the real Reilly, are
'strangers' - not what they may appear to be in the first
act. When we know that Julia's denial that she knows
Reilly is a sham, we should be in a position to understand
that her role of busybody was also a sham, a role consciously assumed in order to test Edward, to watch over
him and the others, to keep him firm in his decision once
he has made it and, most important, to make him face the
implications of his decision - both for himself and the
others. She and Alex manage the exits and entrances of
the others, maneuver Edward's meeting with Celia and
Peter, and watch over the consequences of those meet-
ings. (b) But they must sham since they are aware that,
should Edward suspect he was being 'guarded,' should they
show their hand, their whole plot would backfire and
Edward's decision would probably be reversed. The seeming
ambiguity of the 'Guardians' is their own deliberate creation; they seem to change because we do not know of the
shamming until it is over, and because they actually do
change *in the eyes* of others. In fact, the 'Guardians'
have a fixed purpose and consistent personalities throughout the play; they are not gods, or gods-and-devils, or
the better halves of themselves or of anyone else. These
suppositions have arisen because the play cannot be understood until its *text* has been comprehended and taken into
the experience of the hearer or reader.
I mean by *text* something that is both textual and scrip-
tural. The text of 'The Cocktail Party' is as complex as
it is Christian; in our time, its Christianity is one cause
of its complexity. For the very fact that the play had a
Christian subject would have made it hard for it to get a
wide hearing, and it is for this reason that the thoroughly
Christian aspects of the play exists almost *sub rosa*. This
sounds at first like defeating your purpose (and there is
something to this); but one of Eliot's greatest problems
was, as I have said, just how he should make it possible

for a perceptive (and receptive) hearer to penetrate from
the secular 'front' to the Christian 'interior.' What
Eliot was counting upon was, I think, his conviction that
'we have today a culture which is mainly negative, but
which, so far as it is positive, is still Christian.' It
is this notion of a residual Christianity which Eliot is
getting at in Julia's reference to St. Antony, or in the
exchange between Julia and Edward about 'good Samaritans.'
But at the same time that Eliot is giving a description of
the society in which we live - a society which is Christian if only in its unthinking habits - he is also attempting, I believe, through the very same phrases, to recharge
that Christian experience which is indicated by them, and
to guide the audience which has forgotten their meaning to
understand it anew in the context of the play. This should
make clear the presence in the play of a large number of
those gnomic sayings which still preserve a Christian savor
in our speech: not only 'playing the Good Samaritan,' but
'speak of the devil,' 'playing the devil's advocate,' 'the
one-eyed man in the kingdom of the blind' and so on. Once
these phrases, or their metaphorical or dramatic para-
phrases, are explored for the full range of their meaning,
the play will assume its actual Christian aspect.

Consider the use of expressions involving 'the devil' in
the first part of the play. Celia says of Reilly: 'Then he
must be the Devil! He must have bewitched you.' A champagne cork pops in the kitchen and Edward says, 'What the
devil's that?' The 'devil' happens, in this case, to be
Julia; compare Lavinia's 'I'm puzzled by Julia. That
woman is the devil.' Later, Lavinia asks Reilly: 'Are you
a devil / Or merely a lunatic practical joker?' When
Edward replies to Reilly's method of putting his initial
(devilish) advice that Edward should be thankful Lavinia
has gone, he says: 'Don't put it to me.... And please
don't suggest./I have often used these terms in examining
witnesses'; here I think Eliot is paraphrasing dramatically
what we mean by 'playing the devil's advocate.' And there
are other phrases and other proverbs which seem to have a
tacit dramatic relevance: 'the door is open to the devil,'
'speak of the devil,' 'the devil has all the best tunes,'
'gin is the devil's drink.' Reilly and Julia and Alex
appear 'devils' to the others for obvious reasons: they
show up when they're not wanted, and their advice seems to
have diabolic consequences. What Edward and Celia and Lavinia do not suspect is that their description of Reilly and
Julia as devils is really very much to the point; that is,
although Reilly and Julia are actually not 'devils,' they
are, however, 'playing the devil' and Reilly is 'playing
the devil's advocate' for a fixed purpose. In order that

their purpose should succeed, they wear, each of them, a
devil's mask. I think the sense of that purpose and the
meaning of the mask can be found in another proverb: *to
play the devil for God's sake*. This is what Reilly and
Julia are doing; Reilly, the masked actor, *tempts* Edward
in the matter of Lavinia's return and the Christian meaning of Edward's reply is: *Get thee behind me, Satan!* Eliot
(and Reilly), I think, would say that this reply of
Edward's is possible only because we still have a culture
which is to some extent Christian; but so much has gone
out of our conscious Christianity that the reply has to be
elicited in a negative way: the way of the devil which is
also the way of the world. Edward does not know that he
is being *tempted*, nor does he understand how Christian his
reply is: his Christianity is quite unconscious but nonetheless operative. If we ask why it is necessary to play
'the devil for God's sake,' we can see that had Reilly
appeared flaunting a cross or quoting scripture or choice
passages from 'The Idea of a Christian Society,' Edward
would have been openly hostile and would have perhaps made
a different decision. In this Eliot means that Edward
resembles his society: he is unconsciously Christian but
his reaction is negative when he is evangelized. And, for
just these reasons, 'The Cocktail Party' itself, as a
whole, wears - even in its title - the mask of the secular
world in the service of a Christian society.

Beneath its mask, the play is both a description of
Christian life and the dramatized creation of a possible
Christian society. (c) The 'Guardians' are not saints or
supernatural beings, but merely ordinary people who happen
to hold the Christian belief. What has seemed divine in
their conduct is the fact that they are living the Christian life, the life of Christ. Thus, metaphorically,
Reilly brings the dead to life (Lavinia), or restores their
sight to the blind (Celia, Edward, Lavinia, and, eventually, Peter); thus Celia, after she has renounced 'the
world, the flesh and the devil,' suffers the Passion in
Kinkanja. And all are involved in the attempt of the individual to escape his blindness (self-love) through the communal (Christian) life. By the end of the play, 'Guardian-
ship' (even as unconscious Christians) has been taken up by
Edward and Lavinia whose destiny it seems to be to 'keep an
eye' on Peter. Celia, it is true, becomes a 'Guardian' in
a more transcendent sense. But they are all Guardians,
conscious or unconscious, of two things: each other and the
Christian idea. And, if you happen to share Eliot's convictions, it will follow that the guardians of the Christian idea are 'the one-eyed in the kingdom of the blind';
nothing more exalted than that. According to the practicing

Christian, I believe, men are blind, or have half-sight, or
or perfect vision, to the extent to which they happen to
'see the light'; that light which informs the imagery of
the whole play is to be found in John, VIII, 12: 'I am the
light of the world: he that followeth me shall not walk in
darkness but shall have the light of life.'

Elsewhere Eliot has described in some detail the particular kind of Christian society which I think he is describing in the play:

> The Community of Christians is not an organization, but
> a body of indefinite outline; composed of both clergy
> and laity, of the more conscious, more spiritually and
> intellectually developed of both. It will be their
> identity of belief and aspiration, their background of
> a common system of education and a common culture,
> which will enable them to influence and be influenced
> by each other, and collectively to form the conscious
> mind and conscience of the nation.... ('The Idea of a
> Christian Society', pp. 35 ff)

It is not only a projected society, but a society which,
dramatically, is being made before our eyes. The Christian conspiracy begins at the Chamberlaynes' but as the
play ends, Alex and Julia and Reilly are off 'to the
Gunnings.' And so the society comes to include those who,
like Edward, may not *consciously* hold Christian beliefs:

> I cannot foresee any future society in which we could
> classify Christians and non-Christians simply by their
> pretensions of belief, or even, by any rigid code, by
> their behaviour. In the present ubiquity of ignorance,
> one cannot but suspect that many who call themselves
> Christians do not understand what the word means, and
> that some who repudiate Christianity vigorously are
> more Christian than many who maintain it. (*Ibid.*,
> p. 35)

If this is not enough to make the point, I think the sense
of Eliot's Christian community can be got in the following
extract from an early patristic epistle. The point of
view of the writer is similar to Eliot's (though the direction is reversed); it is that of a Christian in a society
which was not yet Christian (and which might never be):

> Christians are not distinguished from the rest of men,
> either by land, or speech, or their customs, for they
> do not dwell somewhere in their own cities, or use a
> different language, or practise an extraordinary kind

> of life.... They dwell in their own countries, but as
> sojourners; they take part in all things as citizens,
> yet they suffer all things as strangers. Every foreign
> country is their fatherland, and every fatherland is
> foreign.... What the soul is in the body, that the
> Christians are in the world. ('Ep. ad Diognetum.' 5,6)

There is hardly a sentence of this extract which will not
light up some part of 'The Cocktail Party.'

For instance, it would be a mistake to suppose that,
because Eliot's 'Guardians' are conceived as Christians,
they are thereby exempt from normal human failings or from
the general corruption of modern life. The Julia of Act I
('Potato crisps? No, I can't endure them!') is no less
frivolous than the Julia of Acts II and III ('You shouldn't
interrupt my interruptions'). She is a frivolous and
'gluttonous old lady'; she also happens to be a Christian.
Nor should the fact that she and Reilly and Alex are, in
Act I, Christians incognito, lead us to suppose that they
are more intelligent than anyone else in the play. That
Julia imagined she could get to a place in Essex, from
London, on her way to Cornwall, was not part of her disguise or her 'game'; it means merely that Julia, like the
others, belongs to a fractured 'society,' a culture which
has a sense neither of place nor history ('Colchester?
Lavinia just loves oysters'). And this is the meaning of
Lady Klootz, and Mary Mallington (with a monkey) on her
way to Mentone ('I ... go south in the winter') and Princess Bologolomsky and the others. No Christian is exempt
from this corruption, or indeed from most human corrup-
tions:

> I have tried to restrict my ambition of a Christian
> society to a social minimum: to picture, not a society
> of saints, but of ordinary men, of men whose Christian-
> ity is communal before being individual ... a community
> of men and women, not individually better than they are
> now, except for the capital difference of holding the
> Christian faith.... The Kingdom of Christ on earth will
> never be realised and ... it is always being realised.
> ('The Idea of a Christian Society', p. 59)

It is important, for the play, that we should try to
understand the characters as being individuals as much as
Christians. The fact that Reilly speaks a passage from
Shelley has been commonly supposed to be a private aside
of Mr. Eliot's; actually it seems to me to say far more
about Reilly (and this should be all that concerns the
reader): he is the kind of man who, upon occasion, quotes

Shelleyan mysticism and, on another occasion, sings obscene
songs. When a little tight, he is capable of joshingly
'propositioning' Julia (that is what the song means, if you
know the rest of it, and Julia does: 'I've never been so
insulted in my life'). Eliot is rounding Reilly off, trying to make him believable as a whole Christian man, just
as Julia's foibles are intended to relieve what would
otherwise be a dull and abstract pious old Christian
woman. Alex is not only a traveler and a Christian; he is
also a bore. These qualities are neither antithetical nor
complementary; Reilly's Christianity is not meant to cancel
his early obscenity:

> The struggle to recover the sense of relation to nature
> and to God, the recognition that even the most primitive
> feelings should be part of our heritage, seems to me the
> explanation and justification of the life of D.H. Law-
> rence ... we also need to know how to see the world as
> the Christian fathers saw it ... unless we can find a
> pattern in which all problems of life can have their
> place, we are likely to go on complicating chaos.
> (*Ibid.*, pp. 62-3)

Whether or not Eliot has succeeded in this (I do not think
he has) involves a judgment both of the play and of Eliot's
Christianity. And, in this connection, it may be useful to
remember that Eliot has recently stated his conviction that
'we should turn away from the Theater of Ideas to the Theater of Character.'
Before criticism, there is one final point. The charge
has been brought that Alex' description of affairs in Kinkanja is largely irrelevant to the quite straightforward
business of getting Celia martyred. This criticism is
somewhat unfounded. A necessary part of the description of
a Christian society is its relation, not only to the secular states with which it is involved, but to other and non-
Christian societies. Kinkanja, with its mixed population
of Christian natives and natives worshipping a monkey-god,
is such a test-case, both for the colonial administration
and for Eliot's Christian society. The problem is presented as one which is insoluble by ordinary political methods,
since the problem is, in origin, religious and, only afterwards, economic and political. Into this troubled place
come two representatives of an alien culture: Celia, the
thoroughbred Christian, and Alex (with the governor), the
agent of a neutral and benevolent government. 'British
Council' methods, although laudable, produce merely delay
and an 'interim report'; but Celia is martyred and, after
her death, is accepted by the natives and harmonized with

their cult of the taboo 'saffron monkey.' (d) A religious
problem is shown to have a (possible) religious solution.
Eliot's intention is not, I think, dogmatic, but experimental:

> ...missionaries have sometimes been accused of propa-
> gating the customs ... of the social groups to which
> they have belonged, rather than giving the natives the
> essentials of the Christian faith in such a way that
> they might harmonize their own culture with it. ('The
> Idea of a Christian Society', p. 53)

> Into this confused world (of mixed and conflicting reli-
> gious cultures - India) came the British, with their
> assurance that their own culture was the best in the
> world ... and their bland assumption that religion was
> a secondary matter. It is human, when we do not under-
> stand another human being ... to exert an unconscious
> pressure on that person to turn him into something we
> *can* understand: many husbands and wives exert this
> pressure on each other. The effect on the person so
> influenced is liable to be the repression and distor-
> tion, rather than the improvement, of the personal-
> ity.... The benefits of British rule will soon be lost,
> but the ill-effects of the disturbance of a native cul-
> ture will remain. To offer another people your culture
> first, and your religion second, is a reversal of
> values: and while every European represents, for good
> or ill, the culture to which he belongs, only a small
> minority are worthy representatives of its religious
> faith. ('Notes Towards the Definition of Culture',
> pp. 64-5)

From the reference to husbands and wives who 'exert an unconscious pressure on each other,' it will be seen that the
play has traveled full circle: the problem in Kinkanja is
no more, in fact, than the problem of Edward and Lavinia on
an intercultural level. In either case, Eliot would say,
the problem is basically religious, and will have to be
solved, if at all, by religious means.

I have no notion that this analysis exhausts more than a
part of the play. Its resources are as endless as the
language in which it is composed and extend as far as the
gnomic verse will take us into a Christian experience residual in common speech. We may or may not realize the implications of what we say when we say *Speak of the devil* or
God knows!; but we still say them. The problem is not so
much whether these bones live, as whether they can be made
to live again. A play which recreates the experience to

which the words properly apply is one way of finding out
and of getting the answer you want. The fact that the
phrases are current - though unconscious - currency is the
enabling condition of the dramatist's purpose. Look at
the name of the *dramatis personae* once more: not only are
they etymologically meaningful, but they are unconscious
carriers of a certain kind of past. There are the *Christian* names, Celia, Henry, Edward, each bearing the mark
of its patron saint; Lavinia, the bride of Roman history.
And there are the names of place and the British experience: old English in Shuttlethwaite and Quilpe, Scotch in
MacColgie Gibbs, Latin-Norman in Chamberlayne, and that
strange mixture of aristocratic Norman and common Irish,
Harcourt-Reilly. There is also that 'Guardian' who has no
name but lives in Dedham: Lavinia's Aunt. She is a Christian fiction, the kind of excuse we invent - in an unconsciously Christian society - when we want to disguise the
truth; we may be disguising the truth but the disguise is
Christian. When the irony is realized, she becomes the
subject of a toast, binding the group together. Or, on
another occasion, a toast to her may be part of the shamming of a man who, like Edward, lies like a Christian.
Even a Christian society must have its little jokes.

                              III

    In criticism of a play of this kind, I think we are
involved in a larger number of judgments than is normal.
Not only do we have to estimate the play which most people
saw - the rather amusing and bewildering secular comedy
with Christian overtones - but we also have to come to
terms with the total play - the Christian play *and* its
secular mask. Judging a Christian play means, I think,
judging the Christianity of the play as well as the way
that Christianity gets into the drama. If Eliot is dramatically creating a Christian society, you will have to
criticize that society when you criticize the play, for
the play happens to be inseparable from the society and
the Christian experience it creates. Finally, you have to
judge the way in which the exterior is related to the interior: how well has it been made possible for a perceptive reader to make his way from the outside in? I am not
sure that all of these judgments are yet possible in our
present ignorance of the play, but I should like to put
forward several points.
    There is something imprudent about asking whether the
popularity of a popular play is deserved. Given Eliot's
purpose - a profound play in popular disguise - it is

perhaps enough that the play was popular. But it seems to
me a miscarriage of the artist's job if his reputation
does his work for him, and I think Eliot's reputation is
very much at the root of the play's popularity. I doubt
that this was intentional: Eliot could not have foreseen
that his audiences were as anxious to move about on his
level as he was to operate on theirs. But this fact has
made it difficult to estimate whether or not 'The Cocktail
Party' is viable as a popular play. On the whole, I doubt
that it is. True, it is amusing, it is polished, well-
constructed, even 'different,' and it has a readily accessible moral intent. But as a secular comedy it will not
bear comparison to Coward or to Shaw, and it is difficult
to see, on the interpretation of the popular reviews, that
the play has been more than an interesting *tour de force*.
Quite simply, it was not written in the dramatic mode demanded of a popular play, and that demand has to be met,
more or less, if the purpose of the play is to succeed.
It is, of course, a difficult thing to write one play which
has two different surfaces, and still more difficult to con-
connect those two surfaces. But I suspect Eliot's failure
is due to his not having understood just *how much* of some
things a popular play demands from the dramatist; this, I
think, is a part of his judgment, as a Christian, upon the
world of 'a thousand lost golf balls.' It impoverishes
the play.

The poverty may, however, be intentional, may be intended to make the reader look more deeply for his satisfaction, and I think there is something to this, if you consider just how the two plays, Christian and secular, are
connected. That connection has been made with great care
and relies for its effectiveness on the willingness of the
hearer or reader to answer, in terms of the text, the
questions which the play was designed to raise in his
mind. Almost every criticism of the play has been bewildered by the role of the 'Guardians' or the mysterious
champagne bottle or the impression of destiny-at-work, but
it was intended by the dramatist that there should be be-
wilderment. This was not gratuitous: Eliot was counting
upon the hearer's being puzzled *and* upon his readiness to
look for the answers in the text so that, step by step,
question by question, he should make his way from the
exterior to the heart of the play: 'Nobody likes to be
left with a mystery: It's so ... unfinished.' There is
not one of these mysteries which cannot be answered from
the text, and Eliot cannot be held responsible for the
failure of his stratagem. It seems, unfortunately, that
audiences - serious as well as popular - are unwilling to
bring to the play as much detective intelligence as they

would to a 'whodunnit' thriller. Under such conditions,
we shall have only the kind of drama we deserve.

Once, however, the reader has arrived at the interior
of the play and can see that what is taking place is not a
strange conspiracy by mysterious figures, but a Christian
society in the making and a description of the conditions
of Christian life, he should be able to take his stock of
the play. There are a number of dramatic blemishes and
several crucial flaws of structure and characterization.
I think, for instance, that Eliot would have been wise to
give the audience rather more assistance in discovering
the nature of the 'Guardians' and their conspiracy; almost
everything hangs on Reilly's bare statement that he was
asked to the party by Julia, and this is insufficient for
the theater. Again, it is difficult to believe that Eliot
has properly handled the solution of the play, especially
the part pertaining to Celia's martyrdom; up through the
second act, however, Eliot shows himself in firm control
of the play. But no matter how relevantly or fully you
explain the import of the tangled problem in Kinkanja, it
is doubtful that the purpose of the tale comes within the
scope of the dramatist in this particular play. It may
help to justify Celia's martyrdom if you happen to know
that her death was relevant to the solution of a large
problem, and that that problem resembles the central problem of the play, but I cannot think that this justification has emerged dramatically. It is leaving rather too
much to a messenger to report not only a martyrdom but its
import as well, even though the messenger is himself unconscious of its real import. Of course Celia's death
leaves its own mark upon the others, especially upon Peter,
who realizes that his own self-interest is 'not good enough
for Celia.' But it seems to me very much a question - and
a serious one - whether 'The Cocktail Party' itself is
'good enough' for Celia - or, for that matter, for the
Chamberlaynes.

Take the Chamberlaynes first. In the play their lives
represent the alternative to Celia's way - an alternative
which deserves, as Eliot seems to realize, considerable
richness. These alternatives are not a Christian one and
a secular one (for the Christian 'Guardians' have chosen a
life more like the Chamberlaynes' than Celia's) but the
'sainted' life and its day-to-day complement - the life
'without an eagle,' as Trilling puts it. Of these two ways
we are told: 'Neither way is better. / Both ways are necessary.' It is, of course, idle to talk of better or worse
when you are talking of necessities, and recognition of
this fact should have closed the question. But, in fact,
in the play it has not; Reilly may have stated the

solution, but Eliot has not yet met the problem, or, if he
has, his answer is not Reilly's. This seems to me apparent in the qualities which the dramatist thinks are demanded by the 'sainted' life but not by 'the common life';
the extraordinary poverty which he gives the Chamberlaynes' life as compared with the demanding richness of
Celia's stresses the point. One can perhaps disallow
Reilly's description of the common life as his own (short-
sighted) observation, but Eliot's attitude is made clear
in the dialogue between Edward and Lavinia before the final
party starts. Here the solution of their problem seems to
have led to nothing more than an exchange of solicitous
(but eventually self-interested) compliments and a possible pregnancy which presumably stand for such happiness
as their lives can hope for. This simply will not do,
dramatically or emotionally; it is not what we mean by
'making the best of a bad job,' or even a good job, and
the Chamberlaynes' capacity for suffering (Celia has no
monopoly on this) leads one to expect that they are capable of such happiness as this world gives. My point is
not that we should expect Eliot to say that there is no
difference between these two lives (as a Christian he is
bound to enhance the 'sainted' life) but that his Christianity is no more than half the story it should be. He
pretends, intellectually, to the *whole* Christian tradition
but his emotional grasp is only of the extreme ascetic half
of that tradition. It is for this reason that the play
itself does not seem to me 'good enough for Celia,' or for
the Chamberlaynes either.
   Both the Chamberlaynes and Celia are good at suffering;
but when it comes to their release, their happiness, the
play dissolves. Dramatically, there may be reason for
choosing a martyred saint, but not all saints are martyrs,
and many, I believe, like Elizabeth of Hungary and Jane de
Chantal, achieved their sainthood by living 'the common
life' as we know it. And it is difficult to see why the
burdens of that life should not be as great, as demanding,
as the martyrs' momentary anguish and renunciation. I
think Eliot realizes this but he does not yet know it,
and it is this failure of his own Christianity that impoverishes the Christian society the play is trying to create.
A part of that poverty gets into his characters: if you
really look at Reilly, he seems rather ingrown; his wholeness - if that is what Eliot is attempting - still bears
the mark of its willing, and is not natural. He is the
kind of man who thinks he ought to sing obscene songs because he thinks we ought to 'find a pattern in which all
problems of life can have their place.' One admires the
insight, but not the realization. This, of course, does

not damn Reilly as a character, but if Eliot's purpose was
what I think it was, the creation of a Christian society
and not merely a Puritan one, he has not quite carried it
off. His characters, none of them, have the wholeness of
the whole man, or of the whole Christian man, and it is
for this reason that the play is thin and its society an
impoverished one. The characters are imperfect as Christians and as individuals because they bear the marks of Mr.
Eliot's imperfect Christianity, not of his hostility to
the secular world. But in view of the scarcity of the
whole secular man and the imperfect secularism of most of
us, it is difficult to damn Mr. Eliot's Christianity for
having the corruption of the times in it. 'The Cocktail
Party' seems to me by no means a 'great' play, but at
least a good one, and it is by far the best of Eliot's
plays. Those who believe that 'every new literary generation has to begin by killing its father' had better examine both themselves and their intended victim: they may
not be Mr. Eliot's heirs, nor he the infirm father they
thought. He may be a stranger.

IV

I have not intentionally shirked the problem of the
verse. It seems to me that we have to see what the play
is about before we can deal adequately with the play's
means. But sooner or later that problem will have to be
met. For the time being, I should merely like to suggest
that those who have dismissed the verse as unnecessarily
austere, even ascetic, ought to examine its meters and
meanings in the light of what Eliot has said of his own
purpose:

...my ambition was, and is, to write a play in verse
without the audience having to put itself in a special
frame of mind to listen to poetry. I wanted to write a
play in which the audience should be affected, unconsciously, by the rhythm of the verse, without being
consciously aware that it was verse they are hearing.
I wanted the audience to be aware of the poetry only at
intense moments; and I wanted them to feel at such
moments, not that they were listening to lines of
poetry by T.S. Eliot, but that the dramatic situation
had reached such a point of intensity that it was
natural for the characters to express themselves in
poetry.... No poet has begun to master *dramatic* poetry
until he can write lines of verse which are ... *transparent*: that is to say, you listen not to the poetry as
poetry but to the meaning of poetry.

I am not at all sure that I understand what Eliot is trying to do, but my own experience in the theater, hearing
the play, leads me to believe that something was being
done, effectively, something for the analysis of which the
critical training of most of us is simply inadequate. A
large part of this something was metrical, and this can be
roughly confirmed by a comparison of the first and second
halves of the first scene in Act I; but the eventual job
needs to be thorough. Another part, the meaning, is carried in those gnomic phrases like 'speak of the devil'
which have a very precise connotation in their context and
have the enormous advantage of being conversational currency. But in both cases, metrics and meaning, it should
be apparent that the author's purpose has been to write
poetry which is also valid as conversation; that 'The
Cocktail Party,' in its technical aspect, is the attempt of
a poet to come to terms with the conditions of the popular
prose theater in a way that is neither intransigent nor
compromising. But the attempt is more than technical, for
the play is also the effort of a Christian to write a
Christian play in such a way that it can get a wide hearing and yet make its point to those who are sufficiently
neutral and inquisitive to look into it. If you happen to
be both a Christian and a poetic dramatist in an age which
is not overtly Christian and which suspects poetry, you
will eventually have to come to some such stratagem if you
are to go on writing for anyone but yourself.

It is both the practical and the artistic craft of 'The
Cocktail Party' which makes it seem so significant to me,
as significant for verse drama - and other genres - as
'The Waste Land' was for poetry. The position of the
Christian poet in England is actually no different from
that of any serious artist in America: both find themselves unable to say what they have to say directly because
they think they will not be understood, and this produces
the condition called 'alienation.' But a refusal to compromise with a corrupted culture need not entail artistic
intransigence. And if we are going to rescue that culture
we have from its corruption, it is up to the artist to get
his values, his version of a culture, before as large a
public as he can in a way that will not dilute what he has
to say. This means the repossession of popular forms -
like the slick comedy of marital misunderstanding; it also
means a maximum of artistic craft and enough practical
craft to know that there is almost no other way.

Notes

a   I am perhaps stressing what may have seemed obvious to
    many readers. But the two most common misunderstand-
    ings of the play have been (a) that the 'Guardians'
    are divine or semi-divine figures controlling the lives
    of the others, or (b) that the 'Guardians' suffer so
    remarkable a metamorphosis between Acts I and Acts II
    and III that it can only be accounted for by supposing
    that they are ordinary human beings in Act I and demi-
    gods in Acts II and III - or outer selves and then
    inner selves. This last view has claimed the respect
    of a reviewer in so clear-sighted a journal as 'Scru-
    tiny': [see No. 160] 'Julia and Alex have a striking
    metamorphosis from their original selves. This is so
    palpable that it must be intentional, and we are ...
    intended to take Edward's remark about "the guardian"
    as a clue showing how to accept the convention. In the
    light of this the Julia and Alex of Acts II and III are
    presumably the inner selves of their analogues in Act I,
    and not real people at all.' This preposterous conclu-
    sion could have been avoided had the reviewer asked him-
    self: (1) At whose request was Reilly at the party?
    (2) Why, if Julia had invited Reilly, did she deny
    knowing him? (3) Is the Julia of Act I *really* different
    from the Julia of Act III, or is the change ascribable
    to a game she is playing as well as a change in the
    eyes of the others? But see above. It is true, how-
    ever, that Edward's reference to 'the guardian' is
    rather misleading. What Eliot means by this personal
    'guardian' is to be found in Reilly's conversation with
    Celia: she says, 'I don't in the least know what I am
    doing / Or why I am doing it. There is nothing else to
    do: / That is the only reason.' Reilly replies: 'It is
    the best reason.' Or consider Reilly's remark to
    Edward about Lavinia: 'The fact that you can't give a
    reason for wanting her / Is the best reason for believ-
    ing that you want her.' In each case, it is 'the guar-
    dian' ('the obstinate, the tougher self; who does not
    speak, / Who never talks, who cannot argue') which has
    made the decision. Eliot may also intend an analogy:
    what the personal 'guardian' is in the individual, the
    Christian 'Guardian' is in the world.
b   Consider, in this connection, the 'mysterious' bottle of
    champagne. Julia opens a full bottle of Edward's cham-
    pagne but says it is a 'half-bottle.' The point is not
    that she is being malicious or greedy or blind, but
    that she foresees the consequences of Edward's talk with
    Celia and obligingly leaves them an open half-bottle for

their 'farewell drink.' But her action, in context,
appears otherwise.

c   A year before 'The Cocktail Party' appeared, R.P. Blackmur remarked in a shrewd illustration: 'Eliot's religious poetry is a partly utopian and partly direct aesthetic experience of the actual Christian life today.
That is what it is about, and it cannot be judged
aesthetically until full stock has been taken of what
it is about.' 'Hudson Review,' Summer 1948.

d   I confess myself unable to guess what Eliot intends by
these 'saffron monkeys' and their connection with the
New York restaurant where Peter has lunch with Princess
Bologolomsky. It may mean merely that New York is a
pagan place; but why 'saffron'? There seems to me to
be a sacramental idea present, but I find this difficult
since one doesn't necessarily eat saffron monkey when
dining at 'The Saffron Monkey.' Perhaps Eliot is re-
ferring to the actual species of 'saffron monkey'; if
so, some anthropologist will be able to elucidate the
point. Or the source may be some one of the 'Mowgli'
stories; or perhaps the 'ape in saffron clothes' of
Book XI of 'The Golden Ass'; or Portia's little monkey;
or merely an orange version of Hanuman, the Hindu
monkey-god from the 'Ramayana.' In the East, saffron
is the color of the life of renunciation. But 'God
knows'; I don't. The point is obscure.

163. JOHN MIDDLETON MURRY, MR. ELIOT'S COCKTAIL PARTY,
'FORTNIGHTLY'

December 1950, n.s., vol. clxviii, 391-8

This review was reprinted in 'Unprofessional Essays'
(London, 1956), pp. 151-90.

Not unfairly 'The Cocktail Party' calls itself a comedy,
but its theme is the unusual one of salvation. Its relation to Mr. Eliot's previous play, 'The Family Reunion',
which could hardly be called a comedy, is also unusually
intimate. In this essay, I propose to consider this relation.

The dramatic theme of 'The Family Reunion' is the

progressive liberation of a man from 'the awful privacy of
the insane mind'. It is never clearly revealed in the
play whether Harry's belief that he has murdered his wife
is, or is not a delusion. What is revealed is that the
cause of his misery lies in the distant past, in the loveless relation between his father and mother, from which
his father had sought release in love of his mother's
sister, Harry's aunt, Agatha. He had, rather naïvely,
plotted to kill his cold and dominating wife. And it is
powerfully suggested that this murderous impulse of Harry's
father towards his wife is repeated, more terribly, in his
son, who is thus under a 'curse'. To my sense this introduces a perplexing and unsatisfactory element into the
play. I am never sure whether the 'curse' is conceived as
a real power of evil; therefore I am never sure whether
Harry is truly liberated from it. It seems to me that
this perplexing element in the play derives from Mr.
Eliot's intention to re-enact part of the theme of the
Oresteia in a modern setting. There is an element in
the Greek dramatic myth which cannot be reconciled with a
fundamentally Christian scheme of salvation.

Nevertheless, if we imaginatively eliminate from 'The
Family Reunion' this perplexing suggestion of an hereditary
curse, and read it as the drama of the emancipation of a
son from the devastation wrought in him by the loveless
relation between a weak but kindly husband and a self-
righteous and dominating wife, by means of the continuing
and purified love of his father's sister, it becomes not
only moving but convincing too. We can believe alike in
the condition of awful isolation in which Harry is imprisoned, and the reality of his liberation from it.

In 'The Cocktail Party', the theme is again salvation;
but now the subjects of salvation, Edward, Lavinia and
Celia, do not suffer under a 'curse' - at any rate, not
one that is mysterious, questionable and ultimately in-
comprehensible. The cause of their misery is not in the
distant past, like Harry's, neither do they labour, like
him, under any dreadful delusion. Their condition is
ordinary. In consequence there is no need of oracular
utterance in the play: there are no mysteries to conceal
or reveal. This is, no doubt, the chief reason why 'The
Cocktail Party', as compared to 'The Family Reunion', has
achieved a great and deserved success with the general
public. It is, from first to last, eminently credible.
Even the paradox by which the at first sight futile but
richly comic Julia and Alex are subsequently revealed as
confederates with Reilly in the work of salvation strains
our credulity only enough to make us meditate its significance.

At the same time, when we come to essentials, the relation between the two plays is seen to be close indeed.

The affinity between Celia's process of salvation and Harry's is evident, and the relation between her previous state of mind and his obvious. If we abate what is extraordinary in Harry's condition and consider it as one which might, without straining, be universalized, we have more or less exactly Celia's condition.

Celia: No ... it isn't that I *want* to be alone,
         But that everyone's alone - or so it seems to me.
         They make noises, and think they are talking to
            each other;
         They make faces, and think they understand each
            other.
         And I'm sure that they don't. Is that a delusion?
Reilly: A delusion is something we must return from.
         There are other states of mind, which we take to
            be delusion,
         But which we have to accept and go on from.

Celia's condition is awareness of isolation, and a sense of sin - not for anything she had done -

   But of emptiness, of failure
   Towards someone, or something, outside of myself;
   And I feel I must ... *atone* - is that the word?

That is, in essence, Harry's condition at his moment of enlightenment. But Celia has also an affinity with Agatha. She has had a love-affair with Edward, which she does not repent, and which she describes in retrospect very much as Agatha describes her love for Harry's father. Celia says:

                        I haven't hurt *her*.
   I wasn't taking anything away from her -
   Anything she wanted.

which is almost identical with Agatha's words to Amy: 'What did I take? Nothing that you ever had.' And Celia's description of her experience of love:

   I have thought at moments that the ecstasy is real
   Although those who experience it may have no reality.
   For what happened is remembered like a dream
   In which one is exalted by intensity of loving
   In the spirit, a vibration of delight
   Without desire, for desire is fulfilled
   In the delight of loving ...

reminds one of Agatha's: 'There are hours when there seems
to be no past or future...' The affinity between Celia
and Agatha is perhaps not to be stressed, but it is sufficiently marked to warrant the suggestion that Celia is,
in some sort, a combination of Harry and Agatha: a combination which is natural enough, for the spiritual relation
between Harry and Agatha is intimate indeed.

But in 'The Cocktail Party' the guidance which in 'The
Family Reunion' arises as it were spontaneously between
Agatha and Harry, or rather comes to them:

>   Oh, mother,
>   This is not to do with Agatha, any more than with the
>   rest of you.
>   My advice has come from quite a different quarter,

is objectified in Reilly's advice to Celia. This makes
for more explicit dramatic action; it is also necessary in
so far as Agatha and Harry are combined in Celia. The dialogue between Harry and Agatha would have to be soliloquy
in Celia, were it not for the creation of Reilly. And
Reilly has something more to say than is said, or hinted
at, in the dialogue between Harry and Agatha. There is
now a second possibility other than the life of expiation
and dedication. Reilly says to Celia:

[Quotes 'The Cocktail Party', II, CPP, pp. 417-18, 'If
that is what you wish' to 'a good life'.]

But Celia clings to her vision, and rejects, not without regret, the good life that Reilly offers.

[Quotes 'The Cocktail Party', II, CPP, p. 418, 'I feel it
would be' to 'belongs to that life'.]

So Celia chooses the second way, which Reilly describes to
her.

[Quotes 'The Cocktail Party', II, CPP, p. 418, 'The second
is unknown' to 'in the wrong place'.]

That pilgrimage is indistinguishable from Harry's; and
Celia's actual destiny is a factual and painful fulfilment
of Harry's conjecture.

>   Somewhere on the other side of despair.
>   To the worship in the desert, the thirst and depriva-
>   tion,
>   A stony sanctuary and a primitive altar, ...

> A care over lives of humble people,
> The lesson of ignorance, of incurable diseases.
> Such things are possible.

The difference, if difference there is, between Celia
and Harry - abating the Orestean pattern, which is irrelevant when we are considering the poet's doctrine of salvation - lies in the fact that the vision to which Celia
clings is a vision vouchsafed to her in the illumination of
love. Although it is not certain that Harry's vision was
of this kind, there is some evidence to suggest that it
was. For it is central to the drama of 'The Family Reunion', as I read it, that liberation comes to Harry
through Agatha's love and his recognition of it, both as a
fact in the past and an illumination in the present.
That is the purport of his cry to Angela:

> And what did not happen is as true as what did happen
> O my dear, and you walked through the little door
> And I ran to meet you in the rose-garden.

The rose-garden is the symbol of the same ecstasy of love
which Celia describes, when

> what happened is remembered like a dream
> In which one is exalted by intensity of loving
> In the spirit, a vibration of delight
> Without desire, for desire is fulfilled
> In the delight of loving.

Agatha, with Harry's father, 'only looked through the
little door when the sun was shining on the rose garden.'
But when she has told her secret to Harry she 'walks
through the little door' and he 'runs to meet her in the
rose-garden'. I do not think it is pressing the poet's
symbolism too hard to interpret passing through the little
door as the attainment of love beyond desire, and looking
through it only as the vision of love as it comes to one
entangled in desire. Agatha's love for Harry and Harry's
response to it are an instantaneous and eternal passing
through the little door.
   I would surmise, too, that Harry's 'running to meet
Agatha in the rose-garden' is the experience he describes
at the moment of its happening in the words:

> Look, I do not know why,
> I feel happy for a moment, as if I had come home.
> It is quite irrational, but now
> I feel quite happy, as if happiness

> Did not consist in getting what one wanted
> Or in getting rid of what can't be got rid of
> But in a different vision. This is like an end.

Or, if the experiences are not identical, they are complementary. There is, therefore, some solid ground for sup-
posing that Celia's experience is, at the spiritual level,
indistinguishable from Harry's.

What is new, in the scheme of salvation in 'The Cocktail Party' as compared with 'The Family Reunion', is
Reilly's insistence that there are two ways. The possibility of a return to ordinary life with 'a different
vision' is not even faintly indicated in 'The Family Reunion'. There the ordinary life, as presented in Harry's
other aunts, his uncles, and his brothers appears to be one
of stupid mechanism. The vista opened in 'The Cocktail
Party' is new, though it is not new in the history of
mysticism, in which the mysticism of descent as distinguished from the mysticism of ascent has always had an
honourable place. Reilly is true to the tradition when he
answers Celia's question: 'Which way is better?'

> Reilly: Neither way is better.
> Both ways are necessary. It is also necessary
> To make a choice between them.

The absorbing interest of 'The Cocktail Party' and that
which to my mind makes it the more significant play is that
the possibility of the transvaluation and transformation of
the ordinary becomes the main theme: it is not merely suggested but dramatically demonstrated in Edward and Lavinia.
I think the doctrine itself is truer, or at any rate more
comprehensive, and I think the drama gains greatly in
power - even in the power to affect 'our deeper organization' - because there is no penumbra of spiritual uncertainty to perplex. 'The Cocktail Party' is a very fine
play indeed.

On one point it leaves me, not indeed perplexed, but
questioning. I accept the necessity of choice between the
way of renunciation and the way of acceptance; and I can
believe that this is *the* spiritual decision. What I am
doubtful about is the doctrine of human love which is somewhat more than implied in 'The Cocktail Party'. The love
of Celia and Edward was a self-deception.

> And then I found we were only strangers
> And that there had been neither giving nor taking
> But that we had merely made use of each other
> Each for his purpose. That's horrible.

The discovery is humanly true, and no doubt frequent.
But can it be universalized as the inevitable and inexorable destiny of lovers?
That Celia is tempted to universalize it is natural
enough in her moment of disillusion.

> Can we only love
> Something created by our own imagination?
> Are we all in fact unloving and unlovable?

But Reilly himself appears to accept this. The best of
love between a man and a woman, along the way of acceptance, is that

> They do not repine;
> Are contented with the morning that separates
> And with the evening that brings together
> For casual talk beside the fire
> Two people who know they do not understand each other.
> Breeding children whom they do not understand
> And who will never understand them.

Call it tolerant affection. Either that or the impersonal
ecstasy described by Celia, which makes her think at
moments

> that the ecstasy is real
> Although those who experience it may have no reality ...
> But what, or whom I loved
> Or what in me was loving, I do not know.

If there is love, there are no persons; if there are persons, there is no love. Such appears to be the doctrine.
There is plenty of high authority behind it - in fact an
august and venerable tradition. And yet I do not believe
it to be true. Often, terribly often, apparently true: a
doctrine that fits the facts of experience in nine cases
out of ten, or 99 out of a hundred. But for all that not
universally true, either factually or metaphysically. To
make the best of a bad job, by accepting the fact that we
are all unloving and unlovable is not the best thing that
may happen to those who do not choose the way of renunciation, or the best they can achieve. They can learn to love
each other as persons; and become lovable in the process,
which has its own discipline of renunciation. The process
is described in some words of Katherine Mansfield's:

> For a long time she said she did not want to change
> anything in him, and she meant it. Yet she hated things

in him and wished they were otherwise. Then she said
that she did not want to change anything in him and she
meant it. And the dark things that she had hated she
now regarded with indifference. Then she said that she
did not want to change anything in him. But now she
loved him so that even the dark things she loved, too.
She wished them there; she was not indifferent. Still
they were dark and strange but she loved them. And it
was for this that they had been waiting. They changed.
They shed their darkness - the curse was lifted and they
shone forth as Royal Princes once more, as creatures of
light.

I believe that also is a real possibility between lovers.
There is not much room for it in Mr. Eliot's doctrine of
love.

However that may be, it is immaterial to the value of
'The Cocktail Party'. That seems to me definitely superior
to that of 'The Family Reunion', for two main reasons:
first, that the scheme of salvation is satisfying and universal, and second, because (in consequence of this) the
dramatic action is unconfused. Both plays have for their
theme the necessity of salvation; but whereas in 'The
Cocktail Party' what we are to be saved from is clear, in
'The Family Reunion' it is not. The eventually liberated
souls in 'The Cocktail Party' recognizably belong to the
human condition: they are such as you or I. But Harry
under the curse is not. His condition is extraordinary.
That, it seems, would not matter if his extraordinary
situation could be felt to be truly symbolic of the
human situation at large; as it might be if he had not been
persuaded that he had murdered his wife.

It is not easy to be sure of one's own judgment in such
matters. To say that such a condition as Harry's *cannot* be
symbolic of the human condition is obviously excessive.
The inexplicable and mysterious sense of implication and
responsibility for 'the giant agony of the world' which
comes to us all, in moments of awareness, may be symbolized
by an extreme private agony such as Harry's: it is obviously not impossible. The problem is really one of the
dramatic adequacy or plausibility of symbolism. This is,
I think, what Goethe was pondering when he wrote:

There is a great difference between a poet who seeks the
particular for the sake of the universal and one who
seeks the universal in the particular. The former
method breeds Allegory, where the particular is used
only as an example, an instance, of the universal; but
the latter is the true method of poetry. It expresses

a particular without a thought of or a reference to the universal. But whoever has a living grasp of this particular, grasps the universal with it, knowing it either not at all, or only long afterwards.

In these terms, the difficulty of 'The Family Reunion' arises from the difficulty of getting such a living grasp of the particular who is Harry. A condition of mind in which a man verily does not know whether he murdered his wife or not, or for what cause, is impossible for us to enter, to feel as though it were our own. It is insanity, not only in the legal, but in a deeper sense. And the suggestion that this insanity is explicable and 'curable' by the victim's knowledge that his father had meditated murdering *his* wife is spiritually confusing. It recalls the appeal of Baudelaire.

> La vie fourmille de monstres innocents... O Créateur! peut-il exister des monstres aux de celui-là qui sait pourquoi ils existent, comment ils se sont faits et comment ils auraient pu ne pas se faire? (1)

It is as though the poet claimed to know, and to reveal, the genesis of criminal lunacy. This is inordinate; and my mind baulks at the causal connection he suggests. The extremity of Harry's condition is not explained by the origin of wretchedness he discovers. Neither can we believe that he believes it is. He remains the innocent victim, even the innocent monster. What is revealed to him explains why he should be miserable and in exile, but not why he should have been mad, or a murderer.
But it may be said: why distinguish? Harry's sense of isolation and exile is itself a suffering endured by an innocent victim. Screwing it up to the pitch of madness and murder does not alter this; it intensifies the suffering but it does not make the lesser suffering deserved. The answer is, surely, that isolation and exile *is* the common human condition. To become aware is to become aware precisely of this. And even though Harry's wretchedness had a particular origin, it is nevertheless to this extent aptly symbolic of the state of man, just as Agatha's love is symbolic of the means of man's deliverance. But the further condition of madness and murder is not symbolic, in the same way: neither can it be made symbolic by suggesting it is causally linked with a father's desire to murder.
Again, it may be said, this is the mystery of Evil. Then let it remain a mystery. As Mr. Eliot himself has said: 'The mystery of Iniquity is a pit too deep for

652 T.S. Eliot: The Critical Heritage

mortal eyes to plumb.' The poet made a mistake in offering
a half-explanation, which is no explanation. If the cause
why Harry murdered, or believed he had murdered, an apparently unoffending wife, was that his father had meditated
murdering an offending one, and this causal connection due
to the operation of inflexible laws, 'unalterable in the
nature of music', we can only say that the music is no
music to our ear. The laws of Argos and England refuse to
be reconciled. Something has come between.

Anyhow, there is no such radical perplexity to disturb
and confuse one's reaction to 'The Cocktail Party'. In it
the drama seems to arise directly out of the scheme of salvation and the new recognition that there are two ways of
salvation is not only spiritually true, but it makes possible a dramatic contrast which is finally convincing as
well as immediately effective. Compared with it, the contrast in 'The Family Reunion' between Harry and Agatha
and Mary on the one side, and Harry's aunts and uncles and
brothers on the other seems artificial and strained, so
that we seem to be offered a truly desperate choice between complete renunciation and complete idiocy. But in
'The Cocktail Party' the double contrast between Celia on
the one hand and Edward and Lavinia on the other, and between Edward and Lavinia in their former and in their latter condition, is at once illuminating and satisfying.
The drama that has been unfolded is recognizably within
the limits of the human condition; and it is the more dramatic for that. 'The Cocktail Party' represents as great
an advance on 'The Family Reunion' as 'The Family Reunion'
did on 'Murder in the Cathedral'. Considering how original
'Murder in the Cathedral' was, that is saying a very great
deal.

Note

1 'Life teems with innocent monsters ... O Creator! Can
   there be monsters in the eyes of Him who alone knows
   why they exist, how they have made themselves what they
   are and how they could have been other than what they
   are?' from 'Mademoiselle Bistouri', 'Petites Poèmes en
   Prose' xlvii.

'The Complete Poems and Plays 1909-1950'

New York, 20 November 1952

164. V.S. PRITCHETT, AN AMERICAN PURITAN IN ENGLAND, 'NEW YORK TIMES BOOK REVIEW'

30 November 1952, vol. vii, pp. 1, 36

Pritchett (b. 1900), novelist, critic and director of the 'New Statesman', has been visiting professor at several British and American Universities. His extensive publications include 'The Living Novel' (1946), 'Collected Stories' (1956) and 'Midnight Oil' (1971), an account of his early years in Paris and London.

The two great American writers who have settled in England and have taken British nationality in the last half century have been, primarily, persons who inspire awe. Henry James with his austere and indefatigable conception of the novel as a work of art, T.S. Eliot by the always increasing severity of his revolutionary practice of poetry, gave their English contemporaries a tremendous dressing down. Deliberate, circumspect, serious and shocked, almost to the point of being noticeable in the street, these two American men of genius seem aloof from the English imagination which, as a rule, is hostile to intellectual formalizations and is lazy, sociable, sensual and heretical. Even the English feeling for tradition is a feeling for the history of its heresies; in this tradition Eliot and James, on the contrary, have given the sharp call to order. They have both, very strangely, alleviated a certain strain in this attitude by a fertile and irrational weakness: an unreasonable love of London, the most squalid and

disorganized city on earth. And, in Eliot's case, London
has been the seat and occasion of one of the major revolu-
tions in the history of English poetry. He re-created
poetry for new generations and he re-created a city.

It is tempting to see Eliot as an isolated and learned
young man working in a bank. We see a trim anti-bohemian
with black bowler and umbrella, the well-known symbol of
male respectability, ushering us to our seat in hell. But
Eliot belongs to that tremendous boiling over of creative
energy which began in Europe just before 1914 and which
lasted until the Thirties. It is the last of the great
periods in literature and the arts and nothing has happened
since to equal it.

Eliot, Joyce, D.H. Lawrence, Wyndham Lewis in English
literature alone, seem now to be the last fling of liberal
civilization, though at the time they were iconoclasts in
violent reaction against it. In an exciting sense they
were all expatriates from an old order; like their contemporaries on the Continent and in America, they were marked
by the common foreignness to a society which, even after
1914, managed to keep some of its pre-war habits of mind.
Prufrock ('I keep my countenance, I remain self-possessed')
and Sweeney still went around, pertinacious ghosts, until
1931 saw the apotheosis of the former, and Sweeney stood
in the breadline.

The revolution of 'The Waste Land' is matched by
'Ulysses.' There is the same material: the anthropology,
the unconscious mind, the archetypes of a modern city.
The poem, it has been said, contained its time, but that
is also often true of works of little value. What made
'The Waste Land' important was that it also gave us a means
of apprehending time itself. After the spiritual destruction of the first mass war the poem dragged up the past
like a body from the sea bed into the present moment.
Tradition was to be seen by working back into the present.

Eliot has explored this again and again. Twenty years
later the 'Four Quartets' continue the meditation; the
enormous amount of Eliot criticism has explained Eliot explaining it. But when we turn to read Eliot and re-read
him we find that though the reading may be richer, the
dramatic, beautiful and clinching things in him are still
the sliding imagery, the power of the symbols, the power
to make hard thinking sensuously felt, where commonly it
has been 'sicklied o'er.' An intellectual poet without
heart, it is often said.

The animating emotion of 'The Waste Land' is one which
has a stronger place in American than in the purely British contribution to English poetry: I mean nostalgia.
It was first crystalized in Poe and swells to the dominant

emotion in American writing. Eliot begins, as Henry James
did, with the common longing for a lost past, goes on to
raise it to the feeling for the tragedy of time itself and
finally into the longing for God. 'As for man his days
are as grass.'

Upon this emotion Eliot's austere and even agonized
metaphysical strictures have been splendidly designed.
Stricture is not a misprint for structure. For, as time
goes by, we see him as a great but narrow poet. Longing
is an experience of the soul, but to long is to be too
occupied for the entertaining of other kinds of experience.
Eliot is an American Puritan; he prejudges experience.
Hence his very canny assumption of premature old age; the
frosty glint of self-mockery; there are occasional engag-
ing signs of practical Puritan worldliness, which come out
in his startling comic gift. There is the agreeable sad-
ism of letting us down in order to show us up.

When one compares Eliot with the poets of the seventeenth century he is deliberately intellectual where poets
like Traherne or Herbert are men with naïve hearts who do
not think naïvely. They are caught in the rising and tidal
fall of their spirits. Donne is in the grip of a mind, a
body, and senses that struggle for the mastery of him.
The Puritan separation has not taken place. But the
finest moments of the 'Four Quartets' come from an incredible power to separate and to seek. We are led into the
withering landscapes or the wastes of the sea to consider
bones and vestiges, and one image after another, like some
farewell to the flesh, will demonstrate to us the awful
superfluousness of personality and its inexpiable guilt.
Poetry, he has told us, comes of suffering.

At this point many of Eliot's warmer-blooded readers have
retreated. One of the most sensitive and instructed of
his admirers, the late F.O. Matthiessen, has asked whether
Chaucer or Shakespeare exemplifies such a restricted view
of poetry. We can only say of Eliot that the pain is not
a mood, it is an action. Or rather that it is a place
whose topography he sets out. Pain is set out with the
stony light of necessity upon it.

One cannot help glancing back, after reading him, at
the enormous amount of criticism. Some of it is snobbish
and cult-ridden; some of it has tended to degenerate into
treating Eliot as a refined form of crossword puzzle.
One cannot say that the master's own manner has not sometimes encouraged this, but he has more humor than his intense disciples have. The political objections to his
work do not seem to me as serious as they appear at first
sight. Who is not in reaction against what the nineteenth

century conceived progress to be? Where Eliot has seemed
most vulnerable to me is in the belief that he is really
imbued with 'the tragic sense of life.' Certainly, if he
means by that the knowledge that we shall die, he has
that - and sometimes rather like some Anglican Omar Khayam.
But there are moments when one regards the act of putting
one foot in the grave as one of Prufrock's prudences. The
tragic sense of life is felt when the full life meets the
unanswerable death.

The point may be made clearer by a glance at the plays.
In 'The Family Reunion' and 'The Cocktail Party,' with
their common theme of the expiation of guilt, one is
shocked by the disparity in strength between the people and
the sins they committed, as between the sins and the sufferings by which they will expiate them. Mr. Matthiessen
has pointed out that when Harry goes off to follow his
Furies and purge his crime, in the former play, he is a
singularly selfish man who has never felt remorse or love,
and who hardly seems capable of more than a restless passage from one luxury hotel to the next. He can become a
nervous wreck but not a tragic figure. Perhaps we are
foolish to expect that of him.

There is an inturned edge in all Eliot's thought, the
conflict of faith with un-faith in his religion; the sense
of his time and his purpose stirs up the satirist. One is
aware of the practical prescience of one humble enough to
be a church warden and ardent for the gifts of the saint.
One is awed by him because there has been a certain spiritual or intellectual pride in his seeking, as a poet, to
bear the pain of his time, and we would be outraging his
own canon if, for a moment, we were to try to turn his
poetry into a religion - even into his own.

165. MARY COLUM, ST LOUIS OVER BLOOMSBURY, 'SATURDAY
REVIEW'

27 December 1952, vol. xxxv, 17-18

Mary Colum (d. 1957), wife of Padraic Colum, was a prominent literary figure in New York.

'We are country-bred people,' says the Hon. Charles Piper,

brother of the deceased Lord Monchesney, in T.S. Eliot's
'Family Reunion.' This single sentence tells a great deal
as to the difference between Americans and English, between
Americans and Europeans. One of the great American dreams
is to be an urban person with city clothes, city manners,
city habits. One of the great English dreams was to be a
country gentleman, owning a country house of some kind,
with horses, dogs, and guns. This type never minded being
called provincial because, as a matter of fact, they were
not - they were a rural people, but beyond a certain economic line they all wanted to talk with a standard class
accent.

Now, T.S. Eliot loves the English country-house dwel-
lers, and many of his critics, as those of Henry James,
complain that he has too much of a penchant for titles and
people of historic descent. But in old countries these
titles are interesting and romantic, evoking part of the
country's history, and their possessors are frequently
people who understand the arts; in England, the art of
literature particularly. In his remarkable plays Eliot
has undoubtedly made these people oversubtle, but he has
certainly made them characters.

He was always, from his early poems, a character-
creator - Sweeney, J. Alfred Prufrock, the title character in 'Portrait of a Lady,' Burbank with his Baedeker.
To be sure, his characters are all neurotics and neurotics
in the American way. He possesses the American sophistication, the sophistication of cities. Writers like Eliot
and James came into old European cultures with a new type
of intelligence, one that had developed out of a struggle
to tame a continent and which resulted in an overrespect
for social formulas and conventions.

In the writing of his plays, Eliot's American intelligence was able to get him away from the English obsession
about keeping to Elizabethan verse forms. He got back to
the verse of the mystery and morality plays in his striking 'Murder in the Cathedral,' and so made a fresh start
in verse drama. Then, he put himself closer to Racine
than to Shakespeare in 'Family Reunion' and 'The Cocktail
Party,' for these are dramas of conscience as Racine conceived them, nearer to 'Phèdre' and 'Britannicus' than to
'Macbeth' or 'Hamlet.' He knit French and Anglo-Saxon
culture. The shape his early poetry took came out of
Jules Laforgue, though let me stress here my conviction
that he is a far greater poet than Laforgue.

In spite of his love for England and the English tradition, his writing is markedly un-English. The inner
rhythm of his mind, which is what gives any real writer his
style, is something altogether distinct from that possessed

by any English poet; it is a nervous rhythm, short in its
emotional undertones, but capable of taking in diverse influences. Of his poetry, the present reviewer believes
that his earliest is his best, the most distinctive and
with the most personal style. At the same time it is citi-
fied poetry to an extent that no European poetry has been,
no matter how much European poets try to make it so. No
European could, or ever did, write a poem like 'The Love
Song of J. Alfred Prufrock' or 'Sweeney Among the Nightingales.' These two, it seems to the reviewer, are far finer
poems than the much advertised 'Waste Land,' which, in
spite of memorable passages, is not so completely achieved.
What lovely lines are in 'The Love Song of J. Alfred Prufrock':

> We have lingered in the chambers of the sea
> By sea girls wreathed with seaweed red and brown
> Till human voices wake us, and we drown.

and in 'Sweeney Among the Nightingales':

> The nightingales are singing near
> The Convent of the Sacred Heart,
>
> And sang within the bloody wood
> When Agamemnon cried aloud
> And let their liquid siftings fall
> To stain the stiff dishonoured shroud.

But going through the collection before us, we cannot help
feeling that these poems and plays, with all their discoveries and all their great accomplishment, are limited in
their emotional range. The language of his plays becomes a
a cautious speech which never can belong to the great pro-
jections of the theatre. His characters can never rise to
the rhetoric of the great poetic dramatists. Eliot could
not write, and none of his personages could ever speak,
lines like

> A wild dedication of yourselves
> To unpath'd waters and undreamed-of shores

or Yeats's

> The hand that loves to scatter, the life like the
>   gambler's throw.
> And these things I make prosper till a day comes that
>   I know,
> When heart and mind shall darken that the weak pull

          down the strong,
And the long remembering harpers have matter for a song.

But when everything else is said, it must be said that T.S.
Eliot is one of the great poets of the modern world and he
truly deserved the Nobel Prize. He has been able to put
modern man with his anxieties, hesitations, and trivialities into his poetry. He has been one of those poets with
a deep and perhaps almost unconscious urge to link himself
with something outside his private interests. He wanted a
link with English Anglicanism and the old English tradition. Yeats wanted to link himself with the Irish tradition and nationalism. The poetry of both poets benefited
by their enlistment.

'The Confidential Clerk'

First produced at the Edinburgh Festival, 25 August - 5 September 1953;
first edition, London, 5 March 1954;
first American edition, New York, 8 March 1954

166. HENRY DONALD, EDINBURGH FESTIVAL, 'SPECTATOR'

4 September 1953, vol. cxci, 238

Sir Claude Mulhammer, financier, is sitting in the spacious private office of his London house. Enter to him the elderly Eggerson, his former confidential clerk, who has now, except for purposes of consultation, retired. The reason he has been summoned on this occasion is, we learn, so that he can undertake the task of meeing Sir Claude's wife (Lady Elizabeth) shortly due to arrive at Northolt. This is too delicate a matter, Sir Claude explains, to be entrusted to Eggerson's young successor, Colby Simpkins, of whose appointment Lady Elizabeth has not yet been told. But there is something else about the new confidental clerk of which Lady Elizabeth is ignorant. Colby Simpkins is Sir Claude's natural son. And we gather that Sir Claude wishes that he could tell his wife about Colby, wishes, since before her marriage she had a son of her own, that she would accept Colby in the missing boy's place.

As the limpid, often witty dialogue runs smoothly on, the personable Colby comes in. Soon we are hearing of the existence of Lucasta Angel, for whom, it seems, Sir Claude has made himself responsible. And when Lucasta herself appears and is introduced for the first time to Colby, we discover that she is engaged to one B. Kaghan, who follows close on her heels. Kaghan is a business man too, with bowler and umbrella, an amiable rough diamond, but we can easily perceive, before the betrothed couple depart, that Lucasta's meeting with Colby is an event likely to give rise to repercussions. A spark has been struck. And we see too that behind her airy banter there is something

deeper, a melancholy, it may be, a hint of tragedy, something, at all events, beyond Kaghan's ken, something that
the thoughtful Colby might understand and resolve.

Light relief from all this is provided by the premature
arrival of Lady Elizabeth. It is perhaps a little surprising to find not only that she is a silly woman but that we
have met her before. She belongs to 'Hay Fever,' and if
she is not Judith Bliss herself, she must be a close relation. She speaks of mind-control, auras, and the marvellous continental doctors she has been consulting. But she
only stays long enough to inspect and approve of Colby,
and to remind us that she herself once had a son who would
now be about his age. Finally, Sir Claude and Colby are
left alone, and the act ends with a conversation in which
the similar characteristics of father and son and the insecurity of their relationship are drawn with an exquisite
dry-point clarity. The writing here, almost Jamesian at
times in its detail, is the best thing we have heard on the
Lyceum stage since the performance of 'The River Line' last
year. This, clearly, must be the pith of the play.

But there is still what might be called the secondary
theme. The curtain swings up again on Colby's mews flat,
two months later. He is playing the piano to Lucasta.
The spark struck in the first act has begun to glow. A
picture is sketched of two puzzled intelligent young people
searching for a common ground. Once more we are given a
scene of infinite tact, full of lyrical beauty and insight,
flawlessly acted and produced. And it terminates effectively with Lucasta's announcement - shocking news, of
course, to Colby - that she is Sir Claude's natural
daughter.

At this point in the play not only the situation but the
characters are rich with possibilities. How will the
Lucasta-Colby affair be resolved? How soon will she learn
that he is her half-brother? Has Colby really abandoned
all idea of musicianship - for that was to be his ambition?
Is he content to fall in with Sir Claude's plans? Or will
Sir Claude himself, who is also an artist manqué, come to
realize that Colby's talent is worth cultivating? Is this
the meaning of the presentation piano? Above all, to what
deeper revelations is all the fascinating conversation
tending? What more has Mr. Eliot to tell us of music and
craftsmanship, of loneliness, of secret gardens, of God?

It is here that the first ridiculous false note is
sounded. B. Kaghan divulges that his parentage too is un-
orthodox. He is a foundling; he was adopted. Before the
second act is over Lady Elizabeth has gaily refused to
believe, what we have already accepted as fact, that Colby
is Sir Claude's son and claims him as her own 'lost child.'

And as the play's centre of gravity giddily shifts, the
staggering suspicion dawns that the rest of the evening is
going to be taken up deciding who has fathered or mothered
whom. This not only proves to be the case, but the most
obvious forecast turns out to be the right one. The issues
raised in the first half of the play are either perfunctorily wound up or ignored. Lady Elizabeth, dominating the
stage, delights the audience with counterfeit Coward. Her
relatives, she says, 'were so carnivorous - always killing
things and eating them'; or, speaking of her former lover,
'he was run over by a rhinoceros in Tanganyika.' And by
the time Colby's future comes to be decided - for the
greater part of the last act he is either off altogether
or standing in the background - our interest in him has
evaporated, and we have certainly no sighs to spare for
Sir Claude.

In short, this is a maddening, broken-backed play,
which, with every contrivance of art and poetry, raises
the highest expectations and then, perversely, fails to
fulfil them. It is somehow no comfort to be told that it
is based on the 'Ion' of Euripides.

But if the play falls off, the goodness of the acting
is maintained to the end. Margaret Leighton as Lucasta
adds a faultless technique to her incandescent appearance.
Denholm Elliott (Colby) proves himself again to be one of
the most promising and accomplished young actors in the
profession, and Alan Webb plays Eggerson, the only truly
rewarding part, with captivating charm. Isabel Jeans,
Alison Leggatt, Paul Rogers and Peter Jones complete a
cast which must be one of the most talented of any current
production.

The two sets by Hutchinson Scott are ingeniously contrasted. The one is dignified and formal; the other has
planes and perspectives slightly but significantly out of
true.

167. T.C. WORSLEY, A REVIEW, 'NEW STATESMAN'

5 September 1953, vol. xlvi, 256

Worsley (b. 1907), novelist and theatre critic, was literary editor and drama critic for the 'New Statesman' from
1948 until 1960.

With 'The Confidental Clerk,' Mr. Eliot has done it again.
By this I do not mean that he has merely repeated the success of 'The Cocktail Party'; he is not the kind of writer
to repeat his successes. Each work is for him (and consequently for us) an exploration, and initially, if I
understand what he has written about his own methods, an
exploration in technique. 'The Confidental Clerk' explores
new territory and uses methods in some ways quite different
from anything that has gone before, and yet it is able to
rivet the attention of ordinary theatre audiences who could
not - and should not - be expected to be interested in
questions of technique. An audience judges by results, and
though this play is, I believe, very imperfect, Mr. Eliot
has now reached a stage where the authority with which he
puts his questions imposes itself absolutely.

From the very opening of the play we feel we are on
sure ground. Yet it is a very odd sort of sure ground,
this of Mr. Eliot's. It is by no means the conventional
sure ground of problems posed and solutions neatly found
for them. On the contrary, we are never quite sure what
the problems really are; and as for the solutions, they
none of them seem to us to fit at all. Why then we should
be content to follow so fumbling and faltering a guide is
a mystery. But so it is. His authority is such that he
compels us along.

Our exploration is of Sir Claude Mulhammer's curiously
assorted household. Sir Claude himself has inherited a
financial business from his father; he runs it successfully enough but is at heart an artist manqué. Then there
is his wife, Lady Elizabeth, a scatterbrained woman interested in fake religions. There is an ambiguous young
woman whom the faithful old confidential clerk pronounces
'flighty'; and she is engaged to a successful young protégé of Sir Claude's, B. Kaghan. Finally there is yet
another protégé, Mr. Colby Simpkins, a young musician
manqué who is training on as confidential clerk in Eggerson's place. The clue to the plot is not with the rather
Gilbertian revelations of paternal and maternal mix-ups.
It is not a question of who we are, but of what we choose
to be. We must, it is suggested, follow in our father's
footsteps. Young Colby, of doubtful origins, failed
organist but with a talent for finance, can choose one of
several fathers who offer themselves to guide his footsteps. Which shall he choose to be saved? The theme is
decorated with several variations ranging from the poignant
to the farcical. For all of them are, or have been, faced
with related choices, and they are only reminded that once
they have chosen 'we all of us have to adapt ourselves to
the wish that is granted.'

What is new in the play is that for the first time Mr.
Eliot approaches, in his own devious way, the question of
human relationships. We are not yet dealing with people
in the Ibsenite or the novelist's sense, and the fact that
the characters are not people in this sense makes for a
certain confusion. But the human interest is there, and
it gives us a first act which fairly bristles with the
possibilities of development. It gives us too, to start
the second, a scene of great tenderness, a love scene –
or rather a scene which beautifully embodies the reaching
out towards a first shy contact between two young people.
Technically, too, Mr. Eliot has succeeded with his last act
which, even if emotionally it may leave us baffled, is,
with its family conference and its *deus ex machina*, dramatically effective and flowers out of what has gone before.

Yet, amusing, fascinating, oddly disturbing as 'The
Confidential Clerk' is, I cannot help feeling that in
approaching the question of human relationships Mr. Eliot
set himself more problems than he had anticipated. His
present compromise is uneasy. If his characters are to
have relationships which interest us, they must become
less spiritual types and more people – at least so long as
Mr. Eliot, for his own reasons, insists on suppressing the
verse. Nor can the people be in any important relation
with each other so long as the action is on the level of
the absurd. It is all very well to try to reassure us by
founding the plot on classical myth. That doesn't put
right the confusion of modes. The comic exaggerations of
the plot don't fit the terms of contemporary life – or at
least they are not made to fit with these particular
people and their particular problems. Quite a different
form of make-believe is needed for each set. We can perfectly accept a changeling found in a hand-bag, if we are
introduced to it in the fantasy of comedy. But we would be
hard put to it to take seriously the spiritual problems of
such a changeling, or feel solemn over the announcement
that it was to read for Holy Orders.

These confusions have obviously set actors and producer
a difficult task. The problems have been notably well
solved. But, except in two cases, the solution is a compromise. Miss Isabel Jeans is brilliantly funny as Lady
Elizabeth; but she would have had to forgo some of her best
laughs if she were to modulate properly into the seriousness that sometimes seems called for. Yet surely the
author has himself funked the issue in her last scene and
left her with nothing to say and no attitude to strike?
Miss Margaret Leighton has the most difficult part. Her
first act irruption doesn't quite come off in the writing
(ought she not here be quite definitely planted in the

audience's mind as Sir Claude's mistress, if the second act surprise is to work properly?). Her love scene is beautifully written and played with an exquisite pathos; it brings tears to the eyes. But her third act scene is surely another missed chance - too much prosy explanation before the emotional good-bye. Sir Claude is comparatively straightforward (if we accept that he is unexplained), and Mr. Paul Rogers just about achieves him. Young Colby Simpkins is 'different': everyone notices it: everyone says so. But the difference is not very visible or audible in the part (as little as it was with Celia Coplestone); Mr. Denholm Elliott has to be diffident and puzzled and charming; and so he is. Eggerson, the old confidential clerk, and B. Kaghan, the brash young financier, offer no difficulties. Mr. Alan Webb plays the former as a sweet, rather sugary, good old man, and Mr. Peter Jones gives a lifelike lightning sketch of the bounder with a good heart. And finally Miss Alison Leggatt makes a telling entry as the mysterious *Dea ex machina*.

Mr. Eliot has now carried his principles about the kind of verse appropriate to modern verse drama to their logical conclusion. The controlling beat, which could still be faintly heard in 'The Cocktail Party,' is no longer audible at all. It is the abrogation of this control that is, I think, largely responsible for the confusion. Surely he has now reached the point he was aiming at, when 'he can dare to make more liberal use of poetry.'

168. J.G. WEIGHTMAN, FROM A REPORT ON THE EDINBURGH FESTIVAL, 'TWENTIETH CENTURY'

October 1953, vol. cliv, 306-8

Weightman (b. 1915), Professor of French at the University of London, includes amongst his publications 'On Language and Writing' (1947) and 'The Concept of the Avant-Garde' (1973).

The acting of 'The Confidential Clerk,' calls for no comment, because it is perfect. Miss Isabel Jeans and Miss Margaret Leighton put back their heads and spout their words deliciously with many an Edith Evans slur and

squawk. The men are equally good; Mr Denholm Elliott
even achieves the miracle of looking, moving and sounding
exactly like a young Mr T.S. Eliot. The whole performance
is impeccable. It is the play itself which disappoints;
it entertains while it lasts, but instead of growing in
the memory it contracts. (a) This is surprising, because
several critics have spoken of its profundity. Mr Alan
Dent, of the 'News Chronicle', has gone into raptures and
Mr Eliot himself, taking a leaf out of a book by Gide,
has said that any good work has far more in it than the
author himself knows. Shall I proclaim my stupidity by
confessing that I found 'The Confidental Clerk' a limpid,
and almost straightforwardly didactic play? It is a trim,
vicarage lawn, compared to the Nordic forests of 'Hamlet'.
The main theme is that of vocation, and the lesson is
that you should know yourself. We are all, in a way,
foundlings, and have to come to terms with the parents we
happen to have, and with ourselves. If you cannot be a
genius, you may be a decent, second-rate artist. If you
are not an artist at all, you can still play your little
part in life with self-knowledge and (Christian) humility.
The exceptional person, who is painfully aware of the burden of existence and the inadequacy of personal relations,
can become a priest or a saint. It is, in other words,
almost exactly the theme of 'The Cocktail Party'; there,
the married couple came to accept each others' limitations
and Celia went off to die a martyr's death; here, four
characters make progress towards self-knowledge in the lay
world and a fifth turns towards the priesthood.
The verse which Mr Eliot inaugurated in 'The Cocktail
Party' again proves an admirable medium for the rendering
of modern conversation. Mr Eliot has certainly invented a
form. What is doubtful is the quality of the content he
puts into it. After a slow opening, the first two acts
achieve a kind of momentum. They contain two or three
excellent poetic passages; in one, Mr Eliot writes about
the beauty of pure form and seems to be confessing that his
passionate love of poetry is accompanied by a sense of inadequacy as a poet; another is a delicately inhibited love
scene, which, at first sight, appears daringly incestuous.
However, there is a distinct fall in the third act. Mr
Eliot adopts the clumsy solution of bringing in a new
character to facilitate the *dénouement* and all seven sit
down to argue the matter out, without remarkable wit or any
glimmer of poetry. Apart from the patches of lyricism in
the first two acts, the play seems to have no real density.
It is embarrassingly full of echoes of other dramatists,
including Wilde and Shaw; they, belonging to the late
nineteenth century had a grand manner, which allowed them

to get away with the preposterous; Mr Eliot - does the
fault lie with mid-twentieth century Chelsea? - is not
grand; unless I completely misunderstood him, most of the
time he rises to nothing more than resigned whimsy, which
irritates, because we are expecting something better. The
jokes about women not understanding each other, herbal
salads, the Higher Thought and so on, are very mild, to say
the least, and rather old-fashioned. Worse still, the play
perhaps contains failures of taste and sympathy. When Mr
Eliot uses the metaphor of the 'secret garden' to describe
the inner life, is he deliberately forcing us to rehabili-
tate a soiled image, or is he serious? When Lady Mulhammer
gets a laugh by saying that her lover was run over by a
rhinoceros in Tanganyika, is the audience then supposed to
blush and feel that it has been trapped into vulgar mirth?
Mr Eliot is sophisticated enough to play such tricks. But
when Lucasta describes her mother flatly as a prostitute
who drank gin and laid bets, no ambiguity is possible.
The mother, like a character in Victorian melodrama, is
cast into the outer darkness of the unrealizable, where
neither Shakespeare, Shaw nor Wilde would have left her.
And is there not something unbearably coy in introducing
an oblique reference to the priesthood, after a feeble joke
about the badness of a church organ?

These weaknesses are not counteracted by a too deliberate attempt to make the play end on an unresolved tragic
note. Mr Eliot is said to be smuggling spirituality into
the commercial theatre. What is the point, if only a
rather shamefaced curate steps out of his Trojan Horse?
The first and second acts had promised more.

Note

a   In the next article, Mr Richard Findlater gives a rather
    different appreciation.

169. RICHARD FINDLATER, THE CAMOUFLAGED DRAMA, 'TWENTIETH
CENTURY'

October 1953, vol. cliv, 311-16

Findlater (b. 1921), literary editor and drama critic, has
published a number of studies of actors and of the theatre

generally. He was editor of 'Twentieth Century' from 1961
to 1965.
    This review follows the preceding item, by Weightman, in
the same issue of the journal.

Mr T.S. Eliot's new play 'The Confidential Clerk' - first
staged at the Edinburgh Festival this August, four years
after the production of 'The Cocktail Party' - seems likely
to be even more successful at the box-office than its predecessor, and its prosperity may be fostered by the playgoer's sense of Mr Eliot's condescension in being so persistently straightforward. No libations here, or all-
knowing Strangers; no sermons on salvation, and propaganda
for the saints; not a hint of the 'Third Floor Back' -
indeed, 'The Confidental Clerk' was hailed in Edinburgh (I
write before its London production) with relief, surprise
and delight as an unmistakable farce. The names of Robert-
son Hare and Lady Bracknell have been freely invoked by
critics, and comparisons have been made with Wilde and
Labiche, rather than with the 'Ion' of Euripides, to which
the author has acknowledged his debt. Where 'The Cocktail
Party' made its home in the shell of a modern comedy of
manners, 'The Confidential Clerk' masquerades as a kind of
Aldwych farce; the formalized plot is resolutely thick,
where that of 'The Cocktail Party' was precariously thin;
the characters have theatrical substance, and the situations are sprung with deliberate precision and mounting
absurdity; the note of portentous piety, hitherto inseparable from Mr Eliot's plays, is virtually inaudible; and
the verse is even more dexterously presented as eloquently
colloquial prose. In the theatre it is notably well acted,
and provides very good entertainment. But we expect more
of England's leading dramatist: has he more to give?
    Like 'The Cocktail Party', the new play is written on
different levels of attention, and it seeks what Eliot once
described, in an essay on Marston, as 'a kind of double-
ness in the action, as if it took place on two planes at
once'. There is, indeed, 'an under-pattern, less manifest
than the theatrical one' (I quote from the same essay), and
beneath the comedy about the parentage of bastards lies a
drama about the fatherhood of God. So, at least, it seemed
to one observer of the play in Edinburgh; although this
underlying meaning may well be one of which - as Eliot said
of Marston - the author was not fully aware. Eliot indeed
has, as it were, exalted this unconsciousness as a principle of dramaturgy, and in his public statements he has
emphasized, with studied detachment, that his plays are

larger than his own intentions. He said of 'The Cocktail
Party', in 1949:

> Whatever the play's message is, it is as much a matter
> of what message the audience finds in it as what mes-
> sage I put in it, and if there is nothing more in the
> play than what I was aware of meaning, then it must be
> a pretty thin piece of work;

and he has made a similar disclaimer of responsibility for
the contents of 'The Confidential Clerk'. One of the results is the temptation, in the theatre, to multiply the
ambiguitues of the plot. The consciousness that all around
them lie immensities of experience - surely Mr Eliot is
meaning more than *that!* - gives a crossword puzzle fever
to intellectual playgoers, who snap up clues with hungry
solemnity all through this crypto-farce. Such a guessing
game seems to be one inevitable effect of his methods.
Mr Eliot, in fact, has plenty to give besides entertainment; but it is debatable whether he has chosen the right
disguise.

   Before picking up some of the clues, let us look briefly
at the plot of the play, which is all that many satisfied
playgoers will see in the theatre. A successful City
financier, Sir Claude Mulhammer, engages as a new confidential clerk his illegitimate son Colby Simpkins, whose
paternity is kept a secret, for the time being, from Sir
Claude's feather-brained wife, Lady Elizabeth; from Lucasta
Angel, Sir Claude's unhappy, illegitimate daughter; and
from Lucasta's bouncing fiancé, B. Kaghan, a foundling
who never knew his father and mother. During the course
of the play, Lady Elizabeth claims Colby Simpkins as *her*
illegitimate son, whom she 'mislaid' twenty-five years before; she had put the missing boy in the charge of Mrs
Guzzard, of Teddington, who has brought Colby up as her
nephew. In the third act, an investigation is conducted
into the relationships of the cast by the retired confidential clerk, Eggerson (a key-figure in the play), with
the help of Mrs Guzzard. From it emerge the following
facts: Colby is the son of neither Sir Claude nor Lady
Elizabeth, but of Mrs Guzzard herself; Sir Claude's son
died with his mother (Mrs Guzzard's sister) in childbirth;
Lady Elizabeth's son is B. Kaghan, whom she has always despised as a vulgarian; and the play ends with Colby's surrender of his position as Sir Claude's heir, despite all
entreaties, to follow in the footsteps of his father, 'a
disappointed organist' - and, by inference, to become a
son to Eggerson (whose boy has been 'missing' since the
first world war).

Such a summary can only indicate the main lines of action, and here I have space only to unravel a few skeins of meaning. It is notable that the density of the farcical plot emphasizes still more clearly Eliot's concern with the *pattern* in human lives, the mysterious operations of destiny which bring the soul to a moment of choice. 'Greek tragedy is the tragedy of necessity', W.H. Auden has written, 'Christian tragedy is the tragedy of possibility.' 'The Confidential Clerk' which, like all Eliot's plays, is a religious drama, is a tragi-comedy of choice: all of his characters choose their destiny in the moment of crisis. The most significant choice, perhaps, is that of Colby (in whom we may find echoes of Celia in 'The Cocktail Party'): Mrs Guzzard, who appears in the last act as an alarming fairy godmother, asks Colby whose son he would wish to be - Sir Claude's, or the son of a 'dead, obscure man'. Colby rejects Sir Claude, and thus chooses his own inheritance: he must, like Lord Monchensey and Celia Coplestone, work out his own salvation. This will lead him not, like Harry,

To the worship in the desert, the thirst and depriva-
     tion,
A stony sanctuary and a primitive altar,
The heat of the sun and the icy vigil,
A care over lives of humble people,
The lesson of ignorance, of incurable diseases,

nor, like Celia, on a 'terrible journey' to final crucifiction on an ant-heap, but to a post as parish organist in a London suburb.

Yet there are hints that Colby's future may lie in other directions. Eggerson, who seems to be his spiritual father, *knows* that Colby is going to take orders; he is, one feels, doomed to celibacy; and Lucasta describes him as a creature apart from common humanity:

                    You're either an egotist
Or something so different from the rest of us
That we can't judge you.

Is Colby a saint in the making? Is his 'music' a symbol for another kind of harmony? This matters little to the progress of the play in the theatre, for the revelation of his inner life - his 'secret garden', as it is described in one of Eliot's favourite images - stands in its own right as a moment of emotional and theatrical truth. (As acted by Denholm Elliott and Margaret Leighton, it is indeed the most memorable scene in the play.) But on second thoughts

- and 'The Confidential Clerk' provokes these relentlessly
- there is an obvious parallel between the symbolic garden
of Colby's private music, and the actual garden of Eggerson's private life, to which Mr Eliot draws attention.
Colby says to Lucasta:

> What I mean is, my garden's no less unreal to me
> Than the world outside it. If you have two lives
> Which have nothing whatever to do with each other -
> Well, they're both unreal. But for Eggerson
> His garden is a part of one single world.

The achievement of 'one single world' is a major theme
in all religious drama; and when Colby walks out of Sir
Claude's life in the third act of 'The Confidential Clerk',
we may perhaps suppose that he is on his way to it. No
precise meaning is, I think, to be attached to Eggerson or
to Mrs Guzzard, though in this climax of the play they both
assume a supranaturalist importance; these characters are
among Mr Eliot's most successful inventions, and their
haloes are more impressive than those of Aunt Agatha (to
whom Mrs Guzzard bears some resemblance) or Sir Henry
Harcourt-Reilly, because they are revealed in the texture
of the play itself and not by formal, oracular statement.
'The Confidental Clerk' is also concerned, like 'The
Cocktail Party', with vocation and salvation, but these
themes are implied or disguised in the action without in-
dulging in the pompous solemnities of Sir Henry Harcourt-
Reilly:

> You understand your metier, Mr Quilpe -
> Which is the most that any of us can ask for.

Sir Claude is a disappointed potter, who has given up
his passion for ceramics:

> Because I came to see
> That I should never have become a first-rate potter.
> I didn't have it in me. It's strange, isn't it,
> That a man should have a consuming passion
> To do something for which he lacks the capacity?
> Could a man be said to have a vocation
> To be a second-rate potter?

While Colby believes he is Sir Claude's son, he believes
that he too must accept *his* disappointment as a musician,
and he 'fights' the moments when:

> the thing I cannot do,
> The art that I could never excel in,
> Seems the one thing worth doing, the one thing
> That I want to do.

But with the discovery that he is the son of a disappointed musician, Colby accepts his 'second-rate' vocation: to Sir Claude he says

> You have your father before you, as a model:
> You know your inheritance. Now I know mine.
> It's no longer a question of ambition!

The plot involves, too, a discussion of make-believe and
reality, in the lives of Sir Claude and Lady Elizabeth; or
art as a substitute for religion (Sir Claude's ceramics in
a private room); of the acceptance of the human condition
and the incomprehensibility of other people (Sir Claude's
own empirical philosophy, which is turned against himself);
the drama of human responsibility; and, of course, the
questions of paternity, heredity and fatherhood in God -
for what, ultimately, do all these topsy-turvy relationships - whose reality is questioned with a Pirandellian
confusion - matter, beside the fact that, as Lady Elizabeth
reminds us, 'we are nearer to God than anyone'?

> There can be no relation of father and son
> Unless it works both ways,

Colby announces. Here, as elsewhere in 'The Confidential
Clerk', the author releases - consciously or unconsciously
- vast and disturbing suggestions, beyond the literal
statement of the text.

There are densities of meaning, then, in Mr Eliot's new
play which entitle it to some consideration not only as a
money-making farce, but as a religious drama. More than
one visit is clearly required to assess its value, and I
could cheerfully devote an entire issue of the 'Twentieth
Century' to a discussion of its place in Mr Eliot's work.
But it is already obvious, I think, that 'The Confidental
Clerk' may be ranked as another brilliant failure, another
experimental stage in Mr Eliot's progress towards the creation of a great contemporary play. For although the play
is designed with laborious cunning as an intricate theatrical machine, which works on two levels at once, the author
ultimately fails to resolve the action on both its planes;
and once again he fails to achieve the emotional unifica-
tion of the play's meaning, the direct illumination of

experience with the intensity of high drama. Eliot's
elaborate mystification, justified here by the pretext of
the farce, is designed to energize and universalize the
play's action inside the naturalist convention, but it
does not work *in the theatre* with the necessary light and
heat of effective poetic drama. Writing of Massinger, Mr
Eliot said thirty years ago: 'The poetic drama must have
an emotional unity, let the emotion be whatever you like.
It must have a dominant tone; and if this be strong enough,
the most heterogeneous emotions may be made to reinforce
it.' What 'The Confidental Clerk' lacks in the last
resort is precisely this 'emotional unity' - achieved for
example, in 'Murder in the Cathedral', within a very different dramatic convention.

Yet it goes without saying, I think, that Mr Eliot's
failure is of considerably greater importance to the future
of the English drama than the easier successes of other,
luckier dramatists who can touch the audience's hearts
without destroying their preconceived ideas. Slowly and
deliberately, he has created a new kind of theatrical language which, as he shows in 'The Confidental Clerk', has a
flexible, anonymous and lightly hypnotic power; and in the
search for a dramatic convention to express the complexity
of contemporary experience he has moved away from the
trappings of the Chorus, rhetorical and lyrical interpola-
tions, and the direct intervention of the author, leaving
behind him a trail of abandoned poetic properties. He has
found, and held, an audience in the 'commercial' theatre,
and by disguising his subject as carefully as he disguises
his verse, he has tried to solve the problems of the lack
of moral, aesthetic and social conventions that can be
shared by a contemporary audience. Beginning in revolt
against the naturalism of the proscenium stage, he has returned to work inside its limitations, seeking to give
them depth and intensity, fashioning his Trojan Horses
under the sponsorship of Mr Henry Sherek. In this process
'The Confidential Clerk' marks a further stage, and at
the same time illustrates the dangers of his method.

'It seems to me', Mr Eliot said in 1949, with the
magisterial diffidence of a reluctant oracle, 'that we
should turn away from the Theatre of Ideas to the Theatre
of Character. The essential poetic play should be made
with human beings rather than with ideas.' Moreover, he
has made it clear that 'the essential poetic play' should
sound as if it were written in prose: 'a present-day
audience, which realizes that it is listening to a play
in verse, cannot be expected to have the right attitude to
what I am trying to do.' To adjust the attitudes of such
an audience, therefore, the essential poetic play must be

accommodated inside the picture-frame stage, the naturalist
prose drama, and the unholy trade of modern show business.
'If the poetic drama is to reconquer its place, it must, in
my opinion, enter into overt competition with prose drama',
Mr Eliot has said, and it is with this competitive spirit,
for one, that he was imbued in writing 'The Cocktail Party'
and 'The Confidential Clerk'.   In such a contest, he has
decided, the best chance of success is to impersonate one's
opponent, and his two post-war plays may thus be regarded
as ingenious experiments in theatrical camouflage, in which
a religious drama is presented to the secular groundlings
of to-day under an increasingly heavy disguise.

Yet the failure of 'The Confidential Clerk', it seems to
me, illustrates the dangers of this disguise, most of all
the danger that it may be only too successful. Has the
camouflage proved too much for the poetic competitor? Is
Mr Eliot's victory a Pyrrhic one?

> I have before my eyes [he says] a kind of mirage of
> the perfection of the verse drama, which would be a
> design of human action and of words, such as to present
> at once the two aspects of dramatic and of musical
> order.... To go as far in this direction as it is
> possible to go, without losing contact with the ordinary
> everyday world with which drama must come to terms,
> seems to me the proper aim of dramatic poetry.

With this mirage before him, is he content to leave a large
part of his audience unaware that they have watched anything but a melodramatic farce? How far can he afford to
go on compromising with 'the ordinary everyday world'? I
am reminded of Sir Claude's declaration in 'The Confidential Clerk':

> If you haven't the strength to impose your own terms
> Upon Life, you must accept the terms it offers you.

It is time for Mr Eliot to impose his own terms upon the
theatre he has conquered from within.

170. BONAMY DOBRÉE, A REVIEW, 'SEWANEE REVIEW'

January 1954, vol. lxii, 117-31

Whatever the first reactions to Mr. T.S. Eliot's new play
may be, one thing can be claimed for it: it is profoundly
original. Not so much in idea, for as Goethe said, it is
impossible for anyone to have a thought that has not
struck somebody before; all that a man can hope for is to
arrive at such by the motions of his own mind. The originality lies in what has been done with the form. Not that
there is anything new in the way the piece has been built
up; it conforms to the well-tried laws of Sardoodledom -
the exposition, the *scène à faire*, and so on. The play is
original because of the level of existence this kind of
play is made to maintain, for the idea has been presented
through an improbable medium: Eliot has made a serious
thing out of a farce. Or, from another angle, the originality of the play consists in its being a drastic pushing
forward of the old critical comedy which, by making us
laugh at and criticize our neighbors, aimed at making us
see ourselves as others see us. In this play Eliot calls
upon a higher tribunal by demanding that we see ourselves
as our conscience sees us. And what is further original,
is his making us accept as the person who is justified the
individual who in critical comedy would be the butt. In
the old way of writing the young 'hero' of this play would
be the person to be laughed at: he is not fitting into
society, it would be said; he is being presumptuous, he
is guilty of excess, he thinks about himself too much, he
is, possibly, a bit of a prig. But here he is the one
character who has solved the problem of how to live. It
is as though the self-flagellant, or Alceste, or Sir Positive At-All, were to be the model, not the laughing-stock.
The old form has been made to serve a new purpose, and if
this is still moralistic, it is so with a difference.
Eliot has not torn the trappings from society; he has not
given us a fleeting vision of the terror or the glory of
existence; those things are, rather, the province of
tragedy. But he has made a rent in the curtain of complacent assumptions, and whether or not his conclusions seem
valid, he has at least provided something which in its
context is new, and which the imaginative reason can work
upon.

The play is a West End success, which means that Eliot
has achieved something without which any other attainment
is barren; he is daily capturing the ear and the attention

of a large number of people.   Whether what he wants to
say will penetrate to the majority of his audience is
another question, for it may be that he has made the bait
so large that the fish can feed lavishly on it without
swallowing the hook.   To the attentive, it goes without
saying, there all the time exists another play at a deeper
level than the obvious one, perhaps a third at a level
deeper still.   But as an amusing comedy erected on a
basically farcical situation, opening in such a way as to
induce at once that willing suspension of disbelief for
the moment which enjoyment demands, it holds from the
start.   Causing a good deal of laughter by incidental remarks, keeping expectation at full height all the while,
and interspersing the action with quiet, rather sad moments (thus relating the play to a comedy of Molière), it
amounts, apart from anything else, to a piece of theatrical virtuosity which should ensure it a long run.

It may be as well in the first instance to consider what
Eliot has done to gain popularity, how he has done it, and
what price he has had to pay.   He has achieved his result
by making people laugh: well and good.   But, the question
arises, What kind of laughter is it, and does it subserve
or interfere with the penetrating power of the theme?   The
laughter he produces is hardly that of wit in the best
sense, which appeals to the intellect; nor does it arouse
the 'thunders of laughter clearing air and heart,' which
comes from the realization of the antinomies in man's
nature, the absurd contradiction of his being an angel
housed in the body of a timid or lustful or cruel beast;
it is not great, or ritual laughter.   In fact his situations and his remarks are what everybody finds 'funny';
they produce easy chuckles, or even giggles, never on so
low a plane that one need be ashamed of them, but of the
sort with which lesser popular playwrights lard their
plays.   This laughter doesn't plunge you deeper, it doesn't
open the doors of enlightenment, it doesn't release into a
free realm.   Though it must be granted that some sort of
flavoring must be applied as a sauce to the meat of the
serious theme to make it resemble the kind of pabulum the
after-dinner playgoer will swallow, it must be recognized
that Eliot takes a tremendous risk in employing this particular one.   Maybe it breaks down resistances; but does
it make the meaning more transparent?   Or does it obscure
it?   The danger is that more men and women than need be
will remain on the surface level of the play, good, flimsy,
easily digested entertainment.   For some the serious element of the play is so enthralling, that they may find
themselves resisting the laughter, brushing away the jokes
as if they were bothersome flies; for the jokes tend to

distract, to take away the attention from something which
really concerns the auditor. This is the main possible
blemish of the play, but on the whole it survives it.
Eliot has got a public, though it may not be quite the
public that he wants.

It should be said at this point that this review is
based upon only seeing the play, which has not been published at the time of writing; there has been no opportunity to ponder the work, to cast back and forth, to realize
the implications, ironic or otherwise, that earlier scenes
or remarks cast upon later developments, nor to turn over
at leisure what it is that Eliot is fundamentally saying.
Reading and re-reading the play will no doubt alter judgment in many respects, and bring out points too easily submerged in the rapidity of the action; for there are, as is
manifest in merely hearing the play, a good many passages
which will cry out to be lingered over, and of which the
significance can seep in only gradually. Nevertheless
there is something to be said for considering the first
impact of a play seen before being read. After all, a
play's a play, not a document to be fumbled. We ask ourselves what mood or temper has been created in the theatre,
what 'attitude' induced? Do we wish to brood apart, as
after a tragedy? Or does the play, after the manner of
comedy, seem 'to make life spin along more briskly'? The
answer here is uncertain, for 'The Confidential Clerk'
would seem to induce a vacillating mood. Something has
happened to one, but what exactly? That is no adverse
criticism; it is, after all, the first effect of 'Measure
for Measure.' Perhaps the play is a tragi-comedy. Something good has been destroyed by something lesser or accidental, but a fair proportion of good seems to settle down
at the conclusion. All's as well as can be hoped for in a
play that ends not too disastrously.

So to try to assess what is the reason for the uncertainty of response, it seems easiest to go back to first
principles. Thus granting that any work of art is giving
form to the formless, we proceed to ask what in a play is
the material to which form is being given? Is it the bust-
ling, multifarious, passionate life all around us, filled
with all sorts of people, unexpected, contradictory, self-
denying, cruel and generous, from whose confused actions
some meaning emerges, some pattern which enlightens life
or deepens apprehension? Or is it an idea, intuition, or
religious gleam or certainty, or some moral conclusion, for
which the characters of the play and their directed actions
provide the symbols? In the first case, which Shakespeare,
generally speaking, exemplifies (*pace* certain modern critics), creation springs from an abundant love of the human

creature as he is, a glorying in the staggering pageant of
human existence. The pattern develops organically, the
'meaning' oozes as doth the gum from whence 'tis nourished.
In the second, which we meet with on the whole in serious
comedy - think of Molière or Congreve - creation seems
rather to be born from the desire to illustrate the already
conceived pattern; the characters do not exist in life;
they are made as symbols to fit the preconceived moral.
Eliot, as far as can be judged, works in this latter way.
The difficulty with this creative approach is to keep the
simulated life coherent, to impose upon members of the
audience the level at which they are to exist while watching the play. In 'The Cocktail Party' Eliot was not altogether successful so far as this goes; the Guardians were
too puzzling, existing in a dual character; the religious
and the mundane clashed rather than mingled, so that the
audience could never be sure from one moment to another
with what part of themselves they were being asked to
apprehend people or events. In the present play there is
no such uneasiness; it is all of a piece, and no sudden re-
organizations of approach are demanded. The people, though
they vary among and in themselves, can all be grasped on
the level of the world we normally inhabit. The skill re-
sides in having made them at least temporarily plausible,
although the story itself is so fantastically and so
delightfully improbable.

The persons of the play (which bears, if Eliot likes,
some relation to the 'Ion' of Euripides) are Sir Claude
Mulhammer, who has an illegitimate son, Colby Simpkins,
and an illegitimate daughter, Lucasta Angel. His wife
Lady Elizabeth, also has an illegitimate son, whom she has
lost sight of since infancy. B. Kaghan, a business man,
is a foundling. Eggerson, the retired confidental clerk,
to be replaced by Colby, provides the linking element of
the play; and Mrs Guzzard, who appears at the end, rather
as a *dea ex machina*, is a foster-mother who unravels the
tangles. It is, in short, a farce of mistaken or dubious
identity. All that, of course, is only the framework
through which the theme has to be revealed. This, as it
was put by the B.B.C. 'Critics on the Air,' is something
like: 'Unless you know who your father is, you don't know
who you are: and if you don't know who you are you don't
know what you are.' Here is a possible religious significance, if you care to take the play on the third level.
The main theme, however, the 'second level' theme, might be
what it was in 'The Cocktail Party,' namely 'Be the thing
you are' - a Shakespearian theme this too. But whereas in
the earliest play it came as an injunction, as when Reilly
tells Chamberlayne, 'Be content to be the fool you are,'

and Celia has to be led to discover herself to be of the
stuff of martyrs, in the new play the characters discover
for themselves how important it is to find out what they
are, and to pursue the appropriate life regardless of conventional standards, and against the pressure of circumstance. Or it might be a development of: 'Until you rid
yourself of your fantasies, you will never lead a satisfactory life,' the difference being that here we have a
process offered us, rather than a fact we have to accept.

In the first act we learn that Mulhammer, now a highly
successful financier, had really hankered after being a
potter. But realizing that he would never be more than a
second-rate craftsman, he took the opportunity of going
into finance, to which he cannot wholly give himself. He
remedies his frustration by collecting pottery, and withdrawing from time to time into the refuge of his collection, where, though not 'transfigured by the vision of
some marvellous creation,' he can escape from the unreality of his business life. It is, he admits, a kind of
make-believe, but the belief makes it real; he supposes
his devotion to ceramics takes the place of religion.
(We all know what Eliot thinks of that kind of substitute.)
The theme will recur again; but in this act Mulhammer opens
up a second one, that of continuity, not so much of heredity, as it seemed to the critic of 'The Times,' but of
tradition symbolized by paternity. His father had left
him the business, and the son had wished (all this is a
little vague, and would need reading to clarify) to fulfil himself in what his father had wished to fulfil. The
words 'reconcilement' and 'atonement' occur, perhaps - the
suggestion is a little in the air - for the sins of the
father, such as Lord Monchesney in 'The Family Reunion'
had felt the urgency of. All this comes out because the
young man himself would like to be a musician. Both know,
however, that Colby would be only a second-rate musician,
so Sir Claude comforts his son by expatiating on the value
of his own solution. To give Colby the same comfort he
will set him up in a nice flat with a first-rate piano, so
that he also can escape from the hollowness of business
into the realm he would wish to inhabit.

The second act, which takes place in Colby's flat,
develops the theme of the double life in the course of a
touching scene portraying an incipient love affair between Colby and Lucasta, each ignorant of the other's
parentage. Colby, luxuriating in receptive sympathy, describes how his musical life is like a garden to him, into
which he can withdraw locking the gates behind him. A
little sentimental, perhaps, but after all, second-rate
artists often are sentimental. Thus the theme of

loneliness is introduced, a loneliness which can be broken
down only by the continual and progressive understanding
of others. Somebody must join him in his garden, but he
cannot invite anybody; he or she must somehow come in
gradually of their own wish. He is groping after some reconciliation with being - really a religious impulse; for
though he tells Lucasta (from prison?) that he is not religious, she quite rightly tells him that she thinks he is;
and when he speaks of the companion in the garden, there is
a faint suggestion that he is Adam, hoping not only for an
Eve-Lucasta, but remembering that 'Adam in the garden
walked with God.' That level, however, is glanced at
rather than reached, and we are stood firmly on the second
level with a gloss on Mulhammer's thesis, namely that if
you lead two lives which have no connection with each
other, neither of them is real. On the ostensible level,
that of comedy, the love-affair is developing well, until
Lucasta tells Colby that she is Mulhammer's daughter.
This provides the most dramatic, and emotionally deepest
moment of the play. Colby recoils from her as a lover at
the revelation that she is his half-sister, but is unable
to tell her what the revulsion is due to, since he has
promised not to reveal the secret of his parentage: she is
thrown into despair, believing that his evident horror is
on account of her being a bastard. Finding herself thus
permanently outcast, she is prepared to link herself with
the vulgar, breezy, eupeptic Kaghan, who opportunely
appears; being a quite happy foundling he doesn't see that
it matters in the least who your father is. Enter then
Lady Elizabeth, and soon afterwards Mulhammer, and we re-
vert to the sheer imbroglio of farce, enormously entertaining on a very light level. Husband and wife each
claim Colby as their son; and to disentangle the matter,
it is decided to call in the Mrs. Guzzard who fostered
the young man, and who, by a freak of chance, will also
provide a clue to where Lady Elizabeth's son may be found
if he is not Colby. Eggerson, who is intimately acquainted with Sir Claude's affairs, will be summoned to act as
chairman of the meeting.
    The last act resolves the two themes, the resolution
bringing as corollaries a good number of philosophico-
religious considerations, such as the virtue of obedience
to facts, the equal virtue of knowing the limits of one's
understanding of other people, the having to adapt one's
self to the granting of one's wishes. In the event, Lady
Elizabeth's son turns out to be Kaghan, a fact neither of
them recognizes with rapturous enthusiasm; while as to Sir
Claude, Mrs. Guzzard shatters him with the fact that his
son had never been born, Colby being her own by her long

deceased husband who was a second-rate organist. She can
supply substantial evidence. Colby is delighted. He can
drop the silly business of being confidential clerk to a
financier, and can pass his life as a second-rate organist; and, as is proper to farce, he is at once offered a
post by Eggerson. Lucasta is going to marry Kaghan, so
fades out of Colby's picture, apparently unregretted. And
here perhaps is the main dramatic weakness of the play:
expectation has been aroused by the moving Colby-Lucasta
scene in the second act, but the theme drops lifeless from
Eliot's hand. The young man, regardless of earlier passages, with immense satisfaction declares: 'Now that I
know who my father is, I can follow him.' But Sir Claude
is broken (though Lucasta tries to comfort him); the
cherished hope of having a son to follow him is shattered;
further, Lady Elizabeth tells him she would far rather
have had him for a husband as a second-rate potter than as
an important financer who, she fancied, had married her
only because he wanted a hostess. There we touch the
element of tragedy, the something good that is broken.

And now we ask, where has Eliot got to in his fascinating journey as a playwright? What has he accomplished?
What appalling difficulties has he overcome? For he is
not a playwright by nature; the stage was not originally
his chosen medium, and his great triumph consists in
having made himself into a dramatist whose work the great
multitude of playgoers will accept and enjoy. But what
were the problems apart from that *sine qua non* which he
had to tackle?

For one, there was that of embedding in the play itself
the memorable utterances, the *sententiae*, which every
great or even good play must carry. In his earlier plays,
Eliot, in common with other of his contemporaries, went
back to the device of the chorus; forthrightly in 'Murder
in the Cathedral'; with an ingenious modification in 'The
Family Reunion,' where the characters occasionally group
themselves as chorus; and with almost complete camouflage
in 'The Cocktail Party,' where only the big 'libation'
scene is an obvious reminder. He has now completely rid
himself of this device; he gets his general statements
uttered by the characters as such; and if the 'moral sentences' seem to crowd in rather thick and fast in the last
act, the characters can sustain them in the speed and
excitement of the action. For example, there is the comparison of Eggerson's 'escape' with that of Colby.
Colby's garden - at least as far as others are told about
it - is simply a place to go into, a haven in which to
indulge the self-regarding virtues. Eggerson, in his
outer suburb, has a plot of ground into which he escapes

from the little irritations of daily living, the household
chores, the domestic adjustments, wanting simply to be
with himself. The stated difference is this: nothing
comes out of Colby's garden, while Eggerson occasionally
brings back from his solitude pumpkins and beans for his
wife. The moral is plain, it is humorous, and it comes
across charmingly.

Which leads to the question of character. A play is
itself a symbol, and whether the pattern emerges from the
surge of life or is itself the basis, the characters have
to give actuality to the symbol, express it in terms of
living. They must achieve verisimilitude, seem to be common flesh and blood, or if uncommon, appear to possess at
least nerve and sinew. The danger with Eliot, who begins
with the idea and mines for the 'objective correlative,'
is that the characters may obstinately remain vehicles of
an idea rather than have a life of their own, as was too
much felt in 'The Cocktail Party,' not only with the
Guardians. And the difficulty he encountered in his new
play was to give 'reality' to farcical characters so as
to make them more than such, in fact to write a farce with
the texture of comedy. For the people in comedy are
'real' - Portia, Célimène, Millamant, Sir Toby, Orgon,
Tanner - whereas Charley's Aunt or the people in 'The
Importance of Being Earnest' are not. Ben Jonson was
faced with the same difficulty, which he resolved triumphantly by making his characters from Mosca to Abel Drug-
ger almost desperately concerned with the immediate actualities of life as it has to be lived from day to day,
with its complex of duties ('three parts of life'), its
idealisms, its lusts, its laziness, its ambitions, sacri-
fices, and disastrous failures: his are people first and
symbols afterwards. Eliot's beings are not altogether
reassuring. One accepts them at the outset in the eager
curiosity that possesses the happy playgoer; but as the
play goes on the interest shifts from them as fellow-
creatures, to the eagerness of seeing how the tangle is
going to work out. This perhaps is because they do not
solve their problems; their problems are solved for them.
Or perhaps it is that Eliot does not seem to love his
people; and to make his people convincing the dramatist
must either love them, however little he may think of
them, as (since 'Measure for Measure' has been instanced)
Shakespeare loved Pompey; or sympathize with them so
deeply that even his revulsion has a quality of love in
it, as with Shakespeare and Angelo. And because none of
the people who carry the main themes is lovable the idea
is a little weakened, and therefore - since 'the life of
comedy is in the idea' - the play itself. Some of the

characters we greet as knowable - Sir Claude, Colby,
Lucasta; with them we can to some extent experience empathy, though we come away with a little grain of doubt.
Are people in truth and experience like that? Sir Claude
could possibly live as he does. But are the young people
actually young people of today, with similar perplexities?
They neither get far enough in their love-affair to let us
know, nor are they the eternal maid and her wight. So
they don't ring quite true as whole human beings; they
don't enter into the imagination and seize upon it; we
have to make an effort of the imagination to seize them.
And when at the end of the play Colby says that what is
needed is more love - a phrase which at any rate today
needs tremendous pressure behind it to make it mean anything (as Yeats said, 'Things thought too long cannot be
thought at all') - it carries no conviction whatever,
either as a moral sentence or as part of his character.
He at any rate shows little sign of being capable of deep
affection. There is indeed little sentiment of love anywhere in the play. Eliot may love his characters, but if
so it is in spite of their faults, and not (as with Mira-
bel and Millamant) because of them. If the play were just
a farce and no more this would not matter: but since it is
a great deal more, it does in the end count.

A curious point is that on the whole the most lovable
person is Eggerson, who is really little more than a stock
character, though as such an effective vehicle for that
sly genial humour in which Eliot has never been lacking.
He is beautifully 'done,' but belongs to the theatre
rather than to life; he is brother to the elder Boon in
'You Never Can Tell,' the completely understanding old
fellow without ambition for himself, wanting to see everybody happy, the *homme de bonne volonté*. Lady Elizabeth
is a little ambiguous; she is, if not sister, at least
cousin to Julia in 'The Cocktail Party,' the difference
being that though she lives on two planes of 'reality,'
she does so unconsciously. Absurdly amusing figure of
farce as she is, she nevertheless contributes to the
theme as one who tried to break away from family tradition. She even at one time embraced Buddhism, since that
religion allowed her to look upon herself as a self-
existent soul seeking reincarnation through indifferent
parents, mere conveyors, without influence on the essential
self. But regarded as an example of Eliot's technique,
she is very much worth attention. This apparently irresponsible, idiotic-fashionable-'intellectual,' always hunt-
ing after strange gods, can yet be the vehicle of possibly
profound utterances - as the divine simpleton of a very
complex kind! She is, however, so ambivalent that when

she declares 'I don't believe in facts' we do not know
whether the remark is profoundly significant, as it might
be, or merely silly. Lucasta also is a little indeterminate. Self-protectively flippant, but with a potential
depth of which we catch a glimpse in the second act, she
lives in a kind of despair at not knowing what she is,
hardening herself against frustration by going about as
The Girl Who is Always Hungry - a joke which does not
really bear the repetition accorded it. So though Eliot
is, we can think, more successful than ever before in
giving his characters validity on a definite level, he has
not yet quite solved that problem. It is here, possibly,
that we find the key to the indeterminate effect of the
play.

Where, however, he has achieved complete and triumphant
success, is in the matter of stage speech. He has at last
among writers of poetic drama broken away from the notion
that dramatic blank verse is the iambic pentameter, a
silly pedantry that has bedevilled both discussion and
practice for a drearily long period. Since the first two
lines of 'Gorboduc,' dramatic blank verse has never been
the iambic pentameter, a most inappropriate measure for
the stage, for what the dramatist has to do is to give the
actor phrases which he can utter louder than in normal
speech - since he has to fill a theatre with sound - and
which will bring the stress on the right word. It is no
use telling him to let the words come trippingly from the
tongue unless you give him words that *can* come trippingly
from the tongue. The form which tells best in English is
a phrase with normally three stresses, going easily to
four and on occasion to five; and whether the phrases are
chopped off in sausage-lengths of ten syllables or not,
doesn't in the least matter. The advantage of this metre
is that it is enormously flexible, and can, when required,
reflect the tension of poetry proper, create the ethos in
which it can flourish. (a) What Eliot has done, rather
laboriously (as he explains in his extremely interesting
'Poetry and Drama'), is to go back to Shakespearian usage,
that is, a three stress line, though he postulates a
caesura somewhere, which the Shakespearians didn't care a
fig about. What it amounts to is an irregularly anapaestic line, or rather, phrase, for it is of no importance where you end it in print. Take a line or two from
'The Cocktail Party' (the text of the present play not
being available) choosing practically at random:

That was a nearer guess than you
    think.   (3 stress dactylic)
But permit me to remark that
    my revelations   (4 stress anapaestic)

And now, since 'Measure for Measure' has been mentioned,
from that play, where, indeed, Shakespeare uses mainly a
four-stress line such as

>   Stand like the forfeits in a barber's shop. (V, i)

But take:

>   'Tis one thing to be tempted, Escalus,
>   Another thing to fall. I not deny.... (II, i)
>   (Both 3 stress, vaguely anapaestic)

or

>   Intends you for his swift ambassa-   (3 stress irregular)
>   dor (III, i)

When special emphasis is needed there is the three stress
iambic *phrase* (not line)

>   A pond as deep as hell. (III, i)

So Eliot in the present play:

>   And lock the gates behind you,

or Shakespeare in 'The Tempest':

>   And makes my labours pleasures. (III, i)

(It must be duly noted that, as Omond said, counting of
stresses is only a shade less mechanical than the counting
of syllables.)
   The result is beautiful stage speech, neither strict
nor impeccable prose, but the best possible stage instrument. It is delightful to listen to. Eliot's sounds like
ordinary speech, though it is not so; and I venture to say
that in 'The Confidential Clerk' we have the most perfect
theatre measure since Congreve. This sort of verse can do
anything: it can allow Eliot to write the lovely swinging
phrase already quoted - I do not know how he may print it,
nor do I greatly care -

>   Transfigured by / The vision of some marvellous creation

(How does this differ from 'Swell with the touches of those
flower-soft hands'?) and the audience does not notice it at
all as special language. The speeches of Sir Claude and
Colby in the first act would not come with the trenchancy

they do unless they were 'poetry' in this sense; but for
the average listener this will be just talk, not verse,
which is precisely what Eliot wants. To the literary
detective, whose ear listens delightedly for cadences,
what is happening is clear. The verse doesn't in any way
interfere, but it has its effect on the audience without
their knowing it. Here, then, is perfect mastery. To
have swept away the clogging lumber of two centuries itself constitutes an originality. It amounts to the invention of a new verse form, which, as Eliot himself has
remarked in another connection, is the most important
thing that can happen to a nation.

These are the elements as they appear from seeing and
hearing the play admirably performed. What of the final
result?

What exactly, we ask first, was Eliot trying to do?
It's not so easy to say. He is certainly not 'imitating
life' so that his audience may catch the glamor and the
glory of it. He is not presenting a vision of what life
might be to some people, as he was in 'Murder in the
Cathedral,' and to a lesser degree with Celia in 'The
Cocktail Party.' He offers a comedy (disguised as farce);
and comedy is for those who think, tragedy for those who
feel (the old cliché will serve well enough here). He is
trying, in short, to make his audience think. But here
another seeming anomaly, or originality, crops up. Comedy
deals with the relation of people to each other in society,
or with their place in society, with their interactions in
a social milieu: tragedy deals with the relation of man to
God - or whatever name he may be called by. Yet when
Colby at the end says 'Now that I know who my father is, I
can follow him,' the subtler implication is, as the B.B.C.
Critics suggested, that we cannot know what we are until
we recognize our Father in Heaven. When earlier he says
he wishes he could have a father who died before him,
whom he could reconstruct from relics and stories, so that
he might perhaps live the life his father would have
wished to live, it occurs to some that what Eliot means is
that we should model ourselves, as far as is humanly possible, upon Christ. Thus Eliot's play is really (at the
third level, admittedly) a play dealing with man's relation
to God, which would seem to demand tragic form.

In any event the play, on the second level, is a didactic play (in a sense, of course, every good play is such),
and Eliot once again reveals himself as the outstanding
English moralist of our time, at any rate in the literary
sphere. But whereas the moral of comedy is usually 'Fit
yourself into society,' here it is 'Follow the indication
that God has given you of the sort of life you ought to

lead, the sort of person you ought to be.' It is, in
fact, as some have called it, 'a religious farce.' Put in
another way, however, the moral is the Delphic adjuration
'Know thyself!', the Stoic 'Be the thing that you are!'
It is, one might feel, making religion a matter of morality tinged with emotion, however stoutly Eliot might repudiate any connection with Arnold. So now, of course, the
question forces itself upon one as to how far Eliot may
be attacking the assumptions of our day, for this play is,
obviously, a criticism of life. And here our question-
ings become active. Is it really better for a man to be a
second-rate artist or craftsman than a thoroughly efficient
financier or confidential clerk? Which best serves
society, that is, the individual's fellow human beings;
that is to say, God? Isn't the attitude we are asked to
adopt rather that of those who are the prey of a self-
regarding virtue? Are we to follow our desires as admittedly second-raters rather than fit into the larger pattern which the process of society invites us to fill because we are capable of filling it? As Arnold wrote to
his mother, 'we are not here to have facilities found for
us for doing the work we like, but to make them.' Ought
we not to accept the position we find ourselves in, take
up our responsibility to society rather than to our very
noble selves? After all, as Marcus Aurelius said, 'Even
in a palace, life can be led well,' so why not in a City
financier's West End mansion? On the other hand the play,
the moral, may be a protest against the totalitarian forcing of the social atom to sacrifice his individuality to
that nebulous concept 'the general good.' But one must
beware of reading more into the play than Eliot intended;
for though he himself has declared that the poet often
says more than he knows, to extract what one likes out of
any work is surely to miss its vivifying point. But
accepting this possible stricture on our civilization, we
can still ask whether, if we insist on being second-rate
organists rather than good confidential clerks, we are
not being guilty of spiritual pride? For humility is the
greatest of all traps; a man may find with Benjamin Franklin, who hoped to become humble, that he is proud of his own
humility. Yet it may be that Eliot was following an impulse that has been his from the beginning, at all events
since 'Prufrock and Other Observations,' and was here criti-
cizing modern civilization on account of the directionless
people it produces, and its disruptive, fragmented nature.
After all, this play is by the author of 'Notes Towards
the Definition of Culture' and 'After Strange Gods.' But
this last idea, if it was intended, is tenuous and not,
one supposes, the main theme, though it may be there

as an envelope.

So that if now we ask how far Eliot has succeeded in doing what he wanted to do (besides providing an evening's first-rate entertainment, which he has done), the answer must be uncertain. One has once more to ask the question: 'What did I feel on coming out of the theatre? What do I feel - or think - after pondering its impress upon me? Has anything happened to me? Have I had an experience?' It is best to put it in this way to avoid the categorizing habit it is so easy to fall into; present critical fashion tends to forget that a work of art is unique, every time raising the naively fundamental questions. Subjective? Yes, of course. All talk of 'concrete standards' is arid nonsense. Anyone has to ask in the first instance 'What has this work done to me?' - assuming naturally that the 'I' is a fairly normal person. Then if he likes he can relate this experience to others, and with some justification docket and pigeon-hole. And I suppose, judging from myself, that Eliot's intention was to make each member of the audience ask himself 'Am I leading the sort of life I really ought to be leading? Am I not worshipping false gods, and whoring after all manner of inventions?' It is, of course, a salutary question, a question which a man should from time to time ask that particular priest of comedy called Common Sense. If this, as I believe, was the state of mind into which Eliot wished to throw his hearers, then he has been successful. If he wished to persuade us to any sort of doctrine, then, I think, he has failed. We are told to be obedient to facts, in short, to accept; but which of us knows what part of ourselves we ought to accept? and to suppose that we are one kind of thing only is in contradiction with Eliot's own at least partial acceptance of the idea of the fluid personality. We are all of us a great many things; circumstance perhaps has made us one thing rather than another. Of course to swallow the obvious stated moral *au pied de la lettre* would be sheer nonsense. We don't for our salvation necessarily have to follow in father's footsteps; in many cases we clearly ought not to. Should Percy Bysshe Shelley have modelled himself on Sir Timothy? Evidently the father that we ought to follow is the intuitive conscience, the divine spark, however small, that we come to recognize through knowledge of ourselves.

Matthew Arnold has been referred to, explicitly or implicitly, several times in the course of this review, and it is borne in upon one, that however much Eliot may quarrel with Arnold, he is his successor, indeed his close descendant. He is, in fact, the Arnold of our day; and though he is a greater poet - which is saying a great

deal - it may be doubted whether he is so good, so general
a moralist, perhaps because he is not so clear (some might
say, so irritatingly insistent). But then he is trying to
do, at the same time, two extremely difficult things: the
first, to gain acceptance for a morality to which in 1953
most people will be refractory; the second, to create a
new kind of play, new in the form used as vehicle for an
idea, new in the way the impact on the audience is effected. This is admirable. Pick at it as we may among ourselves as men of letters, as men of letters we should
stoutly support the valiant originality. Mr. Eliot may
not be the Shakespeare of our time: but perhaps he is the
Kyd or Tourneur, which after all is a very splendid position to hold.

Note

a   There is no space to discuss this here. I might per-
    haps refer any reader who is interested to my 'Histrio-
    phone.' Hogarth Pamphlets. First Series. 1925.

171. NICHOLAS BROOKE, 'THE CONFIDENTIAL CLERK': A THEATRI-
CAL REVIEW, 'DURHAM UNIVERSITY JOURNAL'

March 1954, vol. xlvi, 66-70

Brooke (b. 1924), Professor of English at the University
of East Anglia, has published extensively on Shakespeare
and on Elizabethan and Jacobean drama.

'The Confidental Clerk' has been seen on the stage before
a printed text is available, a circumstance which chal-
lenges immediate critical consideration based on our
impressions in the theatre, and reflections on them afterwards. In this there is a temporary advantage, for it en-
ables one to be fairly clear as to the development in his
own mind of the impact of the play, and to distinguish
that from guesses at intentions which cannot be said to
have made ány real impact at all. The advantage is only
temporary, for the discrimination implied can and should
be more fully developed on the printed text; the

limitations of this approach are obvious: no two people
will see and realise the same points in the theatre at
one performance; one's impressions are limited to what one
can take in, one's reflections to what one can remember.
There is no text to refer to, and the memory will certainly deceive. Thus it is best to limit this article to
a local and personal occasion: the points developed are
based on the comments my wife and I made to each other in
the theatre and in discussion of the play afterwards.

Let it be said at once then, that the play does provide
a good evening in the theatre and that it does, immediately, achieve more than just that. The first act opens
with a conventional situation: Sir Claude is arranging the
introduction of his illegitimate son to the post of confidential clerk while his psychic eccentric possessive wife is
taking a cure in Switzerland; with the assistance of his
ex-clerk Eggerson, he plans the reception of his wife, the
tactical moves necessary to persuade her to accept the situation. This is banal enough, entertaining without being
interesting. Mr. Eliot has evidently studied more carefully than ever theatrical technique: every entrance and
exit is very elaborately prepared, sometimes over-prepared
(Eggerson's exit is rather clumsy; with a lesser actress
than Isabel Jeans, Lady Elizabeth's entrance could be a
disastrous anti-climax); as in early plays, the commonplace book of stage jokes seems to have been consulted,
this time under the heading 'Ageing Clerk'. The comedy is
not decidedly stylised, so that we are compelled to assume
that some interest is meant to attach to the characters as
human beings, and we are slightly embarrassed to realise
that their treatment can involve no more than the reaction
to a sentimental farce; it is not the farce, but the inherent (and ultimately inescapable) sentimentality that is
disturbing. The explosive appearance of Lucasta Angel
(her name seems to be a private joke to excite one's worst
anticipations of 'The Cocktail Party's' successor; Miss
Angel is not a supernatural figure) makes for more lively
comedy, and her aggressive assumption of the *femme fatale*
is well enough handled to suggest more interesting humanity than anyone yet on the stage. The advent of Lady
Elizabeth on the other hand, suggests a rather different
kind of comedy: she is entirely absurd, a figure of farce
again, but with scarcely enough human reality about her
to stimulate sentimentality; potentially therefore a more
amusing and less risky character than the rest (though
hardly less conventional). But she is intruded on the
sentimental situation, and her treatment is limited by it.
There are passages in the second and third acts that
clearly suggest Oscar Wilde (to the extent I suspect of

verbal echoes); the parallel is not too close, for she is
immediately revealed as a *Grande Dame* of a very different
type from Lady Bracknell, but not from a very different
kind of comedy.

This means then, that the first act introduces a number
of characters from slightly different genres of comedy:
Eggerson the stagey clerk; Sir Claude the plausible
financier with a complicated private life heading for
melodrama; Lucasta the more colourful psychological study:
and Lady Elizabeth hinting at stylized farce. The comment
one is forced to repeat is that these figures can only
mingle on the stage at the level of sentimental drama; this
fact is disturbing in the first act when it is blandly
accepted, and it is disastrous in the last act when Mr.
Eliot attempts to transcend it.

It will be noticed that I have made no mention of Colby
Simpkins the new clerk (Lucasta's fiancé, B. Kaghan, is
not very significant at any stage of the play): in a list
of 'characters' he has no place, for he is an entirely
colourless figure. A reason for this (not satisfactory)
seems to appear in the last act; in the first it only
strikes us as a weakness in dramatic writing, and it perhaps contributes to the partial failure as I see it of the
important interview that ends the act, between Sir Claude
and Colby. Colby, it appears, wanted to be an organist,
but either decided or was persuaded (it is not clear which,
perhaps deliberately) to give that up for Business. Sir
Claude, in a burst of confidence, explains his own conflict
of wills with his father, who forced him away from pottery
to the City; a forcing for which he declares himself grateful because he would have been only a second-rate potter.
He develops from this experience two ideas: firstly, the
respect and curiosity about his father which grew only
after the father was no longer there to satisfy it (a hint
of man's relation with God adequate in its context; but
developed much more elaborately in the last act): secondly,
that the experience of potting is still more 'real' to
him than financing; but that neither is real - both are
worlds of make-believe necessary to make the physical world
tolerable, and he must live in both partial realities because he has not the single-minded power to be wholly alive
in one (reserved for the great artist, and the priest;
there is perhaps a suggestion here of 'Ash-Wednesday':
'Consequently I rejoice, having to construct something
Upon which to rejoice'). Sir Claude's discussion of these
points is satisfying; but such an exposition cannot be
said to arise easily from the rest of the act: it sits on
it as an appendage, vaguely illustrated by the situation
but also limited by it, by the nagging awareness of the

sentimental affair on which this is a comment. The levels
of the first act are not only separate; they are at war.
But what is perhaps finally more damaging is the weakness
of Colby's response: this experience is, he says, just
like his; he feels about his music just as Sir Claude did
about pottery. But the analogy between music and pottery
is not very close, and Colby is given no words to develop
the reality of his experience of music; we are left feeling that his analysis of experience is as vague as his
character. Yet it has been clearly indicated that *he* is
the important figure in the play.

Nevertheless, we have enjoyed the first act: it is
entertaining, and in the end something has been said that
is interesting and if well developed may prove exciting.
The second act is more consistent: the potentiality of the
situation for melodrama is developed with a skill worthy
of something better, indeed we are almost persuaded that
it is something better. Its main length is occupied by a
scene between Lucasta and Colby in the Mews flat which
Lady Elizabeth has furnished and decorated for him to her
own satisfaction; we are not greatly impressed by Colby's
elementary instruction in musical appreciation (though we
remember later, with distaste, his sly trick of playing
inferior music to test her taste) nor by the experienced-
girl-about-town commenting on the shy-young-man's approach
to love. At least this stuff asserts (what is not unexpected) that these two are falling in love; and her new
interest in music is developed as an unconscious urge towards the world that alone is real to him. In fact we are
led back to the terms of Colby's discussion with Sir
Claude: the reality (not here defined as make-believe)
that a man may withdraw to is a mental garden. For Colby
there is the desperate need to have company in his garden
- if he were religious, the companion would be God, if
not...; but of course one cannot issue invitations. For
Lucasta, there is only the search for a garden, and
Colby's assurance (which hardly seems more than polite
and patronising encouragement) that for this one may
deliberately search and be sure of success, there *is* a
garden for every one; thus far, one need not despair.
This is not far from platitude, but it makes its point as
it develops with the emotional tension of the scene; it
has a meaning in the increasing sympathy between the two;
a sympathy whose limitations are effectively demonstrated
from the theatrical situation. Lucasta can declare the
burning shame of the rich foundling and so precipitate a
dramatic misunderstanding. Colby's reaction is horror
(that she is his sister); and her reaction to his horror
is violent, for she believes his shock to be at her tale

of illegitimacy and maternal prostitution. So far, very
effective; the complexity of the scene has reached a point
both moving and interesting; but there is an inherent
flaw. The classical comedy formula requires that Colby
maintain secrecy about his father, hence the misunderstanding must continue; such loyalty (to what? or whom?)
is merely absurd in the dramatic context: Mr. Eliot
having escaped the limitations of puerile melodrama, now
forces himself back into them. The result is that Colby,
never very attractive, is reduced to a mere prig (as the
author himself has called Harry in 'The Family Reunion').
Mr. Eliot does what he can: twice Colby comes to the point
of explanation; on the first occasion Lucasta will not
listen, and on the second they are interrupted. We are
impressed once more by how clever Mr. Eliot has become at
play-writing; but it is of small value, the dramatic weakness cannot be overcome by theatrical contrivance. The
tension is abandoned rather than relieved when B. Kaghan
arrives to rescue his fiancée from what he evidently realises to be a dangerous entanglement; and the shift of
genre is complete when Lady Elizabeth begins to suspect
that Colby is her long lost (illegitimate) son; in the
first act we have been shown (rather tediously) how
quickly Lady Elizabeth can convince herself it was she,
not her husband, who appointed Colby: her memory cannot
now (or in the last act) be treated seriously; the figure
of farce cannot contribute to the plausible drama. After
the dramatic tension of the earlier part of this act we
are merely incredulous that Colby and his father should
take this hallucination so seriously; it makes a preposterous, not a dramatic, curtain for Colby to demand a full
enquiry with his foster mother to settle the 'question'.
     The second interval found us impressed by the ingenuity
with which Mr. Eliot has kept his curious amalgam of different dramatic genres in a balance so nearly convincing;
but apprehensive that a successful last act would require
more than just ingenuity. The difficulties are enormous
and are not lessened by the fact that Mr. Eliot clearly
regarded some of them as advantages. The classical mistaken identities have all to be disentangled without losing the carefully sustained air of commonplace plausibility; and the hints of important understandings have to be
justified. In the event, the plot proves so tangled that
sheer exposition has to be uncomfortably hurried, and
other matters are obtruded perilously and hustled away: it
is skilfully managed (considering the difficulties) but
the result can only be confusion; the accumulation of ex-
positions provokes a large number of questions to most of
which answers are forthcoming afterwards; but in such a

context none of the answers can be very important, and
those that should be seem curiously irrelevant.

Inevitably there are some slight inconsistencies; they
would not matter, except for the persistent illusion of
sentimental plausibility. Lucasta is delighted to learn
that Colby is her brother: it makes respectable the shock
he gave her, and endorses the discovery she made from that
experience, that it was really appropriate (for her) to
marry B. Kaghan; when it is later revealed that Colby is
not after all her brother, it doesn't materially alter her
position; but some reaction is needed for the sake of completeness - a movement or gesture would suffice - yet none
is allowed. Again, the circumstances revealed do not at
all prove that Kaghan is Lady Elizabeth's son, only that
Colby is not. Details of this kind are of very slight
importance, and Mr. Eliot justifiably ignores them; but
they become conspicuous simply because the grotesque im-
plausibilities of the main discoveries are deliberately
underlined in order to hint that behind the whole construction there has been, perhaps, a kind of allegory. Colby's
foster-mother Mrs. Guzzard conducts the proceedings with
the air of a sybil, turning a simple tale of switched
babies into a mysterious matter of choice. Colby is not
Lady Elizabeth's son and he finds that, as he has had no
effective father in his childhood, he would rather not
have a live one now - he would prefer to hunt up the facts
about his father than to know all without trouble; Mrs.
Guzzard, after impressive warnings, is able to oblige him:
he is not Sir Claude's son, he is hers and her late husband's (legitimate after all); and his father was an unsuccessful musician. The stage is now dominated by Mrs.
Guzzard and Eggerson. Mrs. Guzzard comments to our surprise that everyone has had his wish, and must live with
the consequences. The point requires considerable thought:
it is clear that Lady Elizabeth wanted a son and hasn't
got the one she wanted; Lucasta has announced she wanted
security and has it in B. Kaghan; Sir Claude one can only
suppose had his wish when Colby was a baby and he mistook
him for his son: if that is the point - and it is far from
clear - it must presumably modify Sir Claude's theory of
the worlds of make-believe in act one, for his seems to
have been a *mere* illusion and Colby now refuses to patch up
up that illusion by acting as if he were his son. As for
Colby, he can set about searching old letters and photo-
graphs to know his father, and can pursue his hereditary
bent for unsuccessful musicianship; he has discovered that
his nature differs from Sir Claude's, that he must pursue
his one reality however unsuccessfully. But we have not
finished with mechanical gods (or goddesses): Mrs. Guzzard

has done her work and can withdraw; it is now Eggerson's
turn. Throughout the last act he has been growing more and
and more Paternal: he now offers Colby the job of organist
in his village church (he has a peculiar influence in
parochial affairs). There isn't must money in it, but that
will not matter, for he won't stay long; Eggerson can now
reveal what he's always known, that Colby will move from
the organ to the altar, that he has a vocation for the
priesthood which is entirely delightful because he can continue with his music. The fear that has been with us since
we first heard the play's title, but had been cunningly
lulled in the first two acts, is now confirmed: Eggerson
and Colby are both confidential clerks to a greater master
than Sir Claude; the sly powers of 'The Cocktail Party'
are revived, and the same unhappy parlour trick repeated.
The measure of its failure is the measure of Colby's complete unimportance to us; it is true that the hints and
mysteries of the earlier acts have been cleverly worked
out (God does now walk in his garden), even the solution
is clever, but Colby remains the uninteresting figure he
was from the first. Indeed, in this last act, he seems to
be a sort of dumb waiter from whom everyone else can take
his pick. Mr. Eliot (as usual) shows himself aware of
danger, and he resorts again to theatrical contrivance;
twice Lucasta remarks in awe that she had always known
Colby was a man apart. The effect is disastrous: so far
from being persuaded that we had always known this, we are
consciously confirmed in our awareness that we had not.
The point has to be made then, that the important revelations of the last act appear only as irrelevancies: assertions not inherent in the drama that has developed. There
is in fact nothing left of that drama but a sustained (and
absurd) effort to make Sir Claude's reactions 'plausible';
his last despairing question is whether Eggerson really
believes in Colby, and the curtain falls past that wise
old head nodding benevolently in the centre of the stage.
    The carefully contrived structure collapses in the end.
Yet it is in the end that Mr. Eliot offers most of the
ideas that he wants to make interesting - ideas of a kind
which, in other contexts, he has of course made supremely
interesting. It does not follow that they are in their
nature undramatic, but they certainly have no dramatic
force here. It is one thing to take a preposterous plot
and to persuade us that in each new situation there is
something important to be said, a different way of looking
at what has to be said and done; but in that there is evidently the difficulty that the important drama will have
to develop and that its development (as opposed to its
separate situation) will not be aided by the superficial

comedy. Hence the irrelevance of so much that should matter in the last act: it has not developed from what did
matter earlier. But such a comedy might succeed (we may
think) if its surface was stylised; in this sense, Lady
Elizabeth is perhaps the most promising kind of figure in
the play. But Mr. Eliot is not content with stylised
comedy, he attempts to unite his two levels and to develop
them simultaneously by the kind of plausible drama we have
discussed. The reasons are obvious enough: the drama is
to deal with human affairs, so it will move more immediately if human affairs can be shown in action. But the
terms of this action are bounded by what is for convenience called the theatrical (the kind of play at which Mr.
Terence Rattigan excels), and the figure who most completely represents this level is Sir Claude. The demands
of this kind of theatrical writing are exclusive: it does
not admit of mixture with other genres; and because it
makes for easy emotional scenes it dominates the stage
effect. Lady Elizabeth is reduced (if that is the right
word) to the level of her husband, and spends the last act
vaguely hoping that she and Claude will understand each
other better in future (again we remember 'The Cocktail
Party'). Far more serious than that, is the effect that
such trivial emotions must have on the significant ideas
of the play: trivial action can be extended by comment and
suggestion into significance; trivial emotions cannot be
equated on any terms with significant feeling and so
resist any valuable comment whatever. Thus at the end of
the play, Sir Claude's agony is entirely meaningless, but
by its insistent presence precludes any chance there might
have been that Colby's vocation could seem to matter. It
is tempting to adapt Mr. Eliot's own words, and comment
that 'The Confidential Clerk' cannot be poetic, because it
is not truly dramatic; and that criticism will remain even
though, as is most probable, the printed text reveals passages whose potential value has been missed here, because
that potential is annulled by their context.

Our conclusion is, then, that the best of the play is
good prose drama; the high intelligence that manifests
itself occasionally, insisting that Mr. Eliot did have
some part in the writing, is swamped by the very theatri-
cality that will, we have no doubt, ensure a long London
run. The play, we said before, makes a good evening in
the theare, but it makes a depressing one afterwards. The
long search for poetic drama seems to have led only to the
discovering how to write a successful West-end play; a
remarkable achievement indeed, but a bitterly disappointing
one.

172. HELEN GARDNER, A REVIEW, 'NEW STATESMAN'

20 March 1954, vol. xlvii, 373-4

Mr. Eliot's first attempt to write a popular comedy was
naturally an experiment, retaining certain elements from
his earlier work. 'The Cocktail Party' was a blend of two
traditions: the tradition of the comedy of manners, whose
subject is the love-game, and the tradition of romantic
comedy, in which the fortunes of the characters are mani-
pulated by more or less supernatural powers. The whole
conception of the Guardians - comic Eumenides, at first
regarded as nuisances, at the end recognised as 'kindly
ones' - looked back to 'The Family Reunion.' It was as if
those awkward shapes, whose intrusions into the drawing-
room Mr. Eliot has himself mocked, and Agatha, the stern
monitress, had insisted on being present, although in comic
disguise. In subject, too, 'The Family Reunion' and 'The
Cocktail Party' are closely related. 'The Cocktail Party'
is the story of a marriage that breaks down and then comes
right, as 'The Family Reunion' is the story of a marriage
with a tragic issue. Harry discovers, in the wreck of his
human relationships, that he should never have married at
all. His is a different calling. That calling - to solitude and suffering - is present also in 'The Cocktail
Party,' in the story of Celia. At the heart of both plays
lies the doctrine of atonement, of vicarious suffering,
the idea that there is a bill which someone has to pay.
It is treated differently in the two plays. Harry is
guilty; it is his own account as well as his family's that
he is called upon to settle. Celia does not suffer from a
sense of guilt; she has no feeling that she has wronged
Edward or Lavinia. Her story is, therefore, not tragic.
She is conscious of sin; she becomes aware of a burden
which has to be picked up and carried. But with all their
differences, Thomas, the murdered Archbishop, Harry, the
destroyer-saviour of his family, Celia, the self-offerer,
stand in a line. Each is apart from the rest of the characters, called to a favoured lot, an 'exaltation to afflic-
tions high.'
     With 'The Confidential Clerk' a break has been made.
The 'Eumenides' and the martyr have been left behind. The
goddess in the machine, Mrs. Guzzard, holds the role of
Pallas Athene; but she is not that wise virgin, nor any
other. She is firmly rooted in her suburb, Teddington - a
district of slightly higher social standing than Joshua
Park - the widow of Herbert Guzzard, an organist. She is

mother, yet not mother, of Colby Simpkins, not in any mystical or symbolical sense, but because, though she was his
mother after the flesh, she preferred to be his aunt. Mr.
Eggerson, the 'wise one' of this play, does not burst out
with cryptic little runes, pour libations to the gods of
the hearth in his hot milk, or circle round a birthday
cake - and he is mercifully unaware that he is wise. The
lonely figure is still here, the person who is 'different.'
But the desert to which Colby retreats is a comfortable
one. He will be very snug in Joshua Park, more comfortable than under Lady Elizabeth's care in his mews-flat.
     The rather uneasy blend of the comedy of manners with a
kind of divine comedy has given way to another kind of
comedy, something nearer to the comedy of humours. Sir
Claude, with his dreams of himself as a potter, and his
talk about being 'obedient to the facts,' when it is clear
that he has the utmost difficulty in recognising a fact at
all, much more in obeying it; Lady Elizabeth, with her belief in her unconventionality and her search into any
fashionable form of wisdom; Lucasta, with her 'tough
blonde' act; B. Kaghan, with his 'commonness' - these are
humour characters, jolted by the twists and turns of the
improbable plot into acknowledgment of their true natures.
'The Confidential Clerk' has a unity which Mr. Eliot has
not achieved before in a play. No single one of the characters has a monopoly of wisdom or virtue, and no character exists simply to be despised or guyed. Each in his or
her own way has glimpses of the truth and each is capable
of suffering, because capable of love. The plot has an
obvious source in the 'Ion' of Euripides, a fountain-head
of Greek romance, and of the comedy of Menander and his
Roman imitators, and Mr. Eliot has followed good precedent
in his adaptation. As Shakespeare doubled the twins of
his source in 'The Comedy of Errors' to make the fun fas-
ter, so, for the one foundling of the 'Ion,' Mr. Eliot has
provided three. The element of fantasy, necessary if
comedy is to rise above being a mere transcript of daily
life and reach towards general truth, is not, as in 'The
Cocktail Party,' imposed on a particular story by the addition of extraneous characters. It is the plot itself.
     'The Confidential Clerk' differs from Mr. Eliot's ear-
lier plays in having a weak and untheatrical beginning, but
a strong third act and a splendid final curtain. Always
before he excelled in exposition and failed in his _dénoue-
ment_. Here, the last act, with revelation piled on revelation, is a real theatrical climax. The slow exposition is
the price that has been paid for the complications of the
plot and the classically restricted cast. It is a serious
blemish in a play which aims at being theatrical. But,

apart from this defect, the play seems to me, both on the
stage and in reading, an advance dramatically on its predecessor.

The subject of 'The Cocktail Party' was freedom and
destiny, our narrow area of choice. The subject of 'The
Confidential Clerk' is related; but the plot turns less
upon choice than upon the acceptance of choices made long
ago and not necessarily made by ourselves. The 'Know
thyself' of 'The Cocktail Party' is seen here to involve
knowing other people. Mrs. Guzzard chose to be her son's
aunt, not his mother. Lady Elizabeth chose not to be a
mother, except in wish. Sir Claude chose to be a patron
rather than a father: to be in 'a kind of fiduciary relationship' to his daughter, and to keep a son in cold stor-
age, as it were, until he was ready for him. Colby, the
central figure, is the object of other people's choices
and wishes. Personable, intelligent, well-behaved, he is
the ideal son, ready-made, off the peg. At the beginning
he is trying to adapt himself to what he believes to be the
the facts. At the close, asked what he wishes, he
declares he wants what he has had: to have no father and
no mother in this life. The only true father he can have
is a father who died before he was born, who did not refuse him the knowledge of a father's love, because he was
not there to give it. His music is not to be like Sir
Claude's love of his pots. He is not content for it to be
a hobby. The knowledge of who his father was confirms him
in his knowledge that his music is something in his very
being, a key to his nature. His mother must 'rest in
peace'; he has never known a mother and cannot in any true
sense know one now. Colby's 'difference' is something
that has been imposed upon him, which he has made and will
make a source of strength.

If Colby is the central character, at whose choice the
play resolves itself, the point of value in this play is
given by the old clerk Eggerson. He, too, gets his wish,
though he does not voice it. He is the only person in the
play who has truly experienced a parent's 'pains and bene-
fits.' Sir Claude loses the son he thought he had. To
Eggerson, who really had had a son, a second son is given,
a son after the spirit. Everyone else 'wanted Colby to be
something he wasn't.' When Colby decides he wants to be
what he is, he rightly finds his home with the Eggersons,
just as years before little Barnabas, abandoned by his
mother, found a true home with the Kaghans, 'excellent
people, Nonconformists.'

In 'The Cocktail Party' the divine broke into the pattern of human lives in the form of the heroic, and the
heroic is, as Von Hügel said, the most easily recognisable

manifestation of the supernatural. It is not difficult to
respond with admiration to the mystic's search for union
and the martyr's absolute rejection of what this life has
to offer. But to be asked to find a test of the values by
which we live in Mr. Eggerson, pottering about in his garden in Joshua Park, performing commissions for Mrs. E. at
the draper's, and finding everyone has a heart of gold, is
another matter. Mr. Eggerson never opens his mouth without a cliche. The 'monuments of unageing intellect' are,
one imagines, quite meaningless to him. His reading is
the evening paper, and I don't like to think what pictures
adorn his lounge or what tasteful vases stand upon its
what-nots.

For a poet to place such a character at the spiritual
centre of his play is the strongest possible indication
that 'the poetry does not matter.' What the author has to
say here is said in the whole design of his plot, in the
behaviour of all the characters to each other. The play
stands or falls by our acceptance of the characters and
not by any particular scenes or passages of deep significance or high poetic beauty. This is not to say that the
play is not finely written, and that those characters who
properly can do so do not express themselves with an exquisite precision. But whatever message the play holds is
diffused over the whole.

As I see the play, judgment of Mr. Eliot's achievement
must depend on our judgment of his characterisation, on
whether we believe in his characters and whether we care
about them. The queer family party we are left with at
the end, Sir Claude, Lady Elizabeth, Lucasta and B. Kaghan,
both convince the imagination, I think, and touch the
heart. The difficulty lies in Colby and Mr. Eggerson.
For Colby has very little character and Mr. Eggerson perhaps too much. It is difficult to separate the characters
as the poet conceived them from performances one has recently seen. Certainly on the London stage, if not in the
United States, the actor of Colby triumphed over what seems
in reading the coldness and priggishness of the part. As
for Eggerson, I am not sure whether Mr. Eliot has not
strained his chosen medium too far. I can think of only
one English writer who has succeeded beyond question in
presenting the kind of goodness which Eggerson is intended
to embody, Jane Austen in Miss Bates. But the novel can
do things which the stage cannot do, and *vice versa*. The
theatre exaggerates, and in the glare of the footlights
Eggerson may come out as too little a person and too much a
character part. In these two roles Mr. Eliot has asked a
great deal of his actors.

All the same, the gulf that in Mr. Eliot's earlier

plays separated the heroes from their fellows does not
yawn in 'The Confidential Clerk.' In 'The Family Reunion'
Harry and Agatha hardly seemed to belong to the same species as the uncles and aunts of the chorus.   Even in 'The
Cocktail Party,' where different ways of salvation were
shown, the death of Celia and the domestic felicity of
Edward and Lavinia were too far apart for either to seem
true; each infected the other with a kind of unreality.
The obscurely faithful Eggerson is a better touchstone in
the world of comedy than the romantically conceived Celia,
presenting, quite unconsciously, a stronger challenge to
our conception of the good life.

'The Elder Statesman'

First produced at the Edinburgh Festival, 25-30 August 1958;   ^{ican}
first edition, London, 10 April 1959;
first American edition, New York, 13 April 1959

173. HENRY HEWES, T.S. ELIOT AT SEVENTY, AND AN INTERVIEW
WITH ELIOT, 'SATURDAY REVIEW'

13 September 1958, vol. xli, 30-2

Hewes (b. 1917) was a staff writer for the 'New York
Times' until 1952, when he became drama editor, and then
drama critic, for the 'Saturday Review'.

To those who think of T.S. Eliot as clever, cynical,
despairing, and enigmatic, his newest play - 'The Elder
Statesman' - will seem disappointingly simple and much too
full of the milk of human kindness. And to any sophisticated playgoer the 'official' opening of it at the
Edinburgh Festival may have seemed a static and conventional production.
    Indeed, the most conventional and dated scene comes
right at the beginning when we are treated to a love pro-
posal to a young lady named Monica by her very correct
suitor, Charles. But just at the moment when we look at
our program to see if perhaps we have wandered into the
wrong play, there comes a line which suggests that something more than romance is intended. Monica says, 'We
must keep our private world private to ourselves, learn
the path of transition out into the public world and back
again to ours.' This line relates the love duet to
Monica's father, the just-retired Lord Claverton, who has
lost this path of transition. Furthermore, because he is
fatally ill he is being forced to retire from the public
world. He faces this enforced idleness cheerfully 'with

no desire to act, yet a loathing of inaction, a fear of
the vacuum and no desire to fill it.'
   Lord Calverton is deeply troubled as, accompanied by
his daughter, he enters a convalescent home called
Badgley Court. Softly in a Hamlet-like soliloquy he asks,
'What is this self inside us, this silent observer, severe
and speechless critic, who can terrorize us and urge us on
to futile activity, and in the end judge us still more
severely for the errors into which his own reproaches
drive us?'
   And now these errors, embodied as people, return to
haunt him. The first is an unsavory companion of his college days who remembers the night he ran over a man on the
road and did not stop. The companion has changed his name
to Gomez and gone off to prosper through shady dealings in
Central America. But he too faces a lonely old age and
needs to renew his acquaintance with Lord Claverton, because Lord Claverton is the only one who knows all the unpleasant facts about him, and yet cannot judge him because Gomez also knows about him. Next there is a rich
widow, who turns out to be the former showgirl, Maisie
Mountjoy. Maisie once had a brief affair with Lord Claverton, but was bought off by his father. She too wants to
rehash the details of this incomplete first love. Finally,
Lord Claverton's ne'er-do-well son Michael appears. He
has lost his job and wants his father to stake him to a
partnership abroad, something in 'import and export with
an opportunity for profit both ways.' He wants to be
something on his own account, not a prolongation of his
father's existence. After furiously upbraiding Michael,
the ludicrousness of Lord Claverton's position is made
apparent as he says: 'What I want to escape from is myself
in the past. But what a coward I am to talk of escaping!
And what a hypocrite! A few minutes ago I was pleading
with Michael not to try to escape from his own past faithlessness. I said I knew from experience! Do I understand
the lesson I would teach. Well I'll begin to study.
Michael and I shall go to school together, and suffer the
same humiliations at the hands of the same master.'
   In Act III Lord Claverton does learn. He states: 'If a
man has just one person, just one in his life to whom he
is willing to confess everything, then he loves that person, and his love will save him.'
   Thus he is able to confess to his daughter. 'It's impossible to be quite honest with your child. To one's
child one can't reveal oneself while she is a child. And
by the time she's grown you've woven such a web of fiction
about you.'
   This tragedy of non-communication between parent and

child manifests itself in Michael going off to Central
America with the corrupt Gomez, and Eliot is realistic
enough to allow this to happen. However, Claverton receives his son's unwelcome decision with surprising and
new-found compassion. He tells Michael:
'I shall never repudiate you though you repudiate me.
I see more and more clearly the many mistakes I have made
my whole life through. I see that your mother and I, in
our failure to understand each other, both misunderstood
you.'
In this magnanimous spirit Lord Claverton goes off to
die in tranquillity under a beech tree. He has, ironically, found peace at Badgley Court.
The play is Greek in its inspiration. Lord Claverton
and Monica loosely parallel Oedipus and Antigone in
Sophocles' 'Oedipus at Colonus.' Past states are
announced and analyzed. And the lessons are summed up
for the audience.
Under E. Martin Browne's direction the verse is spoken
so naturally that one is scarcely conscious that it is
verse at all, but the performances generally lack sufficient fire and dimension to make us care deeply about the
characters. And since 'The Elder Statesman' contains so
few intellectual surprises, it perhaps needs passion more
than do Mr. Eliot's other plays.
For instance, as Lord Claverton, Paul Rogers gives a
solid portrayal, but there is not enough difference between the unhappy stuffed shirt and the transfigured
being he becomes at the end. Similarly Anna Massey brings
an affectionate good nature to the role of Monica, but she
has not begun to indicate the strain of her relationship
with her father, or the anxiety about her ability to love,
that would make her final cure dramatic.
One suspects that with the right performances and drastic revision of the first act, 'The Elder Statesman' could
be a moving play. For it deals with universals and reveals to us a more human T.S. Eliot than before.

Eliot on Eliot: An Interview

EDINBURGH.
Despite the fact that his seventieth birthday is only days
away, T.S. Eliot seems heartier, more unworried, and more
unafraid of the world than he did when interviewed by this
writer five years ago. (1) This phenomenon he attributes
to his recent marriage (his second) to his former secretary.
'Love reciprocated is always rejuvenating,' he says,
leaning forward in his armchair. 'Before my marriage I

was getting older. Now I feel younger at seventy than I
did at sixty. Any man if he is alone becomes more aware
of being lonely as he ages. An experience like mine makes
all the more difference because of its contrast with the
past.'

Mr. Eliot confesses that when he was young he thought of
fifty as the age at which a writer goes downhill, and fully
expected to be completely finished by seventy. However, he
claims not to be conscious of any diminution of his mental
faculties and is, in fact, planning to write one more verse
play, and some literary or social criticism in prose.

'I'm curious,' he adds, 'to see if I shan't also want to
write a few more poems in a rather different style. I feel
I reached the end of something with the "Four Quartets,"
and that anything new will have to be expressed in a different idiom.'

This experience of reaching an end and making a new
beginning has happened several times in his career as a
poet. It happened after 'The Hollow Men,' which he no
longer likes very much because it represents a period of
extreme depression about his future work. It happened
again after 'Ash-Wednesday,' when it took the commissioning
of 'The Rock' to get him restarted.

Mr. Eliot tends to enjoy his more recent work because it
is closer to the man he now is. He believes that the one
work with which he is most satisfied is the last of the
'Four Quartets.' However, he experiences less dissatisfaction on re-reading his earlier poems than his prose work.

'The poems permanently represent the best that I could
do when I wrote them. But I judge my prose as if I'd written it yesterday and now disagreed with some of what it
said.'

When asked whether he would still write his famous pro-
phecy, ('This is the way the world ends, not with a bang
but a whimper'), Mr. Eliot admits he would not. One reason
is that while the association of the H-bomb is irrelevant
to it, it would today come to everyone's mind. Another is
that he is not sure the world will end with either. People
whose houses were bombed have told him they don't remember
hearing anything.

The original meaning, he explains 'was a subjective dissatisfaction with the pettiness of life. When one is
young, the expression of that mood is simply an effusion of
one's individual situation.'

While this might seem to link him with today's angry
young men, he prefers not to think so. Mr. Eliot feels
that like Rudyard Kipling, who spent his early years in
another country, he has a special feeling for England. On
the other hand, he believes that his poetry belongs more in

the American current than it does in the British.

As for his plays, the poet who likes to be liberated
from both the past and the future rates them in the in-
verse order in which he wrote them. When asked if he now
reads himself in the title role of 'The Elder Statesman,'
he has this to say: 'There are three ingredients in all
one's characters: (1) observation of other people, (2) pure
invention, and (3) something of oneself which includes what
Yeats calls the anti-self. But I find that the character
is most effective when one is least conscious of putting
oneself into it.'

While the word God is never mentioned in 'The Elder
Statesman,' the leading character finds confession to those
he loves the road to salvation and peaceful death, and thus
echoes Mr. Eliot's personal attitude about death and eternity, which is the ordinary Catholic one. He does not believe we can really grasp the concept of the timeless,
although he himself has had intuitive flashes which he's
hinted at in the 'Quartets.' He feels these will only be
communicable to those who have had similar flashes.

'Death is not oblivion,' he says. 'People who believe
that are not afraid of death, they are only afraid of dying.' Mr. Eliot cannot understand people feeling religious
hope without feeling also a religious fear of what their
fate may be.

'For the Christian,' he explains, 'there is that perpetual living in paradox. You must lose your life in order
to save it. One has to be otherworldly and yet deeply
responsible for the affairs of this world. One must preserve a capacity for enjoying the things of this world such
as love and affection.'

Also implied in 'The Elder Statesman' is the pressure on
any famous man to be what other people think him to be, to
become the servant of the myth that surrounds him. Mr.
Eliot knows this influence well through the kind of cult
a great many of his admirers make about him. His formula
for avoiding it is constant struggle against it, plus a
sense of humor with which to see one's own absurdity.

'At seventy I laugh at myself more than I did when I
was young,' he says, 'and conversely I am less and less
worried about making a fool of myself.'

Note

1   'Saturday Review', 29 August 1953, xxxvi, 26-8.

174. J.G. WEIGHTMAN, AFTER EDINBURGH, 'TWENTIETH CENTURY'

October 1958, vol. clxiv, 342-4

This is an extract from a longer article.

The other major commission, besides the ballets, was of
course T.S. Eliot's new verse play, 'The Elder Statesman'.
Although it is not explicitly Christian, the flavour is
much the same as that of 'The Cocktail Party' and 'The
Confidential Clerk'. The first two acts make very good
theatre and contain some slivers of bleak poetry; the
third strikes me as an almost complete failure, contrived
and moralizing. If anything, this play is more clearly a
pièce à thèse than the other two, the lesson being that if
you want to live and die happy, you ought to be honest
with yourself. Lord Claverton, the elder statesman, has
lived a lie all his life. During his wild youth at Oxford,
he ran over an old man but did not stop, not wishing it to
be known that there were two women in the car with him.
After leaving Oxford, he got himself involved in a breach
of promise action with a musical comedy actress whom, in
a sense, he genuinely loved. The memory of these two
early misdeeds has festered within him and prevented him
from being anything more than a near-success. His peerage
symbolizes his acceptance of outward show instead of inner
truth. His conventionally suitable wife has long been
dead. He is at loggerheads with his son, who has hated
growing up in his shadow. He is now ill and living in
retirement with his daughter, an intelligent girl who
cherishes him. It is at this point that two ghosts from
his past come to plague him: a friend of his student days,
a scholarship-boy whom he corrupted and who witnessed the
motor-car incident, and the ex-actress, now a wealthy
widow. Under their taunts he comes to realize his mistakes, and finds peace before death.
    Mr Eliot has always been good at expressing negative
emotion. This play conveys an immense fatigue with life,
tempered in some degree by an apparently new discovery,
embodied in the daughter and her fiancé, of the experience
of shared love. At first, it looks as if this contrast is
going to give a unique interest to the work. But as the
action unfolds, the play, instead of thickening, seems to
become thinner and, as often happens with pièces-à-thèse,
the implied attitude turns out to be rather at variance
with the explicit moral. Lord Claverton, admirably played,
in a stiff, dead-pan way, by Paul Rogers, who is made up
to look exactly like the present Prime Minister, achieves
some progress towards spiritual enlightenment, but not as

708 T.S. Eliot: The Critical Heritage

much as Mr Eliot seems to suggest. Mr Eliot castigates
him, yet all the time surrounds him with a rather unjusti-
fied aura of sympathy. If I may be allowed to moralize in
reply, from the fourth row of the stalls, I should say
that it is not enough to confess one's sins and so slough
off paralyzing guilt. The final test is to realize that
other people actually exist, in the way one exists oneself; this, I take it, is the true meaning of 'love thy
neighbour as thyself'. Mr Eliot himself said as much in
'The Family Reunion':

> We must try to penetrate the other private worlds
> Of make-believe and fear. To rest in our own suffering
> Is evasion of suffering.

Lord Claverton should realize that the ex-musical comedy
star and his old student friend, now a rather shady South
American millionaire, are just as important, spiritually,
as he is. They are, as it happens, the two most interesting characters and, had Shakespeare been holding the pen,
they would have run away with the action. It is true that
in the first half of the play Mr Eliot gives them a promising subtlety. The ex-scholarship boy has not come back to
blackmail Claverton, but to recapture a sense of identity
through talking to the only surviving witness of his past.
The feather-brained musical comedy star remembers the early
love-affair as the one important experience of her life.
But in the third act, this reality is taken away from them,
and they are represented as vindictive schemers, anxious to
revenge themselves on Claverton by helping his son to emi-
grate to South America. The daughter and her priggish
fiancé insult them, with Mr Eliot's obvious approval.
Claverton, having confessed his mistakes, is now able to
dismiss these 'ghosts' from his mind and die happy.
Surely, in the very act of condemning egotistical self-
deception, Mr Eliot is showing himself to be morally snobbish. To put it crudely, he saves the phoney lord at the
expense of the uncultured types, so that he is really repeating the misdeed from which the whole action is supposed to have started.
    The play is quite fascinating in its pattern of confes-
sions and inhibitions. It could have been written fifty
years ago. There is a bell-rope, and a butler who brings
in the tea-tray, and not a single reference to the contemporary world. When Claverton confesses that he was
once the musical comedy star's lover, the fiancé takes the
daughter's arm with a look of concern, as if she will be
distressed by this revelation. Yet there are faintly
Shavian bursts of outspokenness, although Mr Eliot has

always affected to despise Shaw. Strangest of all is Mr
Eliot's feeling for the vitality of the vulgar which gives
life to the first two acts and yet is so fiercely re-
pressed in the third.

175. FRANK KERMODE, WHAT BECAME OF SWEENEY?, 'SPECTATOR'

10 April 1959, vol. ccii, 513

Kermode (b. 1919), King Edward VII Professor of English
Literature, Cambridge University, includes amongst his
many publications 'The Romantic Image' (1957) and 'The
Sense of an Ending' (1967). His edition of 'The Selected
Prose of T.S. Eliot' was published in 1975. In 'Modern
Essays' (1971) he gave a striking account of Eliot's place
in the Modern Movement. He delivered the T.S. Eliot Memorial Lectures at the University of Kent at Canterbury in
1973.

With 'The Elder Statesman' Mr. Eliot has brought us to a
place we could not have expected to reach when we started.
We may see how the road runs from the fragmentary marvels
of 'Sweeney Agonistes' to the finished, fluent *agones* and
subtly complete recognitions of the latest plays, but it
does not follow that this is the necessary, the only possible, or even the right road. Why was this one built,
and not another?
    Mr. Eliot's earliest thinking about the drama for the
most part makes sense only in terms of 'little' theatres
('we should hire a barn or studio'). What you did in your
barn would hardly be fitted to combat the 'listless apathy'
of the 'morally corrupt' middle-class or West End audiences. For the most part, too, one can say of Mr. Eliot's
early dramatic theory that it was anti-naturalist, or,
more positively, Symbolist. One remembers how many interests he had in common with the first-generation Symbolist,
Arthur Symons; to Donne and recent French poetry one may
add the Jacobean drama, ballet, liturgy and music-hall.
Eliot's emphasis is, of course, his own. Thus he finds the
Jacobean drama defective by comparison with a truly classical theatre; but in the last analysis he admires it because
it is more like ballet and more like liturgy than anything

710 T.S. Eliot: The Critical Heritage

in the modern theatre, because its versification was
adequate to its highest intentions yet not too remote from
a colloquial norm, and because its audience would 'stand'
a lot of poetry and so allow the dramatist to satisfy them
while pleasing a minority of finer sensibility. Here, indeed, are Mr. Eliot's two principal and conflicting problems: how to achieve a balletic-liturgical theatre; how to
cope with a mass audience.

At one time he might have given priority to the first
of these problems. 'Is not the High Mass - as performed,
for instance, at the Madeleine in Paris - one of the highest forms of dancing?' he asked in 1925; and in the Dialogue of Dramatic Poetry (1928) he lets 'E' say that the
ballet can give us everything we want in drama 'except the
poetry... If there is a future for drama, and particularly for poetic drama, will it not be in the direction
indicated by the ballet?' Drama cannot afford to lose
touch with the liturgy from which it sprang; perhaps in
a period of chaotic religious and ethical belief it should
be all the more liturgical. Now this choreographic-
liturgical bent was inherited from the Symbolists and their
English followers, who not only took Schopenhauer a step
further and saw the world as ballet but did pioneer research into mediaeval dance-liturgies. Even Mr. Eliot's
passion for 'popular' theatre - Ernie Lotinga, Marie Lloyd
- is inherited from the Nineties; the great 'popular' per-
formers like Lloyd and Guilbert were the darlings of the
élite in both Paris and London. Yet even here Mr. Eliot
has his own emphasis, his 'cultural' qualification, and in
a remarkable essay he represents Marie Lloyd as exclusively
'working-class.' 'The working man who went to the music-
hall and saw Marie Lloyd and joined in the chorus was himself performing part of the act; he was engaged in that
collaboration of the audience with the artist which is
necessary in all art and most obviously in dramatic art.'
Not for him the decadent cult of the music-hall, à rebours,
as it grew up originally in Paris: Eliot sees it in a
sociological context, and its death as a diminution of our
culture. A cult-audience must fall short of what the new
drama would need.

Now it could be argued that the audience of initiates
is the 'best self' of the community, and then the choreo-
graphic-liturgical manner becomes possible. And post-
Wagnerian approaches to a theatre of this kind accepted
Wagner's belief that ordinary speech was no longer a possible way of reaching the soul, since it appealed only to
the understanding, so that speech became an aspect only of
a ritualistic whole, the anti-naturalistic unity of action,
scene and voice proposed by Gordon Craig. Character,

verisimilitude, were banished; the actors went masked and
moved like dancers. Some thought of marionettes; and then
the discovery of the Nō plays seemed to offer the richest
solution. They confirmed all that Yeats had thought and
imagined about a theatre in this tradition, and consequently his incomparably distinguished verse-plays bear,
from then on, the marks of this hieratic influence. But
he wrote for 'an unpopular theatre and an audience like a
secret society' - 'not a theatre but the theatre's anti-
self.' After 'Sweeney' and the unrepeatable compromise of
'Murder in the Cathedral,' Mr. Eliot chose the theatre.
Yeats remained constant to his rejection of naturalism and
the mass audience. And later, pondering, no doubt, the
paradoxical achievement, in Yeats's late plays, of that
spareness and purity of diction at which he himself aims,
Mr. Eliot saw that Yeats had used the theatre none the
less 'as an organ for the expression of the consciousness
of a people.'

Having renounced the anti-theatre, Mr. Eliot was committed to an audience largely made up of middle-class
groundlings, incapable of full participation in his whole
design. This meant operating, in the Jacobean manner, 'on
two levels at once,' and the levels are the 'dramatic' and
the 'musical.' At first Mr. Eliot supplied two kinds of
verse, as in 'The Family Reunion'; now the verse is
strictly monotonous and the 'musical' pattern is a matter
of reverberations within exceedingly careful plots, in
which the author has learned from the Greeks, but also and
perhaps mostly from Ibsen. The task is to 'musicalise'
naturalism, to make poetic an existing, conventional drama.
And such an attempt was adumbrated as early as 'The Sacred
Wood'; perhaps, thought Mr. Eliot, we should not think of
the 'small public which wants "poetry,"' but 'take a form
of entertainment and subject it to a process which would
leave it a form of art.' The author's 'cultural' preoccupation overcame desires far more natural in a poet of
his time.

Space is wanting to discuss the efforts Mr. Eliot has
made recently to achieve the 'mirage,' a perfect confla-
tion of the 'dramatic' and the 'musical.' The audience,
presumably, is engaged in the doomed experiment of forming
'a civilised but non-Christian mentality'; like Celia in
'The Cocktail Party' it has had a conventional upbringing
and has 'always been taught to disbelieve in sin.'
('Sweeney' was *about*, not *for*, this audience.) The naturalistic, 'dramatic' level is theirs. And in the musical
order of the plays we must look for that 'orthodoxy of
sensibility' and pressure of 'tradition' which character-
ise, in Mr. Eliot's view, all possible art. In 'The Elder

Statesman' the dramatic has absorbed the musical more
fully than ever before - Ibsen would have admired it. Yet
it fails to satisfy; if we want to know why, and where we
have got to, we can take our bearings both from Ibsen and
Chekhov and from Yeats. For plot can carry 'music' in a
prose play too; and the poetic drama is another thing
again. In a sense it is the audience he has considered so
carefully that has sabotaged Mr. Eliot's theatre. It does
not give expression to 'the consciousness of a people.'
Yeats seems to have been right in thinking that you do that
by considering only an *élite*, ignoring the 'shopkeeping
logicians' of Shaftesbury Avenue and refusing to supply

> what the blind and ignorant town
> Imagines best to make it thrive.

176. DENIS DONOGHUE, ELIOT IN FAIR COLONUS: 'THE ELDER STATESMAN', 'STUDIES'

Spring 1959, vol. xlviii, 49-58

Donoghue (b. 1928), Professor of English, holder of the
Henry James Chair of Letters at New York University, has
published a number of important studies of Eliot. 'The
Third Voice' (1959) had special reference to the verse
drama, while in 'The Ordinary Universe' (1968) and 'The
Sovereign Ghost' (1976) he gave close attention to Eliot's
poetry, especially 'Four Quartets' and 'The Waste Land'. He
delivered the T.S. Eliot Memorial Lectures at the University of Kent in 1972.

'The Elder Statesman' is T.S. Eliot's sixth play, if we
include 'Sweeney Agonistes'. Like the earlier plays it is
concerned with the possibility of holiness in the modern
world, with duty, responsibility, and moral choice. Most
of the critics who have commented on the play have been un-
easily aware that Mr Eliot is a substantial figure in the
theatre, but I believe they have misunderstood the significance of the play. The main reason for this failure,
I suspect, is that 'The Elder Statesman' is related to a
tradition of comedy which virtually lapsed with Shakespeare
and which reappeared in the English theatre only in the

decadent version exhibited by J.M. Barrie. It is *not* related to the 'comedy of manners', the only form of comedy
which modern theatre-audiences understand. In a full
study one would wish to 'place' 'The Elder Statesman' not
only in relation to Eliot's earlier plays but in its bearing on 'The Idea of a Christian Society' and 'Notes Towards
the Definition of Culture'. The present essay attempts only
to suggest the quality of the play *as drama*: it is based on
the first performances of the play at the Edinburgh Festival last August.

Eliot's plays strive toward the condition of prayer.
In a period in which public or communal prayer has declined, he is tricking his theatre-audiences into an analogue of worship. Thus the opening scene of 'The Cocktail
Party' is a representation of - from a religious point of
view - oaths and blasphemies (politely translated) which
by the dramatist's dialectic will be made over into
prayers: the prayers are enacted in Celia's death and in
Alex's report of that death. Being of our own irreligious
or neutral time, we perpetrate such oaths and blasphemies,
and Eliot takes us as we are before attempting to make us
over in his own prayerful image. He has to begin somewhere: 'If people believe *eight*, I can recommend *nine*; I
can do so by the manipulation of their *eightish* assumptions; I need not justify my *nine* by arguing for *one*.'(a)
These are not Eliot's words, but no matter, they serve.
Eliot's later plays begin with eight oaths, politely disguised, and end with nine prayers.

This transformation is achieved by gentle indirection,
not by apocalyptic admonitions: these plays are not jere-
miads. Eliot may feel as strongly as Increase Mather, but
we have forced him to con a different style. He achieves
his prayers nonetheless. The first Act of 'The Elder
Statesman' has a few beguiling moments of thin young love,
but it is essentially a malign fiesta; bitter, sophisticated, with a grey wit. It is a concentration of Wyndham
Lewis's horror in the more familiar medium of guilt, deception, and emptiness. It is the waste sad time in which
the ghosts of 'The Hollow Men' are more palpable than Lambert who brings in the tea. The 'oaths' in 'The Elder
Statesman' are spoken by the spectres from Lord Claverton's past, the sinister forces which he has carried within himself for many years. Eliot calls them Federico
Gomez and Mrs Carghill. They command a language which he
long ago perfected for such purposes:

You'll be afraid of whispers,
The reflection in the mirror of the face behind you,

> The ambiguous smile, the distant salutation,
> The laughter in the corridor, the snicker in the
>   doorway,
> The sudden silence when you enter the smoking room ...

Lord Claverton himself spends most of the first two Acts
mouthing 'oaths'; putting up a righteous facade against
the bland Gomez, playing a world-weary part to fend off
Mrs Carghill, gesticulating as a maligned father in the
face of a son who has repudiated his inheritance.

Thus the beginning. And the end is a litany of love
intoned for us - as hierophants - by Charles and Monica.
These two are our stylists, 'saying the right thing',
finishing off the play with an essay in practical love now
no longer thin but rich and mellow. Thus the play, changing oaths to prayers, is an uncovering, pulling back the
curtains, breaking up the pieces to put them together
again in new configurations. It is a substitution of new
and deeper pieties, deeper because Lord Claverton, in
exorcising the prudent devil which has 'guided' him for
many years, frees himself from the spectres and emerges
'into something like reality'.

There is a motto for all this; it is a-going-back-to-
the-beginning, a new beginning in a different spirit.
The false gods are rejected and we go back to the point at
which - impiously - we went astray. One of the most moving speeches in 'The Elder Statesman' comes at the end of
the second Act when Lord Claverton, watching his severed
son Michael go arm-in-arm with Mrs Carghill and Federico
Gomez, sees that there is no escape from one's self; and,
seeing this, he sees also that he must go back to the
beginning, and his son in his own way must do likewise:

[Quotes 'The Elder Statesman', II, CPP, pp. 565-6, 'What I
want to escape from' to 'too late for me, Monica?']

This gesture is carried down into the detail of several
speeches: it is a process of constant revision and correc-
tion - as children at school - in the pursuit of truth and
reality. Thus when Monica refers to her father 'thinking
of nothing', he revises the remark to 'contemplating noth-
ingness'.

Everyone has seen that 'The Elder Statesman' bears some
relation to 'Oedipus at Colonus': the relation is both
structural and qualitative. 'Oedipus at Colonus' provides
the 'shape' of the new play, some of its most important
relationships, and a model for its tone. At the centre of
both plays there is the father-daughter relationship,

tesitfying to possibilities that will be realized -
prayerfully - at the end of the play.   These possibilities,
insofar as they express themselves in terms of sexual love,
involve the substitution of Charles Hemington for the
second sister Ismene: Monica is a gracious, if pallid, reflection of Antigone.   Michael-Polynices is the common
ground through which the protagonist and the antagonist
principles come to grips; the 'translation' into modern
terms is in his case entirely convincing.   There is no
Tirisias in Eliot's play, because Lord Claverton in his
role as self-critic, the silent observer who when forced
speaks out, gathers up this role unto himself as Oedipus.
Since the context in which the action of 'The Elder Statesman' is imitated is not very important, there is no need
of a Theseus; and since the gods are to be invoked - if at
all - only obliquely and apologetically, there is no need
of a Creon.   These omissions speak for themselves.
     The tone of 'The Elder Statesman' cannot be described as
if it were something static.   As the play moves from oaths
to prayers it 'spits from the mouth the withered apple-
seed' and yearns toward the autumnal mellowness of the
great beech-tree at Badgley Court.   There is a place for
grey, bitter wit, but it would be a breach of decorum here
in the late afternoon near the beech-tree which is in the-
place-without-a-name at fair Colonus.   Perhaps it is also
'under the larches of Paradise'.   In any event, Eliot has
been graciously loyal to the Sophocles of 'Oedipus at
Colonus'; he has not bruised the late fruit, nor has he
hurt the moving spirit of consolation - Boethian also - in
which Oedipus proceeds on his last journey.   'The Elder
Statesman' is one of the few modern plays which move with
distinction in the realm of Perception.
     In this respect the play is an extension of 'The Family
Reunion', just as 'The Confidential Clerk' is a revised
version of 'The Cocktail Party'.   In this new version of
'The Family Reunion' the issues of the early play are re-
considered in a fresh attempt to accost that guilt-ridden
experience which has been in the shadows of Eliot's world
since before 'The Hollow Men'.   There may seem to be little
connexion between Harry Monchensey and Richard Claverton,
but if we seek an early figuring of the elder statesman do
we not find it in Harry's father, the man who hands on a
smoky inheritance to his son?   It is as if Eliot were to
bring Harry's father out of the shadows into the world
of human relationships, giving him another chance to redeem himself.   In his earlier world 'there was no ecstasy';
the elder Monchensey lived with his wife in a lonely
country house learning the meaning of loneliness.   It is a
fitting context for the awful privacy of Lord Claverton,

imprisoned in guilt and deception: 'only fear of the emptiness before me':

[Quotes 'The Elder Statesman', I, CPP, p. 530, 'But waiting, simply' to 'For nothing'.]

Lord Claverton and the elder Monchensey may not be one and
the same person but they are closer than mere participants
in the same black world; they share the same figure in the
carpet. The difference is that where the elder Monchensey
was doomed to the spectral existence of a 'presence' behind Harry's guilt-ridden life, in the new play he has
been granted a second chance to liberate himself from the
human wheel. When we speak of the 'humanity' of the new
play this is what we mean, that it offers a second chance
which we had been given no reason to expect.
     And of course 'The Elder Statesman' is a more humane
play than 'The Family Reunion', more humane, indeed, than
any of its predecessors. There are no longer any aunts
and uncles whom we can use as scapegoats, burdening them
with our guilt before we cast them off the rocks. There
is no longer a John Monchensey to whom we can bequeath a
rancid world, thereby exhibiting our own fine taste. Lord
Claverton and his Monica do not opt out of the human world
in their pursuit of latter-day felicity; there is in the
new play no urge to deny the integrity of the human world,
or to sell it short. It is a measure of the play's humanity that it preserves the finite world intact - through
Charles and Monica - more generously than 'The Cocktail
Party' or even 'The Confidential Clerk', and that it endorses no inevitable dichotomy between our everyday world
and the world of our most strenuous aspirations. Edward
and Lavinia from 'The Cocktail Party' have now been given
a second chance; as Charles and Monica they find at
Badgley Court a richer love than they were granted in
their London flat. Perhaps the enigmatic Julia was to
blame: she was a severe moralist:

     Everyone makes a choice, of one kind or another,
     And then must take the consequences. Celia chose
     A way of which the consequence was crucifixion;
     Peter Quilpe chose a way that takes him to Boltwell;
     And now the consequence of the Chamberlaynes' choice
     Is a cocktail party. They must be ready for it.
     Their guests may be arriving at any moment.

But Sir Henry Harcourt-Reilly was a little more yielding:

     You will have to live with these memories and make them

Into something new. Only by acceptance
Of the past will you alter its meaning.

and Edward interpreted this as saying 'that every moment
is a fresh beginning'. But Edward was not granted the
illumination of knowing the meaning of love. He could not
have glowed in the insight as Charles does when he says to
Monica:

And no future life is even conceivable
In which we should not be conscious of each other
And conscious of our loving....

The love of Charles and Monica is, among other things, a
mellow critique of the love of Edward and Lavinia, just as
it 'defines' the love which Colby and Lucasta sketched in
'The Confidential Clerk'.
    At the centre of all this is Lord Claverton's vision of
his world. This is the determining focus of the play. We
can understand it best, perhaps, if we chart its development, bearing in mind its earlier manifestations.
    The Ur-hero in Eliot's previous plays was the religious
man defining himself in a secular society. It was part of
Eliot's strategy - and part of the thin humanity of those
plays - to load the dice too heavily in the hero's favour.
Not content to exalt his hero as a man of outstanding
integrity, Eliot made the mistake of regarding as the
Enemy not only the avowedly irreligious factors in the
everyday world but that world itself, in its entirety, in
all its manifestations. Everything went into the same bin.
In the plays up to 'The Cocktail Party' the *scene* itself
was endowed with malignant motives. Hence the tendency of
those plays to denigrate the finite and to associate the
hero's aspirations with some esoteric Essence which demanded, as a prerequisite, that the finite world of
Matter and Body be sloughed off. But Lord Claverton's
role is new in at least one important respect. It is not
a case of a hero, a man of conscience and consciousness,
confronting a hostile *scene* - and then destroying it or
transcending it - but such a man confronting *himself*. The
'argument' of 'The Elder Statesman' is strikingly personal
and internal. The place of the scapegoat *scene* is now
taken by those factors of cowardice, 'prudence', and
emptiness which Lord Claverton sees in himself: he does not
put the blame on Society, or on Matter, or Body, or Nature,
or on any other capitalized malignity. There is no whine
in this play. Claverton does not say, as Harry said in
'The Family Reunion':

> It is not my conscience,
> Not my mind, that is diseased, but the world I have to
>   live in.

That is always an easy way out, at least provisionally, but
it is not available to Lord Claverton; to get to his great
beech-tree he must cut through his own deception.

This involves an act of moral choice, an unfashionable
procedure in modern drama, including Eliot's own. Bearing
in mind the ambiguous representation of such an act in 'The
Family Reunion' we should now acknowledge that 'The Elder
Statesman', penetrating similar experience, commits itself
firmly to the possibility of an individual moral act.
There comes a certain stage in 'The Elder Statesman' at
which Lord Claverton, like Harry Monchensey, decides not to
run away from his spectres; but Claverton's decision, unlike Harry's, issues unambiguously from his own resources
as an individual moral being. The new play asserts, as
clearly as anyone could wish and much more clearly than he
might have expected, that Man has the power of moral
choice, that he holds this power by virtue of his existence
and dignity as a human being, that the exercise of this
power is a matter of incalculable moment. When Monica
urges her father to escape from those obnoxious familiars
Federico Gomez and Mrs Carghill, he corrects her - as we
have seen - warning her that there is no escaping one's
self. This act of moral choice leads not to the conventional 'happy ending' - or to that only superficially -
but to the radical extension of the circumference of insight within which Lord Claverton interprets his world.
And in this new, wider circle there is a mellower place
even for such 'failures' as that of his severed relationship with his son. Michael's flight to San Marco represents the enormous risk attendant upon an act of moral
choice, but the risk is accepted graciously and incorporated into the new circle of interpretation. Lord Claverton, reciting a gentle lesson about reality and make-
believe, says:

> And Michael -
> I love him, even for rejecting me,
> For the *me* he rejected I reject also.
> I've been freed from the self that pretends to be
>   someone;
> And in becoming no one, I begin to live.

The key-word is Love; not indeed a new word even in the
spare landscape of Eliot's plays, but until now a word
used only with a certain embarrassment. 'The Elder

719 T.S. Eliot: The Critical Heritage

Statesman' offers the word with full, grave commitment as
the Meaning of Meanings. Eliot could have found the word
already with a rich meaning in 'Oedipus at Colonus', seiz-
ing it now as the definitive term, not so much correcting
what had gone before as acknowledging a more humane direction. Listing the key-terms of the early plays we have
Conscience, Consciousness, Understanding; and now Love.
And since this is the wisest of Eliot's plays the nature of
Love is defined not by a context of limp 'good deeds' but
by a genuinely won illumination, a flowering of insight
into the relation between reality and responsibility.
Eliot's new testament is endorsed by Love as the Term of
Terms within which all lesser terms find speech.

The words spoken in 'The Elder Statesman' are neither
diffident nor ostentatious; benign, chaste, more relaxed
than those of 'The Confidential Clerk', and more equable
in their partnerships. And it is significant that along
with the more humane version of experience represented in
'The Elder Statesman' there is a greater trust in the possibility of verbal communication. (This is offered at
least as a pious hope, and the gentleman's agreement still
holds; there are certain topics, certain names, which the
dramatist has undertaken not to mention, on pain of 'ex-
communication'.) There is a feeling in the new play that
if our words could only be supported by Love they need not
break under any burden thereafter:

[Quotes 'The Elder Statesman', III, CPP, p. 573, 'It's
hard to make' to 'of all people'.]

In 'The Family Reunion' there is nothing of this; Harry's
psychosis was intensified by the failure, the collapse,
of verbal communication. Agatha encouraged him to speak
in his own language without stopping to debate whether it
might be too far beyond the understanding of his audience;
and he made the attempt, without much assistance from
syntax:

[Quotes 'The Family Reunion', I, i, CPP, p. 294, 'The
sudden solitude' to 'discolouring the bone.']

But he fell back from this awful privacy of insight:

[Quotes 'The Family Reunion', I, i, CPP, p. 294, 'This is
what matters' to 'has no language'.]

Lord Claverton is more fortunate: directed by Love he
finds the words for the confessional act which he performs
in the presence of Monica and Charles. Hence we chart

the following terms, not as synonyms but as mutually en-
dorsing forces: Love, Speech, Communication, Understanding,
Illumination, Consciousness. Monica encompasses this ample
world of possibility when she refers to 'Love within which
all other love finds speech'; at this stage she has divined,
with Charles, that the felicity of one's private world
exists not as a secret place blocked off from the outer,
public world but as the consciousness of 'love unchanging'
in the integrity of the public world. The garden of Monica
and Charles - to speak of it in terms of 'The Confidential
Clerk' - is a part of one single world, its own reality
testifying to the reality of other things. It is a glowing
image to offset many rivalries, dichotomies, and sever-
ances. Lord Claverton's terms are an autumnal translation
of Monica's insight: he speaks of 'the peace that ensues
upon contribution', and 'the illumination of seeing what
love is'; again, 'I have been brushed by the wing of
Heaven'. This is luminous speech and there are luminous
acts, too, as when Lord Claverton says to his severed son,
'I shall never repudiate you, though you have repudiated
me.'

In 'The Elder Statesman' Eliot has stuck to his guns: he
has been scrupulously loyal to those insights which he has
been exploring in the theatre since 'The Family Reunion'.
To some the new play has seemed an 'ironic melodrama', perhaps a sequel to 'The Strange Boarders of Palace Crescent',
but this is to mistake the genre. Keeping before his mind
the development of Shakespeare's later plays, Eliot has
written, in 'The Elder Statesman', an 'ideal comedy' - the
term is Northrop Frye's (b) - gently drawing forth, from
an ambiguous situation, an image of communal order; order
based upon the acknowledgment of responsibility, in a
spirit of piety and love. The mood is optative rather than
indicative, and what the play envisages is not merely individual felicity but an idea of social harmony of which the
Claverton family - in its new circumference of insight -
represents a beautiful instance.
Eliot's problem - or so we conceive it - was to compose
a modern equivalent of 'The Tempest' or of 'Oedipus at
Colonus' - each would serve - while keeping adequately
close to the 'realistic' expectations of his audience.
Perhaps the solution emerged somewhat as follows: starting
with Lord Claverton's psychosis, Eliot broke it down into
its two conflicting parts - the 'negative' or sinister
part, which he divided between Gomez and Mrs Carghill, and
the 'positive', upward-striving part, which he reflected in
Monica and her Charles. Michael the erring son provided
the battleground. Lambert the butler was added to make the

Claverton home more substantial. Mrs Piggott was added
for several reasons; to insinuate the play's contact with
a world outside its windows, a world which, knowing nothing of Lord Claverton's problems, was nevertheless implicated in them; to offer comic relief in those moments in
which the situation might have gone soft; above all, by
providing - for the Clavertons - a local, innocuous dissatisfaction, to modulate between the much more sinister
distresses represented by Gomez and Mrs Carghill. These
are sound rhetorical reasons.

And indeed Eliot is a skilful rhetorician; this is conceded even by those who 'don't like' the later plays or
their 'answer' to the problem of communication in the
modern theatre. 'The Elder Statesman' may be cited as a
case in point: when a Mrs Piggott is required, Eliot is
quick to sense the need and to bring her on. But in one
respect - and that a serious one - he has erred as a
theatre-rhetorician: he has been niggardly in giving 'The
Elder Statesman' the climax for which it cries out. We
have already emphasized the significance of Lord Claverton's moral act: the entire play depends on it; but it
comes too easily. We are asked to acknowledge the soul-
stirrings, the agonizing torments which Lord Claverton
suffers, but we are shown little theatrical evidence of
their existence: a craggy, pained face; a few wise, sad
words; nothing more. Contrition here seems an easy thing,
hardly an 'act' at all, but it can hardly be so. Likewise, confession: it is as if the fears, the misgivings,
and the shame were suffered off-stage; Lord Claverton
enters, resigned, to tell his story to a gentle daughter.
No wonder, then, that we remember as the climax of the
play the moment in which Michael cries out to his father,
'What is my inheritance?' True, the moment is highly
charged, at once poignant and chilling, but it should be
no more than a prefiguring of Lord Claverton's own pained
appraisal. Perhaps Eliot was reluctant to risk injuring
the tone of his play by charging it here with the laments
of a disconsolate chimera; 'The Family Reunion' was a more
ample *genre* for this kind of thing. But even in 'ideal
comedy' a man does not tear himself apart without our hearing the noise.

This is the most serious defect in 'The Elder Statesman' and it injures the play as theatre-poetry. The central relationships, particularly the relationship between
Lord Claverton and his daughter, would be much more convincing if Lord Claverton were shown in agonized recognition of his own emptiness. Monica's answering love would
then seem a rich fulfilment rather than an unearned incre-
ment. Mrs Carghill and Federico Gomez would seem more

palpable servants of Satan. And the process of spiritual
regeneration would seem a truly heroic endeavour.
   Perhaps the fault lies in Monica's role. Gentle, and
'qualitatively' apt, yes, but she makes very little contribution to the play. In one scene in particular she fails
us entirely. Eliot was perhaps foolhardy in having Lord
Claverton confess his sins *twice* - once to us, then to
Monica - but he might have negotiated the hazard if he had
ensured that the second confession would be a *new thing*,
a new phase in the central relationship, or the uncovering
of resources in it beyond our expectation. If Monica had
received the confession with something more intense or
more individual than the elaborate recitation of *It's-
alright-daddy,-I-love-you-more-than-ever,* the scene might
have been saved. As it stands it merely repeats what we
already know, and it has nothing new to enact in the
relationship of father and daughter.

Notes

a   Kenneth Burke: 'The Philosophy of Literary Form'. New
    York. Vintage Books, 1957, p. 309.
b   Northrop Frye: A Conspectus of Dramatic Genres,
    'Kenyon Review', xiii, 4, Autumn, 1951, pp. 543-562.

177. NONA BALAKIAN, AFFIRMATION AND LOVE IN ELIOT, 'NEW
LEADER'

11 May 1959, vol. xlii, 20-1

Nona Balakian, an American critic, has written on modern
American fiction.

'It is my experience,' T.S. Eliot remarked in his 1940
lecture on Yeats, 'that toward middle age, a man has three
choices: to stop writing altogether, to repeat himself ...
or ... to adapt himself to middle age and find a different
way of working.' To do the last, he went on, means 'experiencing new emotions appropriate to one's age ... and
in which the feelings of youth are integrated.'

The 'different way of working' for Eliot since his own
middle years has been the theater. In the 24 years since
his 'Murder in the Cathedral' he has enriched the meager
repertory of modern poetic drama with plays which though
similar in theme, have shown progression and a capacity to
integrate all stages of his experience. At the age of 70,
he has written a new work which, if remote from the Eliot
of 'Prufrock' and the 'Four Quartets' (to mention the two
extremes of his style), unmistakably derives from the
Eliot of the early and middle years.

'The new emotion' he has experienced - love, earthly
love - appropriate at any age, is particularly right for
him now, in the light of his recent, happy marriage. It
can be no mere coincidence that this most serene work of
the elder poet is dedicated to his wife, 'To whom I owe
the leaping delight / That quickens my senses in our wak-
ingtime.'

Indeed, Eliot has confessed to a new hopefulness and
calm since his marriage. To his erstwhile defeatist question, 'Why should the agèd eagle stretch his wings?' Eliot
finds it possible in 'The Elder Statesman' to offer as
positive an answer as he has yet dared to give - and this
time in secular terms, which should pose no difficulties
for modern audiences. In the reading, it seems the inevitable coda to the evolving Divine Comedy of modern life
which Eliot's work as a whole suggests.

Eliot's plays, all written since his conversion to
Anglicanism in the late '20s, have depicted life as a
delusive ritual of appearances in which the essential
struggle is the liberation of the authentic self. Because
his religious and psychological insights have converged,
his meaning, even in such obviously religious plays as
'Murder in the Cathedral,' has never been simply doctrin-
aire. By identifying the religious concepts of contrition
and purgation with the psychoanalytical process involving
the social Persona and the real Self that lies below it,
he has found a new moral approach to character.

What has distinguished his heroes in the past has been
their capacity and willingness to suffer in the hope of
finding the elusive meaning of their existence. Stripped
of their masks, and vulnerable before their fate, they
have accepted the ultimate consequence: renunciation of
their social being and ordinary human relationships. To
suggest their susceptibility to intangible truths, Eliot
has not hesitated to use unrealistic devices such as
Tempters, ghosts and divine confessors in disguise. Mainly
through the mystical overtones of his poetry, he has persuaded us that these are of another order of human beings.

The fact that 'The Elder Statesman' is bare of such

devices is indicative that the demand on the hero has
greatly lessened. In Lord Claverton, the central character, the play has a considerably modified Eliot hero: an
aging public figure, condemned by ill health to retire,
Claverton has only a brief stop to make in his 'purgatory' before he is released from the burden of his
'guilt.' In a lifetime of riding on the high tide of
success, he has never been troubled by his conscience, and
it is only awakened on the eve of his retirement when by
accident he meets two figures from his remote past who remind him of moral failures in his youth. One, a former
Oxford classmate now turned into a cynical Central American businessman, draws a likely parallel between his own
fraudulent life and the statesman's; the other, an aging
musical comedy star, recalling how he had callously jilted
her, pricks his ego by observing:

    The difference between an elder statesman
    And posing successfully as an elder statesman
    Is practically negligible. And you look the part.

But Claverton does not sense his counterfeit image
until he is also confronted by his son, Michael, who protests that as the son of a famous father he has been
denied the right of realizing himself. In the midst of
advising Michael not to run away from his past failures,
Claverton has a sudden illumination about himself, and
growing humble, asks:

    Do I understand the meaning
    Of the lesson I would teach?

Turning to his daughter, Monica, he adds: 'Is it too late
for me?'
    Apparently it is not too late. For in the next act,
having confessed all his transgressions to Monica, Claverton has the courage and insight to acknowledge himself 'a
broken-down actor' who has never loved anyone. Yes, he
has loved Monica, 'but there's the impediment. / It is impossible to be quite honest with your child.'

    How could I be sure that she would love the actor
    If she saw him, off-stage, without
    His costume and his make-up.

Nor could he turn to his wife while she lived:

    How open one's heart
    When one is sure of the wrong response?

725 T.S. Eliot: The Critical Heritage

Only in the realization of Monica's steadfast love can he
finally accept himself. There is potential pathos in his
lines:

> If a man has one person, just one in his life
> To whom he is willing to confess everything...
> Then he loves that person and his love will save him -

In this concept of love as a catalyst in self-
realization, Eliot has come a long way from 'The Cocktail
Party,' where one encountered at every turn the counterfeit faces which lovers create to meet their own needs.

Although the religious implication in this new insight
is muted, the play unmistakably suggests the 'Paradiso'
episode of the poet's 'Divine Comedy.' For here, without
strife or suffering, and in the presence of a loving, for-
giving person, the penitent finds both freedom and bliss.

It is, perhaps, in the nature of a 'Paradiso' to lack
drama. But what adds to the static quality of the play is
a central character who is too abstractly conceived to be
anything more than a mouthpiece for the poet. And in the
absence of his 'special language,' Eliot's leaning toward
Victorian plotting is unhappily emphasized. But as philosophy it marks a turning-point. From the questioning
which began with 'Ash-Wednesday,' Eliot has moved on to an
affirmation which is essentially Dantesque.

178. HUGH KENNER, FOR OTHER VOICES, 'POETRY'

October 1959, vol. xcv, 36-40

Kenner (b. 1923), Professor of English at the Johns Hopkins University, has written extensively on the modernist
revolution in literature. His publications include 'The
Invisible Poet: T.S. Eliot' (1959) and 'The Pound Era'
(1972). He delivered the T.S. Eliot Memorial Lectures at
the University of Kent in 1975.

Mr. Eliot admits no actor to his intimacy. That is one
meaning of the marked change that pervades his verse when
he writes for the stage. His poems, he has nearly told
us, he conceives in some psychic center where the obscure

phatic sensations of his own voice take their origin.
When you are writing such poetry, 'The way it sounds when
you read it to yourself is the test,' and the sensation
of reading to yourself what you have written is permeated
by the way it feels to be speaking: larynx, lips, and
nameless intimate zones of feeling, all affirming, urging,
intertexturing their modulations of a fluid of sound, in a
prolonged ritual courtship of the silence which at last
closes round the utterance.

>   Revive for a moment a broken Coriolanus ...

Not the least of the pleasures such a line implies is the
pleasure of uttering it.

Shakespeare wrote plays in the same way; that is why he
never lacks willing actors to singe their wings in his
flame. He makes thrilling speaking; and often, difficult
hearing. But Eliot's plays reverse the premise not only
of Shakespeare's plays but of Eliot's poetry: they exist
not to be spoken but to be heard. It is true that others
besides the author will experiment with the sensations of
enunciating 'Gerontion' or 'The Waste Land,' but that is
per accidens. But that stage verse shall be spoken by
other people is the essential condition of its existence.
And Mr. Eliot's way of distinguishing and identifying his
characters seems inseparable from a reluctance to allow
any of them access to the central pleasure of enunciating
Eliotic verse. 'In a play,' he has said, 'you write for
other voices, and you do not know whose voices they will
be'; a truth, but one which did not intimidate Shakespeare, whose central act of sympathy was always with the
actor. Eliot is careful to keep his sympathies on this
side of the footlights; he writes (at least after 'Murder
in the Cathedral') on behalf of the audience, whose experience of the play is likely to be not merely more comprehensive than that of anyone on stage, but profounder.

There are small indications that the actor is even
fended off a little by the poet, when the poet has anything to do with the matter, as though the actor whose
vocal apparatus will caress these words constitutes in
some obscure way a threat, to be countered by mobilizing
Old Possum's whole repertory of courteous evasions. Miss
Alison Leggatt, whose responsibility it was to develop for
the first time the part of Mrs. Guzzard in 'The Confidential Clerk,' has recalled the producer's concern to admon-
ish the cast, before a rehearsal at which the author was
to be present, that they were on no account to ask the
author about the meaning of anything; and one or two perplexed spirits who could not forbear to disregard this

warning heard only his claim not to have the least idea.
Miss Leggatt was instructed that in playing Mrs. Guzzard
she was to combine Pallas Athene with a suburban house-
wife, and later received a copy of the play inscribed 'To
the Perfection of Guzzards'. Only Mr. Alec Guinness, who
brings to a part his own ritual of furtive detachment,
seems ever to have been conspicuously intimate with an
Eliot character, less by empathy than connaturality. It
is said that Rex Harrison played the same part in the London production of 'The Cocktail Party' as though baffled
by it, which may help explain 'The Cocktail Party's' relative unsuccess in London.

At the heart of each of the postwar plays lies a problem analogous with this disquieting freedom enjoyed by the
actors. Some mystery to which no one possesses the whole
key condemns everyone on stage to state with explicit can-
dor very little at a time. No obfuscation can be blamed
on the language they employ. It is the clearest verse
ever written, and every discernible poetic means assists
to make it clearer. Parallelisms explicate the structure
of long speeches, diamond-like precisions of diction
clinch shorter ones. A metric, not of recurrences but of
groupings, adjusts salient words to one another. Novelty
of metaphor is eschewed; symbols are absent; epithets do
not astonish but inform. The language of these plays is
upper-middle-class English colloquial speech, raised from
badinage to system. We have only to listen for five minutes to the admirable English cast speaking 'The Cocktail
Party' on the Decca recordings to see how intimate is the
phrasing of the verse with that of English talk: its run
has nothing in common with the deliberate unemphatic
phrasing of any spoken American. It is not 'prosaic'; its
system of communicating is unlike that of prose, which
appeals to shared meanings and agreed areas of understanding. The verse of 'The Elder Statesman,' like the language of Euclid, is coolly adequate to anything that requires saying. Spoken prose is never quite adequate to
what it is saying: hence its ritual of unfinished sentences, gesturing hands, meeting eyes.

'The Elder Statesman' begins with badinage modulating
into a love scene:

Monica: How did this come, Charles? It crept so softly
    On silent feet, and stood behind my back
    Quietly, a long time, a long long time
    Before I felt its presence....

Before long the world of the lovers offsets the loveless
world of Monica's father, The Elder Statesman, whose

speech (we are to listen, not doze between rhetorical
thrills) has a kind of bloodless adequacy because he is a
ghost:

> Perhaps I've never really enjoyed living
> As much as most people. At least, as they seem to do,
> Without knowing that they enjoy it. Whereas I've often
>   known
> That I didn't enjoy it.

That is the way Lord Claverton talks. It is 'poetry' by
no definition but this one, that it embodies the exact
meaning that requires embodying, at this point in this
fable. The same is true of this ghost's conversation with
one of the ghosts who return from his past:

> Lord Claverton: Why should I feel embarrassment? My con-
>   science was clear.
>   A brief infatuation, ended in the only way possible
>   To our mutual satisfaction.

> Mrs. Carghill: Your conscience was clear.
>   I've very seldom heard people mention their consciences
>   Except to observe that their consciences were clear.
>   You got out of a tangle for a large cash payment
>   And no publicity. So your conscience was clear.
>   At bottom, I believe you're the same silly Richard
>   You always were. You wanted to pose
>   As a man of the world. And now you're posing
>   As what? I presume, as an elder statesman;
>   And the difference between being an elder statesman
>   And posing successfully as an elder statesman
>   Is practically negligible. And you look the part.
>   Whatever part you've played, I must say you've always
>   looked it.

This extraordinary explicitness isn't making a point of
throwing cards on the table, or dramatizing its own can-
dor; it is simply a function of the language Eliot gives
characters to speak in the most matter-of-fact way. Mrs.
Carghill neither *wields* this talk nor is subsumed by it;
she utters it and is detached from it. A Lear, a Cassius,
an Antony, by being preternaturally articulate becomes a
function of the capacity of the English language for expressiveness: an upwelling: an overflow: anything, in fact,
but an embodiment of human privacy articulating what it
chooses to articulate. One cannot conceive of a silent
Othello, and Cordelia's silences are a mode of speech; but
Lord Claverton and Mrs. Carghill have their reticences and

their blighted areas.

The tension of 'The Elder Statesman,' in fact, is located in the very idea of human privacy. It is a tension between privacies of two sorts: the sort which withholds itself behind a rôle and one day withers into a ghost -

> If I've been looking at this engagement book, to-day,
> Not over breakfast, but before tea,
> It's the empty pages that I've been fingering -
> The first empty pages since I entered Parliament.

- and the blessed sort which can give itself into communion with another person precisely because it *is* a privacy, a self, a serene personal entity, this and not an interfering determination to make its existence felt. 'I've been freed,' Lord Claverton sums up a few minutes before the end of the play,

> ...from the self that pretends to be someone;
> And in becoming no one, I begin to live.
> It is worth while dying, to find out what life is.

Then the lovers, Charles and Monica, close the play as they opened it:

> Monica: We will go to him together. He is close at hand,
>   Though he has gone too far to return to us.
>   He is under the beech tree. It is quiet and cold there.
>   In becoming no one, he has become himself.
>   He is only my father now, and Michael's.
>   And I am happy. Isn't it strange, Charles,
>   To be happy at this moment?

The play's form is as simple as mediaeval music: a precarious compromise between something as sparely intimate as 'At the Hawk's Well' and the innocent pretensions of a formal theatre. The actors who can combine the authority and self-effacement it demands are to be found, one supposes, in some ideal world not very different from ours but less avid of brilliance. The work will never attract Mr. Elia Kazan. Mr. Eliot can be forgiven if he doesn't much care. He has written, perhaps under the illusion that he was serving a theatre that exists, the most intimate of his works, so much so that the lyric dedication of the book to his wife is perfectly in keeping. That drama is the most personal of forms is one way of stating this play's theme. As Lord Claverton was able to enter into reality only through others, through a daughter he had hitherto tried

to keep to himself, a son he had constrained, and a former
lover he had allowed to be bought off, so his poet is set
free from the lyric flame by writing for other voices, not
knowing whose voices they will be.

'Collected Poems 1909-1962'

London, 25 September 1963; New York, 26 September 1963

179. DONALD DAVIE, MR ELIOT, 'NEW STATESMAN'

11 October 1963, vol. lxvi, 496-7

Davie (b. 1922), a British poet, critic and teacher, is
Professor of English at Vanderbilt University. He
published his 'Collected Poems' in 1972. Among his critical studies are 'Purity of Diction in English Verse'
(1952), 'Articulate Energy' (1955), 'Ezra Pound: Poet as
Sculptor' (1965) and 'Thomas Hardy and British Poetry'
(1972). He is one of the editors of 'PN Review'.

This review was reprinted in Donald Davie, 'The Poet in
the Imaginary Museum: Essays of Two Decades', edited by
Barry Alpert (1977), pp. 117-21.

In 1928, introducing Pound's 'Selected Poems', Mr Eliot
protested against 'those who expect that any good poet
should proceed by turning out a series of masterpieces,
each similar to the last, only more developed *in every
way*'. On the contrary, he went on, though 'it may be only
once in five or ten years that experience accumulates to
form a new whole and finds its appropriate expression',
yet, to be ready for these accumulations when they come,
the poet has to keep in training 'by good workmanship on a
level possible for some hours' work every week of his
life'. And the implication is that the poet has the right
to publish some of these practice pieces. Pound has taken
advantage of this right perhaps outrageously; Mr Eliot
seems not to have taken advantage of it at all.

What is striking all over again, leafing through his

poems, is how little he needs to enter the plea. Not that
each of his poems is a masterpiece, nor that he has advanced simultaneously on every front. The second collection, 'Poems 1920', advances beyond the 'Prufrock' volume
of 1917 in very few ways, and in many ways is a falling-
off. 'A Cooking Egg', for instance, deserves nothing much
better than the fate which has come upon it - of being the
occasion for a protracted critical wrangle; and in 'Gerontion' the relation between poet and persona is far more
fluctuating and frustratingly evasive than in 'The Love
Song of J. Alfred Prufrock'. All the same, if we think of
Mr Eliot putting in a few hours' work each week of his
life, we boggle, appalled, at the sheaf on sheaf that must
have been destroyed, and at the austere self-control which
decided time and again what, and how little, should be
preserved.

The extraordinary fact is, surely, that Mr Eliot has
published between hard covers not a single poem which he
now needs to blush about reprinting. This is a fantastic
achievement; an achievement not of poetry (for greater
poets have not proceeded like this and we don't think any
worse of them), but of judgment, taste, self-knowledge,
self-control. We are not prepared for this rigour of
self-criticism in poets. In 'Poems 1909-1935', and again
now, Mr Eliot consigns to the austere category, 'Minor
Poems', such exquisite pieces as 'Cape Ann' and 'Rannoch,
by Glencoe'; and one's admiration for them quails and
stammers before the conclusiveness of his deprecation.
And in the new collection, which gathers into the major
canon only the belated Ariel poem, 'The Cultivation of
Christmas Trees', I similarly want to rescue 'A Note on
War Poetry' from the rubric, 'Occasional Verses', which
stands over five uncollected poems of wartime and since.
If, reluctantly, we set aside the poems herded into these
carefully subordinated categories (one is called, explicitly, 'Five-Finger Exercises'), what we have from Mr
Eliot is pretty much what he said in 1928 that we could
not expect from any one - the accumulations of five or
ten years at a time, conclusively discharged in one considered poem or group of poems, with no near-misses, no
ranging shots, no labour-pains, no afterbirth.

What's particularly remarkable is the way in which the
poems and the critical essays are sealed off from each
other. The variously cock-eyed or idiosyncratic readings
of cultural history which in Pound lay waste whole areas
of the Cantos, which in Yeats infect past redemption a
poem like 'The Statues' - these appear in Mr Eliot's
essays without once spilling into his poetry. Now that
many of the essays, having served their vast polemical

purpose, seem dated or out-dated, the poems soar on completely undamaged. The criticism never fitted the poems
anyhow. And more and more it looks as if it couldn't fit
because it tried to assemble, using only English products,
a reader's kit which needed, to be serviceable, many tools
of foreign and especially French manufacture. From 'Prufrock' to 'Little Gidding' is a movement from Laforgue to
Valéry; the body of poetic theory which illuminates and
explains it is not in Mr Eliot's essays nor anywhere else
in English, but in French. Comically, of recent years
we've been detecting in this professed classicist, this
admirer of Donne and Dryden and Johnson, elements which we
call Tennysonian. Is this to find Mr Eliot out? Hardly.
His is a late-Romantic sensibility, and the poems are late-
Romantic poems. Written when they were, how could they be
anything else? In particular, how could they have escaped
the late-Romantic ambition, which according to Valéry over-
rode all else in French *symbolisme*, the will to make poetry
approach the condition of music? They did not escape this
ambition, in the end they realised it - as the title, 'Four
Quartets', triumphantly declares.

Normally literature lives in two times at once. 'I
wandered lonely as a cloud' lives in the time which we
take to speak it, rhythmically shaping that time as we
read; but it lives also in the imagined time which Wordsworth took on the walk he is telling us about. Music on
the contrary lives in only one time, the time it takes for
its performance, time which it shapes as we listen. One
way to make poetry into music is to collapse the two times
of literature into the one time of music, by making the
poem refer to no time except the time it takes in the
reading; and this means making the only events in the
poem be the happening of its constituent words as one by
one they rise and explode on our consciousness. Thus, in
'The Love Song of J. Alfred Prufrock':

Shall I say, I have gone at dusk through narrow streets
And watched the smoke that rises from the pipes
Of lonely men in shirt sleeves, leaning out of
    windows?...

I should have been a pair of ragged claws
Scuttling across the floors of silent seas.

This is Prufrock's poem: everything he says before or after
this in Eliot's poem isn't Prufrock's poem but only talk
about it, mostly about the impossibility of writing it.
This is Prufrock's poem, or as much of it as he was able
to stammer out. He got even so far with it only because

he took himself by surprise. 'Shall I say...' what? And
of course in saying what he has to say, he says it. The
eventfulness of language is on him before he is prepared,
the future tense ('Shall I say') is overtaken by the present tense of verbal happenings, much too fast for him to
control. Suddenly language is happening through him. And
before he can gather his wits (which is to say, his crip-
pling self-consciousness), the language carries him beyond
what he meant to say, into saying what he didn't know he
wanted to say, didn't know he had it in him to say:

> And watched the smoke that rises from the pipes
> Of lonely men in shirt-sleeves, leaning out of
>   windows?...

For this moment Prufrock, as he steps cat-like but with
mounting apprehension through the 'certain half-deserted
streets' of the poem's own maundering development, is suddenly carried out of himself, to feel that others exist
besides himself, to pity the loneliness of others even as
he pities his own loneliness. This is the moment when the
Ancient Mariner, seeing the sea-serpents, 'blessed them
unaware' - but with this difference, that the unawareness
isn't stated but takes place before us, as a verbal event,
Just because, in asking, 'Shall I say such a thing?' such
a thing gets said, language can take us unawares, blurting
out precisely what we were wondering about perhaps not saying at all. To compare that moment in Coleridge's poem
with this moment in Eliot's is to compare Romantic poetry
with late-Romantic or *symboliste* poetry, poetry like
music with poetry that aspires to *be* music.
    An effect like this appears to correspond to what
Mallarmé demanded, in translation by Symons:

> The pure work implies the elocutionary disappearance
> of the poet, who yields place to the words, immobilised
> by the shock of their inequality; they take light from
> mutual reflection ... replacing the old lyrical affla-
> tus or the enthusiastic personal direction of the
> phrase.

It is language which happens through the speaker, not the
speaker who expresses himself through language. And this
seems to have been what Mr Eliot was groping for when he
talked about impersonality in his essay, Tradition and the
Individual Talent. If so, he made a bad botch of it, for
instead of talking about impersonality as a poetic effect,
a valuable illusion, he talked about the psychology of
artistic creation, and has rightly been taken to task for

735 T.S. Eliot: The Critical Heritage

seeming to advance the quite unbelievable proposition that
the quality of an artist's products has nothing to do with
the richness or poverty of the artist's emotional life at
times when he isn't composing.

Yeats also knew this tag of Mallarmé and echoes it in
early essays. But as soon as he decided that actor and
orator were nearer to the poet than the musician could be
(and this he did explicitly in his Abbey Theatre years),
Yeats was committeed to precisely that 'enthusiastic personal direction of the phrase' which Mallarmé condemned.
And this is why, later, Donne could be a strong immediate
influence on Yeats as he could not be on Mr Eliot. It
means too, so far as I can see, that Yeats's connection
with French *symboliste* poetry had to be altogether looser
and more remote than Mr Eliot's.

It is only with 'Four Quartets' that we reach the logical conclusion of this line of speculation and experiment.
There, just as the only happenings in the poem are the
occurrences of its own words, so the poetry talks about
nothing but itself, continually gnawing its own vitals -
though, language being what it is, it can be argued that
poems which talk only about their own language by that
token talk about everything else. How this can be we see
foreshadowed in many places in 'The Waste Land'. For
instance:

> At the violet hour, when the eyes and back
> Turn upward from the desk, when the human engine waits
> Like a taxi throbbing waiting,
> I Tiresias, though blind, throbbing between two lives,
> Old man with wrinkled female breasts, can see
> At the violet hour, the evening hour that strives
> Homeward, and brings the sailor home from sea,
> The typist home at teatime, clears her breakfast, lights
> Her stove, and lays out food in tins.

This is a sentence, grammatically flawless, which is
nevertheless designed to trap the reader more than once.
'I Tiresias ... can see (at the violet hour, that is to
say, the evening hour...) the typist.' But in this case,
there is no subject for the next verbs, no one left to
clear the breakfast, light the stove, lay out tins. So,
when we get to 'clears her breakfast', we make a rapid
retrospective revision, and pretend that what we read from
the first was 'I Tiresias ... can see ... *the evening
hour*'. In this way we get a subject for the later verbs
because we make it the evening hour which, besides striving homeward etc., also clears breakfasts, lights stoves,
lays out tins. But of course 'clears' and 'lights' follow

'the typist' too closely for us not to think that it's
still she who does the clearing, the lighting, the laying
out. Because in this way we have to revise our expectations continually as the sentence unfolds, the effect is
that the typist is both an object of two distinct verbs
(of Tiresias's seeing and the evening hour's bringing) and
also the subject of 'clears her breakfast'.

When we turn the page and come upon her pathetically
squalid seduction, we see the point of all this: for she
has not chosen to surrender, but has permitted time and
the circumstances to make the choice for her. It is,
indeed, the evening hour that has done everything, even
to seducing her. And (this is the point) we are made to
feel that it is in the very structure of language that
this should be so. This is why the syntax has to be flawlessly correct. When we had to revise our notions of how
the sentence was going, we also, and by that very token,
revised our notion of how people are free agents. It is
language that trapped us into our wrong notions, and it is
language that makes us put them (dejectedly) right. It is
language that does this, not the speaker manipulating language to his own purposes. (Tiresias helps because, being
bi-sexual, he is as a speaker unimaginable.)

In an important sense we, the poets of now, have nothing to learn from Mr Eliot. There is no following him
down the roads he has taken because he has been right to
the end of them himself, once and for all. As Dryden
said of Shakespeare, he has laid waste his whole territory
simply by occupying it so conclusively. We can learn from
a poet so different as Yeats, and a poet so imperfect as
Pound, in a way we cannot learn from Mr Eliot. The one
lesson he might teach us - of inhuman accuracy and self-
control in publishing only those poems we need never be
sorry for - this we shall never learn because the lesson
is too hard.

180. JOHN FREDERICK NIMS, GREATNESS IN MODERATION, 'SATUR-
DAY REVIEW'

19 October 1963, vol. xlvi, 25-7

Nims (b. 1913), educated at the universities of Notre Dame
and Chicago, is a teacher and writer. His publications
include 'The Poems of St John of the Cross' (1959) and

'Sappho to Valéry: Poems in Translation' (1971). He received the American Academy for Arts and Sciences award
for creative writing in 1968.

Published last month on the occasion of T.S. Eliot's
seventy-fifth birthday, the new 'Collected Poems 1909-
1962,' shows only trivial changes in already published
work. A period tidies up the syntax toward the end of
'Gerontion,' though there is something to be said for the
earlier flurry of words. The line 'Views of the Oxford
Colleges' has lost its 'the.' Those cat things are
omitted. Sweeney himself must have set up the Greek:
there are four brutal errors in as many lines.

A handsome volume, 'Collected Poems' represents the
work of half a century. During that time Eliot has loomed
above our landscape like an Everest, his crags and glaciers
crawling with explicators who have chipped their way to the
top, or sometimes, dazed by the rarer air, gone clear beyond the top and on into the 'circumambient gas.' Eliot
himself warns us against ranking contemporary poets: the
most we can say is that they are genuine. Well, he is genuine: no molehill. If asked what contemporary poets he out-
ranks, we would have to say: just about all of them.

It is true he has written nothing so thrilling as 'Le
Cimetière Marin'; nothing so richly varied, so deeply
thought and felt as the 'Duineser Elegien.' He cannot hold
a candle to Yeats. Frost concealed a profounder art with
greater artistic cunning, and, using less, did more.
Cummings, Stevens, Thomas, and probably others, though
their eminence is less imposing, have written finer poems.
Even on a diamond jubilee, it would be vain to pretend
that Mr. Eliot is without defect. 'There is a large class
of persons,' he once said, 'including some who appear in
print as critics, who regard any censure upon a "great"
writer as a breach of the peace ... or even hoodlumism.'
If we find his own achievement straitened, he has anticipated us with mention of his 'meagre poetic gifts.' Distinguished in many fields, he should perhaps be considered
more writer than poet, more man of letters than writer.
We might even describe him as he described Matthew Arnold:
'in some respects the most satisfactory man of letters of
his age.'

As such, he will not be dishonored if we suggest that
his pre-eminence is neither of such kind nor so great as
earlier admirers believed. My impression has been that he
is less respected among poets than among non-poets, those
who seek not literature but certain impurities that may be

found with it: culture or religion, or the social sciences.

Ezra Pound, sending 'Prufrock' off to Miss Monroe, called Eliot 'the only American I know of who has made what I can call adequate preparation for writing.... It is such a comfort to meet a man and not have to tell him to wash his face, wipe his feet, and remember the date (1914) on the calendar.' And, in 1914, 'Prufrock' must have seemed a bright and trenchant manifesto. News from where people were living. Or partly living.

But it has not been 1914 for a long time now. The question is: how does Eliot look among the immortals, to whose company he has been promoted? A little drab, perhaps, next to his favorites. A little prim next to Dante. A little colorless next to Villon, or Donne, or Marvell, who did not have world enough; next to Blake or Baudelaire or the wild old wicked man; next to Valéry who, facing his brilliant void with no consoling creed, could still cry out 'Debout! Dans l'ère successive!'; or next to Rilke, who transcended the worst in a glory of *Jubel und Ruhm*.

If the range of experience is between ecstasy and agony, with boredom at the center, Eliot has hovered midway. When he vacillates it is downward; if not in shantih-town he haunts the dumps and doldrums. What we miss is the exhilaration of great poetry, which even if it deals with what is weary, stale, flat, and unprofitable, even if it calls on us to absent ourselves from felicity or leave all hope behind, persuades us that we are larger, more alive than we thought. But we hardly enter Eliot's world without shrinking a bit, without being aware of carbuncles and falling hair, without drawing our coats a little closer about narrowing shoulders. There are wistful visions of a loveliness out of reach, lost or renounced or adrift on allegory. There is much antique charm in 'Ash-Wednesday,' much luxurious music in the tell-tale anaphoras of 'Prufrock,' many images bright as lenses, though most of them diminish rather than magnify. The very things that depress Eliot, Yeats sees as a splendid challenge. The one prepares 'a face to meet the faces that you meet'; the other exults:

> Put off that mask of burning gold
> With emerald eyes.

The one, in an account of the gifts reserved for age, concludes with

> the rending pain of re-enactment
> Of all that you have done, and been; the shame
> Of motives late revealed ...

The other glories:

> I am content to live it all again
> And yet again ...

When Eliot quotes St. John of the Cross, he quotes only
what is negative; one would never guess that love and
ecstasy were St. John's goal, nor that what he saw in the
world was the shimmer of infinity. Exhilaration, a sense
of increased life, is the theme and effect of his work.
So with all great poetry, even the most tragic. Eliot,
however, woos the lugubrious. I am closer to his beliefs,
if not their spirit, than to those of Wallace Stevens, yet
'Sunday Morning' involves and enchants; Mr. Eliot's devo-
tions are a bore, obtruding and exhorting, button-holing
us with 'Redeem the time' and so forth.

Even in hell Dante found nobility. But how many handsome characters can we recall from the whole range of
Eliot's poetry? Yeats's great lover Hanrahan is a hero;
Sweeney, squatting on his hams, is a slob; Yeats, thinking
of a woman, notes 'the fire that stirs about her, when she
stirs'; Eliot detects in Grishkin a catlike smell and
makes a joke about breasts. Perhaps such is his triumph:
his world of grotesques is 'distorted to scale,' as he said
of Tourneur's; it constitutes in its intensity a unique
vision of life, possibly something like a 'mystical experience' of human mediocrity.

Nor does Eliot's technique quite exhilarate. He is a
fine metrist, but not an exciting one; for all his freedom,
he sounds more like Debussy's metronome than like a human
heart. We miss the rough-and-tumble between meter and
rhythm that we get in Donne, or, differently, in Frost.
His diction is not stirring; it is merely impeccable; a
certain lack of character is shown by the fact that it
translates so easily. We can imagine 'Let us go then,
you and I ...' without loss in any of several languages, as
we cannot imagine 'Suddenly I saw the cold and rook-
delighting heaven ...' or 'Back out of all this now too
much for us....'

Is 'Prufrock,' written fifty years ago, really the
'portrait satire on futility' that Pound thought? Or
something else? Perhaps a dramatic lyric of the swooning
psyche, half-relishing, in those sensuous rhythms and
langorous sentences, its own self-immolation? Whatever
it is, it made sense against the hated 'cheerfulness,
optimism, and hopefulness' of the nineteenth century. It
makes sense today: anyone who has 'taught' the poem knows
it as a bonanza to students who little expected such fun.
If a poem is indeed, as Valéry said, a machine made out of

words, this is a sleek, ingenious, fine-running contrap-
tion. It has a few bugs (it shrinks people), but it comes
equipped with many shiny inventions. Consider that most
celebrated image of modern poetry, as Donne's compass
image is the most celebrated of his school:

>   the evening is spread out against the sky
>   Like a patient etherized upon a table.

An evening pale, still hushed like a thing asleep. But to
Prufrock's neurotic sensibility not naturally asleep. No
'sweet dreams and health and quiet breathing.' Asleep as
Prufrock's will was asleep - for he projects his moods on
nature as we all do. A morbid and enforced sleep, a para-
lysis with the prognosis unfavorable. Eliot had to find a
visual image *like* the sky; he had to find one true to his
state of mind and way of seeing; had to find it in modern
life, not in the tradition. It had to be in key with the
laboratory image of the bug pinned to the wall, the ana-
tomical slide of the nervous system. What he finds is
perfectly apt: simple, shocking, with that sense of surprise that Poe, as Eliot reminds us, demanded of poetry.
'Prufrock' indeed gives pleasure. Yet if it represents
the 'greatest emotional intensity of our time,' as Eliot
says it is the poet's business to do, the worse for us.
  And what of 'The Waste Land,' for decades one of our
favorite parlor games? The poet himself ridiculed the
'bogus scholarship' of the 'Notes' which keep us from
reading it as the moving poem it can be. Since Eliot gave
the cue, everyone gets into the act. (Anyone noticed that
every word in

>   The barges drift
>   With the turning tide
>   Red sails ...

occurs on the first page of 'Heart of Darkness'? etc.)
'April is the cruellest month...,' one remembers how different - ahah! - Aprille was for Chaucer, and how, for
Malory, just as flowers burgeon in spring, so 'every lusty
harte that ys ony maner of lover ... buddyth, and floryssh-
yth in lusty dedis.' Ironic contrast. Or one turns to
Frazer's sonorous periods on 'the spectacle of the great
changes which annually pass over the face of the earth,'
and sniffs at those who go south in the winter or call for
a closed car if it rains. Even enemies of the poem must
concede its propaedeutic value. But it has more: there are
wryly beautiful growths on the sandflats:

> Out of her window perilously spread
> Her drying combinations touched by the sun's last
>   rays ...

Lines no less richly 'poetic,' no less evocative, than

> Charmed magic casements, opening on the foam
> Of perilous seas, in fairy lands forlorn.

I would even defend the logic (not the poetry) of Eliot's
breaking the language barrier at the end, particularly
since, by evoking the insane Hieronymo, he admits that his
seems a voice not only out of cisterns and exhausted
wells, but out of the madhouse itself. Imagery is vivid,
diction simple, rhythm persuasive. Why then regard the
poem as the Rosetta Stone of our civilization? Why go
picking over its picturesque desert, nose to the ground,
intent on 'meaning'? Why not take it merely as the scary
incantation it ought to be? The commentators, all over
the place, make it hard for us. And the poet does, too,
for the reproving figure of 'Mr. Eliot' is perhaps his
most convincing creation. With that sharp-nosed ghost at
our shoulder, it seems *lèse-majesté* to read for fun, even
though he said - said it himself! - that the first function of poetry is to give pleasure.

'Earnest, earthless, equal, attuneable' - the opening
of Hopkins's sonnet describes 'Ash-Wednesday,' again best
taken as incantation. A key to its defect is in the opening echo - a translation of Cavalcanti, dying in prison:
'Because I have no hope of ever returning to Tuscany, a
little song, go to my lady and say...' The original is
about a girl and a place; Eliot uproots the line, floats
it in ruminative good plays with its meaning, makes it
rhyme with a tag from another poem. The girl is gone and
the earth is gone; we are left dangling in the vast inane,
perhaps musing on Eliot's remark that 'A man does not join
himself with the Universe so long as he has anything else
to join himself with.'

The same slackened grip on the physical shows in 'Four
'Quartets.' Eliot has become a self-disparaging Prufrock
on Parnassus; what is a critic to do when a poet shrugs:
'The poetry does not matter'? Much does not, for it comes,
here, from an almost disembodied voice. There are no
people in this floating world: some dancing wraiths who
speak Middle English, a corpse in the river, Krishna and
Arjuna, a composite ghost out of Dante. What few concrete
objects there are lie askew in a cold aspic of abstractions. Instead of finding his image, his 'objective correlative,' instead of *trattando l'ombre come cosa salda,*

Eliot reverts to what may have been the manner of his
Ph.D. thesis: 'It seems, as one becomes older, that the
past has another pattern, and ceases to be mere sequence -
or even development: the latter a partial fallacy, encouraged by superficial notions of evolution, which becomes, in the popular mind, a means of disowning the
past....' This is the kind of writing that Gerontion,
with his failing senses, might have managed; no way of
printing it makes it 'poetry.' Or Eliot is slackly adjec-
tival: within eight lines *tumid, cold, unwholesome, un-
healthy, faded, torpid, gloomy*. How slowly he moves can
be seen by looking at

> The river is within us, the sea is all about us;
> The sea is the land's edge also, the granite
> Into which it reaches, the beaches where it tosses
> Its hints of earlier and other creation ...

and recalling Yeats:

> Once more the storm is howling, and half hid
> Under this cradle-hood and coverlid
> My child sleeps on ...

'To get *beyond poetry*, as Beethoven, in his later work,
strove to get *beyond music*,' Eliot once said, is 'the
thing to try for.' The quartets, in trying to go beyond
poetry, beyond humanity, have simply gone apart from both.
This longing for beyondness is quixotic: like wishing to
live without a body. Music is already sensuous, if it
exists. But language can send us directly to abstraction;
it is no more spiritual for being colorless. Still, for
those who find it possible to be happy with their feet off
the ground, the quartets are probably the best abstract
ruminative verse ever written.

Ours is an age, Eliot tells us, of moderate virtue and
of moderate vice. Recalling certain horrors of the time,
and certain men and women who defied them, we may refuse
to share this opinion. But for the age, as he sees it,
Eliot may well have provided the appropriate spokesman.
A great poet, yes. But a moderately great one.

181. FRANK KERMODE, READING ELIOT TODAY, 'NATION' (NEW YORK)

26 October 1963, vol. cxcvii, 263-4

'Little Gidding,' which was published in the dark middle
of the war, concluded not only the 'Four Quartets' but
Mr. Eliot's poetical career (or so it seems). The
British, who value stability in their immortals, decided
that nobody would ever again accuse him of raving like a
drunken helot - a charge leveled against him in 'The Waste
Land' days - and in 1948 gave him the Order of Merit,
which is certainly the highest honor to be had by British
men of letters. Mr. Eliot at sixty (Nobel laureate, royalist, Anglo-Catholic, O.M.) had seen his lifetime's effort
crowned. His life had taken a course curiously different
from those of his old friends and co-plotters, Pound and
Wyndham Lewis.
     Now he is seventy-five, and to mark the occasion there
is a new edition of the 'Collected Poems.' Since 'Little
Gidding' there have been six poems, mostly occasional in
character and of no great importance; but this is an obvious moment for interested parties to overhaul their views
on the most famous living poet. His personal standing in
the English world of letters is high and steady; maybe he
attracts some dislike as a pillar of the Establishment,
but, rather characteristically, you find that in speaking
of him you use that term in a purer sense than it nowadays
has in the language of the tribe. His opinions on the
poetry of the past and the theoretical basis of his own
poetic are increasingly subject to question, but an extraordinarily high proportion of useful modern debate origin-
ates in them. As to his views on other matters, they are
sometimes found, in the words of Northrop Frye, 'fantastic'
or 'repellent.' For example, he is an imperialist, though
in a weirdly pure sense that Dante would have commended and
that Mr. Krushchev can afford to ignore. He is a tradi-
tionalist who invented his tradition. He thinks it impossible to be civilized and at the same time non-Christian,
to live in a period of social mobility and enjoy a culture
of any merit; but he writes plays for the benefit of heretics who disagree on this, and who continue to regard him
as one of the major expressions of their impossible
civility.
     'Modern poetry' still connotes Eliot, and 'The Waste
Land' is still, after forty years, a modern poem, if only
because 'Modern' has partly turned into a periodic

concept, like 'Baroque.' But although the poem has kept
so much of its original power to surprise and delight first
readers, the critical campaign which accompanied it, and
provided theoretical justifications, is probably no longer
much of a force. We don't see Eliot in quite the relation
to the past that he proposed; in fact, it is becoming a
commonplace that he belongs in the Romantic tradition he
so excoriated. Without contesting the fineness and authority of the early essays, one may have doubts about many of
the doctrines proposed: the dissociation of sensibility,
the objective correlative. Then there is the matter of Mr.
Eliot's learning. Of course he is a learned man; but he
himself authorizes skepticism concerning the notes to 'The
Waste Land,' and as a poet he seems rather a subtle preda-
tor on learning than a curious and universal scholar.

The technical devices first used in 'The Waste Land' are
now matters for cool historical explanation; the attempt to
give literature a spatial instead of a temporal mode by
simultaneous presentation or time-defeating juxtapositions
of image is largely a matter for historians who might
think it only the last important incursion of painting
(Cubism) into the domain of poetry. And although I've said
the fresh reader can still feel a shock of recognition on
meeting it for the first time, it remains true that Eliot's
early poetry is classic as well as modern; rhetoricians
have perfected ways of expounding it which are in daily
use in a hundred classrooms. You could make it seem that
Eliot is already fading into literary history, a kind of
late Great Victorian.

So whoever acquires this handsome book should try to
forget the ritual responses of the classroom: read it as if
you'd never seen the poems before and certain facts which
nobody mentions emerge as still true. For instance, 'The
Waste Land' is a damned difficult poem. Also, it was and
is obviously good even if you don't know what it means, or
spot the quotations from Dante and Baudelaire, or see the
point of the Sanskrit. The first readers must have seen
the 'Unreal City' passage, or the passage on Philomel in
'A Game of Chess,' as absolutely original and beautiful
blank verse. As to the whole thing, they were simply bewildered, yet - one supposes - not without confidence that
fuller understanding would come. For though it can be
argued that this is not so much a poem as a sequence of
poems, there *is* a sense of unity - below the level of
explanations - and it is available now as it was then,
when the most knowledgeable reader had only 'Gerontion' to
guide him.

'Ash-Wednesday,' written at the point in Eliot's career
when he began to lose the support of some who mistook their

own misunderstanding for some sort of desertion on his
part, remains, as it ought, a very mysterious poem. But
if you read the third part (for instance) freshly, you
have the sense of living in an unfamiliar but coherent
world whose geometry you will happily learn.   It is an
accurate world, like that of the 'Four Quartets.' Those
great poems are not uniformly successful; but they are
full of mind and have at their best a crystalline purity
of language which is the real reward of a lifetime's
effort. The truth is that Eliot is matched only by Pound
and Yeats (both present in the 'familiar compound ghost'
of 'Little Gidding') in the intensity of his effort,
'under conditions that seem unpropitious,' to give a whole
mind to poetry - so that we feel

        a lifetime burning in every moment
    And not the lifetime of one man only
    But of old stones that cannot be deciphered.

Select Bibliography

ACKROYD, PETER, 'Notes for a New Culture' (1976).
BERGONZI, BERNARD, 'T.S. Eliot' (1972). Also edited 'T.S.
Eliot: "Four Quartets"' in the Casebook series (1969, re-
printed 1975).
BLAMIRES, HARRY, 'Word Unheard: A Guide through Eliot's
"Four Quartets"' (1969).
BROWNE, E. MARTIN, 'The Making of T.S. Eliot's Plays'
(1970).
COX, C.B., T.S. Eliot at the Cross-Roads, 'Critical Quar-
terly' (Winter 1970).
COX, C.B., and HINCHCLIFFE, ARNOLD P., eds, 'T.S. Eliot:
"The Waste Land"', a Casebook (1968, reprinted 1972, 1975).
DAVIE, DONALD, Anglican Eliot, 'Southern Review' (January
1973), reprinted in 'Eliot in His Time', edited by A.W.
Litz (1973). 'Articulate Energy' (1955, reissued with a
new preface in 1978) contains various suggestive considera-
tions of Eliot's poetry. Eliot in One Poet's Life,
'Mosaic' (Fall 1972), was reprinted in '"The Waste Land" in
Different Voices', edited by A.D. Moody (1974). 'The Poet
in the Imaginary Museum: Essays of Two Decades', edited by
Barry Alpert (1977), contains three essays on Eliot.
DONOGHUE, DENIS, 'The Ordinary Universe' (1968). Chapter
12 is A Reading of 'Four Quartets'. 'The Sovereign Ghost:
Studies in Imagination' (1976) contains in chapter 6 a
penetrating study of 'The Waste Land', an earlier version
of which had appeared in A.D. Moody's '"The Waste Land"
in Different Voices'.
DYSON, A.E., 'There The Dance Is': Notes on T.S. Eliot's
'Burnt Norton', 'Christian' (All Souls 1978).
EDWARDS, MICHAEL, 'Eliot/Language' (1975).
ELIOT, VALERIE, ed., '"The Waste Land": A Facsimile and
Transcript of the Original Drafts' (1971, reprinted 1972).
FORREST-THOMSON, VERONICA, 'Poetic Artifice: A Theory of
Twentieth Century Poetry' (1979).

GALLUP, DONALD, The 'Lost' Manuscripts of T.S. Eliot,
'Times Literary Supplement' (7 November 1968). 'T.S. Eliot:
A Bibliography' (1969, revised and extended version of the
edition that first appeared in 1952).
GARDNER, HELEN, 'The Art of T.S. Eliot' (1949, new edition
1968, reissued in 1969, 1972 and 1975). 'The Composition
of "Four Quartets"' (1978). Noteworthy amongst the reviews
of this book were Eric Griffiths, Fiery Refinements, 'Cambridge Review' (23 March 1979), and Bernard Bergonzi,
Ghostly Voices: Eliot's 'Four Quartets', 'Encounter'
(July 1978).
GORDON, LYNDALL, 'Eliot's Early Years' (1977).
HOWARTH HERBERT, 'Notes on Some Figures behind T.S. Eliot'
(1965).
JOSIPOVICI, GABRIEL, Linearity and Fragmentation, 'Pros-
pice' (November 1973). Extended and revised, this appeared
as 'But Time Will Not Relent': Modern Literature and the
Experience of Time, in 'The Modern English Novel', edited
by Josipovici (1976). The essay appeared a third time,
again revised, in 'The Lessons of Modernism' (1977).
KENNER, HUGH, Eliot's Moral Dialectic, 'Hudson Review'
(Autumn 1949). 'The Invisible Poet: T.S. Eliot' (1959,
frequently reprinted). Kenner edited 'T.S. Eliot: A
Collection of Critical Essays' (1962), a volume in the
Twentieth Century Views series.
KIRK, RUSSELL A., 'Eliot in His Age' (1971).
KNOLL, ROBERT E., ed., 'Storm Over "The Waste Land"'
(1964), a collection of essays by well-known critics such
as Leavis, Kenner, Brooks and Hough.
KOJECKY, ROGER, 'T.S. Eliot's Social Criticism' (1971).
LEAVIS, F.R., Eliot's Permanent Place, 'Aligarh Journal
of English Studies' (October 1977), the text of a previ-
ously unpublished lecture delivered at the Catholic Univer-
sity of Milan on 18 April 1969. 'English Literature in
Our Time and the University' (1969, the Clark Lectures of
1967). 'The Living Principle' (1975); chapter III is
devoted to 'Four Quartets'.
LEAVIS, F.R. and Q.D., 'Lectures in America' (1969).
Includes Eliot's Classical Standing by F.R. Leavis.
LEE, BRIAN, What Eliot Means, 'Haltwhistle Quarterly'
(Summer 1980).
LITZ, A.W., ed., 'Eliot in His Time' (1973).
LUDWIG, RICHARD M., T.S. Eliot, 'Sixteen Modern American
Authors: A Survey of Research and Criticism', edited by
J.R. Bryer (1974). A concise account of Eliot's reputa-
tion and of the critical writings available on him up to
the time of writing.
MARGOLIS, JOHN D., 'T.S. Eliot's Intellectual Development'
(1972).

MARTIN, GRAHAM, ed., 'Eliot in Perspective' (1970).
MARTIN, MILDRED, 'A Half-Century of Eliot Criticism: An
Annotated Bibliography of Books and Articles in English,
1916-1965' (1972, reprinted 1973). An invaluable and
exhaustive guide.
MAXWELL, D.E.S., 'The Poetry of T.S. Eliot' (1952,
reprinted in 1959 and 1961).
MILLER, JAMES E., JR, 'T.S. Eliot's Personal Waste Land'
(1977).
MILLER, J. HILLIS, 'Poets of Reality' (1966). Chapter IV
is devoted to Eliot.
MONTGOMERY, MARION, 'T.S. Eliot: An American Magus'(1969).
MOODY, A.D., 'Thomas Stearns Eliot: Poet' (1979). Also
edited '"The Waste Land" in Different Voices' (1974), subtitled the Revised Versions of Lectures Given at the
University of York in the fiftieth Year of 'The Waste
Land'. Contains work by Davie, Donoghue, Harding,
amongst others.
RIDDEL, JOSEPH N., 'The Inverted Bell' (1974). Contains an
extended discussion of Eliot's work in relation to that of
William Carlos Williams, a discussion much influenced by
the ideas of Derrida.
ROSENTHAL, M.L., 'Sailing into the Unknown: Yeats, Pound
and Eliot' (1978). An illuminating discussion of this
book and of contemporary attitudes to modernism, especially
'The Waste Land', is Theodore Weiss's The Many-Sidedness of
Modernism, 'Times Literary Supplement' (1 February 1980).
SCHNEIDER, ELIZABETH, 'T.S. Eliot: The Pattern in the Car-
pet' (1975).
SCHUCHARD, RONALD, T.S. Eliot as an Extension Lecturer,
1916-1919, 'Review of English Studies' (May and August
1974). Eliot and Hulme in 1916: Towards a Revaluation of
Eliot's Critical and Spiritual Development, 'PMLA' (Octo-
ber 1973). 'Our Mad Poetics to Confute': The Personal
Voice in T.S. Eliot's Early Poetry and Criticism, 'Orbis
Litterarum' (1976), xxxi, 208-31. 'First Rate Blasphemy':
Baudelaire and the Revised Christian Idiom of T.S. Eliot's
Moral Criticism, 'ELH' (Summer 1975).
SCOFIELD, MARTIN, 'A gesture and a pose': T.S. Eliot's
Images of Love, 'Critical Quarterly' (Autumn 1976).
SHARROCK, ROGER, 'Four Quartets' as a Post-Christian Poem,
'Aligarh Journal of English Studies' (October 1977).
SMIDT, KRISTIAN, 'Poetry and Belief in the Poetry of T.S.
Eliot' (1961).
SMITH, GROVER, 'T.S. Eliot's Poetry and Plays: A Study in
Sources and Meanings' (1955, reprinted in 1961. Second
edition 1974).
SOUTHAM, B.C., ed., 'T.S. Eliot: "Prufrock", "Gerontion",
"Ash-Wednesday" and Other Shorter Poems', a Casebook (1978).

SPENDER, STEPHEN, 'Eliot' (1975), in the Fontana Modern
Masters series.
TATE, ALLEN, ed., T.S. Eliot (1888-1965), 'Sewanee Review'
(Winter 1966). Reprinted with additional material as
'T.S. Eliot: The Man and His Work' (1966).
UNGER, LEONARD, ed., 'T.S. Eliot: A Selected Critique'
(1948, reissued 1966).
WARD, DAVID, 'T.S. Eliot: Between Two Worlds' (1973).
WOODWARD, KATHLEEN, 'At Last, The Real Distinguished
Thing' (1980). Chapter 1 considers 'Four Quartets'.

Select Index

The index is divided into three parts: I Works by Eliot;
II Themes and Thematic Groupings; III General Index.

I WORKS BY ELIOT

'After Strange Gods', 32,
33, 310-12, 382, 453,
687
'Anabasis', 265, 266-7
'Animula', 26, 261, 283,
355, 361
'Ara Vos Prec', 15, 16,
102-18, 119, 193
'Ariel Poems', 37, 335,
336, 338, 340, 358,
578-9, 732
'Ash-Wednesday', 25-30, 31,
32, 33, 36, 37, 38, 56,
62, 249-79, 281, 282,
283, 289, 290, 311, 328,
332, 336, 337-8, 340,
342, 345, 351, 352, 354,
355, 356, 357, 358, 361-2,
365, 368, 390, 401, 415,
434-5, 458, 459, 460,
462, 470, 473, 477, 500,
560, 561, 562, 568, 574,
578-9, 580, 587, 600,
691, 705, 725, 738, 741,
744-5
'Aunt Helen' ('Miss Helen
Slingsby'), 6, 7

'Before Morning', 2
'Boston Evening Transcript,
The', 6, 7, 75, 84, 85,
89, 90, 111, 125, 131-2
'Burbank with a Baedeker:
Bleistein with a Cigar',
14, 116-17, 214-15, 263
'Burnt Norton', 37, 38, 39,
41, 42, 43, 335-6, 338,
340, 342-3, 345-6, 352,
354-5, 358-9, 362, 363-4,
366, 367, 390, 391, 409,
410, 415, 417, 434, 435,
436-7, 438, 443-50, 455,
460, 463, 467, 471, 472,
474, 477, 481, 484, 485,
492, 500, 501, 505,
508-9, 510, 519, 521,
522, 523, 527-8, 531,
539-40, 543, 548, 554-5,
555-6, 561, 562, 565,
580-1, 582, 583-5, 590

'Cape Ann', 352-3, 358, 732
Catholicism and Inter-
national Order, 343
'Charles Baudelaire:

Intimate Journals'
(Introduction by T.S.
Eliot), subsequently
Baudelaire in 'Selected
Essays' (1932), 434, 436
'Choice of Kipling's Verse,
A', 530
'Choruses from "The Rock"',
37, 335, 336, 337, 342,
345, 355, 357, 360, 365,
440, 473, 561, 562
'Circe's Palace', 2
'Cocktail Party, The',
47-50, 53, 591-652, 656,
657, 663, 665, 666, 668,
669, 671, 674, 678-9,
681, 682, 683, 684, 686,
690, 695, 696, 697, 698,
699-700, 701, 707, 711,
713, 715, 716-17, 727
'Collected Poems 1909-1962',
42, 54-5, 731-45
'Collected Poems 1909-1935',
37-9, 41, 335-68, 522,
562, 732
'Complete Poems and Plays
1909-1950, The', 653-9
'Complete Poems and Plays of
T.S. Eliot, The', 2, 71,
73, 75, 85, 86, 89, 92,
105, 107, 108, 109, 111,
114, 115, 125, 126, 128,
129, 150, 171, 192, 194,
214, 222, 270, 271, 298,
313, 327, 357, 359, 387,
394, 397, 410, 411, 417,
419, 428, 439, 450, 451,
452, 455, 456, 461, 462,
484, 491, 492, 497, 503,
507, 513, 518, 526, 538,
539, 540, 541, 542, 543,
554, 562, 568, 571, 585,
588, 610, 646, 714, 716,
719
'Confidential Clerk, The',
50-2, 660-701, 707, 715,
716, 717, 719, 726
'Conversation Galante', 3,
8, 71, 78

'Cooking Egg, A', 14, 16,
116, 120, 132, 237, 290,
732
'Coriolan', 37, 336, 354,
458, 459-60, 464
'Cousin Nancy', 6, 132
'Criterion' (edited by T.S.
Eliot), 18, 25, 32, 59,
134, 138, 162, 287, 290,
428, 516
'Cultivation of Christmas
Trees, The', 732

'Dans Le Restaurant', 14, 15
'Dante', 261
'Death of St Narcissus,
The', 6
Dialogue on Dramatic Poetry,
A, 40, 325, 400, 608, 710
'Difficulties of a States-
man', 282-5, 290, 352,
354, 358, 561
'Dry Salvages, The', 41, 43,
451-95, 505, 521, 527,
540-1, 548-9, 552-3, 555,
561, 562, 571, 581, 582,
586-7, 588

'East Coker', 41, 42-3, 46,
409-42, 443-5, 447,
451-4, 456, 457, 460,
461, 462, 463-4, 465,
466, 470, 471, 472, 475-
6, 477, 486, 491, 500,
505, 509, 511, 513, 521,
554, 555, 557, 561, 563,
565, 568, 581, 582, 584,
585-6, 588
Eeldrop and Appleplex, 8,
14, 63
'Elder Statesman, The',
52-4, 59, 702-30
'Elizabethan Essays', 343
'Essays Ancient and Modern',
339, 343, 355
'Ezra Pound: His Metric and
Poetry', 14

'Family Reunion, The',

39-41, 48, 369-405, 445,
466, 470, 472-3, 474,
475, 476, 479, 481, 482,
540, 562, 568, 580, 587,
591, 597, 607, 612, 613,
614, 616, 617-18, 622,
623, 643-4, 646-7, 648,
650, 651, 652, 656, 657,
679, 681, 693, 697, 701,
708, 711, 715, 716,
717-18, 719, 721
'Five-Finger Exercises',
354, 357, 732
'For Lancelot Andrewes', 26,
27, 31, 261, 343, 421
'Four Quartets', 37, 38,
41-7, 52, 55, 56, 59, 60,
61-2, 62, 64, 552-90,
591, 593, 599-600, 612,
654, 655, 705, 706, 723,
735, 741, 743, 745
'Frontiers of Criticism,
The', 63
Function of Criticism, The,
25, 243

'Gerontion', 15, 60, 61,
104, 105, 115-16, 119,
132, 188, 193, 214, 216,
217, 235, 237, 248, 261,
263, 283, 290, 361, 425,
426, 464, 580, 726, 737,
744
'Gus: the Theatre Cat', 55

Hamlet and His Problems
(later Hamlet), 39, 370-1
'Hippopotamus, The', 14, 15,
98, 100, 120, 125, 128,
261, 290
'Hollow Men, The', 22, 23,
24, 25, 26, 37, 38, 216,
234, 237, 239, 243, 246,
259, 261, 262, 265, 283,
290, 337, 354, 357, 360,
365, 410, 464, 498, 578,
587, 705, 713, 715
'Homage to John Dryden',
263, 343

'Humouresque', 3
'Hysteria', 7, 15, 132

'Idea of a Christian
Society, The', 421,
426-7, 428-9, 434, 436,
631, 632, 634, 635, 713

'Journey of the Magi', 26,
261, 263, 295

'La Figlia Che Piange', 8,
13, 71, 78, 84, 86, 90,
91, 94, 95, 217, 283, 467
'Le directeur', 14
'Le Serpent par Paul Valéry'
(introduction by T.S.
Eliot), 419
'Lines for Cuscuscaraway and
Mirza Murad Ali Beg', 350
'Literary Essays of Ezra
Pound' (edited and intro-
duced by T.S. Eliot), 75
'Little Gidding', 41-2, 44,
45, 46, 47, 496-551, 552,
558-9, 561, 562, 563,
569, 581, 582, 584, 587-
90, 733, 743, 745
'Love Song of J. Alfred Prufrock, The', 3, 4, 5, 6,
11, 12, 13, 56, 60, 67,
71, 72, 73, 74, 75, 84,
85, 88, 88-9, 91-2, 93-4,
103, 108, 109-10, 114,
117, 120-1, 122, 124,
125, 126, 127, 129, 132,
135, 151, 157, 166, 187,
188, 216, 217, 220, 237,
248, 253, 261, 262, 290,
319, 335, 340, 341, 342,
350, 354, 365, 401, 447,
464, 486, 559, 578, 611,
658, 723, 732, 733-4,
738, 739, 740
'Lune de Miel', 14

'Marina', 29, 30, 280-1,
282, 283, 311, 354, 355,
441, 458-9

'Mélange adultère de tout',
14, 138
'Minor Poems', 37, 336,
356-7, 732
'Miss Helen Slingsby' ('Aunt
Helen'), 6, 7
'Mr. Apollinax', 8, 73, 124,
130, 187, 252
'Mr. Eliot's Sunday Morning
Service', 14, 261
Modern Education and the
Classics, 343
'Morning at the Window', 8,
126, 220
'Murder in the Cathedral',
34-7, 39, 40, 41, 48,
313-34, 336, 346, 348-9,
350, 352, 355, 365, 381,
382, 387-8, 390, 393, 397,
460-1, 462, 465-6, 533-4,
561, 562, 573, 580, 584,
591, 597, 600, 607, 613,
616, 622, 623, 652, 657,
673, 681, 686, 711, 723,
726
Music of Poetry, The, 574-5

'New Hampshire', 580
'Nocturne', 3
'Note on War Poetry, A', 732
'Notes Towards the Definition
of Culture', 47, 635, 687,
713

'Occasional Verses', 732
'Ode', 15, 20
'Old Possum's Book of Prac-
tical Cats', 406-8
'On a Portrait', 2
On the Place and Function of
the Clerisy, 59

'Pensées' of Pascal, The
(formerly 'Introduction'
to 'Pascal's "Pensées"'),
343
'Poems' (1919), 14, 15, 16,
96-101, 109
'Poems' (1920), 15, 16, 17,

119-33, 135, 138, 148,
151, 179, 341, 578, 732
'Poems 1909-1925', 22,
213-48
'Poems Written in Early
Youth', 2
'Poetry and Drama', 684
'Points of View', 43
'Portrait of a Lady', 3, 7,
11, 84, 90, 107, 109,
110, 114, 117, 120, 121,
127, 128, 132, 135, 151,
154, 157, 354, 464, 657
'Preludes', 3, 4, 7, 11, 84,
85, 104, 107, 110, 111,
122, 131, 220, 235, 361
'Prufrock and Other Observations', 3, 6, 8-13, 22,
67-95, 100, 109, 119,
131, 137-8, 187, 345,
354, 687, 732

'Rannoch, by Glencoe', 732
Religion and Literature,
343
'Rhapsody on a Windy Night',
4, 7, 11, 73, 81, 84, 85,
122, 125, 126, 156, 220,
361
'Rhetoric' and Poetic Drama,
400
'Rock, The', 32-4, 59,
294-312, 313, 325, 328,
331, 332-3, 334, 335,
336, 337, 342, 345, 346,
350, 355, 356, 388, 435,
447, 464, 465, 467, 613,
619

'Sacred Wood, The', 15, 19,
102, 136-7, 138, 145,
163, 171, 190, 243,
246-7, 310-11, 343, 355,
419, 711
'Salutation', 25
'Selected Essays 1917-1932',
31, 514
'Selected Poems', 47
Some Notes on the Blank

Verse of Christopher Mar-
lowe, 122
'Song' ('The moonflower
opens to the mouth'), 2, 3
'Song' ('When we came home
across the sea'), 2
'Song for Simeon, A', 26,
261, 264, 357, 365, 514
'Spleen', 3
'Sweeney Agonistes', 32, 37,
55, 286-93, 295, 325,
334, 336, 337, 354, 365,
608-9, 611, 613, 709, 711,
712
'Sweeney Among the Nightingales', 14, 98-9, 100,
120, 124, 125, 128, 213,
217-18, 241, 263, 361,
658
'Sweeney Erect', 120

'Thoughts After Lambeth',
31, 282
Tradition and the Individual
Talent, 147, 243, 310-11,
419, 514, 578, 734
'Triumphal March', 282-5,
290, 352, 354, 366, 460

'Use of Poetry and the Use of
Criticism, The', 24, 32,
350
'Usk', 336, 352

'Waste Land, The', 17-22,
23, 25, 26, 31, 36, 39,
45, 50, 51, 57, 60, 61,
62, 63, 70, 93, 134-212,
235, 236, 237, 240, 241,
243, 246, 248, 249, 252,
253, 254, 259, 261, 262,
263, 264, 269, 270,
275-7, 283, 289, 290,
307, 311, 317, 319, 327,
332, 336, 337, 338-9,
340, 341-2, 345, 347,
349, 351, 354, 355, 357,
360, 365, 368, 384, 390,
391, 395, 401, 402-3,
404, 411, 413-14, 418,
419, 425, 442, 447, 460,
462, 464, 467, 470, 471,
472, 498, 504, 514, 533,
550-1, 562, 566, 574,
576, 578, 579, 587, 612,
654, 658, 726, 735,
740-1, 743, 744
'"Waste Land, The": a Facsimile and Transcript of
the Original Drafts',
58, 63, 144
'Whispers of Immortality',
14, 128, 157

II THEMES AND THEMATIC GROUPINGS

allusion/erudition, 20-1,
43, 96-8, 100, 106, 109,
112-13, 117, 119, 157-8,
159, 162, 165, 183, 184,
187-8, 191, 194, 195,
206, 211, 219, 235-6,
241, 345, 351, 355, 365,
411, 418-21, 472, 512,
541, 542-3, 544, 550-1,
562-3, 564, 579, 589-90,
740, 744
ambiguity, 22, 29-30, 236,
269, 358, 395, 548, 669,
718
American qualities, 13, 18,
24, 58, 91-2, 93-4, 137,
146-7, 210-11, 239, 242,
273, 401-2, 405, 653,
654-5, 657-8

beauty, 22, 46, 67, 74, 85,
103, 115, 122, 139, 149,
161, 169, 171, 178, 182,
189, 197, 200-1, 206,

215, 221, 245, 252, 258, 264, 269, 281, 283, 311, 336, 441, 452, 503, 528, 537, 538, 542, 562, 573, 574

Christianity/Roman Catholicism/Anglo-Catholicism, 22, 28, 31, 35, 38, 44, 49, 61, 62, 254, 261, 267, 297, 304, 331, 332, 333, 348, 376, 389, 391, 395, 413, 458, 460, 468, 474, 489, 493, 498, 511-12, 624-41

Church, 24, 25, 27, 28, 111, 227-8, 230-1, 251, 253, 255, 267, 273, 274-5, 300, 302, 303, 305, 306, 307, 310-11, 343, 346, 365, 465, 486, 487, 545-6

complexity, 20, 38, 114, 120, 130, 142, 158, 160, 214, 219, 277, 501, 522, 547, 550, 567, 597, 629; 'metaphysical', 547, 550

criticism, 23, 25, 30, 31, 109, 136-7, 146-7, 162-4, 190, 226, 243, 245, 270, 273, 299, 310, 343, 400-1, 417

decadence/despair/disillusion (also bitterness/decay/desolation), 17, 133, 151, 169, 183, 186, 188, 198, 202, 208, 238, 259, 262, 263, 267, 289, 315, 337, 341, 345, 358, 365, 456, 464, 485, 486, 516, 611

development and change, 336, 337-8, 340-1, 342, 343, 345, 347, 348, 350, 353-4, 355, 356, 357-8, 359-64, 365, 367, 368, 410, 412-13, 470, 484, 494, 562, 578-9, 612-13, 616, 705, 732

dramatic qualities, 33, 39, 40, 47, 50, 51, 53, 221, 287, 295-8, 317, 320-2, 324-5, 333, 339, 370, 372-5, 377, 379, 381, 382-3, 387-90, 391-2, 394, 397, 400, 401, 404, 591, 592-3, 595, 597, 599, 600, 604, 605, 608, 612-13, 614, 618, 623, 628, 646, 652, 657, 661, 664, 666, 673, 675, 681, 707-9, 711-12, 714, 715, 721; comedy, 592, 593, 594, 602-3, 609, 613, 614, 616, 668, 676, 697-8, 713; 'theatrical contrivance', 693

emotion and feeling, 15, 17, 20, 38, 45, 47, 73, 103-5, 114, 143, 155, 158, 160, 170, 177, 184, 193, 205-6, 219, 237-8, 239-40, 244, 247, 255, 346, 360, 436, 445, 468, 516, 517-18, 520, 654, 658, 707, 739; split between emotion and intellect/belief, 520, 523-9, 616-17; 'experience ordered into significance', 526

European qualities, 17, 18, 24, 25, 58, 137, 146-7, 208, 210-11, 242-3, 405, 733

failure/defects/limitations, 23-4, 43, 48, 53, 56, 142, 150, 156, 188, 195-9, 208, 218-19, 225, 227, 254, 264, 283, 290, 311, 328, 342, 349, 377, 389, 393, 395, 400-1, 405, 410, 411-12, 420, 465, 466, 484, 501-2, 519-21, 568, 571, 606-7, 620, 622, 637, 639,

651-2, 662, 665, 666-7,
673, 674, 695-6, 707,
721-2, 741-2
fragmentation and discon-
tinuity, 19, 23, 24, 37,
149, 152, 158, 159-60,
161, 167, 172-82, 183,
186, 192, 205, 207, 235,
238, 243-4, 284, 351,
357, 366, 519, 524-5,
526, 616-17, 620
French influences, 3, 9, 17,
20, 72, 132, 244-5, 299,
340-1, 365, 733

humility/wisdom, 259, 276-7,
304, 353, 413-14, 436,
437, 444, 452-3, 456,
457, 469, 505, 507, 508,
532, 600, 687

impersonality, 19, 27, 33,
147, 207, 245, 308, 503,
504, 580, 734

language/imagery/juxtaposi-
tion/paradox/simultaneity,
22, 23, 28, 35-6, 38, 54,
60, 106, 118, 127, 153,
179, 188-9, 198, 204, 217,
218, 244-5, 253, 260, 265,
278, 299, 308, 319, 334,
338, 349, 351, 354, 358,
362-4, 366, 367, 377,
379-80, 383, 395, 414,
421, 425, 440, 445,
471-2, 487, 497, 498,
501-2, 505, 508-9, 511,
521, 526, 538-9, 540,
541, 548, 566, 568, 575,
576, 585, 596, 603, 604,
623, 635-6, 658, 673, 719,
726, 727-8, 733-6, 740,
742, 745; 'Eliotese', 621
literariness, 20, 106, 157,
260, 285, 516, 528, 683;
'artificial', 567; cliché,
520-1
liturgy, use of and interest

in, 260, 271-2, 297, 300,
307, 309, 313, 334, 384,
478, 709-11
love, 532, 533, 534, 557-8,
610, 645, 648-50, 683,
704, 719, 721, 725

modernity and modernism, 5,
20, 30, 37, 46, 52, 54,
78, 100, 121-5, 132, 227,
229, 261, 276, 306, 329,
353-4, 460
musical structure, 471, 499,
503, 504, 509, 574-5,
576, 578, 583, 729
myth and symbolism, 39,
40-1, 52, 132, 139-41,
148-9, 158-9, 185, 191,
196, 202, 205, 221, 237,
243, 247, 255, 256, 259,
263, 264, 275, 278-9,
351, 370, 372, 373-4,
378, 386, 398, 399,
403-4, 424, 444, 460,
462, 474, 477, 509, 510,
520, 526, 568, 580, 582,
589, 612, 647, 650, 671

obscurity and meaning, 11,
13, 17, 37, 41, 84, 86,
109, 143, 154, 157, 160,
164, 190, 192, 193,
200-1, 204-5, 211, 221,
236, 240, 252-3, 256,
333, 336, 337, 363-4,
452, 453-4, 470-81, 484,
501, 503, 509, 510,
530-1, 537-9, 541, 544-5,
563, 614, 670, 744

personality/maturity/sensi-
bility, 14-15, 21, 33,
46, 54, 81, 116, 147,
155, 157, 163, 179, 184,
275, 283, 284, 309, 362,
415, 456, 464, 470, 498,
499, 502, 578-9

realism and ugliness, 12,

40, 52, 77–8, 85–7,
106–7, 111, 154, 177–8,
197, 202, 205, 214, 215,
243, 275, 276, 291, 372,
399, 460, 738
refinement, 23, 29; refining
fire, 507, 512, 513, 515,
517, 587, 589–90
religious concerns/spirit-
uality/detachment/renun-
ciation, 26, 28, 34, 37,
43, 45, 47, 134–5, 140,
149, 169, 211, 228, 230,
233, 246, 250, 255,
263–4, 267, 273, 275,
306, 346, 355–6, 358,
382, 389, 392, 421, 423,
427, 429–35, 460–1, 463,
473, 474, 476–81, 485,
488, 492–3, 498, 500,
507, 511–14, 516, 517,
531, 532, 533–6, 565–6,
574, 576, 580–1, 586,
588, 599, 604–5, 615,
617–18, 648, 656, 706,
707, 723; un-Christian
qualities, 569–70, 571;
via negativa, 463, 474,
476, 533–6, 564, 576,
580–1; vision and illu-
mination, 626–9, 631;
sin/sanctity, 531, 532,
572, 598, 639
reputation/popularity/
success, 15, 23, 25, 27,
30, 31, 50, 60, 84, 113,
126, 145, 163, 170, 176,
191, 198–9, 215, 220,
282, 295, 338, 339–40,
364, 446, 470, 500, 551,
607, 611, 621, 637, 644;
box-office success, 668,
675
revolutionary qualities/
novelty/innovation, 8, 9,
57, 69, 74, 126, 174,
178, 219, 220, 222, 311,
328, 355, 593, 654, 675,
744
rhythm, 10, 11, 36, 38,

78–80, 110, 120, 124,
151, 177, 189, 217, 219,
238, 250, 271, 277–8,
279, 293, 305, 312, 319,
340, 348, 351, 352, 362,
375, 425, 441–2, 459,
461, 462, 464, 471–2,
474, 530, 540, 568, 596

self-consciousness/self-
awareness/self-scrutiny,
3–4, 29, 45, 61, 88, 102,
105, 239, 248, 262, 284,
290, 464, 528
sense of place, 473–4, 475,
477, 485, 544, 561, 583,
585, 586, 587
social/cultural/political
attitudes, 35, 207–8,
209, 211, 223, 254,
306–7, 326, 327, 343,
355, 359, 360–1, 390–1,
392, 415–17, 418, 421,
426–7, 428–9, 436, 460,
485, 488, 490, 630, 632,
656, 743; 'classicist,
royalist, anglo-
catholic', 488–90
sophistication/cleverness/
dandyism, 17, 19, 67–8,
74, 89, 99, 100, 128,
148, 151, 170, 184, 185,
207, 208, 211, 221, 235,
259, 287, 345, 486, 657,
702; 'intellectual', 655
sterility, 24, 25, 28, 32,
39, 42, 108, 148, 197,
205–6, 207, 208, 227,
229, 234, 241, 262, 739,
741

technique/versification, 14,
19, 29–30, 36, 40, 48,
77, 78–80, 86, 88–9, 108,
116, 120, 143, 205, 216,
221, 237, 238, 244, 295,
308, 319, 327, 351, 383,
420, 501–2, 504, 512,
513, 539, 569, 571, 583,
588, 612–13, 684–6, 726,

739; verse almost imper-
ceptible, 596, 601, 606,
607, 622, 623, 640
time/eternity, 338, 346,
354, 355, 391, 409, 453,
454, 455, 457, 458, 460,
461, 462, 465-6, 472-3,
475, 478-80, 481, 494,
498, 502, 503, 507-8,
512, 513, 514, 517, 531,
532, 534, 548, 549, 557,
565, 572-3, 581, 583-9
tradition/classicism, 8, 9,
10, 19, 26, 43, 47, 85,
145, 156, 182, 210,
222-34, 243, 245, 247,

250, 263, 304, 310, 312,
328-9, 422, 466, 516,
578-9, 654; past and pre-
sent, 468-9, 473, 475,
479, 512, 513, 514, 516,
527

wit/irony/parody/satire, 9,
15, 16, 17, 21, 28, 75,
89, 90, 111, 121, 125,
128, 130, 151, 160, 178,
187, 199, 217, 218, 235,
239, 252, 275, 276-7,
281, 284, 288, 324, 327,
346, 354, 358, 361, 403,
464, 660, 713, 740

III   GENERAL INDEX

Ackroyd, Peter, 3-4, 61, 62,
63
Addison, Joseph, 184
'Adelphi', 23, 222-34,
288-9, 384-7, 451-7
AE (George E. Russell), 353
Aeschylus, 332, 389, 395,
623
Aiken, Conrad, 5, 9, 11, 12,
20-1, 33-4, 59, 64, 80-1,
156-61, 193, 246-8,
310-12, 574; 'Letters',
59, 80
Aldington, Richard, 6, 17,
22, 51, 63, 179, 265
Anacreon, 71
Anderson, Sherwood, 135, 143
Andrewes, Lancelot, Bishop,
263
Anouilh, Jean, 612
Apollinaire, Guillaume, 244
Aquinas, St Thomas, 265,
286, 570
Archer, William, 608, 622
Aristophanes, 286, 287, 288,
290, 292
Aristotle, 145, 318, 351,
381
Arnaut Daniel, 142, 325,

391, 512, 513
Arnold, Matthew, 42, 55,
243, 246, 261, 415,
688-9
Arrowsmith, William, 49, 53,
624-43
Ashbery, John, 61
'Athenaeum', 15, 16, 102-5,
109
'Atlantic', 182-3
Auden, W.H., 56, 60, 294,
297, 315, 344, 345, 377,
383, 392, 398, 464, 670
Augustine, St, 142, 149,
191, 194, 197, 206, 219,
347, 462, 535, 550, 582
Aurelius, Marcus, 687
Austen, Jane, 700

Babbitt, Irving, 2, 31, 233
Bacon, Sir Francis, 421
Balakian, Nona, 722-5
Balzac, Honoré de, 12, 88
Barber, C.L., 40, 443, 445
Baring, Maurice, 422-3
Barker, George, 32, 288-9,
344
Barrett, William, 48, 606-12
Barrie, J.M., 713

Barthes, Roland, 62
Baudelaire, Charles, 17, 93,
    142, 170, 194, 240, 263,
    264, 275, 341, 349, 407,
    410, 434, 436, 550, 651,
    738, 744
Bazin, René, 482
Beckett, Samuel, 61
Beethoven, Ludwig van, 190,
    569, 576, 742
Bell, Clive, 17, 22, 117-18,
    186-91
Bell, George (Bishop of
    Chichester), 34
Benét, William Rose, 27,
    153, 192-3, 267-8
Benlowes, Edward, 98
Bennett, Arnold, 189, 223
Berdyaev, Nicolas, 582
Bergonzi, Bernard, 42, 64
Bergson, Henri, 4, 174, 582
Bernard, St, 532
'Bhagavadgita', 472, 479,
    562, 564, 569
Birrell, Francis, 33, 251-3
Bishop, John Peale, 20
'Blackfriars', 304-5, 500-2
Blackmur, R.P., 36, 38, 64,
    366-8, 643
Blake, William, 60, 105, 117,
    246-7, 260, 458, 481, 618,
    738
Blanchot, Maurice, 61
Blanshard, Brand, 56
Blunden, Edmund, 240
Bodenheim, Maxwell, 193
Bodkin, Maud, 384-7
Bohr, Niels, 211
'Booklist', 16
'Bookman' (London), 265-7
'Bookman' (New York), 31,
    130-1
Borges, Jorge Luis, 61
Bosschère, Jean de, 12
Bossuet, Jacques Bénigne,
    510
Bradbrook, Muriel, 44, 47,
    458-68, 510-14
Bradford, Curtis, 43, 418

Bradley, F.H., 5, 7, 174,
    181, 200, 426
Bramhall, John, Archbishop,
    263
Braybrooke, Neville, 53
Bridson, D.G., 32, 286-8
Brooke, Nicholas, 51,
    689-96
Brooke, Rupert, 344
Brooks, Cleanth, 32, 39-40,
    390-2
Brooks, Van Wyck, 43, 468,
    469
Brown, Ivor, 47, 375-7
Browne, E. Martin, 33, 34,
    48, 50, 57, 59, 64, 303,
    305, 376, 596, 600, 704
Browne, Irene, 493-5
Browne, Sir Thomas, 477
Browning, Robert, 10, 72,
    77, 83, 85, 96-7, 98,
    112, 113-14, 131, 133,
    366
Bryer, Jackson R., 59
Brzeska, see Gaudier-
    Brzeska
Buddha, 140, 142, 149, 194,
    197, 219, 472, 550
Bunyan, John, 557
Burke, Kenneth, 722
Burns, Robert, 79
Butler, Edward Cuthbert,
    Abbot, 535
Butler, Samuel, 246
Byron, George Gordon, Lord,
    70, 79-80, 165

Caesar, Julius, 154
'Calendar of Modern Let-
    ters', 23, 184, 215-19
Campbell, Roy, 272
Carlyle, Thomas, 72
Carroll, Lewis, 554
Cary, Phoebe, 130
Catullus, 93, 94, 195
Cavalcanti, Guido, 741
Caxton, William, 626
Cecilia, St, 626
Céline, Louis-Ferdinand, 570

'Chapbook', 22, 162-6
Chapman, George, 536, 537,
    538, 543, 551
Charles I, 545, 580, 587
Chaucer, Geoffrey, 232, 323,
    421, 655, 740
Chekhov, Anton, 372, 382,
    712
Chesterton, G.K., 192
Chopin, Frédéric, 79
'Christian Century',328-32
Churchill, Winston S., 456
Cinna, 195
Claudel, Paul, 42, 183, 409
'Cloud of Unknowing, The',
    45, 476-7, 499, 532, 533,
    534, 535, 590
Cocteau, Jean, 27, 371, 569
Coffin, Robert Tristram, 575
Coleridge, Samuel Taylor,
    55, 174, 220, 222, 493,
    734
Collins, Seward, 31
Collins, William, 232
Colum, Mary, 656-9
Colum, Padraic, 16, 17, 53,
    75, 131-3
'Commonweal', 290-1
Congreve, William, 146, 678,
    685
Connolly, Cyril, 344-6
Conrad, Joseph, 238
Corbière, Tristan, 9, 17,
    71, 244, 263, 341
Coward, Noël, 593, 609, 637
Cowley, Abraham, 547, 550,
    551
Cowley, Malcolm, 38, 46,
    244, 347-9, 563-6
Cowper, William, 407
Cox, C.B., 64
Craig, Gordon, 710
Crashaw, Richard, 26, 250,
    304, 343, 533, 534, 587
Creeley, Robert, 58
Cummings, E.E., 16, 121-5,
    737

Dante Alighieri, 26, 29, 35,

    46, 57, 79, 95, 140, 141,
    142, 154, 170, 183, 194,
    232, 233, 247, 263, 265,
    273, 326, 338, 366, 427,
    481, 490, 491, 512, 532,
    550, 558, 559, 569, 582,
    588, 590, 593, 738, 739,
    741, 743, 744
Darlington, W.A., 39
Davie, Donald, 38, 54, 61,
    731-6
Davies, W.H., 85
Dawson, Christopher, 423,
    424, 425, 582
Day, John, 142
Day Lewis, Cecil, 344, 345
Debussy, Claude, 739
della Mirandola, Pico, 421,
    435
Denham, Sir John, 216, 274
Dent, Alan, 666
Derrida, Jacques, 60, 61
Deutsch, Babette, 12, 88-9
Devine, George, 50, 55
De Voragine, Jacobus, 626
Dewey, John, 174, 181
'Dial', 11, 18-20, 90,
    121-5, 134, 135, 136-44,
    145, 151, 162, 172, 193,
    246-8, 562
Dibdin, Thomas John, 223
Dionysius the Areopagite,
    St, 45, 533, 535, 536,
    564
Dobrée, Bonamy, 31, 33, 49,
    50-1, 57, 222, 612-15,
    675-89
Donald, Henry, 50, 660-2
Donne, John, 26, 98, 154,
    157, 216, 241, 250, 253,
    261, 263, 495, 554, 655,
    709, 733, 735, 738, 739,
    740
Donoghue, Denis, 53, 62,
    712-22
Doolittle, Hilda (H.D.), 6,
    402
Dos Passos, John, 273
Dostoevski, Fyodor M., 134,
    238

'Double Dealer', 170-2
Douglas, Major C.H., 300, 302
Doyle, Sir Arthur Conan, 427
Dresser, Paul, 152, 366
Dryden, John, 26, 55, 188, 217, 250, 481, 733, 736
'Dublin Review', 552-60
Duncan, Robert, 58, 60
Duncan, Ronald, 623
Dunne, J.W., 355
'Durham University Journal', 689-96
Dyson, A.E., 60

Eagleton, Terry, 61
Ecclesiastes, 140, 142, 256-7, 550, 586
Eckhardt, Meister, 463, 535
Edison, Thomas A., 168
Edward, St, 627
Edwards, Michael, 21-2, 62, 64
'Egoist', 8, 9, 10, 72, 83, 119, 138
Einstein, Albert, 211, 490
Eliot, H.W., Jr, 43
Eliot, Mrs Valerie, 18, 52, 58, 60, 63, 66, 144
Elliot, Denholm, 662, 665, 666, 670
Elyot, Sir Thomas, 420-2, 424, 425-6, 428, 431, 482, 564, 586
Emerson, Ralph Waldo, 197
Empson, William, 30, 51
'Encounter', 56
Engels, Friedrich, 359
'English Review', 13, 91-2
Erasmus, Desiderius, 421
Erigena, Scotus, 564
Euripides, 137, 402, 662, 668, 678, 698
'Everyman', 72, 303-4
Ezekiel, 142, 191, 194, 257, 271, 550

Ferguson, Francis, 40
Fernandez, Ramon, 31

Ferrar, Nicholas, 496, 499, 533, 544, 545, 546, 561, 579, 587
Findlater, Richard, 50, 667-74
Firbank, Ronald, 345
Fitts, Dudley, 268
FitzGerald, Edward, 113
Flaubert, Gustave, 286, 454
Flecker, James Elroy, 344
Flemyng, Robert, 591, 596, 600
Fletcher, John Gould, 46, 573-6
Flint, F.S., 12, 162
Florio, John, 548
Forrest-Thomson, Veronica, 62, 65
Forster, E.M., 30, 48, 64, 485, 602-4
'Fortnightly', 643-52
France, Anatole, 181
Francis, St, 570
Frankau, Gilbert, 200, 203
Franklin, Benjamin, 687
Frazer, Sir James, 139, 158, 191, 194, 196, 197, 206, 550, 740
'Freeman', 126-30, 151-3
Frere, John Hookham, 287
Freud, Sigmund, 180, 394, 489, 514, 610
'From Ritual to Romance', 139, 148, 200, 206, 236, 551
Frost, Robert, 369, 737, 739
Froude, J.A., 142
Fry, Christopher, 622
Frye, Northrop, 720, 722, 743
'Future', 14

Gallup, Donald, 18, 58, 63
Galsworthy, John, 223, 376
Gardner, Dame Helen, 41, 42, 44, 47, 48, 51, 57, 58-9, 66, 335, 469-83, 696-701
Garnett, David, 223, 225
Gary, Franklin, 31

Gascoyne, David, 44
Gaudier-Brzeska, Henri, 83
Gautier, Théophile, 14, 15
Géraldy, Paul, 89
Gibson, Wilfred Wilson, 81
Gide, André, 666
Gifford, William, 82-3
Goethe, J.W. von, 42, 175,
    247, 413, 650-1, 675
'Golden Bough, The', 139-40,
    142, 196, 198, 206, 550
Goldsmith, Oliver, 142, 185,
    194
Goodman, Paul, 46, 570-3
Gordon, Lyndall, 6, 18, 59,
    63
Gosse, Edmund, 163
Gourmont, Remy de, 71, 75-6,
    78, 81-3, 95, 148, 181
Grant, Duncan, 19
Graves, Robert, 21, 25,
    51-2, 173, 181
Gray, Thomas, 190, 232, 246
Gregor, Ian, 61
Gregory, Horace, 40, 45,
    400-5, 560-3
Guinness, Sir Alec, 47, 591,
    596, 600, 727

Haigh-Wood, Vivien, 5, 6
Hale, Lionel, 39
Harding, D.W., 33, 38, 44-5,
    306-9, 359-64, 515-18,
    519, 521, 522, 523, 525,
    527
Hardy, Thomas, 62, 238, 261,
    353, 586
Harrison, Rex, 727
'Harvard Advocate', 2, 39
Hawthorne, Nathaniel, 24,
    35, 239, 326
Haydn, Franz Joseph, 411,
    420, 578
Haye, Helen, 371, 375, 376,
    377
Hayward, John, 2, 37, 335-6
Heard, Gerald, 26, 249-51
Hedley, John C., Bishop, 535
Hegel, G.W.F., 582

Henley, W.E., 84, 85
Heraclitus, 355, 367, 423,
    424, 426, 432, 436, 542,
    569, 580, 582-3, 590
Herbert, George, 304, 466,
    655
Herrick, Robert, 455
Hewes, Henry, 53, 702-6
Heyl, Bernard, 31
Higinbotham, R.N., 45,
    519-21, 521-5, 526, 527,
    528
Hinchcliffe, Arnold P., 64
Hobson, Harold, 48
Hodges, H.A., 59
Hodgson, Ralph, 344
Hogan, J.P., 43, 451-7
Hogarth, Paul, 86
Hogarth Press, 15, 18, 96,
    192, 213
Holroyd, Michael, 59
Homer, 93
Hope-Wallace, Philip, 49
Hopkins, Gerard Manley, 250,
    513, 554, 587, 741
Horace, 484-5
'Horizon', 344, 415-18
Horton, Philip, 40, 393-5
'Hound and Horn', 32, 272-9,
    282
Housman, A.E., 261, 344, 353
Houston, Donald, 591, 596
Howard, Brian, 27, 269-72
Howson, Rev. Vincent, 33,
    301-2
'Hudson Review', 49, 624-43
Hueffer, Ford Madox, 6
Hügel, Friedrich von, 699
Hulme, T.E., 434, 436
Hume, David, 177
Humphries, Rolfe, 38, 356-9,
    468-9
Hutchinson, Mary, 17
Huxley, Aldous, 225, 563

Ibsen, Henrik, 39, 183, 372,
    396, 403, 612, 711, 712
Isherwood, Christopher, 315,
    377, 383

James, Henry, 24, 35, 146, 239-40, 326, 378, 653, 655, 657

James, William, 174, 242

Jeans, Isabel, 662, 664, 665

Jeans, Ursula, 591, 596, 600

Jeffers, Robinson, 358, 402

Jepson, Edgar, 13, 91-2, 93-5

Joachim, Harold, 5

John of the Cross, St, 45, 227, 289, 290, 292, 336, 365, 430, 431, 432, 433, 437, 477, 500, 532, 534, 535, 564, 569, 574, 586, 739

Johns, Orrick, 68

Johnson, Samuel, 55, 198, 273-4, 545, 547, 550, 551, 733

Jones, Peter, 662, 665

Jonson, Ben, 205, 616, 682

Josipovici, Gabriel, 22, 61

Joyce, James, 10, 61, 72, 77, 150, 151, 154, 192, 462, 489, 490, 610, 654

Julian of Norwich, 45, 499, 531, 532, 533, 535, 564, 574, 576, 581, 588

Jung, C.G., 430

Kafka, Franz, 61

Kandinsky, Wassily, 95

Kant, Immanuel, 174, 181

Kazan, Elia, 729

Keats, John, 12, 70, 82, 181, 230, 271

Kenner, Hugh, 38, 53, 56-7, 61·, 725-30

'Kenyon Review', 45, 172, 180, 393-5

Kermode, Frank, 53, 55, 57, 709-12, 743-5

Kierkegaard, Søren, 582, 584

Kipling, Rudyard, 84, 130, 203, 344, 495, 575, 705

Kirkup, James, 42, 43,· 412-15, 505-10

Kojecky, Roger, 59, 64

Kreymborg, Alfred, 7, 11

Krushchev, Nikita, 743

Krutch, Joseph Wood, 276

Kyd, Thomas, 51, 142, 194, 689

Labiche, Eugène, 668

Lacan, Jacques, 61

Lacey, Catherine, 371, 375, 377

Laforgue, Jules, 3, 9, 10, 14, 16, 17, 71, 110, 116, 132, 148, 153, 186, 244-5, 263, 340-1, 345, 358, 568, 657, 733

Landor, Walter Savage, 189-90, 267

Lanman, Charles, 4

Lao-tzu, 453

Larbaud, Valéry, 283

Lasky, Melvin J., 45

Lasserre, Pierre, 233

Laud, William, Archbishop, 546

Laughlin, James, 34, 37, 317-19

Lawrence, D.H., 30, 60, 198, 401, 452, 467, 468, 634, 654

Lear, Edward, 357, 366, 593

Leavis, F.R., 29-30, 31, 42-3, 44, 45, 60, 64, 502, 521-9, 593

Leggatt, Alison, 662, 665, 726-7

Leighton, Margaret, 662, 664, 665, 670

Lessing, Gotthold Ephraim, 572

Lewis, C.S., 44, 468

Lewis, Wyndham, 6, 7, 83, 286-7, 462, 582, 654, 713, 743

'Life and Letters', 64, 111, 400-5

Limbour, Georges, 282

Lindsay, Vachel, 93

'Listener', 33, 56, 294-5, 377-8, 385, 406-7, 602-4

'Literary World', 9, 74

764   Select Index

'Little Review', 8, 12, 13,
    14, 63, 81-3, 83-8, 92-5,
    145
Liveright, Horace, 18
Lloyd, Marie, 710
Locker-Lampson, Godfrey, 130
'London Mercury', 163,
    191-2, 240-1, 268-9,
    320-2, 379-81, 410
Lotinga, Ernie, 710
Lowell, Robert, 55
Lucas, F.L., 22, 27, 195-9
Lucretius, 582, 586
Ludwig, Richard M., 59
Luke, St, 142
Lycophron, 195
Lyly, John, 167

McAfee, Helen, 22, 182-3
MacCarthy, Sir Desmond, 15,
    27, 39, 111-17, 371-5,
    385, 544-5
Machiavelli, Niccolò, 343
MacKenzie, Mrs Orgill, 255-9
MacLeish, Archibald, 332
MacNeice, Louis, 344, 381-4
Maeterlinck, Maurice, 93
Mallarmé, Stéphane, 54, 62,
    575, 734, 735
'Manchester Guardian', 8,
    194-5, 591-2
Mangan, Sherry, 27
Mannheim, Karl, 59
Mansfield, Katherine, 102,
    649-50
March, Richard, 80
Margolis, John D., 59
Marlowe, Christopher, 97,
    122
Malory, Sir Thomas, 740
Marston, John, 235, 668
Martin, Graham, 61
Martin, Mildred, 58
Marvell, Andrew, 152, 165,
    191, 194, 263, 433-4,
    543-4, 550, 738
Marx, Groucho, 55
Marx, Karl, 300
Mary, Queen of Scots, 422-3,

424, 475, 586
Mason, H.A., 324
Massey, Anna, 704
Massinger, Philip, 137, 245,
    673
Massis, Henri, 242
Mather, Increase, 713
Mathews, Elkin, 7, 67
Matthiessen, F.O., 32, 35,
    45-6, 324-8, 564, 655,
    656
Maupassant, Guy de, 454
Maurras, Charles, 43, 242
Maxwell, James Clerk, 209
'Meanjin', 581-90
Melville, Herman, 482
Menander, 287, 698
Mencken, H.L., 5
Meredith, George, 30, 188,
    353
Meynell, Francis, 7
Middleton, Thomas, 142, 194,
    206
Miller, J. Hillis, 60
Milton, John, 26, 57, 96,
    97, 118, 142, 194, 206,
    232, 246, 250, 251, 274,
    325, 348, 410, 414, 429,
    430-1, 490, 499, 546,
    573, 587
Mirsky, D.S., 356, 358
Moberly, W.H., 59
Mogin, Jean, 614-15
Molière, 678
Monro, Harold, 5, 7, 162-6
Monroe, Harriet, 5, 6, 7,
    166-70, 738
Montaigne, Michel de, 343,
    542, 548, 549-50
Moody, A.D., 61, 62, 63
Moody, William Vaughn, 353
Moore, G.E., 111
Moore, Marianne, 12, 32, 37,
    64, 89-90, 280-1, 291-3,
    350-3, 568
Moore, T. Sturge, 135
More, Paul Elmer, 31, 32, 64
More, Sir Thomas, 421
Morgan, Charles, 39

Morgan, Louise, 219-22
Morley, Frank, 33, 41, 57
Morris, William, 251
Morton, A.L., 25
Mottram, Eric, 60-1
Moult, Thomas, 265-7
Muir, Edwin, 23, 34-5, 37, 242, 245, 320-2, 336-9, 502-5
Munson, Gorham B., 22, 203-12
Murry, John Middleton, 16, 23-4, 27, 49, 96-8, 99, 102-5, 222-34, 236, 643-52

'Nation' (New York), 23, 125-6, 144-51, 242, 323-4, 350-3, 567-70, 743-5
'Nation and Athenaeum', 23, 186-91, 213-15, 251-3
Nerval, Gérard de, 142, 263
Nesbitt, Cathleen, 592, 596, 600
'New Adelphi', 27, 255-9
Newbolt, Henry, 25
'New English Weekly', 41, 47, 286-8, 298-302, 317-19, 438, 577-81
'New Leader', 45, 570-3, 722-5
'New Masses', 356-9
'New Republic', 20, 26, 56, 88-9, 117-18, 131-3, 156-61, 193, 239-40, 242-6, 259-60, 347-9, 381-4, 563-6
'News Chronicle', 666
'New Statesman', 8, 9, 10, 24, 31, 33, 37, 47, 54, 55, 57, 75, 78, 83, 84, 88, 111-17, 195-9, 234-8, 269-72, 339-43, 371-5, 385, 409-12, 419, 502-5, 594-6, 662-5, 697-701, 731-6
Newton, Sir Isaac, 209
'New Writing and Daylight', 44, 469-83

'New Yorker', 34, 610
'New York Evening Post Literary Review', 63, 153-6, 172-82, 193
'New York Post', 48, 601-2
'New York Sun', 335-6
'New York Times Book Review', 18, 135-6, 253-5, 560-3, 653-6
Nichols, Robert, 15, 16, 108-11, 127
Nicholson, Norman, 623
Nims, John Frederick, 54-5, 736-42
'Nine', 47, 592-4
'Nineteenth Century', 536-51
'1924', 203-12
Norman, Charles, 121

'Observer', 47, 52-3, 56, 108-11, 375-7, 385
O'Casey, Sean, 297, 306
Olivier, Sir Laurence, 55
Olson, Charles, 52, 57-8, 60, 62
Omond, T.S., 685
O'Neill, Eugene, 39, 142, 332, 372, 373-4, 402, 403, 404
Oppen, George, 58
Origen, 590
Orwell, George (Eric Arthur Blair), 43-4, 483-8, 490, 492, 493-4
'Others', 7, 8, 11
'Outlook', 17, 63, 219-22
Ovid, 10, 77, 131, 133, 142, 191, 194, 206, 366, 536
Owen, Wilfred, 451

'Pagany', 27
Paige, D.D., 64
Parsons, I.M., 34, 315-17
'Partisan Review', 35, 48, 390-2, 438, 574, 606-12
Pascal, Blaise, 343, 380, 437, 474, 482-3, 512
Pater, Walter, 245, 358

Patmore, Coventry, 553
Paul, St, 272, 472, 489, 590
Pearson, Gabriel, 61
Perse, St-John (Aléxis Léger), 265, 266
Peter, John, 48-9, 615-22
Petronius, 141, 142, 196
Picasso, Pablo, 19, 122, 283, 489-90
Pinero, Arthur Wing, 52, 402
Plato, 421
Pliny, 129-30
Poe, Edgar Allan, 108, 137, 402, 407, 654, 740
'Poetry', 5, 6, 8, 10, 26, 45, 53, 64, 67, 75-80, 89-90, 119-21, 166-70, 261-5, 280-1, 282-5, 291-3, 310-12, 366-8, 396-400, 468-9, 529-36, 573-6, 725-30
'Poetry London', 43-4, 412-15, 483-95, 505-10
'Poetry Review', 438-42, 446-50
Pope, Alexander, 189, 439, 440
Pottle, Frederick, 39, 332-4, 387-90
Pound, Ezra, 5, 6, 7, 9, 10, 11, 14, 15, 16, 18, 20, 37, 51-2, 54, 55, 57, 60, 62, 64, 67, 68, 70-3, 75-80, 81-3, 83, 92, 93, 94, 112, 123, 131, 143-4, 152, 154, 157, 162, 166, 191, 204, 247-8, 283, 325, 344, 345, 346, 402, 454, 502, 593, 731, 732, 736, 738, 739, 743, 745; 'Cantos', 20, 52, 143-4, 157, 402, 502; 'Hugh Selwyn Mauberley', 10; 'Instigations', 75, 131; 'Literary Essays of Ezra Pound', 75; 'Lustra', 14; 'Selected Letters, 1907-1941', 64

Powell, Charles, 22, 194-5
Prescott, Frederick Clarke, 173, 181
Pritchett, V.S., 653-6
Prokofiev, Sergei, 411, 420
Prothero, G.W., 82
Proust, Marcel, 29, 283, 284, 462, 501
Prynne, J.H., 61

'Quarterly Review', 8, 9, 12, 67-9, 70, 71, 73, 82-3, 83-4, 88
Quennell, Peter, 37, 339-43
Quinn, John, 18, 63

Rabelais, François, 624
Racine, Jean, 657
Rahv, Philip, 35-6
Raine, Kathleen, 44, 488-93, 494-5
Ransom, John Crowe, 21, 37, 40, 64, 172-9, 180-2, 396-400
Rascoe, Burton, 31, 152, 170
Read, Herbert, 16, 31, 57, 127
Redgrave, Michael, 371-2, 375, 377
Reed, Henry, 482
Régnier, Henri de, 9, 71
Reid, B.L., 63
Rhys, Ernest, 72
Richards, I.A., 24, 30, 57, 234-8, 247, 306, 308, 419
Rickword, Edgell, 23, 184-6, 215-19
Riding, Laura, 25
Ridler, Anne, 623
Riley, Peter, 61-2
Rilke, Rainer Maria, 42, 43, 413, 418, 457, 570, 738
Rimbaud, Arthur, 17
Roberts, Michael, 39, 379-81
Robinson, E.A., 193, 239, 265, 353
Roche, Denis, 61
Rodker, John, 15

Rogers, Paul, 662, 665, 704, 707
Rosenthal, M.L., 62
Rossetti, Dante Gabriel, 191, 199
Rousseau, Jean-Jacques, 233
Royce, Josiah, 4, 7
Ruskin, John, 235
Russell, Bertrand, 59, 111, 149, 187
Russell, Peter, 47, 592-4

Saintsbury, George, 135
Salmon, André, 244
Sandburg, Carl, 143
Santayana, George, 2, 181, 199
Sappho, 89, 142, 197, 550
Sarett, Lew, 166-70
Sartre, Jean-Paul, 600, 612
Sassoon, Siegfried, 270, 344
'Saturday Review of Literature', 26, 53, 64, 267-8, 324-8, 656-9, 702-6, 736-42
Sayers, Dorothy L., 44
Sayers, Michael, 298-302
Schopenhauer, Arthur, 710
Schuchard, Ronald, 59, 64
Schwartz, Delmore, 46, 567-70
Scofield, Paul, 55
Scott, Geoffrey, 222
Scott, Hutchinson, 50, 662
'Scrutiny', 30, 32, 33, 44-5, 47, 48, 306-9, 359-64, 515-29, 615-22
Seillière, Ernest, 233
Seldes, Gilbert, 18-20, 144-51
Seneca, 217, 579
'Sewanee Review', 25, 57, 675-89
Shand, John, 536-51
Shakespeare, William, 37, 96, 97, 118, 137, 142, 165, 170, 188, 194, 201, 221, 230, 233, 291, 301, 348, 366, 403, 404, 407, 458, 537, 541, 550, 588, 608,

616, 622, 623, 655, 667, 677, 678, 682, 684, 685, 689, 698, 708, 712, 720, 726, 736
Shaw, George Bernard, 223, 358, 396, 401, 404, 637, 666-7, 708-9
Shawe-Taylor, Desmond, 47, 594-6
Sherek, Henry, 673
Shillito, Edward, 328-32
Shelley, Percy Bysshe, 109, 238, 415, 416, 596, 608, 622, 633-4, 688
Shorthouse, J.H., 545, 561
Sinclair, May, 12, 83-8, 135, 191, 198
Sitwell, Edith, 272, 344, 592
Sitwell, Osbert, 16, 127, 344
Smart, Christopher, 304
Smiles, Samuel, 72
Snell, Reginald, 46-7, 577-81
Sophocles, 318, 332, 376, 389, 704, 715
'Southern Review', 32, 37, 40, 43, 57, 61, 64, 353-6, 418-38, 443-5, 563
Southey, Robert, 71
Speaight, Robert, 47-8, 57, 497-500, 597-600
'Spectator', 33, 50, 111, 315-17, 336-9, 612-15, 660-2, 709-12
Spender, Stephen, 56, 57, 61, 344, 345, 406-8, 415-18, 493
Spengler, Oswald, 208, 242, 582
Spenser, Edmund, 142, 165, 170, 194, 206, 410, 411, 420
Spicer, Jack, 58
Squire, Sir John, 22, 163, 191-2, 240-1
Statius, Publius Papinius, 101

Stead, C.K., 8, 63
Stein, Gertrude, 230, 260,
    357
Stendhal, 611
Stephenson, Ethel M.,
    438-42, 446-50
Stevens, Wallace, 11, 39,
    61, 737, 739
Stevenson, R.L., 84
Stock, Noel, 63, 64, 144
Stonier, G.W., 42, 409-12,
    419-20, 421, 432
Storman, E.J., 581-90
Strachey, Lytton, 59, 111,
    222, 223, 225
Strafford, Earl of, 546
Stravinsky, Igor, 25, 55,
    118, 239, 283
Strobel, Marion, 119-21
'Studies', 62, 712-22
Sullivan, J.W.N., 209
'Sunday Times', 48, 305-6,
    344-6
Sweeney, James Johnson, 43,
    45, 418-38, 529-36, 563,
    574
Swift, Jonathan, 217, 499
Swinburne, Algernon Charles,
    97, 105, 142, 269, 283,
    353, 429, 533
Symons, Arthur, 3, 709, 734

'Tablet', 33, 303, 597-600
Taggard, Genevieve, 268
Tailhade, Laurent, 71
Tasker, John, 64
Tate, Allen, 19, 20, 21, 25,
    27-8, 29, 55, 57, 180-2,
    242-6, 272-9
Tennyson, Alfred, Lord, 71,
    86, 96, 97, 113, 283,
    343, 355, 733
Thackeray, William Make-
    peace, 130, 456
Theocritus, 10, 77
'Theology', 33, 44, 302-3,
    458-68, 510-14
Thomas, Dylan, 737
Thompson, Francis, 84-5,

    250, 261
'Time and Tide', 48, 49
'Times', 33, 47, 50, 52,
    55, 679
'Times Literary Supple-
    ment', 9, 15, 16, 18, 25,
    34, 39, 42-3, 46, 51-2,
    54, 56, 58, 62, 73-4,
    96-9, 102, 105-8, 134,
    184-6, 282, 295-8,
    313-15, 369-71, 496-7,
    604-6, 622-4
Tolstoy, Count Leo, 183
Tomlinson, Charles, 58
Tourneur, Cyril, 15, 51,
    245, 689, 739
Toynbee, Philip, 56
Traherne, Thomas, 655
Trilling, Lionel, 638
'Tristan und Isolde', 149,
    152, 197, 550
Turner, Luke, 500-2
Turner, W.J., 344
'Twentieth Century', 50,
    665-74, 707-9
Twitchett, E.G., 268-9
Tynan, Kenneth, 52-3

Unger, Leonard, 57, 63, 64
Untermeyer, Louis, 16, 46,
    126-30, 151-3, 219, 220,
    364-6, 576-7
Upanishads, 149, 159, 366,
    430, 550, 579

Valéry, Paul, 242, 419,
    530-1, 733, 738, 739
Van Doren, Mark, 35, 125-6,
    323-4
Vaughan, Henry, 429, 590
Vedic Hymns, 140, 142, 564
Velasquez de Silva, Diego
    Rodriguez, 10, 77
Verdi, Giuseppe, 594
Verlaine, Paul, 17, 93, 142,
    194, 206, 261, 366, 440,
    550
Verschoyle, Derek, 33
Villon, François, 17, 738

Virgil, 142, 194, 199, 205, 550
Voltaire, 301

Wadsworth, E.A., 109
Wagner, Richard, 142, 191, 710
Waley, Arthur, 6
Waller, Edmund, 216
Walton, Eda Lou, 26, 253-5
Wanning, Andrews, 43, 443-5
Wardle, Mark, 419
Watkin, E.I., 532
Watson, George, 22, 59, 64
Waugh, Arthur, 8, 9, 11, 12, 67-9, 70-2, 82-3, 83-4
Weaver, Harriet Shaw, 6
Weaver, Raymond, 16, 130-1
Webb, Alan, 662, 665
Webb-Odell, Rev. R., 33
Webster, John, 15, 140, 142, 157, 194, 206, 241, 245, 263
'Weekend Review', 249-51
'Weekly Westminster', 200-3
Weightman, John, 50, 53, 665-7, 707-9
Weil, Simone, 57
Weiss, Theodore, 62
Wells, Carolyn, 182
Wells, H.G., 223
Werfel, Franz, 283
West, Rebecca, 31, 315
'Westminster Gazette', 102
Westminster Theatre (London), 39, 369, 371
Weston, Jessie L., 139-40, 142, 148, 194, 196, 198, 200, 206, 236, 551
Wharton, Edith, 239
Wharton, Gordon, 52
Whibley, Charles, 230
Whistler, James McNeill, 12, 90
Whitehead, A.N., 355, 582
Whitman, Walt, 109, 211, 238, 402
Whittemore, Reed, 56

Wickstead, Philip Henry, 535-6
Wilde, Oscar, 50, 457, 593, 666-7, 668, 690-1
Williams, Charles, 44, 552-60
Williams, William Carlos, 13, 48, 56-7, 57-8, 60, 62, 92-5, 568, 601-2
Williamson, George, 25, 31
Wilson, Edmund, 18, 19-20, 24, 26, 64, 136, 138-44, 154, 162-3, 165, 193, 239-40, 246, 259-60, 277
Winters, Yvor, 21, 32
Wolfe, Humbert, 22, 200-3
Woods, James, 4
Woodward, Daniel H., 63
Woolf, Leonard, 15, 17, 18, 59, 111, 213-15
Woolf, Virginia, 15, 17, 18, 23-4, 225, 226, 233-4, 372
Wordsworth, William, 21, 56, 71, 112, 179, 182, 220, 222, 458, 466, 493, 495, 556, 561
Worsley, T.C., 50, 662-5
Worth, Irene, 591, 596, 600
Wundt, Wilhelm, 180
Wylie, Elinor, 153-6, 192, 193

'Yale Review', 56, 182, 192-3, 332-4, 364-6, 387-90, 576-7
Yeats, William Butler, 16, 38, 53, 54, 55, 60, 62, 68, 79, 93, 132, 154, 260, 327, 344, 410, 458, 462, 499, 502, 658-9, 683, 711, 712, 722, 732, 735, 736, 737, 738, 739, 742, 745

Zabel, M.D., 26, 32, 38, 261-5, 282-5, 290-1, 353-6

THE CRITICAL HERITAGE SERIES

GENERAL EDITOR: B. C. SOUTHAM

Volumes published and forthcoming

ADDISON AND STEELE	Edward A. Bloom and Lillian D. Bloom
MATTHEW ARNOLD: THE POETRY	Carl Dawson
MATTHEW ARNOLD: PROSE WRITINGS	Carl Dawson and John Pfordresher
W. H. AUDEN	John Haffenden
SAMUEL BECKETT	L. Graver and R. Federman
ARNOLD BENNETT	James Hepburn
WILLIAM BLAKE	G. E. Bentley Jr
THE BRONTËS	Miriam Allott
BROWNING	Boyd Litzinger and Donald Smalley
ROBERT BURNS	Donald A. Low
BYRON	Andrew Rutherford
THOMAS CARLYLE	Jules Paul Seigel
CHAUCER 1385–1837	Derek Brewer
CHAUCER 1837–1933	Derek Brewer
CHEKHOV	Victor Emeljanow
CLARE	Mark Storey
CLOUGH	Michael Thorpe
COLERIDGE	J. R. de J. Jackson
WILKIE COLLINS	Norman Page
CONRAD	Norman Sherry
FENIMORE COOPER	George Dekker and John P. McWilliams
CRABBE	Arthur Pollard
STEPHEN CRANE	Richard M. Weatherford
DEFOE	Pat Rogers
DICKENS	Philip Collins
JOHN DONNE	A. J. Smith
DRYDEN	James and Helen Kinsley
GEORGE ELIOT	David Carroll
T. S. ELIOT	Michael Grant
WILLIAM FAULKNER	John Bassett
HENRY FIELDING	Ronald Paulson and Thomas Lockwood
FORD MADOX FORD	Frank MacShane
E. M. FORSTER	Philip Gardner
GEORGIAN POETRY 1911–1922	Timothy Rogers
GISSING	Pierre Coustillas and Colin Partridge
GOLDSMITH	G. S. Rousseau
THOMAS HARDY	R. G. Cox
HAWTHORNE	J. Donald Crowley
HEMINGWAY	Jeffrey Meyers
GEORGE HERBERT	C. A. Patrides
ALDOUS HUXLEY	Donald Watt
IBSEN	Michael Egan